The Interpretation of II Corinthians

R. C. H. LENSKI

Augsburg Fortress
Minneapolis

THE INTERPRETATION OF II CORINTHIANS
Commentary on the New Testament series

First paperback edition 2008

Copyright ©1946, 2008 Augsburg Fortress. All rights reserved. Except for brief quotations in critical articles or reviews, no part of this book may be reproduced in any manner without prior written permission from the publisher. Visit http://www.augsburgfortress.org/copyrights/contact.asp or write to Permissions, Augsburg Fortress, Box 1209, Minneapolis, MN 55440.

Richard C. H. Lenski's commentaries on the New Testament were published in the 1940s after the author's death. This volume was copyrighted in 1937 by the Lutheran Book Concern, published in 1946 by the Wartburg Press, and assigned in 1961 to the Augsburg Publishing House.

ISBN 978-0-8066-8080-4

The paper used in this publication meets the minimum requirements of American National Standard for Information Sciences—Permanence of Paper for Printed Library Materials, ANSI Z329.48-1984.

Manufactured in the U.S.A.

Second Epistle
To the Corinthians

TO

THE THEOLOGICAL SEMINARY

OF THE

JOINT EVANGELICAL LUTHERAN SYNOD
OF WISCONSIN AND OTHER STATES

AT

THIENSVILLE, WISCONSIN

ABBREVIATIONS

R. = A Grammar of the Greek New Testament in the Light of Historical Research, by A. T. Robertson, 4th ed.

B.-D. = Friedrich Blass' Grammatik des neutestamentlichen Griechisch, vierte, voellig neugearbeitete Auflage, besorgt von Albert Debrunner.

C.-K. = Biblisch-theologisches Woerterbuch der Neutestamentlichen Graezitaet von D. D. Herman Cremer, zehnte, etc., Auflage, herausgegeben von D. Dr. Julius Koegel.

C. Tr. = Concordia Triglotta. The Symbolical Books of the Ev. Lutheran Church, German-Latin- English. St. Louis, Mo., Concordia Publishing House.

R., W. P. = Word Pictures in the New Testament, by Archibald Thomas Robertson. Vol. IV.

NOTE. — The translation is intended only as an aid in understanding the Greek.

INTRODUCTION

One fact in regard to Second Corinthians must be strongly emphasized at the very beginning: all, literally all textual evidence proves this letter a unit. No abbreviated text has ever been discovered that might raise a question on this score, and no text that showed an omission or omissions has ever been found. This fact alone stands as a bulwark against the hypotheses of our day.

With regard to Romans this is not the case. We have a textual question regarding the last two chapters, regarding the doxology, Rom. 16:25-27, regarding 16:24. This question is not at all serious, it is easily answered, although it cannot be solved so that all of the forms of the text as it is extant are explained. The facts in regard to the text of Second Corinthians are the opposite, there is no abbreviation, no excision whatever. That fact stands, its significance is plain.

This epistle has three parts, and they have always been recognized as such: Chapters 1 to 7; 8 and 9; 10 to 13. "Tradition makes the epistle a unit. ... In spirit the reader follows Paul from Ephesus through Troas to Macedonia (1 to 7); then he lingers with him for a moment in the churches of Macedonia (8 and 9); finally, he is led to the consideration of conditions in the church at Corinth from the point of view of Paul's coming visit there. The three sections of the letter treat respectively, the immediate past with its misunderstandings and explanations, the present with its practical problems, and the near future with its anxieties." Zahn, *Introduction* 312. It is the distinctness with which these parts stand out that gave rise to the avalanche of hypotheses, which has now exhausted about every possibility.

In 1776 Semler hit upon the idea that the last four chapters were not an integral part of Second Corinthians. The various hypotheses were, however, not seriously advanced until much later. Criticism of the letter has run this course: chapters 10-13 are not a part of Second Corinthians, are not even Pauline; chapters 8 and 9 cannot belong together, chapter 9 was not a part of the letter, chapter 8 likewise; then 6:14 to 7:1 were regarded as an interpolation and then as not coming from a writing of Paul's; finally the whole letter is turned into a mosaic and made a late compilation, in other words, we finally have no letter left to be interpreted!

It is, however, not a textual question which furnishes the basis for these hypotheses; it is the relation of Second to First Corinthians, the time intervening between the two and the events that occurred during that time. Three occurrences are postulated, one of which is a fact, namely that Paul was going to Corinth for the *third* time when he wrote Second Corinthians (12:14; 13:1). The hypotheses place the second visit *between* First and Second Corinthians and make the interval between the two visits six months or extend it to a year and six months. Then a new case is developed: II Cor. 2:1-11 no longer deals with the case of incest mentioned in I Cor. 5 but is made a case of meanest insult offered to Paul or to Paul through Timothy. This insult occurred while Paul was in Corinth on his brief second visit. Thirdly, an additional letter, which was written to the Corinthians by Paul, is postulated, and this letter is found in II Cor. 10 to 13. Here there is room for hypotheses, the room is even enlarged by other suppositions and possibilities.

The movements of Timothy and of Titus are introduced: Timothy, who was sent to Corinth by Paul before Paul wrote First Corinthians, did or did not get to Corinth, or got there ahead of this letter and left again before it arrived or after it was received. What Timothy reported to Paul is thus made hypothetical. The same is true with regard to Titus; what he reported to Paul when he returned to Paul in Macedonia is also hypothetical. Did or did not further news from Corinth reach Paul while he was writing Second Corinthians?

The whole is capped by additional hypotheses to the effect that Paul's theology underwent a decided change: he advanced from his Jewish theologumena to Hellenistic philosophoumena. He gave up the expectation of witnessing the Parousia during his lifetime. He gave up his earlier teaching, the dreary state between death and the final resurrection; he dropped the idea of a final resurrection of the body. He turned from the Pharisaic to a Hellenistic eschatology; did this on the strength of his Christ-mysticism and his Pneuma-doctrine and in consequence of the mortal danger through which he had recently passed (II Cor. 1:8; 5:1-8). A totally new Paul emerges.

We might note still other contributions to this critical structure. A *consensus criticus* has been established, which means that the critics have proven their contentions. Zahn quietly calls this a *consensus criticorum*, namely a consensus of only these critics. It is not even that, for theirs is not a *consensus*, it is a discordant *dissensus*. Each critic has his own hypothesis. While each applauds that of the other, yet by setting up his new hypothesis each really upsets those of the rest. They destroy each other to a large extent, and those who are living at any one time expect to be answered by others who are yet to arise. The possibilities have, however, been practically exhausted. It is now rather difficult to find a new "problem" which may be made the basis of a new hypothesis.

This is regarded as the "historical" method of interpretation in contrast with the old, superseded "unhistorical" method. The historical method is undoubtedly the correct one to follow; it is an advance on every method that disregards the historical setting of any ancient piece of writing. But it is not historical when it loses the genuine historical facts and substitutes hypothetical, i. e., imagined facts. It is not historical when it fills in silences and blanks which no man can at this late date fill with data. It is dishonest when it alters, shifts, manipulates, or denies the still available historical facts in order to make room for hypotheses.

Natural science has learned, in part at least, to use hypotheses in a fruitful way. Guesses are made where no data are as yet at hand, but guesses for which later research and discovery may find the data, which may then make some guess a certainty or junk it as being false. But in the case of Second Corinthians the discovery of such data is practically excluded. We have what we have, and we shall never have more, or at best very little more. So to operate with hypotheses means to end with nothing but hypotheses. Instead of being a means to an end, as is the case in the natural sciences, the hypotheses themselves constitute the end.

The "historical" method thus often turns out to be the method of the novelist and romancer. The *consensus criticus* becomes a paper house. The more hypotheses are needed to support a hypothesis, the flimsier the structure becomes. It is generally a work of supererogation to refute them. Nothing can ever be proved by an array of unverifiable hypotheses. Are these critics operating in the scientific, scholarly way? Is their attitude justified when they deny scientific and scholarly standing to those who dissent from their *consensus criticus* and work without hypotheses? We answer with a challenging "no." It is unscientific, unscholarly to build up hypotheses to fill in gaps of history for which no hope of securing further factual data exists, no matter how much detailed learning one may possess for doing this thing.

Pardon the excursus; consider the provocation. Something to this effect, if it were said oftener, would check the jungle growths of Biblical interpretation and would plant more orchards with fruit-bearing trees. Sober historical exegesis of Second Corinthians, as of the other sacred writings, has produced the richest results for the church. Into this inheritance we propose to enter.

None of the blanks regarding the history are serious. None affect our understanding of this Second Epistle to the Corinthians. We know much about the conditions that were existing in Corinth when about Easter of 57 Paul wrote First Corinthians while he was laboring in Ephesus. The second visit which Paul made to Corinth was quite brief — all that we know about it is found in the brief references in 12:14, and 13:1 — and must be placed somewhere during the three years of Paul's labors in Ephesus. We do not know how long before the writing of First Corinthians it took place. Paul apparently went by ship directly from Ephesus to Corinth, hence not during the winter of 56-57 but before this time. The chief point is that the details of this visit are wholly immaterial for Second Corinthians and its historical interpretation. Paul says that he made such a visit, that is all. If he had said nothing whatever about it, we should understand Second Corinthians just as well. To place this visit into the six months that intervened between First and Second Corinthians, to speak of insult to Paul, physical illness and mental inefficiency, bitter defeat and then helpless departure, opens the way for further hypotheses. To extend the interval of six months between First and Second Corinthians into eighteen months is another hypothesis which would make room for a visit by Paul between First and Second Corinthians, since it is impossible to find a place for it during these six months. Six months is too short a time because Paul starts about Pentecost, sends Titus to Corinth, and expects his return at Troas.

Before First Corinthians was written, Paul had sent Timothy by land with instructions for the churches en route and with orders to go to Corinth. In I Cor. 16:10, etc., he informs the Corinthians regarding Timothy's coming. He expects Timothy to arrive after his letter has arrived but asks that he be allowed to return to Paul promptly. We have no reason to suppose that this program was not carried out. It is unlikely that Timothy for some reason turned back before he reached Corinth, for his orders were to go as far as Corinth. It is equally unlikely that he did not find First Corinthians when he got to Corinth and then, as directed in I Cor. 16:11, did not hasten back to Paul in Ephesus. When Paul left Ephesus at Pentecost, Timothy was with him.

The information brought by Timothy regarding the situation at Corinth induced Paul to send Titus to Corinth with instruction as to how to proceed in righting things there and with orders to time his return so as to meet Paul in Troas. Titus was not sent on this mission because he was a better man than Timothy. Timothy was more serviceable than Titus for the business which Paul had to transact in the churches along his route; that is all. He had, for one thing, been circumcised, Titus had not; then he had been in these churches with Paul when they were founded during Paul's second missionary tour.

Titus was delayed; Paul, anxious because of the delay, fearing the worst, and thinking that conditions in Corinth had detained Titus, went on from Troas into Macedonia, and there Titus met him. Paul was overjoyed because of the many good things which Titus reported although some things were still bad enough.

Paul promptly and wisely sent Titus back with Second Corinthians. He instructed him to proceed with the righting of matters and also with expediting the great collection. Paul expected to arrive in Corinth two or three months later, evidently because he still had much to do en route and felt assured also that a little longer time would be good for Corinth while Titus was there to direct matters.

This explains why Titus alone is mentioned as the source of Paul's information. Timothy himself is joint author of the epistle (II Cor. 1:1). Being such, any information that he had brought to Paul was utilized in this joint letter and could not be especially labelled as having been contributed by Timothy. Only if Paul had written under his own name alone would one have the right to expect special references to information which he had secured from Timothy. Titus could not be made joint author with Paul and with Timothy because he was to hurry back with the epistle. The propriety of Timothy's joint authorship is enhanced when we remember that he was with Paul on his second missionary tour when the church at Corinth was founded. Regarding Titus see 2:13; 7:6, 13, 14; also 12:18, where we learn that a brother had accompanied him on his mission. Regarding the return of Titus to Corinth with the epistle see 8:6, 16, 23.

All that needs to be said with regard to chapter 2 and 7:12 is that I Cor. 5:1-5 presents the historical basis. A flying visit to Corinth by Paul, a disgraceful scene plus other additions such as a violent letter immediately after Paul's return, are not in accord with historical sense. Since Timothy had returned and had reported to Paul before they left for Troas, etc., since Titus had been sent on a mission to Corinth, and since an agreement to meet Paul at Troas and to report had been made, no flying visit, no intervening letter are likely. The brief interval of six months would also preclude these suppositions. When, therefore, a whole year is added to these six months on conjectural grounds, such an extension is unwarranted.

At what place in Macedonia Titus joined Paul cannot be determined. Consider Philippi, which is as good as any surmise; Paul is satisfied to say only "Macedonia." On the basis of 8:6, 16, 23 we are certain that Titus at once returned to Corinth with Second Corinthians and attended to the matter of the collection. The supposition that Paul intended to conclude his letter with chapter 9, that in some way further news arrived from Corinth, and that Paul then added four severe chapters is unwarranted. Paul arrived in Corinth at the end of the year, remained there for three months (Acts 20:3), at the end of which period he wrote Romans, and then started on his journey for Jerusalem with the bearers of the collection. As far as one is able to gather from the tone of Romans and from the mental condition of Paul which it reflects and from the plans which Paul was making to work in Spain, Paul's two letters and his other efforts had restored order, peace, and sound conditions in Corinth.

What originally led to a number of hypotheses is the apparent diversity of the three parts of Second Corinthians. In defending the unity of the epistle it would be a mistake to minimize this diversity although it would be a mistake only in a right cause. The critical commentators call the last four chapters the *Vierkapitelbrief* and describe it as a compact "Philippic" which they say has no place in a letter that contains chapters 1 to 7 or even chapters 1 to 9. Objection is raised to the placement of chapters 8 and 9 into the same letter between such other parts as chapters 1-7 and chapters 10-13. A letter that is composed of three such main parts, and these in such a sequence, is regarded as an impossibility. The same reasoning is applied to 6:14-7:1 in order to eliminate also this section.

This is the method applied to other writings of the New Testament, here it is applied on a large scale.

As one reads Paul's chapters from beginning to end, one is not conscious of the great gulfs that are said to exist in at least two and even in more places. Each part and each lesser part seem to follow in natural order. The last part does not read like a Philippic or a denunciation. The bulk of it concerns Paul himself, it is an effort to bare his life, sufferings, and the grace vouchsafed to him in order to win the Corinthians and, as far as opponents are concerned, to warn them that he will face them. This is not a Philippic, it has more of the nature of an ἀπολογία, a most effective self-defense which ends with the fear of what Paul may find and does not want to find (12:20, 21) on his arrival and with a warning of what he may have to do and yet does not want to do (13:2, 10).

In part one Paul writes about his happiness because, as Titus reports, matters are clearing up in Corinth, and Paul adds to this clearing up. In part two we see Paul's concern regarding the matter of the collection. This is again beginning to move forward, and Paul writes to speed it forward successfully by sending Titus and two additional brethren for this purpose. This leaves Paul's arrival which is to follow two or three months later. Paul writes about it in part three, tells of his fears, of what he does not want to meet unless he absolutely must (chapter 13), and, in order that the last opposition to him may be removed, writes at length about himself in a way that seems foolish to him yet is necessary under the circumstances. Parts one and two thus deal with what has been accomplished, with the understanding that has been reached, and touch what is yet to be achieved, and part three deals with the last obstacles, the final opposition yet to be overcome. We thus see the unity of the whole. The three parts appear in natural order.

In Second Corinthians Paul bares his heart and his life as he does in none of his other letters. This lends a special value to the letter. Combined with this self-revelation is the wonderful way in which Paul reaches out to the Corinthians. He lets all the love of his heart speak, and its language is perfection. Paul's psychological judgment of his readers never errs. His arms reach out. He touches the secret springs in his readers who certainly could not help but respond. Even the sterner tones in the last chapter voice this compelling love. These inward things that run through the entire letter deserve far more attention than they have received. Other apostles may have been like this, but none of them has left us a document which reveals this as does this one dictated by Paul. Second Corinthians is precious indeed.

CHAPTER I

The Greeting, 1:1, 2

"Paul and Timothy ... to the church, etc. ... grace and peace!" nominatives to indicate the writers — a dative to indicate the church to whom the letter is sent — nominatives to express the terms of the greeting. This arrangement is stereotyped. It varies only slightly from the common secular formula which has the infinitive χαίρειν to convey the word of greeting (James 1:1; Acts 15:23; 23:26). Each of the three terms may be amplified, and the amplification then becomes important because it is an indication of what the letter conveys. Paul's amplifications are invariably significant, even his omissions are noteworthy (note the unmodified dative in Gal. 1:2).

1) Paul, apostle of Christ Jesus through God's will, and Timothy, the brother, to the church of God which is in Corinth, with all the saints who are in whole Achaia: grace to you and peace from God, our Father, and the Lord Jesus Christ!

In this greeting the addition to Paul's name and that to Timothy's form an intentional contrast. It is, of course, Paul who dictates the letter; he regularly dictated his letters to a scribe. He might have called Timothy "my fellow worker" or given him some other designation to indicate his assistantship in the work of the gospel. He is instead named only "the brother" who in this capacity alone is associated with Paul in the sending of this letter.

By calling Timothy "the brother" Paul does two things: he places into relief the addition of his own name "apostle of Christ Jesus," etc., and fixes the exact measure of responsibility for all that follows. His own relation to the churches addressed is far more than fraternal as will appear throughout the letter, it is apostolic. Paul's high and holy office is involved directly and completely in all that is contained in this letter. Timothy's office of assistant to Paul is not so involved. As in the case of Sosthenes mentioned in I Cor. 1:1, whatever pertains to Timothy's office as assistant Paul assumes as Timothy's superior. Paul relieves him of all but his fraternal responsibility for this letter. Since brotherhood is the fundamental relation, this responsibility is by no means small; that it is greater than it was in the case of Sosthenes in I Cor. 1:1 appears from 1:19 and from Timothy's personal relation to the Corinthians.

"Apostle" is "one sent from" a superior on a commission; he thus represents his superior, is his ambassador. The word is here used in its narrow sense as "through God's will" also indicates. Associates of the apostles were called apostles in a wider sense but not "apostles of Christ Jesus through God's will," for this designation refers to their immediate call while those assistants had only a mediate call. The genitive "of Christ Jesus" is more than "belonging to Christ Jesus"; it indicates origin and agency: "called and sent by him." "Through God's will" = not accidentally by a set of fortuitous circumstances, or temporarily, or growing into this position. God's θέλημα is his volitional act which placed Paul into his office. See I Cor. 1:1 regarding this phrase. We note no contrast with false apostles although we shall see that men of this type had invaded Corinth, and that Paul takes issue with them. It is sufficient here that the Corinthians know that Christ's own representative is writing to them.

An additional word needs to be said especially in regard to this epistle. It is often thought that Paul places his authority upon the scales, and that "apostle" intends to stress *authority*. This view is not borne out by the letter. At times preachers thus expect their mere authority to produce submission. "Apostle of Christ Jesus" is, first of all, written with regard to Paul himself and expresses his own consciousness of bearing a most *heavy responsibility* with regard to the Corinthians. He writes as one who feels this weight. It is his first concern to discharge his own apostolic obligation. He is accountable to Christ Jesus.

Moreover, the letter shows that his whole soul is in his office. We see his deep emotions throughout the letter, this is more evident than even in Galatians. These emotions, this deep concern for the Corinthians, this fervent reaching out for them — it is this that is truly apostolic. Place authority in this light and it will appear more truly how Paul expected it to affect the Corinthians. They were to respond, not by compulsion, but by a satisfied, even by an enthusiastic following, not to say submission.

As "brother" places "apostle" into relief, so it also does the reverse. Paul's apostolic concern has Timothy's brotherly concern at its side. The fact that Timothy is not called by an official name lets the Corinthians feel that not mere authority is dictating to them. While Paul necessarily cannot call himself merely "brother" lest that convey the suggestion of giving up apostolic authority, responsibility, and obligation, his making this "brother" the joint-writer of the letter brings out the full fraternal appeal that is intended by the letter. The apostle and the brother have talked over the contents, have agreed on all of them. The apostolic and the brotherly word blend into one. In I Cor. 1:1 we read "Sosthenes, the brother," exactly as here, it is like a title of honor. Brethren will heed a brother. We see that it is not the weight of authority that Paul urges but one that is even heavier and harder to resist.

With this corresponds the dative: "to the church of God which is in Corinth," which is explained in I Cor. 1:1. The church of God, no matter in what locality it is found, will certainly heed the words of one who is Christ's apostle by God's will. Here we have Paul's estimate of the Corinthians, and it indicates what their estimate of themselves ought always to be: no less than "the church of God." It is well that we ponder the designation, both we who hold positions of responsibility in this church, and we who are brethren in the assembly. In I Cor. 1:2 Paul has further additions which define the membership of this church of God. Now he is more succinct and leaves the two nominatives and the dative focused fully upon each other.

Regarding Timothy's presence with Paul and his recent visit in Corinth see the Introduction. The view that Timothy's last commission to Corinth was a failure is unwarranted. If that were the case, Paul would not have invited him to join him in writing this letter. Neither here nor elsewhere does Paul try to vindicate or to re-establish Timothy. It has been well said that the naming of Timothy as the co-writer is neither a challenge to the Corinthians nor a satisfaction to him. He had helped to found the congregation, he was conversant with its present situation, for he had recently been there. The fact that he is not personally involved in the troubles that are now subsiding is seen from the letter itself in which he is not named save in 1:19. Paul does not need to refer to Timothy's recent commission since that is known to the Corinthians, and since Timothy is now joining Paul in this letter.

This letter is intended also for "all the saints who are in whole Achaia." But Paul writes σύν and not καί; he does not address these saints in the same way in which he addresses the Corinthian church. There has been no trouble between Paul and these others, nor were they party to the trouble in Corinth. "With" means that some things such as the matter of the collection pertain to all the saints in the Roman province of which Corinth was the capital. All that pertains to the former difficulties in Corinth and to their settlement concerns these saints indirectly. They may have heard or may yet get to hear about them. The troublemakers who had invaded Corinth may also try to intrude themselves elsewhere. Then, too, Paul is not shunning publicity; the entire trouble in Corinth had been public from the very beginning, its conclusion should likewise be public.

"Saints" is in Acts 9:13 used already by Ananias of Damascus as a designation for the Christians, and this designation was current in the early days of the church. It means "separated unto God by faith in Christ." It is the sainthood of true faith that indicates the cleansing of pardon through Christ's blood, the beginning of a new life in Christ, the putting away sin more and more. This term never indicates total sanctification in the sense of perfectionism so that these "saints" never sin after becoming saints (Phil. 3:12, Paul; I John 1:8-10, John).

When Paul writes "all the saints in whole Achaia" he does not mean that only unorganized believers and no churches existed outside of Corinth. Scattered believers may have resided in some localities, but Cenchrea had a church which employed Phœbe as a deaconess (Rom. 16:1), Athens had a church, and although we cannot name others because the records are so sparse, it is only fair to believe that a good many existed. The very phrase "in whole Achaia" demands no less. Paul had worked on a large scale, with several assistants, and thus covered much territory. His first stay in Achaia was for a period of a year and one half. We have no right to exclude Athens from consideration. Achaia is the senatorial province which was under a proconsul with its capital at Corinth and included Epirus, Thessaly, Middle Greece, the Peloponnesus, and notably Eubœa among the islands.

But Paul's letter is not intended, on the one hand, as an encyclical — "with all the saints" excludes that view; nor, on the other hand, is it the intention that only parts of the letter (say chapters 8 and 9) are to be communicated to the saints who live outside of Corinth. An encyclical would be addressed equally to all the churches; this letter is occasioned by conditions that existed at Corinth and is intended for Corinth and is only thus intended for the Achaians in general.

2) The words of greeting are the same as those found in other epistles: "grace to you and peace from God, our Father, and the Lord Jesus Christ." Χάρις = the *favor Dei* as it is found in God's heart together with all the gifts of this favor. "Grace to you" means: May God and the Lord give you an abundance of their undeserved gifts. Εἰρήνη, the Hebrew *shalom*, the German *Heil*, denotes the condition that prevails when God is our friend and all is well with us. The objective condition of "peace" is the essential, from this the subjective feeling and enjoyment of "peace" will flow. The former remains although the latter fluctuates and at times disappears. Paul desires both for the Corinthians and for the Achaians. The order is always "grace and peace," the former is the source of the latter. Without grace there is no peace, but with grace peace is certain. The grammarians supply εἴη with these nominatives, but why supply anything? The greeting is exclamatory.

The exalted value of these gifts is expressed by the phrase "from God, our Father, and the Lord Jesus Christ." Ἀπό conveys the idea that these gifts are to flow down from God and thus involves also the thought of origin. Since only one preposition is used with the two objects "God, our Father," and "the Lord Jesus

Christ," the two are made a unit source of grace and peace and are placed on an equality. The Greek is so plain that no scholar will deny these facts. How subordinationism seeks to destroy this equality of our Father and the Lord Jesus we have noted in I Cor. 1:3. Both names express the revelation which these persons have made of themselves in connection with the work of saving us. "Our Father" = we his children through faith in Christ Jesus; "the Lord Jesus Christ" = he who redeemed, purchased, and won us so that by faith we are now his own, live under him in his kingdom, and serve him in everlasting righteousness, innocence, and blessedness (Luther). Both terms express deity, but deity in the blessed, soteriological sense, the sense in which grace and peace, too, are meant.

The greeting is brief, but the terms employed are in their combination so weighty that they constitute the basis of the entire Biblical and Christian theology. They were so understood when they were written and sent and when they were received and read.

The First Part of the Epistle

Seven Chapters

Greatly Comforted and Cheered, Paul Clears away the Last Difficulties and at the same Time Glorifies His Office with Its Work and Its Suffering

I. *Comforted for Comforting*

3) **Blessed the God and Father of our Lord Jesus Christ, the Father of the compassions and God of all comforting, he who is comforting us in all our affliction so as to enable us to be comforting those in every affliction by means of the comforting with which we ourselves are being comforted by God!**

Meyer's simple *herzgewinnender Eingang* (warmly affectionate introduction) is truer and worth more than all the cold grammatical and literary analyses of this opening exclamation. The fundamental emotion of Paul and of Timothy bares itself to the Corinthians. It underlies the entire epistle. Other emotions flow into this main stream; they only add to its volume and make it richer. To understand and to appreciate this letter, its spirit, its purpose, and its details, we must enter into the feelings of the two writers; the more we do so, the more we gain. In order to do this mere intellectuality is insufficient, and critical approach is fatal. The fact that Paul felt more deeply than Timothy is certain, but the fact that Timothy shared Paul's emotions is equally certain. They reach out to the hearts of their readers, and those hearts surely responded.

The very designation used with reference to God accords with the emotion expressed. God is thrice named in the greeting, and now he is at once again and again and more fully named. As the letter begins, Paul and Timothy raise their eyes and their hearts to God and to Christ. Benediction and praise move their pen. The readers' hearts are carried upward. All that follows is dictated as being in the presence of the blessed God and Father of our Lord Jesus Christ, the Father of compassions and the God of comforting.

Tribulation and consolation are wound together. The ministry always meets the former yet always finds the latter, and the latter exceeds the former (v. 5). The church and the saints, together and individually, have the same experience. Yet here there is more than a parallel and a likeness, for the ministry is to be a channel to conduct God's consolation to the membership of the church in its tribulation. The second person "you" is not at once employed, it does not occur until v. 6. 7. Paul and Timothy minister to many others besides those in Corinth and in Achaia, hence they at first write in general: "so as to enable us to comfort those in all affliction" whoever they may be. But already here the saints and the ministry are drawn together. In a moment we see the arms of the writers embracing their readers in the divine consolation.

Here we have the ministerial and pastoral object of the affliction and the subsequent consolation that are experienced by the ministry of the church. God sends both for the personal sanctification of his ministers but also for the purpose of enabling them more truly, more richly, more effectively to minister unto others, for that is their very office. We indeed know it well: *oratio, meditatio, tentatio faciunt theologum*; but when the *tentatio* and its affliction come, many a minister is surprised and acts as though something untoward is happening to him. This is often true also with regard to the saints. Let us learn from Paul.

With heart lifted up he exclaims: "Blessed the God," etc. The verbal εὐλογητός is regular in such ascriptions of praise. The grammarians feel that something should be supplied. They debate as to whether it should be ἐστί, declarative, or εἴη or ἔστω, optative (wish) or imperative, the LXX has the former (R. 396). Is anything needed in an exclamation? We bless, i. e., speak well of God when we truly say what he is and does in his attributes and his works, and no task should be more delightful to us. There is too little contemplation of God and too little praise of him. This entire ascription is choice in wording, the very beauty of the expressions is intended to match the excellence of praise here offered to God.

Thus we have the full liturgical name: "the God and Father of our Lord Jesus Christ." It names God in connection with Christ in the fullest soteriological way: the God with whom our whole salvation in Christ is bound up. This name is really a concentrated confession; it puts into this glorious name all that the Scriptures reveal regarding our Savior-God. The discussions of the commentators regarding the point as to whether Paul intends to say that God is only the Father of our Lord Jesus or also his God generally lose the main import just expressed.

The A. V. translates here and in Rom. 15:6: "God, *even the* Father," etc., and in II Cor. 11:31; Eph. 1:3; I Pet. 1:3: "*the* God *and* Father," etc.; the R. V. translates all these passages in the same way. The plea that we may translate in either way is a Gamaliel's counsel of indecision; Paul had only one thought in mind. The remark that "Paul was not conscious of creating a peculiar Christological dictum" is misleading. This designation was standard in the church, Paul is not creating it. When it was first used, this was done consciously.

The Greek has one article: "*the* God and Father," this is its regular way of joining two concepts into a unity; thus the genitive "of our Lord" naturally belongs to this unity, to God as much as to Father. Even when no unity is intended, when the article is used with each noun, a following genitive may belong to both nouns if the sense permits. The remark that "blessed be God" is a Semitic formula that is complete and needs no genitive, and that "Father" is incomplete and needs a genitive, is specious. Both may be used alone, both, too, with genitives; see both with one article and no addition in I Cor. 15:24. To assert that because in I Cor. 15:24, and in Eph. 5:20 no genitive follows, and that when a genitive is added it belongs only to the second noun, is unwarranted.

Jesus himself calls God his God in Matt. 27:46; John 20:17. Eph. 1:17 says in so many words: "the God of our Lord Jesus Christ." For Jesus in his human nature God is his God, and for Jesus in his deity God is his Father; his God since the incarnation, his Father from all eternity. But let us not fail to note "*our* Lord," which connects us with Christ and through him with God. "Lord" is again wholly soteriological: he who purchased and won us, to whom we belong as our Savior-King.

"The God and Father" is repeated chiastically in the apposition: "the Father and God," and again with a unifying article although each noun now has a genitive. He is first designated from the viewpoint of our Savior, the Lord Jesus Christ; next from the viewpoint of his feeling and his action toward the saved. This God and Father of our Lord Jesus Christ is "the Father of the compassions and God of all comforting." We at once see that the genitives cannot be exclusive as though as Father and not as God the compassions belong to him, and as God and not as Father the comforting; for the compassions produce the comforting, neither is ever without the other. This shows still more that "our Lord" belongs to "the God and Father." He is compassionate and active in comforting us through our Lord Jesus Christ. The two great designations are bound closely together.

"The Father of the compassions" (or "pities") recalls Ps. 103:13: "Like as a father pitieth his children, so the Lord pitieth them that fear him." Οἰκτιρμοί is an idiomatic plural and may be rendered with our singular "compassion," the tender feeling of pity for those in distress. The article points to all of the pity in the Father. The word itself, although it is plural, does not refer to acts. The acts are expressed by the second genitive, "all comforting," "all" expressing totality.

Παράκλησις and the verb παρακαλέω may mean admonition, encouragement, or consolation according to the context; here the last is referred to because the reference is to affliction. The genitives are sometimes thought to be identical, but one *has* the feeling of pity (genitive of possession) and *puts forth* an action like comforting (effective genitive). In "the Father of pity" we have tenderness; while in "God of comforting" we have effectiveness, the comfort is divine. It has been noted that Paul's expressions are not so much doctrinal in describing God as due to actual recent experience (v. 7-11).

4) Still more must be said as the second apposition makes plain. This description of God pertains to the writers and to the readers of this epistle. God is praised on behalf of all of them. As Paul and Timothy are needing God's pity and comfort, so also are the Corinthians. As the troubles in Corinth were an affliction for Paul and for Timothy, so those troubles are viewed by the writers as an affliction also for the Corinthians. For all concerned God is providing help and comfort. Paul and Timothy are ministers, Paul is even an apostle; hence God is using also them and enabling them to transmit his comfort to the Corinthians and to any others in every kind of affliction. In a beautiful way, in order thereby to praise God the more, Paul weaves together παράκλησις and the verb forms of παρακαλέω and uses these words no less than ten times. The whole opening paragraph is thus made to ring with comfort — comfort — comfort, all in praise of God.

Ὁ παρακαλῶν κτλ., the substantivized present participle, is appositional and like another noun: "the One comforting," etc., or "he who is comforting," etc. The tense is durative: "engaged in comforting," we may say, "always comforting." And "us" refers to Paul and Timothy. Much of the discussion regarding "I" and "we" in this epistle is untenable as we shall find. "I" always designates Paul in distinction from Timothy, and "we" is never the editorial or majestic plural to designate Paul alone. It should be recognized that no competent writer would refer to himself with "I" and then with "we."

Timothy shared the affliction with Paul. Here Paul uses ἐπί, the comforting comes "upon the affliction";

then he uses ἐν, "in the affliction." The Greek word means "distress" that is caused by painful pressure, and the comforting consists in the help that removes that pressure so that one breathes again or so that one is able to bear the distress without fainting. The article is added: ἐπὶ πάσῃ τῇ θλίψει ἡμῶν, but not only because specific distress is referred to (R. 772), but also because ἡμῶν is added and makes the reference specific; ἐν πάσῃ θλίψει = "in every distress" in general. "Our whole distress" that has come upon us; then "every distress" that may come upon those whom we are to comfort.

The two are tied together: Paul and Timothy are comforted in distress "so as to enable us to be comforting those in every affliction by means of the comforting with which we ourselves are being comforted by God." Εἰς τό with the infinitive expresses purpose, intended result, or actual result. Any one of these three would serve here although some prefer purpose. "Those in affliction" is general and extends beyond the Corinthians, for Paul and Timothy had extensive fields of labor; yet the readers are included, and they will be mentioned presently.

God's comforting of Paul and of Timothy did more than to help them; it enabled them to comfort others "by means of the comforting with which we ourselves are being comforted by God" (ἧς is attracted from the accusative of the cognate object, R. 716; some think of the dative). "By God" brings out the idea that all of the comforting is done only *by him*; Paul and Timothy are only God's instruments through whom he comforts others who are in distress.

Some commentators refer to pagans and Jews in this connection. Seneca and Cicero are introduced who state that only he can help others who has experienced the same need, and Philo is cited to the same effect that when the first-born in Egypt were slain, none could comfort the others because everyone had the first-born dead in his house. But what *comfort* has a pagan or a Jew to offer, who has been in distress and speaks to another who is in similar distress? *He* had no true comfort; how can *he* then point another to true comfort?

We see the vast gulf between Paul and Timothy and all others. They have the God and Father of our Lord Jesus Christ, the Father of the compassion and God of all comforting, are comforted *by him*, and are enabled to comfort others by bringing them God and *his* comfort. What can a pagan or a Jew bring? Only what they had in their distress — *nothing!* This is a text for a funeral, it points to the full, open fountain of Christian comfort, *Deus Consolator*. Let the preacher contrast him with the emptiness of all other comforters and the sham comforts they offer. How this will draw poor sinners who seek comfort and find only husks elsewhere!

Some say that Paul here offers himself as the "mediator." His suffering is made vicarious. He is said to stand for others "in Christ's stead." The comfort is mediated by him to others. He is the "apostolic-pneumatic" leader who superabounds in the experience of God and in possession of the Spirit. But these comments are farfetched. Διά expresses means, but this means is not the mediator Paul; it is the comforting act, the agent of which is carefully expressed by ὑπό, the regular preposition to indicate the agent, and he is "God." *God* does all the comforting. As he did so in the case of Paul and Timothy, he also does in the case of the others in all their distress. He uses his ministers for this as he uses them for preaching, teaching, etc., and in no other way.

5) When ὅτι is translated "because" and v. 5 is regarded as the *reason* for v. 4, difficulty arises, and one can understand why v. 5 has been considered super-

fluous, a mere sidethought, and the like. We put the break in thought, not after v. 5, but after v. 4 and read together v. 5-7 so that ὅτι becomes the *consecutivum* (R. 1001): "seeing that." Then the exclamation of praise voiced in v. 3, 4 will be "in view of" (ὅτι) v. 5-7, not as proving it by a reason (there really is none), but as pointing still further to the *result* of God's blessed comforting, namely in particular the result for "you," the readers of the epistle. Thus v. 3-7 become a unit, a closely knit paragraph.

We adopt the text followed by the R. V. in preference to that used by the A. V.: **seeing that as the sufferings of Christ abound for us, so through Christ also our comforting abounds; besides (δέ), whether we are afflicted, (it is) for your comforting and salvation; whether we are comforted (it is) for your comforting, that which works in endurance of the same sufferings which we, too, are suffering. And this hope of ours is firm for you, we seeing that as you are partakers of the sufferings, so also of the comforting.**

The stress is on καί: as the sufferings, so *also* the comforting; secondly on "through Christ." The fact that "the sufferings abound" has already been stated in v. 4 where the expression "*all* our affliction" was used; and the fact that "the comforting abounds" has likewise been indicated in the expression "God comforting us in all our affliction," he, the "God of *all* comforting." What is new is that in the very nature of our relation to Christ the comforting corresponds to the suffering. It is a case of "even as — so also"; and the connecting link which makes the two agree is Christ. We see why God who does this comforting is so effectively called "the Father of our Lord Jesus Christ" (v. 3). He comforts us "through Christ," διά = he being the Mediator in all this comforting. "For us" and "our" = Paul and Timothy; in "our comforting" note that "our" is the objective genitive: the comforting that comforts "us."

This correspondence of the sufferings that come "for us" and of the comforting extended to us is due to the fact that both the sufferings and the comforting are connected with Christ. "Of Christ" and "through Christ" are placed chiastically and match. As to the comforting, that is mediated (διά) by Christ, mediated by all that he has done as "Christ." Our comfort and our passion hymns constantly dwell on this mediation; the church has produced no better commentary. M. Loy sings, *American Lutheran Hymnal* (277):

> "The way of life is by the cross,
> The glowing fires along,
> Which serve to purge away the dross
> And make the spirit strong.
>
> "To me, O Lord, Thy grace impart
> Each trial to abide.
> And ever let my fainting heart
> Find refuge at Thy side."

Bernard of Clairvaux (417):

> "Ah, let me grasp those hands,
> That we may never part,
> And let the power of their blood
> Sustain my fainting heart."

Add Paul Gerhardt, from whom many a line might be quoted (383):

> "Be Thou my consolation
> And, when I die, my shield;
> Let me behold Thy passion
> When I my breath must yield.
> Mine eyes, to Thee uplifted,
> Upon Thy cross shall dwell,
> My heart by faith enfold Thee:
> Who dieth thus dies well."

But all our tribulation is also connected with Christ in such a manner that Paul calls it "the sufferings of Christ." In what sense the genitive is to be understood Jesus himself explains in John 15:18-21, especially in the statement: "All these things will they do unto you for my name's sake." Παθήματα (generally plural) has a passive sense, *Leiden*, injuries inflicted upon us. The genitive may be regarded as subjective: the sufferings which Christ endured. These same sufferings, Paul says, now "abound for us" (Paul and Timothy). The thought is not that in glory Christ continues to suffer these sufferings, but that his original sufferings which, as far as his suffering is concerned, were completed at the time of his death continue after a fashion in those who are connected with him. The very same hatred that killed him on the cross now hurts his believers who are one with him by faith in his name. This thought explains such passages as Matt. 20:22, 23; Rom. 8:17; Gal. 6:17; Phil. 3:10; Col. 1:24; Heb. 13:13; I Pet. 4:13.

Deissmann mentions a "mystical genitive," and others speak about Christ's still suffering because of his mystical union with us by referring to some of the passages quoted and adding those which speak of us as his body, members of his body, (I Cor. 12:12; 6:15; Acts 9:4, 5). In I Cor. 12:21 the head is not Christ but one of the members, and in v. 26 all the members suffer, and yet v. 27 does not intimate that Christ suffers. In the *unio mystica* Christ is never *identified* with us, his spiritual body; we are not = Christ, nor is Christ = we. There is only a *unio*. So the human nature of Christ does not = the divine, nor is the reverse true; yet there was a *unio* of the two. As to Acts 9:4, 5, it is plain that the glorified Christ was persecuted in the Christians, and that nothing is said to the effect that Christ was still undergoing pain.

Some also state that this mysticism follows the Hellenistic mystery cults, for instance, the expressions used by the Attis and the Osiris mystics. The suffering god is identified with his devotee mystics. More than this, what the god is to the mystic, the mystic is to his fellow. "As Christ bore *our* sins, we bear *his* diseases and sufferings; he has by no means taken them from us, on the contrary, he loads on us what he still has to bear and lets us suffer with him." "Also he (Paul) is for his own a 'preceder,' an 'Attis,' a 'Christ,' at least the mediator of the saving operations of Christ." Paul has borrowed from the pagans!

Some of these exegetes point to a Jewish apocalyptic source. But the Jewish apocalyptic "birth pains of the Messiah" do not match the θλίψεις and the παθήματα of Christ as Paul speaks about them. For the ungodly those "birth pains" were a penalty; these exegetes say they were this also for the godly, and the Messiah comes only after these pains have been completed. So it is said that Paul modified the idea but kept the main point: insofar as the παθήματα of Christ represent the sufferings of the last times and thus precede the Parousia and furnish assurance for the reception into the Messianic eon, the Jewish idea is preserved. But Paul was a Christian.

6) From the third person: "those in all affliction" (v. 4), Paul passes quietly to the second and to the direct address with the two genitives "your." Δέ is not adversative but continuative: "besides," "moreover"; and the addition to the abundance of the sufferings and of the comforting through Christ (v. 5) is that both are experienced by Paul and by Timothy ὑπέρ — ὑπέρ, *"in behalf of"* the Corinthians and the Achaians. Paul is faulted because he divides the affliction and the comforting: "whether — whether." The fact is that the affliction and the comforting are purposely

divided from the beginning (v. 4) and remain so, and each is spoken of with reference to the other. Both are made to stand out.

Conditions of reality are used; we do not translate with English subjunctives as our versions do. Paul and Timothy *are* afflicted, *are* comforted, and in these clauses they speak thus regarding both experiences. The idea of substitution should not be inserted into the two ὑπέρ phrases; yet this is done by some. Only in certain connections does this preposition convey the idea of substitution, namely when an act must be "instead of" in order to be "for." In the apodosis we supply "it is," which the Greek does not need. Already the fact that Paul and Timothy bear affliction is "for your comforting and salvation," the two are regarded as a unit because of the one article (R. 782); compare the designations for God in v. 2, 3.

Salvation is here not to be taken in the restricted sense of deliverance from afflictions but in the regular sense of being saved from sin, death, and damnation. It is lacking in the next "for" phrase, for the first phrase is objective: the comforting and the salvation which *God* works; the second is subjective: the comforting which works in endurance, in perseverance *in us* so that we hold out amid afflictions and in this way reach the goal, final salvation. Both of these purposes and these effects start with the divine comforting hence both phrases begin: ὑπὲρ τῆς ὑμῶν παρακλήσεως; then, however, they diverge, the one to the final effect "salvation," the other to the means in us, our "endurance of the same sufferings which (ὧν attracted from ἅ) we, too, are suffering."

What the readers see in Paul and in Timothy, how much they must bear in their work of spreading the gospel, is to benefit these readers, is to be "for your comforting and salvation" as showing them "that we must through much tribulation (διὰ πολλῶν θλίψεων, the noun that is derived from the very verb used here) enter into the kingdom of God," i. e., final salvation, Acts 14:22. It is always so. If the leaders would have an easy life, one that is free from affliction, what would the general membership think when it finds itself in much affliction? But when it sees how the Lord burdens the leaders with the greatest affliction, that very fact is comforting to the members and aids their salvation when they, too, feel affliction. So Christ himself attained the crown through the cross. Again and again he marked out the same path for his apostles and also for all his true followers. It is unwarranted to fault Paul for dividing, for speaking first about the purpose of his afflictions in regard to his readers.

Naturally and necessarily the other side is now added. Paul and Timothy are comforted, in fact, this epistle starts with the strongest praise to God for this comforting (v. 3, 4) and is throughout written from the viewpoint of the full experience of God's comforting. When it is witnessed by their readers it is and will be "for your comforting (namely that comforting) which works in endurance of the same sufferings which we, too, are suffering." To see Paul and Timothy comforted will surely help their readers the better to endure the same kind of suffering. It is always so: the comfort seen in the leaders, the assurance, faith, and joy with which they endure are of great benefit to the members for making them hold out in the same kind of suffering.

Paul does not say that the comforting works endurance but works *"in* endurance." That point is worth noting, for the phrase implies that the readers are already "in" this endurance, and that the divine comforting operates in it by strengthening and increasing it. Ὑπομονή = the remaining under, brave, steady holding out, perseverance. The sufferings must, of course, be such as can be called "the sufferings of Christ" (v. 5). Read I Pet. 2:19-23 and note that being buffeted for our faults is a quite different matter.

The thought and the wording are above criticism. As the double statement begins with "we are afflicted," so it ends with "we are suffering," and between the beginning and the end all the comforting and its benefit are mentioned. Still finer is the chiastic thought: suffering — salvation; then comforting — in endurance of suffering. Moreover, this chiasm is not artificial; it reproduces the facts as they are.

We need not ask about affliction and sufferings among the Corinthians and the Achaians. They were certainly no exception when they were compared with other Christians. The only question is whether Paul refers to griefs that were caused him by the Corinthians and then also to griefs of the Corinthians, both such as unruly and misled brethren caused the faithful brethren in Corinth and such as Paul had to cause by correcting them. We may remember how much Jesus had to endure from the Twelve. Think of the pain which Philip caused him (John 14:8, 9), of Peter's frequent rashness which was so trying to Jesus, of Peter's denial, of Judas. Many a rebuke had to be spoken by Jesus' lips. These things are in a way constantly repeated. The injuries inflicted by those who are outside are less painful than the injuries inflicted by those who are inside.

7) In typical Pauline fashion the two chiastic lines of thought are now brought to their unity in the hope of Paul and of Timothy for their readers. The advance is not from ὑπομονή to ἐλπίς. The article is practically demonstrative: "this hope of ours for you." It is "firm" as it has ever been. Why so firm? Because back of it is "the Father of the compassions and God of all comforting." It thus rests on the knowledge "that as you are partakers (the adjective used as a

noun) of the sufferings, so also of the comforting." These two merge into one. The duality unfolded in v. 4 and already there in a measure woven together, now comes to its unity.

We find no anacoluthon in εἰδότες since "our" precedes; even grammatically all is in smooth order, and no apology is in place. In order to be really firm hope must rest on knowledge. Some think that this knowledge is the information that was brought from Corinth by Titus. "This hope of ours" has a more solid basis. It was in the heart of Paul and of Timothy before Titus arrived; it was only confirmed by his good report. If Titus had brought bad news, he who wrote: "Love hopeth all things" (I Cor. 13:7), would still have hoped on and in this hope have worked for Corinth. Paul and Timothy knew how the sufferings and the comforting go together, as in their case so also in the case of the Corinthians, in the experiences through which they were passing. The two genitives are objective.

II. Deliverance and Thanksgiving

8) A recent deliverance from mortal danger still fills the writers' hearts with its effects, and these help to explain to the readers with what feelings this epistle is being written. This paragraph is thus still introductory and secondary to v. 3-7. "For" = that you may the more understand our feelings.

For we do not want you to be ignorant, brethren, concerning the distress of ours which occurred in Asia, that we became weighted down exceedingly beyond ability so that we got to despair even of living on; yea, we ourselves have had the verdict of death within our own selves in order that we may not get to placing confidence on our own selves but on the God who raises up the dead: he who did deliver us out of so great a death and will deliver us, in

whom we have been hoping (ever since) **that he will also still deliver us: you also joining in help in our behalf with petition in order that, as** (coming) **from many persons, the gracious gift** (obtained) **for us by means of many may get to receive thanks on our behalf.**

All of the key words are repeated: "death" twice, the verb "deliver" three times, "many" twice, "in our behalf" twice. The deliverance thus looms above all else. The story itself is not told, for not its details but the divine purpose apparent in it is the main point together with the cooperation of the readers in this purpose. Something that was almost fatal had recently happened to Paul and to Timothy while they were still in the Roman province of Asia; they had resigned themselves to death; God had practically raised them from the dead. His purpose in doing so is all too plain. Too many of the readers cannot join in fervent thanks on behalf of the two who were brought from the gates of death.

"We do not want you to be ignorant" is a kind of litotes for "we want you to be informed." "Brethren" reaches out to the readers and counts on their concern. Here they have a sample of what Paul and his assistants must at times undergo. Here was a θλῖψις, "pressure" indeed, actual mortal "distress." The same word has been used three times before (once as a verb) together with its synonyms. Here, too, is a sample of deliverance and of the comfort and the sure hope which it yields. Some of the tenses show how vividly the memory of it remains in the writers. They had just recently come out of the province of Asia via Troas.

When Paul writes "Asia," we are left without a clue as to the city. Some think of Ephesus and the tumult incited by Demetrius before Paul left. Aside from other features that fail to fit, this takes us back several months, and Paul is writing about something recent. Some mention Troas but do not note that it lay neither in the province of Asia nor in that of Mysia but was an independent city. Paul's vagueness is also thought to be due to the fact that the readers, at least the Corinthians, knew; but this, too, is unsatisfactory, for "we do not want you to remain ignorant" (present infinitive) means that this is the first information which they are receiving. Titus had not known until he reached Paul and Timothy; Titus would give the details to the Corinthians.

Let us confess that all that we know is what is written here. Many guesses have been made; we shall not even list them. The ὅτι clause is appositional to "the distress of ours" and states in what this distress consisted. Θλῖψις = pressure, and this was so intense "that we became weighted down exceedingly beyond ability." The aorist is ingressive, and this verb is always passive in the New Testament. The pressure got to be such a weight that Paul and Timothy crumbled under it. It was καθ' ὑπερβολήν, hyperbolical, excessive, actually ὑπὲρ δύναμιν, "beyond ability," and we should remember that at least Paul's ability was not small. When he gave up hope, his case was grave indeed. The result clause states outright: "so that we got to despair (again ingressive) even of living on" (τοῦ with the infinitive after verbs that take the genitive, B.-D. 400, 3; R. 996 calls this an ablative). We venture only one assertion here: this was not a court trial, for "even of living on" suggests an entirely different kind of mortal danger. Paul and Timothy had resigned themselves to death.

The question has been raised regarding the force of "we" in this paragraph. Does Paul refer only to himself, only to himself and to Timothy, or are others included, his entire party? He generally traveled with several companions. The exegetical answer is that Paul and Timothy are speaking for themselves. If others *were* involved, these two speak only about themselves.

9) Ἀλλά is not "but" (A. V., commentators), it only carries the story on (R. 1186), it is the nonadversative or continuative use of this word: "yea" (R. V.). With vivid recollection the perfect tense states what happened and is still present to the mind. R. 896, etc., calls it the dramatic perfect; John loves it and uses it frequently. "We ourselves have had the verdict of death within our own selves" and still feel this dire experience. Some debate as to whether ἐσχήκαμεν may, perhaps, have the force of an aorist and be like the preceding aorists; there is no need for such a view when the use of the perfect is understood.

Τὸ ἀπόκριμα τοῦ θανάτου is a technical juridical term: "the death sentence" (A. V.) and not "the answer of death" (R. V.); see B.-P. 146; M.-M. 64; C.-K. 633 is less good. Here again the wording, although it is juridical, points us away from a court trial. They themselves in their own selves have had the death sentence = they themselves pronounced it in their own hearts. In this way they despaired of living on. They were staring death in the face as men do on whom the death penalty has been pronounced, a penalty that is to be executed forthwith; for in those days it followed immediately as it did in Jesus' case. They had come that close to death.

Paul is not telling how low they were brought in order to excite his readers with the tale or to arouse their sympathy but from this his recent experience to show them the great purpose which God had in letting him and Timothy despair of living on, in letting them tell themselves that their end had come. It was "in order that we may not get to placing confidence on our own selves but on the God who raises up the dead." Or, putting it in the wording of the first paragraph, in order to go to the God of real comforting in distress.

Paul and Timothy had been brought to the point "beyond ability," to the point of despair, where all struggle, even mental struggle, was useless, where they waited only for the deathblow to fall. Not even the least confidence in themselves or in their own resources was left to them. If they had such confidence in anything which they might do, it had utterly deserted them. They were absolutely naked and stripped. That was the very purpose of God.

More than that. They had not only reached a point where only trust in God was left to them, but even God was able to save them by nothing less than a miracle, yea, the greatest miracle, his power to raise up the dead. So close to death were they that their deliverance was identical with raising them from the dead. They had the alternative of utter despair or this supreme trust. We have the periphrastic perfect subjunctive: πεποιθότες ὦμεν, which R. 908 lists as intensive. As a subjunctive it is future, as a perfect it is punctiliar-durative, the start is marked and then the continuance: ——>, which we try to convey by rendering: "get to placing confidence."

This divine purpose is the high point of Paul's narration. The readers feel that Paul and Timothy were taught this confidence providentially at this time, and not without reference to the work in Corinth. Trusting in God who raises up the dead, who so recently demonstrated in the case of Paul and of Timothy themselves that he is, indeed, such a God, they were to trust him in regard to all future difficulties at Corinth or elsewhere. When hope has left us and death is the only prospect, then God stands forth, the God who raises up the dead. Such situations are his opportunity, for he, and he alone, is able to meet them.

Wenn die Not am groessten, ist Gott am naechsten (When the need is greatest, God is nearest). One reason that distress must reach the extreme point where all human help is utterly gone and we ourselves realize that and give up completely is "that we get to placing confidence, not on our own selves, but (with finality) on the God who raises up the dead." When that experience is needed, God provides it. Paul really confesses that he needed it, needed it at this time. That is comfort for us lesser men.

The view that the expression "who raises up the dead" is originally Jewish, that it is found in Jewish prayers, etc., and is derived from the Old Testament, is acceptable. But why call it a "formula," and why deny that it is here Christianized when every Christian reader automatically thinks of the fact that Christ raised the dead and was himself raised on Easter morning? But when Babylonian paganism is brought in with its Marduk and its Ninib as raisers from the dead, the Christian must object, for this does not agree with I Cor. 2:13 (see the author's exposition).

10) With a simple relative we are told about the deliverance: "who did deliver us out of so great a death," the historical aorist indicates the fact; yet the relative has demonstrative force: "he who," etc. In the New Testament the adjective always refers to size, R. 710. Nothing but the mighty deliverance itself as well as nothing but the mortal danger are recorded. We have only the essentials with no detail to divert our attention.

But the verb "to deliver" is now driven home; it is repeated two additional times. These writers who were delivered love the very sound of this word. Their wonderful deliverance, which is still so vivid in their minds, makes them see God's deliverance in the days to come: "did deliver us and will deliver." After such a supreme deliverance will God ever fail them? God, the Deliverer, is his name. When he then does let us die, when his work with us on earth is completed, he removes us with a final deliverance, the most blessed of all. Luther in regard to the Seventh Petition of the Lord's Prayer: "Finally, when our last hour has come, grant us a blessed end and graciously take us from this vale of tears to himself in heaven."

We pass by the changes in the text and in the punctuation that have been offered, none of which commend themselves. "And will deliver" is to be repeated and to be emphasized by the relative clause: "in whom we have been hoping that he will also still deliver us." Ever since that great deliverance, when God so signally proved himself the Deliverer, Paul and Timothy achieved new strength of hope for deliverance from anything that might still come upon them. Hope grows in a twofold way: by means of the promises in the Word, by means of signal experiences of God's deliverance, especially such as reveal the delivering hand of God in a manner not to be mistaken. Here the latter is meant. The perfect tense implies the present continuance of this hope.

11) In concluding Paul and Timothy reach out to their readers who will join them by means of petition and thanksgiving. The unspoken thought is the bond which connects the writers and their readers, which is significant in this epistle because in the case of the Corinthians this inner bond had been strained and was now again being brought to full strength. "You also joining in help in our behalf with petition" means adding their prayers to those of the writers for their deliverance in any future need. Δέησις is "petition" to have some need supplied, "supplication" as when a beggar asks alms; it is used with reference to asking from men as well as with reference to asking from God. The thought is that the readers can add help by means of their petition (dative of means).

One purpose which the readers and the writers will have in this joint appeal to God is to multiply the thanks to God for the gracious response which God will make to their petition. The subject is τὸ εἰς ἡμᾶς χάρισμα διὰ πολλῶν, "the gracious gift (obtained) for us by means of many," i. e., by the petition of many. The verb is passive and is modified by the phrase which is placed forward for the sake of emphasis: ἐκ πολλῶν προσώπων — εὐχαριστηθῇ ὑπὲρ ἡμῶν, "from many persons — may get to receive thanks on our behalf," i. e., get a multitude of thanks. R., *W. P.*, finds the clause difficult to understand; it is also called *schwulstig*, overloaded, etc. We do not agree. This difficulty is due to making wrong combinations of the expressions used and thus getting an irregular sense of the meaning. There is no need to take up these wrong constructions that create difficulties where none exist.

"The gracious gift (coming) to or for us by means of many," when it is considered together, refers, not to the past deliverance of Paul and of Timothy, but to God's future gracious help in response to the prayers of the many readers; the gift is future and not past, and διά is the proper word to refer to the many petitioners. The ἐκ phrase is to be construed with the passive verb: the thanks (certainly not the gift) are to come "out of" the hearts and the mouths of many persons. And it is this that Paul and Timothy and their readers should purpose.

The word χάρισμα does not refer to a charisma or endowment like those listed in I Cor. 12:8-10. Of linguistic interest only is the question whether πρόσωπα = "persons" or "countenances," and whether πολλῶν is an adjective or a noun. Arguments are offered pro and con. The one that convinces some more than anything else is the idea that the thanks come from (out of) the *faces* that are upturned to God in prayer. "From many *persons*" is good Koine and fits the sentence exactly.

An unacceptable thought has been found in this verse, namely that God is ready to help out only when he is acknowledged as the Helper, and that the greater the number of those is who cry to him for help and then join in thanking and praising him for his help, the more readily will God help. So, we are told, the psalmist literally summoned all creation to join in a maximum chorus of praise and thanksgiving, cf., Ps. 103:20-22. This thought implies that God selfishly wants all the credit and all the glory and in reality is so mean that, unless he gets what he wants, he will let men perish miserably. The fact that God is infinite love and mercy, that he so reveals himself, that he saves to the uttermost those who deserve to perish in their sin and guilt, all of this truth passes unnoticed. The fact that God *is* the one Helper, and that he *can* help only when we give up the lie and the delusion that we can help ourselves, is also ignored.

Can anything be more blessed *for us* than fully to recognize who he is and what his love and his mercy are for us, and who and what we are in our mortal need? Can anything be more blessed than the knowledge that this recognition should extend to all believers, yea, to all creatures, so that with united voice they cry to God as their one true helper, give up the folly of seeking help where none is possible, and glorify God in praise and in thanksgiving for his grace and his mercy? Yea, *can* God give "the gracious gift" ($\chi\acute{a}\rho\iota\sigma\mu a$) when men treat him as did the slave in Luke 19:20, 21 or as did the despicable guest in Matt. 22, 11, 12?

III. *Conscience and Sincerity*

12) Instead of calling this the real beginning of the body of the epistle, we take it that the two preceding paragraphs merge into all that the two writers desire to communicate in this epistle. So $\gamma\acute{a}\rho$ = let us explain why it is that we count on your prayers and

your thanksgiving to God for us (v. 11). We, Paul and Timothy, are of value to you as you are to us.

For our glorying is this, the testimony of our conscience, that in God's holiness and sincerity, not in fleshly wisdom but in God's grace, we have conducted ourselves in the world and especially toward you. For we write no other things to you, other than what you read, than also you understand, and I hope that to the end you will continue to understand even also as you did understand us (at least) **in part that we are your subjects of glorying just as also you are ours, in connection with the day of our Lord Jesus.**

We shall not speak of a disharmony of terms, that while καύχησις is the act of boasting or glorying, μαρτύριον and ὅτι κτλ. are the matter of the boasting, i. e., the boast. Nor shall we erase the distinction between καύχησις, the act, and καύχημα (v. 14), the matter, in order to remove the disharmony. To be sure, the act is here not described as being merely an act. But many acts automatically involve their subject matter; boasting always has something about which it boasts. Of such an act one may predicate the matter with which it deals. The advantage is that the act itself is mentioned and retained. That is the case here. The writers say that they do engage in boasting, and that when they do, it is the testimony of their conscience, etc., with which the act deals.

A certain type of pietism tells the Christian never to boast, at least not about anything in himself. Paul is free from this inhibition. He boasts of his good conscience and his good Christian conduct; in v. 14 he makes the readers of this letter his boast and himself and his assistants in the work the boast of his readers. It is one way of glorifying God for what he has produced in us and through us. Some people are so humble that their humility fails to acknowledge with joy what God has done. The boasting that is reprehensible glories in what we are and what we achieve of ourselves (Luke 18:11, 12). We shall find a great deal of genuine boasting in this epistle.

"The testimony of our conscience" (subjective genitive) is the predicate (not an apposition), and ὅτι states the substance of the testimony. Μαρτύριον = substance; μαρτυρία = quality; the one, *what* is testified, the other, the *nature* of what is testified. On "conscience" see the discussion in Rom. 2:15. Etymologically it means *Mitwissen* (a knowing with), and the very word implies a duality: I myself know, and conscience knows. It knows, and I cannot deceive it, and it at the same time judges me and is a judge that cannot be bribed. Conscience is that in us which holds us to a norm of right and damns us when we violate that norm. It is not itself this norm, but it always has its norm. In the case of Paul and of Timothy it had the true and the perfect norm supplied by God in his Word. Their conscience was properly enlightened. "The testimony of our conscience" refers to the *conscientia consequens*, to what conscience testifies concerning an act or a course of conduct after it is finished; the antecedent conscience pronounces on acts or on conduct contemplated and proposed.

Now the conscience of the writers gave them this testimony: "that in God's holiness and sincerity, not in fleshly wisdom but in God's grace, we have conducted ourselves (the Greek aorist to indicate the past fact) in the world and especially toward you." It approved of their entire past course, it condemned nothing in that course and that conduct. The second passive is used as a middle, the Koine prefers these passive forms and even creates new second passives.

The reading ἁγιότητι, "in holiness," has better attestation than ἁπλότητι, "in simplicity," (A. V.) or singleness of heart, although the latter would also be fitting. The former word is rare and for that reason, too, is more likely to be the correct reading. The genitive "of God" is overstrained when it makes this holiness and this sincerity the attributes of God, a possessive genitive; this is the genitive of origin or author: by his grace God works holiness and sincerity in us. Conscience testified that Paul and Timothy had confined their conduct within the sphere drawn by these qualities. Holiness is a broad term which covers the whole relation to God and the devotion to him. Sincerity signifies honesty and uprightness, without duplicity, and refers to the relation toward men.

"Not in fleshly wisdom" is the denial of the opposite. Σαρκικός = κατὰ σάρκα ὤν, what accords with flesh, with man's sinful nature, here that which is still left in the believer. Such "fleshly wisdom" seeks its own selfish ends in its own cunning ways. In contrast with it is "but in God's grace," which is now a divine attribute, the one that is operative in all believers (see v. 2). All three ἐν = "in union and connection with"; the view that they signify place is incorrect. Fleshly wisdom and God's grace are the sources, the former making holiness and sincerity in us impossible, the latter producing both. Paul might have used two genitives: "wisdom of the flesh" — "grace of God"; but that would parallel "flesh" and "God," a procedure which the adjective "fleshly" purposedly avoids. That debased wisdom is the evil source in us, God's grace is the divine power from above. This wisdom fits means to an end and thus looks wise, looks attractive because it looks wise, and thus deceives us. It is the devil's invention which deceived Eve. God's grace, which is itself the pure favor of undeserved love, draws us upward into a life that is holy and sincere.

Thus Paul and his assistants had conducted themselves. That statement is here made only regarding Paul and Timothy, but we know that it applies to Paul's assistants as well. "In the world" = among men generally. The comparative adverb "more abundantly" is our "especially." Πρός, "toward you," refers to relationship; in some instances this preposition conveys something that is almost intimate and personal (R. 624). Are Paul and Timothy boasting unduly? The testimony of their conscience is certainly fully supported by all that we know about them. In fact, when it comes to specifying under the term "holiness," much more might be added besides "sincerity."

13) "For" now specifies; γάρ = "for to mention one thing." The reference is plainly to Paul's letters to the Corinthians and to charges that were brought against Paul on the basis of these letters. His character had been attacked. He had been maligned as being a man who did not always mean what he wrote. From what he intimates we conclude that his opponents had not even carefully noted just what he did write, and that they went about and spread false reports regarding what he had written, misled others by their talk, and, when they were then corrected, blamed him.

We have an instance of this kind in I Cor. 5:9-11. Paul there refers to something he had written in an earlier letter, one that is lost; and we see that it was not read properly, and that Paul was compelled to correct the misunderstanding, one that was wholly unwarranted as his correction of the Corinthians shows. Whether other instances of a similar nature occurred we cannot say. But it is a common experience that opponents misread or are averse to understanding even plainly written statements and then begin making charges and spreading them. The hypothesis that reference is here made to what the critics call the *Zwischenbrief* or the *Traenenbrief* (2:4) is untenable.

"We write" includes the present letter and the two previous ones of which we know. It might include also any letter which Paul would write in the future. The "we" in the verb has the same force that all of the preceding "we" had. Paul and Timothy were the writers, Paul was the principal writer; in I Cor. 1:1 it was Sosthenes who joined Paul in writing that letter. What these letters say in writing is exactly what the readers read when reading the writing, and what those who hear the writing read to them understand; and for himself Paul says that they will also always so understand. Ἀλλ' ἤ repeats ἀλλά pleonastically (R. 1187); we have imitated it in English: "no other things . . . other than," etc. No covert meanings, no ambiguities, which permit the readers and the hearers to think that one thing is meant and allow Paul later to evade the issue by claiming that he meant another, and no tricks of language which allow all sorts of reservations, no such things are found in the letters but only what one actually reads or, if it be read to him, actually and naturally understands. The latter is added because a letter to the congregation was read aloud so that all might hear it. This is still done today in the case of letters that are intended to be read in public.

With "I hope" Paul incidentally speaks for himself. Ἕως τέλους is an adverbial phrase which, like many other such phrases, needs no article. "Moreover (δέ), I hope that to the end you will continue to understand" (the future tense is naturally durative here) is no mere pious or optimistic wish but a gentle reminder of past, unjustified misunderstanding that ought never to reoccur. "To the end" certainly does not mean "to the end of the world," nor specifically "to the end of my life," but "as long as any of you live," for Paul is speaking about *their* understanding. The verb never means "to acknowledge" (our versions), but three times in this connection and thus pointedly it means "to understand" (C.-K. 252). We see no reason for making the καθώς clause parenthetical: "I hope that to the end you will continue to understand — even also as you have understood us in part — that we are your subject for glorying." Verse 14 simply continues the thought; "will continue to understand" needs no object. Note the fine paronomasia: ἀναγινώσκετε — ἐπιγινώσκετε — ἐπιγινώσεσθε — ἐπέγνωτε.

14) The Greek simply marks the time as past and hence uses the aorist; we desire to indicate the relative time and hence use our perfect: "even also as you did know us in part, i. e., have known us at least in part." Paul had worked in Corinth for eighteen months, founding and thoroughly establishing the congregation; Timothy and other assistants were with him. Then no cloud had arisen to darken the understanding by disaffecting the minds. When Paul and the others spoke, the Corinthians understood. Paul adds truthfully ἀπὸ μέρους, which has the force, "at least in part." This does not mean a part of the Corinthians so that at least a few understood. This phrase never means *stueckweise* as is still suggested, which implies that the Corinthians understood a fragment here and there. They understood "in part" means that the Corinthians did not penetrate completely into the profound truths which Paul and his assistants preached to them. In I Cor. 3:1, 2 Paul says that they were then only babes and had to be fed milk. He is not blaming the Corinthians, for it is natural at the beginning to understand only "in part." So to understand is not to misunderstand. What had happened recently was that a spirit of opposition had arisen which was intent on finding fault with Paul and his assistants and was putting meanings into his and into their words which were not there.

Second Peter 3:16 is sometimes referred to, especially the statement that some things in Paul's letters are hard to understand, but Peter's addition is omitted: "which they that are unlearned and unstable wrest, as they do also the other Scriptures, unto their own destruction." Note "unstable" and the fact that these people wrest the other Scriptures as they do Paul's words. Peter commends "the wisdom given to Paul" in what he had written. This wisdom from God naturally contained some things that were profound and not immediately easily understood. Peter knew what ignorant and unstable men had done with these statements of Paul. Here, however, such more difficult things are not involved; the reference is to trusting that Paul and Timothy mean whatever they say and write. Both remind the Corinthians that they at one time had had no difficulty, that they had understood their teachers well; and these teachers have not changed a particle in that respect, something about the Corinthians had changed. The source of past misunderstanding lay in them.

The ὅτι clause does not state the reason that the Corinthians at one time understood Paul and Timothy. The tense disagrees with that sense; it ought then to be: "because we *were* your subject of glorying," were really then considered so by you. The clause is epexegetical to the pronoun "us"; "did understand us . . . that we are your subject of glorying," καύχημα is explained in v. 12. The tense is the same as the Greek would use in direct discourse. The thought is: you Corinthians once understood us well enough and thought: They are our pride and glory — as we indeed still are. They felt a sacred pride in Paul, Timothy, and the others because such gospel heralds had been sent to them by God. These men are still unchanged today. It is no undue claim on the part of Paul to imply that the Corinthians should still boast about them, about their connection with them. The former estimate was, in fact, restored in good part, and this letter is to complete the restoration.

Paul's great heart at once reverses the thought: "just as also you are ours" — to this very day you

Corinthians and all believers in Achaia are our great pride and boast, of whom we are sacredly proud. The writers think about all that, by God's grace, they have been privileged to accomplish in their readers, and this swells their hearts. This is not a mutual admiration society — you kiss me, and I kiss you. A true basis, an actual reason for glorying exists, one that was produced by God. Attention was fixed on that, for it is the best means of removing all still lingering misunderstanding and lack of appreciation on the part of the Corinthians. Note the force of the genitives and how they bind the writers and the readers together: we *your* subject of glorying — in the same way you also *ours*. Καθάπερ = κατὰ ἃ πέρ, "according to what indeed" = "just as."

Both subjects for glorying are now suddenly placed into the divine light: "in connection with the day of our Lord Jesus," the last day, when our Lord Jesus shall appear for judgment, and when all of us shall stand before him. There is considerable confusion regarding ἐν. It is said to fix the date when this mutual glorying will occur. And then Paul's eschatology, his viewing this glorying as a "dogma" and not as a present experience, and the like are referred to. Ἐν = "in connection with," and the connection is in the hearts and in the minds of the writers and the readers. Everything of which they boast — and let us add of which they fail to boast — they put into the light of the last day. That clarifies the vision; that removes faultfinding, wrong motives, tainted purposes. In all that Paul and Timothy think about the Corinthians, say to them, and do regarding them, they keep that day in mind; and the Corinthians should ever do the same in regard to Paul and Timothy. How many hostilities, misunderstandings, unbrotherly actions would never occur if we ever kept in mind our connection with that day? How much love, good-will, and graciousness would strew roses along the path of our brethren if each of us always saw that day as the goal of our mutual path?

IV. *Yea Is Yea*

15, 16) Paul refutes the charge that, as far as we can conclude, was bruited about in the past and not entirely silenced as yet, that one could not depend on his word, that his yea, yea and his nay, nay were confused so that one could not tell which he really intended when he used either. He had made a material change in his plans regarding his coming to Corinth; he had not adhered to his original plan. We at once see how flimsy a ground there was for challenging his veracity and his reliability; how only ill-will or something worse could prefer such a charge against any man on such grounds, to say nothing about one who was so proved as was Paul among the Corinthians. He had even informed them about his change of plans. He had not assigned reasons for the change, had not thought it necessary, he had expected enough good-will on the part of the Corinthians to suppose that he was acting on the basis of good reasons. But no; from the report of Titus he now learned that he was still being attacked on this score.

He takes up this point first. It is so easy to settle. Yet the charge is an odious one, especially when it is brought against an apostle. It belongs to that type which opponents love to make against ministers: He is not a man of his word, in fact, when it suits him, he lies. We now see why Paul writes as he does in v. 12-14 regarding the testimony of his conscience, regarding his conducting himself in holiness and sincerity and not in fleshly wisdom, about writing just what his readers read and understand him to say in his writing, etc. Here we have the first application of all of this.

And with this confidence I decided formerly to come to you in order that you might get to have a second grace, namely to go on through you into Macedonia and to come again from Macedonia to you and (then finally) **to be sent on forward by you into Judea. Now in deciding on this was I then using fickleness? or was I deciding on what I was deciding in a fleshly way so that with me there is** (at the same time) **the yea, yea and the nay, nay?**

The dative of manner "with this confidence" refers to v. 13, 14, the confidence that the Corinthians would understand and appreciate his motives for making the change. We now have the first person singular. In this connection the verb βούλομαι does not mean "to wish" but "to decide," it is here used three times in the identical sense. The tense is the imperfect, and this is quite important, for it implies that the decision was not carried out. Paul was holding to this decision until he at last found reason for altering it. He wrote to the Corinthians about his altered plan in I Cor. 16:4-8 and told them that he intended to go through Macedonia to Corinth, hence not by sea directly from Ephesus to Corinth, that he would then visit Macedonia and return to Corinth.

The plan to go by sea was given up when First Corinthians was written. It seems that this plan had been made known to the Corinthians, this was in all probability done in the letter which preceded First Corinthians, the letter which is lost but is mentioned by Paul in I Cor. 5:9. The new plan, regarding which I Cor. 16 informed the Corinthians, was in process of execution as Paul writes Second Corinthians.

There is some difference of opinion as to whether πρότερον belongs to ἐβουλόμην or to the following infinitive ἐλθεῖν. But adverbs are commonly placed next to their verbs: "I decided formerly." If this adverb were to be construed with the infinitive it would follow the infinitive: "to go to you formerly," i. e., before this. The original plan was that the visit would bring "a second grace" to the Corinthians. The first grace was the stay of one and one half years when the congregation was founded (Acts 18), the visit that was now planned was to be long enough to be reckoned as a second blessing. Since Paul had to go to Macedonia also, his plan was to go by sea to Corinth, then to Macedonia, then back to Corinth, in order to make his stay at Corinth as extended as possible; for he could also sail from Macedonia (Philippi, its harbor town being Neapolis) to Judea. Some think that "a second grace" was this proposed return from Macedonia to Corinth; if "second" meant "double," this would be satisfactory. As it is, "second grace" refers to the entire visit in Corinth, the clause that follows adds only that it would consist of two parts.

Χάριν has better attestation than χαράν, "joy." "A second grace" should not be reduced to a *Freundlichkeitserweis*, a favor shown by Paul. He would come as an apostle whose office it was to dispense *God's* grace wherever and whenever he came. When he plans to visit Rome he writes about getting some fruit there by gospel preaching (Rom. 1:13-15). He does not visit churches in order to dispense personal favors. We may note that according to both plans Macedonia had to be visited. We know one reason for this, the matter of the collection. "To be sent forward by you" (see I Cor. 16:6) refers to the custom of fitting out the traveler and of having men from the congregation accompany him at least a part of the way. In Acts 17:14, 15 the men of Berea conducted Paul the entire way to Athens.

Some have characterized these two verses as "belonging to the most difficult and most controverted in Corinthians." Five possible alternatives are opened up, and these are increased beyond five if combinations are made. We refuse to enter upon a discussion of these.

These facts are well established: 1) that v. 15, 16 present the earlier decision of Paul which was made prior to First Corinthians; 2) that the imperfect tense ἐβουλόμην implies that this decision was altered; 3) that I Cor. 16:5-8 presents the new plan which Paul carried out. Add I Cor. 4:18, 19 to I Cor. 16:5-8. Some thought that Paul would not risk coming at all because he was afraid; in First Corinthians Paul tells them that he is coming shortly, that he will start at Pentecost (he wrote First Corinthians before Easter). He did start at Pentecost. He took the route that he said in I Cor. 16 he would take. He wrote Second Corinthians while he was traveling that route, while he was in Macedonia. This cannot have occurred a year and a half after First Corinthians was written. The interval between First and Second Corinthians was six months.

17) Paul now asks the Corinthians, and not them alone but all of the Achaians (v. 1): When he made that first decision which he later altered, did he then use fickleness; did he decide what he then decided in a fleshly way so that no one could tell his yea from nay, could tell whether he meant what he said in one way or another, because he dropped his first decision and made another? The questions answer themselves even as the interrogative particle μή implies a negative answer. Only an evil-minded person would charge Paul with fickleness, with violating the word he had given.

We have a right to think of I Cor. 4:18, 19 where it is implied that in Corinth some had charged Paul with cowardice, with being afraid to come. After Paul actually started, after this charge could no longer be made, they turned to the equally odious one that he was not a man of his word — he had changed his route; he was not dividing his visit in Corinth; he was now intending to make just one stay in Corinth! What a crime! Note well I Cor. 16:6: "It may be that I will winter with you," winter with you after leaving at

Pentecost (v. 8). Can this be the second winter after that Pentecost? Never.

Μή τι (or μήτι) are to be taken together as the interrogative particle, and ἄρα "then," refers to the participial clause: is the legitimate deduction this that Paul was using "lightness," the opposite of serious "sincerity" (v. 12)? The article in τῇ ἐλαφρίᾳ does not mean "the fickleness" involved in this case, or the one charged against me, or the one you in general look for in me; the article is only the generic article with abstract nouns, and χράομαι governs the dative. Note the steps: fickleness of mind, a moral character defect — κατὰ σάρκα, "in a fleshly way," i. e., wrong motive and purpose with fleshly, selfish interest — "yea, yea, and nay, nay," wrong act, yea turning out to be nay, which is lying. This is true analysis. We need not shrink from regarding ἵνα as expressing result, especially where the result is in the form of a mental deduction (R. 997-9). The article with "yea, yea" and "nay, nay" marks them as nouns, and the repetition indicates plurals: yea statements, nay statements, so that in regard to Paul ("with me") no one can tell them apart. Paul's opponents generalized from his change of decision and claimed that you could not rely upon anything that he said.

18) Instead of explaining at once why he changed his plans Paul scorns to do this, and rightly. To have explained thus would have been a mistaken defense. Paul has stronger artillery. Men of evil minds would seize upon the explanation, would call it a cunning invention that was made to evade the charge against him. Paul does later on explain why he changed his plans of travel, but these explanations are not intended for his friends who trust him. Explanations regarding motives and purposes only arouse opponents to new attacks. So Paul makes the following answer to friend and foe alike.

But (aside from questions about my decision that I changed) **faithful** (is) **God in respect to this that** (ὅτι) **our word, the one to you, is not yea and nay. For God's Son Jesus Christ, who was preached among you by means of us, by means of me and Silvanus and Timothy, was not yea and nay but has been yea in him. For, however many promises of God** (there are), **in him** (they are) **the yea; wherefore also through him** (they are) **the amen to God for glory by means of us. Moreover, he who is making us firm with you for Christ and anointed us** (is no less a one than) **God, he who sealed us for himself and gave us the pledge of the Spirit in our hearts.** It will, indeed, take more than changing a decision once made to destroy the good name and the character of people such as this!

Much comment does not observe the force of the great argument here made. It does not explain why Paul uses the plural and draws into the plural "we" also his readers, "you." Nor does it explain why he says not a word about his own case, about the decision which he changed. Hence it is said that his rejoinder does not fit the case, or fits it only in the vaguest way. The only point made is that because the gospel is yea, Paul, too, must be so — which is no proof in regard to him.

What Paul says is this: Just stop and think a moment! Here is God, absolutely trustworthy; his Son Jesus Christ, ever yea and not yea and nay; all God's promises in his Son forever yea and amen. And here are *we*, God's own instruments (διά, three times) for conveying this very yea and amen. And here are *we with you*, established by no less a one than God himself and made firm in him and in his Son and in all this yea of his promises, anointed, sealed, pledged with his Spirit (the whole Trinity is thus involved), *you* as well as *we*. What a farce to fault any one of *you and us* for no better reason than that a plan was changed and forthwith to brand that one as not being held by all this yea, as being false and lying in spite of it all! What a monstrous charge to base on such evidence! What a crime even to breathe such a thing, to say nothing of broadcasting it among the rest of us! Who are those that could conceive such a thing in their hearts?

"Faithful is God" is not an oath although it has been thought to be. Paul uses it too often and never as an oath. Ὅτι specifies in what respect the assertion is made: "in respect to this that our word to you is not yea and nay," that when we say a thing we do not really mean it. "Our word to you" = all that we say in dealing with you. "Our word to you" is not limited to the gospel. This statement about God relative to "our word to you" is general and comprehensive. It is at once elucidated at length. Both *"our* word" and "to *you"* are important. Timothy is equally involved with Paul, and not Timothy alone but all of Paul's associates, whom God employs. And all of Paul's readers are involved, the Achaians in general (v. 1) as well as the Corinthians, for through these his ministers God has brought all of them into connection with himself.

19) Here are God's faithfulness and his reliability: "for God's Son Jesus Christ, who was preached among you by means of us, by means of me and Silvanus and Timothy, was not (at any time) yea and nay but has been (ever and always and now is) in him (in connection with God, his Father) yea (and nothing but yea)." When the God of truth conveyed to you readers the Christ of truth he used *us* as his instruments. Could he possibly have used instruments that were devoid of truth? Could they have served as channels for conveying God's Son Jesus Christ who is himself Truth? The readers know God's Son Jesus Christ, him "who was preached among them." Because of their soul's contact with him they know that he was

never (ἐγένετο) yea and nay but has always been (γέγονεν) and thus now is yea, yea only. Nothing in him or in his Word was ever or is now even questionable.

We preached him, says Paul, preached him "among you," and you believed, trusted him as what he is, absolute and blessed yea. *We* were the instruments (διά), Paul says, and you received *our* ministration. He even specifies: "by means of me and Silvanus and Timothy." Three names are used as if three witnesses are referred to. These three started the work in Corinth (Acts 18:5). Silvanus = Silas, which is probably the same Semitic name Græcized and then Latinized, B.-D. 125, 3. If more men helped in Corinth, the mention of these three is enough here.

The point is that the Corinthians had trusted these instruments of God, had trusted their message and their character, for the two went together. No mighty yea-Christ could have been transmitted by yea-and-nay heralds. That certainly counts heavily for their leader Paul. But he was not alone. If he is a yea-and-nay man, what about Silvanus and Timothy? Did they know his character and still work with him? Were they yea-and-nay men too? For one and one-half years the work went on, the Great Yea and Amen was put into the hearts of the Corinthians by these instruments of God. Does that say anything about these instruments, the God who employed them, the Son of God, Jesus Christ, for whom they were employed?

20) How God's Son, Jesus Christ, is ever "yea" is now stated by adding all the promises of God and combining them with God, Christ, and the human instruments: "For however many *promises* of God (there are), *in him* (in Christ they are) the yea; wherefore also *through him* (they are) the amen to *God* for glory by means of *us*." Compact, brief, including everything save "you." Ὅσαι = as many as, all of God's promises. God is faithful (v. 18), and he shows himself to be so

in keeping all of his promises to the letter. In connection with (ἐν) Christ all of them are sealed with "the yea" of verity; wherefore we must also say that through him (διά added to ἐν), through his instrumentality or mediation, they are stamped with "the divine amen." "Truth" is thus Christ's very name (John 14:6). All of the promises center "in him" as their yea; wherefore they are fulfilled "through him" as their amen. "Amen" is the transliterated Hebrew word for "truth" and is used by Paul after doxologies and benedictions; it is used after prayers and in other ways to express the conviction of verity. Here it is made a noun by the article and is used as the predicate.

They are *God's* promises, and Christ's mediatorial fulfillment of them redounds *"to God* for glory" but does this "through us." The two διά phrases match: through Christ — through us. *Through* him the promises are amen, verity, for he fulfills them; *through* Paul and his assistants they produce glory for God, for these are the men who preach Christ and this verity to all whom they can reach, and all such believers praise, honor, and glorify God. The two διά phrases are essential, and the last "through or by means of *us"* contains the point of the argument.

Some say that "us" "includes the congregation," the supposition being a congregational service in which not only the liturgist but the whole congregation with him say: "Amen!" But Paul writes that he as an apostle and his helpers are God's instruments to win "glory" for God by establishing Christ, "the Yea," "the Amen," in men's hearts. Although he is glorious in himself, and there is no possibility of augmenting his glory, God receives glory from his creatures when they recognize who and what he is and when they think and speak of him accordingly. An apostle and the helpers of an apostle, whom God chose and employs for this work, who deal with the everlasting Yea and Verity itself in all God's own promises — can they be charged with playing fast and loose with truth on grounds such as were used for the charge made in Corinth?

21) But the Corinthians themselves belong to this sacred circle. And it is not the apostolic work alone that fills Paul's and his assistants' heart with "God's holiness and sincerity" (v. 12) beyond all playing in fleshly fashion with yea and nay (v. 17), God himself sanctifies their hearts together with the hearts of those who believe through their preaching. This last is added by δέ, "moreover." The emphasis is on Θεός, the predicate, which is without the article, the copula is omitted to add to the emphasis. Now, however, the objects are: "us with *you*" (σύν associative), *us*, the preachers of Christ, the Yea and Amen, and associated with us *you*, the believers of this Christ, the Yea and Amen. This association (not μετά, accompaniment) is that *we* preach and *you* believe. Thus "through us" (v. 20) is explained.

As always, Paul sees the whole, here the whole relation to God, Christ, the gospel promises, and the whole number of those who are in this relation. To make Paul *truthful* involved making him much more; truthfulness is never alone. To make Paul truthful involved making also his assistants truthful and much more (hence the plural "we" since v. 18). And doing all this for these, his ministers of the gospel, involved still more, namely God's doing the same for *you*, the membership of the church. For this reason "to you" and "among you" occur in v. 18, 19, and for this reason "with or in association with you" is made prominent at the end.

Many things are seen rightly only when they are viewed in connection with the whole. The whole office, yea the whole church, God's work in both were attacked by these opponents who assailed the reliability of Paul's word. Paul is making no mere doctrinal statement when he so emphatically says what *God* is doing and has done for "us in association with you" but is penning an eminently practical statement which goes straight to the point at issue. As God could not have employed a liar to convey Christ, the Yea and Amen of truth, in all the gospel promises, so, if God's great apostle who is at the head of all this work of God were indeed a liar, God could not have done and now be doing what he does and has done in the Corinthians in association with Paul and Paul's assistants. One would have to forget all this regarding *God* to credit the base slander against his chief instrument; one would likewise have to forget the very nature of what God was *doing* by means of this instrument, doing in his chosen instruments as well as in the Corinthians themselves.

The first substantivized participle is present and durative: "he who is engaged in making firm us in association with you for Christ." We need not make εἰς = ἐν, "for Christ" is correct. And we must hold fast what has just been said about Christ as God's Son, who was preached by Paul, Silvanus, and Timothy, God's instruments, this Christ who is ever yea and not nay, the Yea and the Amen of all of God's promises. In this light we see what God's making us firm with you signifies, namely rooting and grounding us and you ever more solidly in the Yea and Amen Christ. "For Christ" is not general but specific: the Christ of Verity, and thus covers the very point at issue, veracity.

One article combines into one designation for God his continuous making firm and his past act of anointing, the two belonging together. From what God still does we think back to what he did. Note εἰς Χριστὸν καὶ χρίσας ἡμᾶς, Christ, the "Anointed," and we also "anointed." Because "us" is not again followed by "with you," some suppose that "us" refers only to Paul and his assistants; but then the next "us" and "our" would be equally restricted. This cannot be correct, for all three divine acts apply to "you" as well as to "us" just as does the first act. We have also seen that there is an advance of the thought in this very inclusion of the Corinthians with Paul and his assistants. "Us," which follows "us with you," is only briefer; it would be pedantic to write "us with you" four times.

"Anointed us" means: made us like the Anointed One, Christ. We are being made firm for him because in the very first place God sanctified us as he sanctified Christ, by an anointing. Christ and we are anointed with the Spirit. After the act was once performed, the Spirit remains upon us. The act occurred in our baptism as it did immediately after Christ's baptism. By means of his anointing Christ was placed into his high office and position; our anointing did the same for us. He was made King and Priest in the supreme sense, hence the supreme way in which God anointed him. We were made kings and priests under him, hence the way in which our anointing took place by means of baptism. Those who conceive of baptism as a mere sign and symbol must place the anointing elsewhere than in baptism, a thing that it is most difficult to do.

Now there follows the predicate, the one word Θεός, "God," which is highly emphatic: "is no less a one than *God* himself." And because it is *God*, neither his act of anointing us nor his confirming us can be anything but truly effective.

22) Souter disappoints us in regard to the reading which is either ὁ καί or only καί; Westcott and Hort bracket ὁ, Tischendorf does not. If ὁ is omitted, the ὁ before βεβαιῶν would seem to govern also these last two participles and make them continuations of the subject. In other words, the long subject, which consists of four participles, would be divided by having the predicate "God" thrust into the middle. This strange

construction is removed when the well-attested ὁ is retained, for this makes the last two participial designations appositions to the predicate "God"; "he who sealed us for himself (middle) and gave us the pledge of the Spirit in our hearts."

A seal is affixed for various purposes, for security, concealment, distinction, authentication, attestation, and confirmation. Several purposes are sometimes combined. The idea is here that of ownership: by the seal God marked us for his own (hence the middle voice). The next participle shows how God did this. Although it is added coordinately with καί, God's giving the Spirit in our hearts is his sealing of us for himself. We know of no sealing except by the Spirit. Anointing, sealing, giving the Spirit all occurred in baptism, in a single act.

The ἀρραβών is the first down payment by which he who makes it assures the recipient of final payment in full. The genitive "of the Spirit" is appositional: the Spirit is the pledge. Christ — God — Spirit: the Trinity. From baptism onward, in holy anointing, sacred sealing, and gift of the Spirit, followed by constant confirming, God himself connects us with Christ, the divine Yea and Amen. When evil-minded men vilify us, this is the impregnable bulwark of our defense.

Confirming, sealing, down payment, but not anointing, have been referred to as legal and juridical terms that are technical or semitechnical. It is true that these terms sometimes appear in legal connections, but only sometimes, they occur far more often in altogether nonlegal connections. The terms have also been connected with the pagan mysteries, sealing also with Jewish circumcision. Yet Paul wrote I Cor. 2:13: πνευματικοῖς πνευματικά, and claimed that he spoke, not in words taught by human wisdom, but that he used "spiritual words for spiritual things."

The force of Paul's argument is misunderstood when he is thought to be proving that he did not play with the truth in the matter of his plans for travel because God had done in him all that he here records. That would be proof if it meant Paul's total sanctification and his inability to sin after his baptism (Phil. 3:12, 13; I John 1:8, 9). Besides, why does he say "us," "you," "us in association with you," and never "I, me, mine" in this section? No single charge of sin is refuted by pointing to what God has done for and in me and in all other Christians in baptism and since baptism.

Paul's opponents were using the instance of his plans for travel as proof against his entire character. His change of plan was employed to brand him as one whose yea could never really be trusted in regard to anything. Against this, the worst part of the charge, Paul defends himself first of all. He was being discredited completely. Now the full pertinency of his reply appears, and we also see why it had to draw in all of his helpers, even all true believers in Corinth. Every one of them could be overthrown in the same way if Paul could be convicted on this plea. Every one of them knew that such a thing could not be done in his own case, and thus he was compelled to see that it could not be done, as these opponents desired, in the case of Paul, the very man who had brought them what made them God's own.

The little charge is thus permitted to stand for the moment. The terrible implication insinuated into it is first annihilated. That was the big thing to be removed. It was big and vital for Paul's own person, but with his heart of love he sees that all of the others are involved and thus defends all of them. This love, that at the very beginning of the letter embraced all and raised the mighty shield of "God" over them, had to win a strong response. From all doubt concerning

Paul they should and surely also would turn in full love and confidence to him, they would revive the old love and confidence that bound them together during that first year and one half. Objectively and subjectively no bettter, no more effective defense could have been made. The Spirit guided Paul's words.

With the greater task done, he turns to the lesser, and he does it equally well. Why did he change his plan for travel?

V. *The Desire not to Come in Sorrow*

23) This is the reason that Paul changed his plans of travel. He presents it in such a manner that we see that it is intended, not for the opponents who tried to make him a prevaricator, speaking and acting "in fleshly fashion" (v. 17), fickle and following "fleshly wisdom" (v. 12), no apostle at all, but for the Corinthians as such who were still well-minded toward him. We see that his reason is of such a nature that he could scarcely have stated it at the time when he first changed his plan and informed the Corinthians of the change (I Cor. 16:5-8). We see that he is now entirely free to speak, apart from the vilification which he has had to suffer. Much more that is of decisive value for understanding this epistle appears in this short section.

Δέ is merely transitional. **Now I for my part appeal to God as witness on behalf of my soul that, as sparing you, I did not again come to Corinth.** The A. V.'s translation "moreover" is more correct than that of the R. V. which translates as adversative "but." Paul had originally planned to go by sea from Ephesus directly to Corinth, then to visit Macedonia, to return to Corinth, and to go to Judea (v. 15, 16). This would have brought him to Corinth soon after Pentecost. Because of the case of incest (I Cor. 5) and the generally untoward situation obtaining at Corinth when Paul wrote First Corinthians he had changed his plan, had decided to go to Macedonia, then to Corinth, and then to Jerusalem (I Cor. 16:5-8). Since there was much to be done along the route overland, this plan would bring Paul to Corinth much later than he had at first announced. In fact, because he had carried out this plan Paul was now in Macedonia, and it was already autumn.

Charged by opponents with not being a man of his word (v. 17) after having before that been charged with being afraid to come (I Cor. 4:18), he now tells the Corinthians why he changed his plan so as to arrive much later. It was chiefly for their sakes, because he wanted to spare them (φειδόμενος ὑμῶν, causal). In I Cor. 4:21 he had asked whether he should come with a rod. As things stood when he wrote First Corinthians, with the case of incest, the puffed-up pride of many, the party wranglings and all, if Paul had come by the direct route immediately after Pentecost, how could he have proceeded except with severity? He debated the matter, resolved to delay his arrival in order to allow the Corinthians by God's help to remedy the evils, and then to arrive in their midst. This is the simple story.

We at once see why Paul could not have told his real reason in First Corinthians. We see the pureness of his motives for delaying his arrival. Things were now fairly righted in Corinth. Paul would even now not have revealed why he had planned on delaying his coming if it were not for the opponents who had attacked his veracity; so the congregation must now indeed be told. This was not an altogether simple matter because the opponents were still active. Paul's motives and his purposes had been formed in his own soul. He probably told his assistants about them at the time, but he does not want to involve his own helpers. Those opponents might seize on what he feels that he must now reveal regarding his reasons, they might call them inventions that were now made to save his veracity, and they might thus discredit him anew. For this reason Paul calls God to witness as he does. God is, indeed, his real and his only witness to what transpired in his soul when he resolved to change his plans of travel.

It is then not "the importance of the statement" that Paul is trying to emphasize by his appeal to God; he has said many things that were more important without such an appeal. It is because the thing is one that transpired in his own soul and was without human witness. We have the same case in Rom. 9:1-3: Paul's grief for his nation and his readiness to save it at the cost of his own soul. Hence he uses the emphatic ἐγώ: "I for my part." In v. 18-22 he used "we" throughout since Paul's assistants were also involved, and even "you" (Corinthians) is added, they, too, were involved. Now, when it is a matter of his own thoughts and intents, he must say "I." This "I" is not opposed to "God" in v. 22 or to Paul's readers with their thoughts.

"I appeal to God as witness" is not an oath although some think that it is. Critics have regarded it as one of those oaths that are forbidden by Christ in Matt. 6:34-37 but have excused Paul because he was probably unacquainted with this prohibition of Jesus. Deissmann has some following when he has this supposed oath include an actual curse. But a glance at his pagan parallels in *Light from the Ancient East* 306 (compare 427) shows the reverse. Those pagans cursed, Paul calls a witness. On page 305 Deissmann points to another curse in Paul's words as recorded in I Cor. 5:3-5, which are a legal verdict couched in strictly legal language (see the author on that passage). Anything that is cited from Deissmann must be tested before it is used; his ardor for pagan parallels takes him too far.

The curse is thought to rest on ἐπὶ τὴν ἐμὴν ψυχήν, as if this means that Paul calls down the wrath of God "upon my own soul," to damn his soul if he is lying. But such an ἐπί has never been found in an oath or a curse. This ἐπί merely repeats the ἐπί that is found in the verb. Instead of meaning "upon my soul" in the hostile sense, to damn it if I lie, it means the opposite: "upon my soul" to support its testimony. For this reason, too, Paul writes the strong adjective ἐμήν and not the slight enclitic μου.

His own soul stands alone when he is testifying. We find that Jesus and also Paul never offer only their own testimony; they always cite two or three witnesses, one or two besides themselves; take John 5:31-37 as a sample. It is a Scriptural principle; unsupported testimony does not stand. In v. 19 Paul names two witnesses besides himself. Who shall here testify along with his soul? He appeals to the only other witness he has, and that is God.

Much is said about the various uses of ἐπικαλοῦμαι (middle), "to call on someone in one's own behalf." In the Biblical Greek this word is almost a technical expression for calling on God and Christ so that this act (even when no object is named) marks the believer (C.-K. 569). It is here employed in a sort of legal way, "witness" also being legal: "I appeal," the same use is found in Acts 25:11: "I appeal to Caesar."

Οὐκέτι has also been weighed in the scales. It may be read as one concept with ἦλθον: "I forbore" (R. V.); but that is in effect as if we read: "I came not as yet" (A. V.). To be most exact, it would be: "not again, not still," promising nothing in regard to the future; οὔπω would be: "not yet," promising "but soon or eventually." But οὐκέτι also gets to mean "not yet," Augustine translates it *nondum*. The point is of minor importance, for Paul was now on his way to Corinth. He had wanted to spare the Corinthians for the time being.

24) Paul excludes every wrong implication that some opponent might attach to the word "sparing you," as though Paul and his helpers were high lords over the Corinthians and as such exercised clemency when they pleased. All lordship is disavowed: **Not that we are exercising lordship over your faith, but we are co-workers of your joy; for as regards the faith you are standing.** It should be noted that Paul drops back into the plural "we" and includes his assistants with himself. This means that, as far as lordship over anybody's faith is concerned if there were such a thing, it would not belong merely to an apostle but to all teachers and preachers. But no such thing exists. Everything hierarchical on the part of an office and on the part of all officers in the church is here disavowed. The importance of this fact needs to be stressed in doctrine and in practice, Paul was practicing here. We may translate the verb as conative: "not that we are trying to exercise lordship," etc.; verbs of ruling take the genitive.

Lordship over people's faith is exercised when in any matter of faith whatever human authority demands obedience, whether it comes openly as human authority or disguises itself and pretends to be divine authority. We read, as we did in Rom. 1:5, "faith's obedience"; trustful obedience is one definition of faith. It, however, obeys only one Lord, "our Lord Jesus Christ" (v. 3), only his authority. It makes no difference who brings us our one Lord's word and authority, apostle, minister, lay brother; faith obeys, not the bringer, but the divine authority brought.

Human lordship is exercised when faith is made to be or to do what some man demands; the Lord's lordship is exercised when he by his Word and his ministers and his church tells us what our faith should be and do. The church still suffers from self-appointed lords and spurious authority. It is easy to detect, for these lords either presume to dispense our faith and its doing from some word of our Lord, or they presume to add some requirement to our faith and our practice that is contrary to or beyond the Word of our Lord. Here belong Deut. 4:2, and Rev. 22:18, 19.

The suspicion had been raised that Paul had hitherto acted the lord. Therefore some commentators seek to find out when and how this was done. So they suppose that this must have occurred on the occasion of a visit and in a letter that was written during the interval between First and Second Corinthians. Then the hypothesis is advanced that this letter is II Cor. 10-13, that these four chapters are appended to Second Corinthians but were really a separate prior letter, etc. The suspicion which this hypothesis supposes is unjust to Paul. So also is the further assumption that Paul is now not exercising lordship but that he certainly will if his sparing leniency gets no response. What a fleshly apostle Paul is thus made; he who knew no lord and no authority except the one Lord and his authority, to which he himself bowed and to which he asked all men to bow as he did!

No, he says, the word "sparing you" has no thought of an authority of ours back of it; back of it lies something that is vastly truer, namely that "we are coworkers of your joy" (objective genitive), men who in our divinely appointed office and work are associated (σύν) with you in working to produce spiritual joy and happiness for you by fostering everything in you that pleases our one Lord and removing everything that he must resent and that would thus end in grief for you. Such grief we wished to spare you. First Corinthians shows how the Corinthians had ruined some of this joy and were running into grief for themselves; take the case of incest (I Cor. 5), the fornications, the abuses of the Lord's Supper (I Cor. 11:17, etc.), etc. First Corinthians was Paul's effort to restore true joy in the Lord in Corinth.

Paul's delay in going to Corinth was made in order to give the Corinthians time to right the evils that had crept in, to right them by heeding his first letter. If he had hastened to come in person he would have had to come with a rod (I Cor. 4:21), with the Lord's discipline. That would have been painful for both Paul and the Corinthians. That was what he wished to spare them by hoping that they would right themselves. Let us say that Paul's wise and tactful plan was succeeding; he had excellent news from Titus. While all was not yet joy in Corinth, it eventually came to be. When he arrived in Corinth several months after he had written Second Corinthians he had an unmarred three months' visit.

Συνεργοὶ τῆς χαρᾶς ὑμῶν is the true conception of the Christian ministry. Its great task is to dispense the Lord's grace and the gifts of grace, all of which are productive of the purest and the highest joy, and by that grace to remove all that would decrease and mar that joy and bring grief. To do both effectively includes wisdom, care, and carefulness such as Paul exercised so that joy may ever be the result.

"For as regards the faith you are standing," the perfect of this verb is always used in the present sense. Opinion is divided regarding the dative; as to whether it is instrumental or means: "by the faith"; place: "in the faith"; indirect object: "for the faith"; or our choice, dative of respect: "as regards the faith." Since it is placed forward and thus made emphatic, this last type of dative seems correct.

It is stated that we must take this acknowledgment of the faith of the Corinthians with a grain of salt; v. 13 answers that, Paul writes what he truly means.

The fact that the Corinthians are standing as regards the faith completes the thought that Paul and his assistants are co-workers with them in producing joy for them. Only with regard to those standing can they be co-workers in any sense, in particular also fellow producers of joy. To stand "as regards the faith" means "the faith" objective, *quae creditur;* the standing itself is believing, subjective faith, *qua creditur.*

CHAPTER II

Continuation:

The Desire not to Come in Sorrow

1) In 1:23, 24 Paul writes regarding consideration for the Corinthians, now regarding a simultaneous consideration for himself; hence he uses δέ which adds, but adds something that is somewhat different. **Moreover, I came to this judgment as regards myself, not to go back to you in grief.** The ingressive aorist ἔκρινα is juridical: as a judge, after hearing a case, pronounces his verdict, so Paul, after thoroughly probing the situation, arrived at this verdict. He had decided what was best in the interest of the Corinthians, namely by delaying his visit to spare them (1:23); he found also, as far as he personally was concerned (dative of respect), that such a delay was by far best: he could not bring himself to the idea of going back to Corinth "in grief." "In grief" certainly refers to grief in Paul's own heart. Grief is, however, always caused by something. So here Paul's grief was due to the deplorable conditions that were obtaining in Corinth.

Because of his grief-laden heart Paul, who felt that his ministry was to bring joy (1:24), did not want to appear in Corinth. He did not want to do this on his own account. But this is his second and thus his secondary motive; his first and primary one had to do with the Corinthians (1:23). If their interest had been best served by Paul's promptly getting to them, heavy though his heart was, he would have gone. But this was not the case, and he could thus think also of himself. He would not need to say anything about himself here. He is, however, entirely honest and open. He had thought also about himself and not only about the interest of the Corinthians; and so he does not write as though their interest alone swayed him.

More than this. Paul is baring his heart. We shall see that he does this completely. Injury to the Corinthians grieved him, grieved him to tears (v. 4). He was neither womanish nor an emotionalist. So many regard him as an intellectualist and a dialectician. The real Paul had his whole heart and soul in his work. Personal suffering and insult were never his grief, but any injury to the church was. He was ready to suffer, to give up and sacrifice, to do any work to help save souls, to help the church onward to prosperity and joy. Things had gone wrong in Corinth, and this grieved him to the heart. His hope was that, given a few months of time, the Corinthians would right themselves.

Here is food for thought for all ministers. What grief do they experience over deplorable conditions in their congregations? How many grieve only over what they must personally suffer? How many just settle down to the bad conditions, heave a sigh, adjust themselves, and let it go at that? How many thus become a worse cause for grief than their congregations with their grievous conditions?

We are sure that Paul had been in Corinth on two previous occasions: the first time when he founded the congregation (Acts 18) and a second time during his long stay in Ephesus *before* he wrote First Corinthians (see the Introduction). On the strength of πάλιν Paul's second visit to Corinth is dated *after* First Corinthians and is made a grief visit from which Paul, badly insulted and hurt, hurried back to Ephesus and wrote "the tear letter." Thus on the basis of πάλιν the critics build up their hypotheses and remove Second Corinthians from its connection with First Corinthians.

The critics contend that πάλιν modifies only ἐν λύπῃ. If πάλιν modifies ἐλθεῖν or — what amounts to the same thing — ἐν λύπῃ πρὸς ὑμᾶς ἐλθεῖν, a grief visit did not occur at any time. The word πάλιν means "back," its modified meaning is "again" or "back again." It is used with many verbs and notably also with ἔρχομαι, "to go back," and here we have the aorist ἐλθεῖν. This is one of those adverbs that does not need to be placed next to the verb in order to modify that verb. According to the rhetorical emphasis it may be placed forward in the sentence. It is so placed here because the point is Paul's going "back" to Corinth or, if we wish, his going "again" to Corinth. He did not want to go back for his third visit "in grief." In regard to this second visit to Corinth we know nothing but the simple fact gathered from 12:14 and 13:1. It occurred *before* First Corinthians was written and may well have taken place more than a year before, even as much as two years before that writing. It is of no importance for either of Paul's canonical letters. Dating this second visit far ahead, after First Corinthians, and filling it with a terrible experience of grief because of insults by the Corinthians is not necessarily suggested by Paul's πάλιν. For some reason the dictionaries and the grammars offer no information regarding the force of πάλιν in this passage.

2) Paul wanted to go back to Corinth, not with a grieved, but with a relieved heart. Hence he devised the plan of a time-consuming journey through Macedonia, which would delay his arrival at Corinth. His grief had been caused by the Corinthians. Hence how was he to go to Corinth with a relieved heart unless those who had caused his grief removed this cause and so gladdened him again? Paul was delaying his arrival while waiting for this happy outcome.

For if I on my part (emphatic ἐγώ) **grieve you, who, then, is he that makes me glad save he who is receiving grief from me?**

Paul touches the whole interaction. Paul's grief was caused by the situation obtaining at Corinth. Because of his grief *he* had to grieve the Corinthians in turn, namely by correcting them in no uncertain terms. This correction constitutes a large portion of First Corinthians; and the mission of Titus, no doubt, also included a good deal of correction. The fact that he was compelled to grieve the Corinthians was also a part of Paul's grief. How was he to be made happy again? Who could remove this grief from him? Evidently only *those* who had caused it. Others might do what they could for Paul in order to bring him happiness, none but the Corinthians themselves could remove the grief which he felt at every thought of them. But if *they* changed, how happy they would then make Paul! In other words, Paul tells them that his whole happiness depends on *them*.

Both the thought and the expression are genuinely Pauline: this dwelling upon grieving, the grieving that he was doing and that which others were receiving from him, and the reference to his own happiness; this uniting of the Corinthians with himself so that his very happiness is entirely bound up with them and with what they do. It is the voice of true love.

Καί before the apodosis seems to be merely pleonastic although B.-D. 442, 8 and our versions regard it as "then"; R. 1182 as indicating an unexpressed thought. Instead of concluding with the plural: "save *you* who are being grieved by me," Paul is considerate and uses a third person singular. This avoids all bluntness; it generalizes: in a case like this, where one has grieved Paul, and he must grieve him in turn, this man so grieved is the only one who can make Paul happy again. One should not miss these refined, considerate touches, for they reveal Paul's character.

The singular does not refer to some special person. Paul could also have used the plural "who save they"; it is a matter of choice. Carefully, too, he does not write ὑπό, "by me," but ἐξ with the passive participle. His grieving of the Corinthians came only "from" him; it was not a deliberate act in any way but one that was forced "from" or "out of" him. He *had* to make the correction although it would hurt those who received it and him while making it.

3) We now get the complementary thought, which is expressed as Paul's conviction, that his own joy is also the joy of the Corinthians. We once more see how Paul's mind takes in all of the angles whereas so many minds would go only halfway. **And I wrote for this very purpose that on coming I should not get to have grief from them from whom I ought to be getting joy, still having confidence in you all that my own joy is that of you all.**

We do not regard ἔγραψα as an epistolary aorist, either here, in v. 4 and 9, or in 7:12 (R. 846). Paul is not speaking about the letter which he is now in process of writing but about one that he wrote before this time. We think that he is referring to First Corinthians. It is possible that when Paul sent Titus to Corinth he gave Titus a letter that was addressed to the Corinthians, a letter that is now lost like the one mentioned in I Cor. 5:9; but this view is no gain, for it would deal with the same situation in Corinth which is revealed in First Corinthians, the very situation with which Paul is now again dealing. A letter that was sent along with Titus could not contain anything beyond what First Corinthians contains, nor is Paul now referring to anything that is of a different nature. On the **hypotheses** regarding this letter see v. 4.

The present connection leads us to regard τοῦτο αὐτό as an adverbial accusative: "for this very thing, i. e., purpose" (B.-D. 290, 4), and not as an accusative object: I write "this very thing." In the preceding verses (1:23-2:2), as well as in the statement that follows in v. 3, Paul is not stating *what* he wrote in his previous letter but *why* he wrote as he did. He is now revealing his purpose and object for writing as he did; when he wrote as he did he had withheld this object. We have explained in connection with 1:23 why Paul could not have stated this purpose in First Corinthians (16:5-8) when he changed his plans of travel. His purpose was, if possible, not to return to Corinth in grief (v. 1). It is this purpose regarding which he now says still more. If we translate: "I wrote this very thing," namely that I did not want to return in grief, this is the very thing he did not write; he is telling about this for the first time. He could not have told this even in a letter which was sent along with Titus. On the other hand, if "this very thing" refers to something else that Paul wrote, nobody can guess what this was, we are left at sea. The objection that in v. 1 τοῦτο is the object, and that in v. 9 it is εἰς τοῦτο that states purpose, is invalid, for purpose can be indicated in various ways.

Ἵνα is subfinal and tells us what "this very purpose" was which Paul had in mind when he wrote as he did (I Cor. 16:5-8) and arranged for a later date of arrival in Corinth. He did not, on his arrival, want to get to have (σχῶ, ingressive aorist) grief from those from whom he ought to be getting joy (χαίρειν, present, durative). In ἀφ' ὧν the antecedent is absorbed: "from whom" = "from them from whom." The Greek uses the imperfect, here ἔδει, to indicate an obligation that has remained unfulfilled (R. 887, 920). The Corinthians ought, indeed, always to have brought joy to Paul, the founder of their congregation, one of Christ's own apostles. They had not been doing that and are gently reminded of the fact. Things had been so ill among them, as First Corinthians fully shows, that he could hitherto not have come back to them save with great grief. Titus brought a better report after weeks of the greatest depression on the part of Paul, and we shall see how Paul is now greatly rejoiced (v. 14). His hopes and his prayers were now coming to fulfillment, namely that he could, after all, enter Corinth with joy.

Here we again see that Paul thinks about himself only in connection with the people whom he serves. He wants joy for himself from the Corinthians, but never merely for himself alone but only as it includes them, his joy being theirs. The perfect participle says that during all this time, despite all his grief, he has held even as he now holds this confidence, that his joy is at the same time theirs. It would not be joy to him, it would lose all of its sweetness if this were not the case. The thought becomes exceedingly beautiful as we are thus again permitted to look into Paul's heart. The grief which the Corinthians had caused him was such grief to him because it robbed him of the joy that he should have had, that joy which should rejoice also the Corinthians and be their joy. They conducted themselves instead so that only grief resulted.

Paul says: "I have been holding fast to this confidence"; it is exactly the proper word. It does not say too much, but it does say a good deal. Best of all, by means even of the very tense used it invites the Corinthians to hasten to justify this confidence which Paul has been holding, justify it to the full. 'Επί means that Paul rested his confidence "upon" them; yea, spreading his arms wide for an embrace, he says: "upon you all" and repeats "of you all" when he is referring to the joy. Note, too, how "joy" begins in 1:24: the whole office of the ministry is the work of dispensing joy. Can one spread joy when he has a heart that is steeped in grief? In v. 2 he therefore asks, who but he who took the joy from him and gave him grief instead can make him glad again by returning his joy to him.

4) The explanation offered by γάρ as to how and with what object Paul wrote his former letter, refers to all that he has said about his own grief and about his grieving the Corinthians. He describes the first flood of his grief and the motive that, nevertheless, moved him when he was writing First Corinthians. **For out of much affliction and anxiety of heart I wrote to you through many tears, not (just) in order that you might be grieved, but that you might realize the love I have especially for you.**

Paul himself tells under what conditions he wrote First Corinthians. Ἐκ has the idea of source. "Much affliction" = the grief out of which the letter flowed, Paul's own pain which was caused him by the Corinthians. This is what he had instead of joy. Mingled with it was his "anxiety" about the Corinthians, namely as to the effect his letter would have on them, whether they would heed him, or whether they would just get angry at his sharp admonitions and perhaps turn completely against him. The word means "a holding together" and thus might mean "anguish" (our versions) and be only a synonym of the preceding "affliction"; but an advance in thought is better (compare v. 12), the pressure of worry regarding the effect of his letter. This is how his heart felt. Διά = "through" and is said often to denote accompanying circumstance. Paul's tears flowed again and again, and through them he wrote. Regarding his tears compare Acts 20:19, 31, and Phil. 3:18. We have already (v. 1) said that he was not womanish but was most deeply affected by his work, which filled his whole heart.

In v. 3 he states the purpose regarding his own person, which purpose reacted on the Corinthians; now he speaks about the purpose regarding them directly, first negatively: "not that you might be grieved," then positively: "but that you might realize the love I have especially toward you." It is pedantic to take "might not be grieved" in an absolute sense. The Greek regularly omits qualifiers when, as here, the opposites are not entirely exclusive. The plain sense is that when Paul wrote, although he himself was so deeply hurt, so anxious about the Corinthians, wrote even amid many tears, it was not, in fact, could not have been done just to hurt them. His was not a penal letter. To be sure, it hurt, it grieved. Is it pleasant to hear rebuke? When we are confronted with grave wrong and serious moral conditions, our guilt pains us. Contrition without an inner pang has not yet been invented; the deeper the pang, the truer the contrition. But the grief is never inflicted for its own sake but for what it is to produce, namely amendment. The law is not used except in conjunction with the gospel. The thought is not that the hurt is to be made less by the gospel but is to be healed by the gospel.

The emphatic word in a ἵνα clause is frequently placed before the conjunction; it is so here in the case of τὴν ἀγάπην (R. 423): "my love, that you might realize it," etc. The very grief which Paul had to cause the Corinthians when he wrote to them was a manifestation of his love for them. Only a man who had great love in his heart could have written First Corinthians. Recall its imperishable chapter (the thirteenth) regarding love itself.

The verb means "to know" from actual contact and realization. It is the way in which the loved really know the love that is loving them. It was true that Paul loved the Corinthians "especially" (the comparative adverb is to be taken in this sense). One and one-half years Paul had labored in Corinth, and since his time and his labor as an apostle had to be distributed, this was a long time. His success had been great. The congregation was of vital importance for the whole of Achaia. Special love was rightly devoted to Corinth.

But this was not mere φιλία, the love of affection such as we have for people who are congenial to us, for friends. This was ἀγάπη, the love of understanding and comprehension coupled with corresponding purpose. So God "loved" the world. How could he affectionately embrace the foul, stinking world? He comprehended what the world was and purposed to cleanse it by sending his only-begotten Son. So we are "to love" our enemies. They would strike us in the face if we came to them with affection; but we are to see their state of hate and are to carry out the purpose of freeing them from that state. This, in brief, pictures the New Testament ἀγαπᾶν. It is sometimes conceived as seeing value in the loved object. But such a view is too limited.

The history of the word should also be studied, especially the fact that in the LXX it was still used to designate the lower forms of love, even erotic love. In the New Testament it appears in full glory, pure and high, even when it is used with reference to publicans' and sinners' loving their own kind, for its marks are always comprehending intelligence and corresponding purpose. See John 21:15, etc. This is the love that may hurt the beloved in order to bless and to benefit even as Jesus hurt Peter in that loving questioning regarding love.

We take the letter to which Paul refers to be First Corinthians. The critics disagree. They fail to find the tears about which Paul speaks. They catalog the passages where Paul may have and where he could not have shed tears when he was dictating First Corinthians. The view that the whole letter must be dripping with tears, that all of the emotion of the writer must lie revealed on the surface, in fact, that his tears ought to be mentioned in the proper places where he had shed them is unwarranted.

First Corinthians reflects conditions in Corinth that were sad enough to depress any Christian heart, to say nothing about the heart of the apostle who had founded that congregation and whose whole heart was wrapped up in its welfare. There were ugly party divisions that might tear the whole congregation to pieces; unholy pride that is the forerunner of a fall and boasts of wisdom that were sheer folly; the horrible case of incest, and the whole congregation sitting by indifferently, cases of fornication multiplying; litigations of members before heathen judges; a tangle of questions about marriage; eating idol meats no matter how this affected weak brethren. So much of this sort is found already in the first eight chapters. Need we repeat the rest? Even the Lord's Supper had become well-nigh impossible at Corinth. How much more would need to occur before tears would be wrung from Paul's eyes? If tears were ever justified, a situation like that prevailing in Corinth justified them.

First Corinthians seeks to bind up the wounds, bruises, and sores. The emotions are restrained in order to perform this difficult and trying task. To fill the letter with cries and exclamations of grief would not heal nor help. It is now, weeks and months afterward, that Paul can speak to the Corinthians about his own heart which was so distressfully bruised at that time and so anxious ever since that time regarding the results of his efforts to right things in Corinth. Do matters in First Corinthians and in Second Corinthians agree? They do.

What is the critics' view? Sometime after First Corinthians had been written Paul hastened to Corinth in person. He was ill and incompetent, and after disgraceful scenes and personal insults to him hurried back, a defeated man. And when he got back to Ephesus he wrote the so-called *Traenenbrief*, "tear letter," whose contents are unknown, but according to another hypothesis thought to consist of II Cor. 10 to 13, which was afterward somehow attached to II Cor. 1 to 9. We read II Cor. 10 to 13 and look for the tears that are thought to be there — and fail to find them.

VI. *The Case of Incest Is Closed*

5) The worst incident that had occurred in Corinth was the case of incest mentioned in I Cor. 5:1, etc. Its worst attending circumstance was the indifference of the congregation; no action whatever had been taken, and thereby the whole congregation showed its low moral tone and thus became partaker of this man's most grievous sin. We see that Paul was compelled to write in I Cor. 5:1, etc.; it was necessary almost to force the congregation into action. He gave it even the formal wording of the resolution by which the guilty man was to be expelled from the congregation (I Cor. 5:3-5). In order to understand what he now says regarding the case, one should understand just what that resolution contained as it was offered and formulated by Paul, etc. See the author's exposition in the *Interpretation of First Corinthians*. The erroneous ideas held in regard to this case begin with this resolution which was offered by Paul. Hence first of all clearness in this matter must be sought.

When Paul wrote First Corinthians and corrected so many of the gravest faults found in Corinth, the chief questions were: "Will the Corinthians respond? Will they change their evil ways, or will they resent Paul's letter, repudiate him, cause a terrible division in the whole church, etc.?" The gravity of the situation is often not fully appreciated. In Corinth things were forced to a mighty decision by First Corinthians. It was an either — or; either heed Paul's letter or repudiate Paul and his letter. Everything hung in the balance, and we can readily imagine Paul's worry.

Prominent in the critical situation was this frightful case of incest. The real test would in a way be made in regard to this case. It was so prominent, it was also so vicious; it required formal action on the part of the congregation. Paul had written out even the formal resolution which the church should pass. If Paul had failed in this case, if the congregation had voted adversely on the resolution he had asked it to pass, the awful breach would have been made: Corinth would have been lost to the church.

Second Corinthians shows the happy turn which events took. Two facts are clear: the congregation had passed the resolution written out in I Cor. 5:3-5 and had expelled the incestuous member; this member had repented most thoroughly. Paul had received this report from Titus. It was vastly more than good news regarding this one case alone, and it should not be considered in this partial light. The acutest issue had yielded to the truth and the right of the gospel; that meant gospel victory as far as the rest of the errors and abuses noted in First Corinthians were concerned. Paul had the brightest prospect that his grief would be completely dissipated. No wonder he writes as he does. The congregation had not, however, as yet reinstated the repentant member. The details are immaterial. Perhaps the vote of expulsion and the repentance were of recent date. Since this was the first case of so grave a nature, the congregation hesitated to effect too prompt a reinstatement. Whatever these details may have been, Paul now advises the congregation to reinstate the offending member and to do so wholeheartedly.

The treatment of this case under apostolic direction has become classic for the church of all time, the divine guide for all grave cases of church discipline. If the church is to derive guidance from this case, a correct exegesis of I Cor. 3:1-5 and of all that Paul says in Second Corinthians is necessary. Some commentators have failed the church although we are happy to say her teachers have stood her in good stead. Regarding the views of the commentators we shall have something to say at the end of our consideration of v. 11.

We now appreciate even the manner in which Paul speaks when he advises the congregation to bring this case to its proper Christian close. He no longer dwells on the grievous sin, does not even name it; he is through with it, thank God. He does not mention the man's name but writes "such a one" and generalizes; for every such person, not merely just this one person, should be dealt with as Paul has directed and now further directs. Paul eliminates himself from the case; it is one that comes under the jurisdiction of the congregation. He regarded it so at the beginning (I Cor. 5:3-5) and still regards it so. He guides the congregation, he is not lord of the church (1:24). Tact and good sense are combined with refinement and considerateness, and these grace the true Christian principles along which the congregational action is directed. Let us appreciate this; all of it lies on the high plane on which the church and all her guides should ever remain.

But if one has been grieving (anybody), **not me** (alone) **has he been grieving but more or less—in order that I may not burden him unduly — you all.**

Δέ has its slight adversative sense, to indicate which our "but" serves inadequately. From all that has been said about grief and grieving Paul now turns to this most acute grievous case. The thought is that it alone had grieved Paul; by taking up this case he certainly does not imply that other things in Corinth had not grieved him.

The indefinite τίς has the meaning "one," not "any" (our versions). "One" merely indicates, "any" generalizes, and a definite person is referred to here, and he is tactfully left unnamed. The perfect "has been grieving (sc. anybody)" or "has been doing any grieving" has no present connotation such as this tense often has but refers to the past, not to one act (aorist), but to an extended period in the past, a period that is now happily closed. The condition of reality regards the case as one that occurred in the past. And it is this person who was guilty of spreading grief.

This is another case in which the Greek οὐ — ἀλλά is not exclusive. Our idiom requires an addition: "not me (alone) has he been grieving." It is plain that this man did, indeed, grieve also Paul, but primarily he grieved the congregation of which he was a member. This point is rather important. Paul does not occupy a position above the congregation, apostle though he was. All hierarchical notions are far from Paul's thinking and acting. Throughout the case the primary position belonged to the congregation. *It* had to pass the resolution that expelled the man (I Cor. 5:3-5), *it* had to pass the resolution to reinstate the man (v. 6, 7); Paul could and did only guide the congregation in the matter of these resolutions, he acted and acts only as their συνεργός or helper (1:24), or, we may say, as their διάκονος, "minister." We at once see the pertinency of the statement which Paul makes regarding himself, for in v. 6, 7 he guides the congregation in what it is now to do since its members are the ones in whose hands the matter lies.

This man's grieving concerned "you all" primarily so that taking action belonged to the congregation. It was the supreme court to judge the case (under the Lord, of course) and not the apostle or any other of the apostles, not the ministry whether this term be taken as referring to one or to all ministers.

We find much discussion regarding ἀπὸ μέρους and regarding the ἵνα clause. There is no need to review all of it. The phrase does not mean that only a part of the congregation had been grieved, for the verb is not passive and thus does not indicate who felt grieved so that Paul implies that some in the congregation, being indifferent, felt no grief. At first, in fact, no one in the whole congregation felt grieved, and Paul had to arouse its members to an understanding of what had been done to all of its members (I Cor. 5). Despite his efforts all of them were not immediately aroused. Perhaps even now some were still unmoved.

The verb states what the man had done: he has grieved "you all" whether "you all" realize it or not. The phrase "in part" means "more or less," some felt the grief more, some less, each in some part or to some degree. It is always thus when someone sins against a whole congregation: some are deeply wounded, some less so, some feel scarcely anything. Yet the sinner's grievous action nonetheless extends to every member, even to the little children. Paul speaks with exactness.

The parenthetical purpose clause obviously states why the phrase is added. By the use of this phrase Paul does not intend to fault a part of the congregation for not having felt the grief deeply enough; he is now not dealing with that feature of the case. He is speaking about what the sinner has done to the membership in Corinth. God knows it was terrible enough. When he now speaks about it Paul says, "I do not want in the least to exaggerate the effect which the sin has had on you Corinthians in regard to the grief now felt by you."

Ἐπί in the verb intensifies: "to put pressure or a burden upon," i. e., more than I have to, thus, "to burden unduly." The Greek needs no object; but the object involved is not the following "you all," nor can it be drawn from "you all," which would result in a queer thought. The object implied is the subject of the two main verbs, namely this sinner, "him." Paul says: "This man grieved you in varying degrees, and

I say in varying degrees only in order not to put upon him more blame than is necessary, his guilt is serious enough as it is and as you all know." Paul keeps a perfect balance in every word he says about this case. He does so although this man's sin hurt him very much because of the shameful indifference with which the congregation at first treated this sin and this sinner. The more terrible a member's sin is, the more viciously are some inclined to speak about the sinner and about his deed just as others act and speak with too little concern. Paul does neither.

6) After stating, "You he has grieved, you all!" and once again implying that it was *their* matter to take all action in the case, Paul states what this action should be and adds its purpose. **Sufficient for such a one this penalty** (inflicted) **by the majority, so that contrariwise you** (now) **rather forgive him and comfort him lest by any means such a one be swallowed up with his excessive grief. Wherefore I urge you to ratify to him love.**

"To such a one" = to the man in question, not because it is he, but as you would deal with any man in a similar case. When Paul worded the indictment against the man in I Cor. 5:3-5, he employed a legal form and phraseology. Now he again uses various legal terms. One of these seems to be ἐπιτιμία (found only here in the New Testament) in the sense of penalty. "This penalty by (inflicted by) the majority" (plural comparative) is the one stated in I Cor. 5:3-5. It amounted to expulsion from the Christian membership and entailed a loss of all rights of membership.

This resolution which had been formulated by Paul had finally been adopted by the congregation. The result had been of the very best: the sinner had thoroughly repented. Titus had just reported these things to Paul. These, it seems, were the recent developments in Corinth. First Corinthians had been written about

Easter time, fall was now approaching. Thus, one may conclude, it had taken some time before this result had been obtained in Corinth. It seems also that the repentant sinner had not as yet been reinstated; Paul is asking that this be now duly done.

It is not amiss to assume that, since Titus was going from Corinth to Paul, the Corinthians had asked him to request Paul to advise them regarding reinstatement, and that Paul therefore instructs the Corinthians as to what to do. Ἱκανόν is neuter although the noun is feminine; this is due to the generalization expressed in "such a one," the predicate adjective referring not merely to this one case of penalty but abstractly to every such case, B.-D. 131. In view of Acts 17:9, and Mark 15:15 ἱκανόν may also be juridical.

What arrests attention is the fact that Paul writes "by the majority." The action had evidently not been unanimous. We should, however, note that Paul has nothing to say about the implied minority. Was their dissent innocent, due to absence from the meeting, to timidity in voting, or to hostility to Paul? We cannot say.

7) In what sense "sufficient" is to be understood is now apparent. The desired result of the expulsion has been attained, namely the sinner's repentance. With ὥστε the result upon the congregation is now stated. There was no need for Paul to insert δεῖν, what "must" or "ought" to be done. Paul states what the normal and the right result *is* for the Corinthians, and there is no implication of reluctance on their part in regard to accepting this result. Compared with the expulsion, it is an opposite act: "contrariwise," to which "rather" is added, in which we, however, find no reference to a tension in Corinth but only the preference which Paul thinks the Corinthians would show by taking this opposite action. And this is: "that you grant him favor (or, as we may translate, 'forgive'

him) and comfort him," two effective aorists. They point to one act, namely to a congregational resolution to reinstate the repentant sinner into his forfeited membership. The vote to pardon him will also comfort him. It would, of course, include the discussion that would lead up to that vote and the resultant treatment of the sinner; all would be a mighty comfort.

In I Cor. 5:3-5 Paul formulates the resolution for the Corinthians. It was similar to offering a motion in a public meeting; but Paul transmits it in writing since he can be present only in spirit. As things stood in Corinth at that time, Paul had to follow this course. Since things are now more favorable, and the congregation is very willing, it is enough and also very tactful that Paul only state what the result of the repentance is for the church, and that he leave to it the formulation of the motion which it will naturally vote on and pass.

Paul adds what purpose will strongly prompt the Corinthians to take this action: "lest by any means (μήπως) such a one be swallowed up with his excessive grief." Paul is concerned for this man's soul. It is beyond the English idiom to reproduce the effect of ὁ τοιοῦτος, "such a one," which is placed at the very end in the Greek and thus voices Paul's deep sympathy and concern for the repentant sinner.

Nor should we miss this final mention of "grief" in the present section. At one time this sinner was grieving so many with his sin, now he was grieving himself in deep contrition for that sin — a blessed change. And yet he could not be abandoned to this excessive grief lest with or by it "he be swallowed up." There is no need to debate about the meaning of the figure as to whether it means suicide or this and that. It means to sink into despair no matter how the despair might manifest itself.

It has been asked why Paul says nothing about God's forgiveness of this man's sin. Again, it is assumed that Paul is dealing only with the congregation's forgiveness, with pardon for the great wrong done to the congregation. Both need clarifying. By again receiving the repentant sinner through forgiving and comforting him the congregation did absolve him in God's name and by that absolution brought and sealed God's remission to him.

On the other hand, every Christian and thus also every congregation are to forgive a wrong done *to them personally* at once, the moment it is committed, no matter whether the wrongdoer repents or not, whether he be a church member or a bloody persecutor. Paul is not speaking about this forgiveness; he does so in v. 10 as far as his own person is concerned, which see. He is speaking about reinstating a fallen and repentant church member. This can be done only by formal congregational resolution. And this resolution is in every case equal to pronouncing God's absolution in God's own name to the sinner for his sin against God. The sin against the congregation alone was forthwith forgiven irrespective of repentance; but God held this sinner guilty also for wronging the congregation as he held him guilty for his sin *in toto*, and the congregational reinstatement was thus God's full and complete absolution.

Who are you, sinner, to hold a sin that is done against you against any sinner? You yourself sin against others daily. Do not place yourself on a level with God! But when, especially as a congregation, we act in God's name we convey God's own absolution, but never to any save to the contrite and repentant.

8.) Διό, "wherefore" = in order that this purpose may be attained and the repentant sinner preserved from despair Paul urges the Corinthians "to ratify" love to him, κυρῶσαι, a legal term: to ratify by formal decree or vote, M.-M. 366. B.-P. has the correct meaning of this word in the passage Gal. 3:15: a legally ratified will or testament, but in the case of this passage he gives the meaning *beschliessen, entscheiden.* The sense of the word is the same in both passages. Hence the aorist: the legal ratification of love is to be made "for him" by formal resolution and vote. "Love" is enough (see v. 4): as a man who is repentant, absolved, and reinstated in God's name all that ἀγάπη includes is now once more his. This "love" is now no more only that with which we love even our enemies but that with which we are able to love our brethren as brethren, I Pet. 2:17. As God's *agape* is able to bestow vastly more upon his children than it is able to bestow upon the ungodly, so it is in the case of our love to our brethren.

9) With γάρ Paul indicates why he is so free to urge the Corinthians to follow a certain course of conduct in this sinner's case; Paul has tested them out when he wrote to them to expel the man (I Cor. 5:3-5), which they also did — although after some delay. **For this purpose I also wrote in order that I might get to know the** (real) **genuineness of you, whether you are** (really) **obedient in all regards.**

Καί is to be construed with "wrote": "also wrote" the former time as I am now again writing in regard to the same case. Then I wrote and made the test; you proved genuine; and knowing this, I now write again and urge you to take the reverse action toward the sinner. Εἰς τοῦτο = not "for this reason" but "for this purpose," ἵνα stating what it is. The aorist γνῶ means "get to know, realize, experience," namely by seeing how you would respond to my letter and to what I bade you to do about this case.

Paul frequently uses δοκιμή and its cognates. This word is derived from the testing of metals, coins, etc., in order to prove their genuineness. The translations try to convey as much of this as is possible, the difficulty being in finding one word which expresses both the facts that a test was made and that the test was successfully passed. Our versions offer "proof," we venture to offer "genuineness" and to add parenthetically "real"; ὑμῶν is the objective genitive because the Corinthians were proved and found genuine.

The test made in I Cor. 5:1, etc., was applied to the Corinthians in regard to this one case; but this was an eminent case that would bring out fully "whether you are (really) obedient in all regards." Paul wrote about many matters in First Corinthians, any one and all of which were likewise tests. Because it was such an acute, definite case, the case of incest was one which probed and tested the obedience of the Corinthians most completely. If they passed this test — and they finally did — they proved that they would be equally obedient in other and lesser cases.

Let us note that Paul here acknowledges the genuineness of the Corinthian congregation in an unobtrusive way. We should remember how anxious he had been regarding the tests to which he had to put the Corinthians, in particular also regarding this most decisive test (v. 13). What a relief it was to find that they were genuine! So the implication is that in regard to what he now bids the Corinthians do he is fully assured that they will again respond. We feel that saying what he does, and saying it in this telling way, will surely move the Corinthians the more obediently to respond to Paul's bidding, both in now absolving the repentant sinner and in carrying out whatever else Paul may ask.

Some have thought that this question is one regarding Paul's personal apostolic authority and obedience to that. Others say that he held back his apostolic authority until this point of his letter was reached and did not assert it until this point; or that he advocated congregational autonomy in the present case only for diplomatic reasons while his aim in reality was unquestioning, blind obedience in every respect. Paul is also said to be *klug* (sagacious) for speaking about a "proof" when "conversion" would be the proper word.

But the only apostolic authority that existed was that which had been delegated by Christ. No apostle and no apostolic church knew of any other, obeyed any other. In I Cor. 5:4, where the formulation of the resolution which was submitted to the Corinthians by Paul is given after the preamble stated in v. 3, there follows: "In the name of our Lord Jesus Christ." To that authority Paul bowed, to that he asked the Corinthians to bow. "Obedient in all respects" = to Christ in all things. An apostolic hierarchy never existed.

This shows that each congregation is autonomous but that it is ever under Christ when it is exercising its autonomy. Expulsion and reinstatement, the ban and absolution are powers conveyed to the congregation by Christ (Matt. 18:17). Paul treats the congregation accordingly. Matt. 18:18, and John 20:23 do not make apostles or ministers "lords" (1:24) of the church, they are given to the church (I Cor. 12:28; Eph. 3:11), their office is granted to the church in order to show what Christ's authority is and conveys to the church so that the church may exercise it under Christ's guidance through the holy office. Finally, to find fault with Paul for speaking about genuineness and its testing is to deny the facts of both epistles, which present an ἐκκλησία of God (I Cor. 1:2; II Cor. 1:1) that has faults, indeed, but proves itself a church nonetheless by allowing itself to be cleansed of its faults.

10) When Paul formulated the resolution regarding the expulsion of the sinner, which was sub-

mitted by him for adoption by the Corinthians (I Cor. 5:3-5), he wrote as being present with them in spirit and as thus voting with them, so now in the matter of voting the absolution of the repentant sinner Paul again joins the congregation and once more votes with it. He does not in this instance (as he did in I Cor. 5:3-5) formulate the motion, he only indicates its contents. Being absent in body, he, as it were,. submits his vote for forgiveness in writing with the assurance that the vote of the congregation will be unanimous or practically so. **Moreover, to whom you forgive anything, also I on my part** (forgive).

Δέ adds this casting of Paul's vote. "To whom" and "anything" are general as are the two "such a one" in v. 6, 7. These indefinite terms thus cover the case in question. But they cover far more, for they show that Paul now has such confidence in the congregation that he votes with it in the case of whomever it may absolve for whatever sin. The implication is that the congregation, which is now awake to its obligation under Christ, need not wait and first submit each case to the apostle before voting reinstatement. It seems to have done this in the case that was pending.

Let us note that the action is one of the congregation alone, of course under Christ; it is not that of an individual apart from the congregation, be he an apostle, a general officer of a church body, or a pastor. As being a part of the church these may advise and direct, but they can do no more. It is the church that acts. It expels, it forgives and reinstates under Christ.

In the present case Paul was, however, personally involved. This case had also caused him grief, not indeed directly, but indirectly, namely through the previous indifference of the Corinthian congregation which took action only after Paul had coerced it to do so. Note the explanation in regard to Paul's grief in v. 5. Paul now adds (καί) what he has long ago done in regard to the grief which this sinner had caused him personally. Paul had at once forgiven the man. See the explanation of this point in connection with v. 7. **For also I on my part, what I have forgiven** (this long while, perfect tense), **if** (indeed) **I have had anything to forgive, on account of you** (have I forgiven it) **in the presence of Christ in order that we may not be taken advantage of by Satan; for,** etc.

Paul had done what every Christian should do. He had at once forgiven this sinner the hurt which he had caused him and now tells the congregation so. That injury done to Paul was forgiven by Paul from the very beginning. Paul, indeed, felt the injury throughout, but only as one that was wholly forgiven. Paul has not been withholding his personal forgiveness until the sinner who had offended him should repent. The Corinthians are not to think that, before they may reinstate the man, he must first beg Paul's pardon. The man has always had Paul's personal pardon. How the man stood in the sight of God is another matter, one between himself and God. Paul's soul was innocent, he had never harbored resentment, he had prayed the Lord's Prayer aright.

In this spirit Paul speaks about his hurt as he does: "what I have forgiven, if I have (really) forgiven anything," i. e., if, indeed, I have had anything to forgive. The man's sin was not committed against Paul directly; Paul had very likely not as yet met the man. We know how the grief had come to Paul, namely indirectly. Therefore Paul says: "In a way I had nothing to forgive him; he involved me only distantly and in that way hurt me; he probably never realized that I, too, would be hurt." This is perfect fairness on the part of Paul in his personal feelings toward the man.

We need not discuss other views of the commentators who think that Paul's forgiveness has been conditional; or that he is now willing to forgive provided the Corinthians are; and the like. Paul says "what we read" (1:13) and not something else.

"On your account in the presence of Christ" is to be construed with the purpose clause: "in order that we (namely you Corinthians and I) may not be taken advantage of by Satan." If it were not for the fact of Paul's connection with the Corinthians, sin and a crime committed by a member in the Corinthian church would have had no effect upon him, would probably not even have come to his ears, and, even if he had heard about it, would not have caused a grief and a hurt that called for personal forgiveness on the part of Paul. But since Paul was connected with and thus bound up with the Corinthians, this fact made his grief regarding this man's sin what is was and thus also necessitated Paul's personal forgiveness. It concerned the Corinthians, could not but concern them. Paul's forgiveness of the man was automatically "on account of you" Corinthians. How it was this on account of them the ἵνα clause shows. "In the presence of Christ" neither marks the sincerity of Paul's forgiveness nor names Christ as a witness of the forgiveness; nor is this phrase a sort of oath. It modifies "on account of you." Paul's relation to the Corinthians was "in the presence or in the sight of Christ." Christ had made him the apostle who founded the Corinthian church, who had thus bound them and him together.

11) And now we see what this sinner's sin might have done to this relation between the apostle and the congregation of his founding. Satan was seeking greater game than the soul of that one sinner. Satan's schemes (his νοήματα or "devices," the word is used in an evil sense) were to alienate the Corinthians from Paul. He intended to turn Paul against them by means

of the injury that had been caused to Paul personally and to turn them against Paul by means of what Paul would be compelled to demand of the Corinthians, namely that they take proper congregational action against this sinner. Satan saw a double opportunity for making his schemes succeed, for "getting the advantage" of Paul and of the Corinthians. He hoped to frustrate the whole blessed work that had been done in Corinth and to deliver a stunning blow to Paul. These evil results would spread to even other congregations.

As far as his own person and the personal hurt he had suffered were concerned, Paul at once forgave the sinner. No wrong reaction came into Paul's heart for even a moment. He wrote First Corinthians without so much as a trace of bitterness regarding this sinner. His main concern was for the Corinthians themselves, that as "in the presence of Christ" he might lead them, too, not to play into Satan's hands, for they might have easily done so. Satan, no doubt, counted chiefly on them for the success of his "devices." Would the Corinthians, too, as "in the presence of Christ" act properly as Paul bade them? This it was that brought such worry to Paul (v. 13) throughout those long weeks of waiting to learn what effect his epistle had had in Corinth. It had the right effect. Satan's devices had been frustrated. Even the sinner had been snatched from him. The "we" of the verbs are perfectly plain; they refer to Paul and the Corinthians. And Paul can say: "We are not ignorant of his devices," since the Corinthians, too, had seen through them and had helped to frustrate them.

Luther translated: *Das vergebe ich um euretwillen an Christus statt,* see also A. V., v. 10. This has led to a wrong application of our passage as though it proved that, when a minister pronounces absolution, he does so *an Christus statt,* in Christ's place. This phrase does not have that meaning. Paul is not speaking about the absolution that is pronounced by a pastor in the name of Christ, in this clause and phrase he is speaking only about the personal forgiving that took place in his own heart. Let us add that v. 10, 11 have been misunderstood in various ways. Public absolution and Paul's private, personal forgiving are often confused.

We are now ready for a word regarding the question as to whether Paul speaks about the case of incest that is known to us from I Cor. 5. Every detail of our paragraph (v. 5-11) not only corresponds with that case but cannot be understood if that case is not referred to. If II Cor. 2:5-11 does not speak about the case mentioned in I Cor. 5, we must invent a duplicate of that case (save only that it need not be a case of incest) which would otherwise have the same characteristics. The critics do that. They disregard I Cor. 5 and set up a hypothetical case that fits II Cor. 2:5-7 plus 7:12. The results have been confusing. Paul himself has made it impossible to substitute a hypothetical case. He does it in the simplest way by writing in such a manner that, unless one is acquainted with the actual case (I Cor. 5), one cannot understand a number of the expressions which he employs in v. 5-11. First Corinthians 5 is so completely the key to II Cor. 2:5-11 that, when this key is disregarded, the door remains locked.

VII. *Thanks and Triumph*

12) Verses 12-17 form a paragraph; we do not divide at v. 14. The success of First Corinthians and of the mission of Titus to Corinth found their climax in what the Corinthians did in regard to the case of incest and were now ready to do since the sinner had repented. Paul's worry about the Corinthians after writing First Corinthians and dispatching Titus had centered in this case as being the real test for the Co-

rinthians (v. 9). So now after the Corinthians are obedient in this gravest matter, after Paul has been able to tell them how to proceed to reinstate the sinner (v. 5-11), what is more natural than to tell the Corinthians how he had worried, how he had gone forward to Macedonia to hasten his meeting with Titus, how he thanked God when Titus came with the good news from Corinth, how he felt triumphant and yet attributed all the success and the triumph to God, he and his assistants ever holding to God's word in Christ?

Δέ makes the natural transition. **Now having come to Troas for the gospel of Christ, and a door having been opened for me in the Lord, I have had no relief for my spirit because I did not find Titus, my brother, but after taking my leave of them I went forth into Macedonia.**

The picture of what transpired in Paul's spirit during the anxious wait for the return of Titus from Corinth is realistic in every way. According to the plan projected in I Cor. 16:5 Paul had come from Ephesus as far as Troas in order to go on from there to Macedonia and finally to Corinth. The tour was not rapid, work was to be done along the way. On arriving at Troas, Paul expected to find Titus there. We see that he had sent Titus to Corinth long enough before that so that Titus might have returned with a full report about conditions in Corinth. We see that Troas had been agreed upon as the place of meeting. But when Paul arrived there, Titus had not come, and no news had been sent by him. One can imagine Paul's feelings. Had the worst happened at Corinth? Was Titus detained in Corinth because nothing had as yet been achieved? We have seen, not only that Paul's very soul was in his work, but also what the great troubles and dangers in Corinth meant to him and to his work. See v. 11 regarding Satan's devices. Paul found no rest in Troas, he resolved to wait there no longer but to go into Macedonia, hoping thus the sooner to be joined by Titus and to get the news that, whether good or bad, meant so much and would end his uncertainty.

As far as the history of these experiences is concerned, we need not raise questions such as that, in sailing from Troas to Neapolis, Paul might have passed Titus who was sailing in the other direction and such as failing to meet Titus in Macedonia. Give these men credit for as much sagacity as we should use under like circumstances. When Titus was sent, exact routes were planned, eventualities were provided for in advance so that, if Troas could not be the meeting place, the two would meet elsewhere. As far as sailing past each other is concerned, it was an easy matter to send a messenger ahead in time to detain Titus in Neapolis, Paul's leaving Troas being timed accordingly. So it came about that Titus joined Paul in Macedonia (7:13); we do not know in what city they met. Here is our evidence that Second Corinthians was written in Macedonia.

Paul is describing only his great anxiety and is not dispensing general information. He intended to stop in Troas "for the gospel of Christ," in its interest, εἰς denoting aim or purpose, R. 595. "Gospel" means "gospel," the message; there is no need to introduce the idea of "gospeling." The fact that the gospel is always preached is understood. The statement is made that Paul came to Troas for this purpose; then, after he arrived there, he found a door standing wide open for him (perfect tense) which invited him to enter, i. e., a favorable and a promising opportunity for success. "In the Lord," a phrase that is used so often by Paul, has no mystical sense here. Since it is connected with the standing open of the door it conveys only the idea that this favorable opportunity was connected with the Lord without stating just what the connection was.

It was thus not an accidental opportunity. "Lord" needs no article, Κύριος is used as a proper noun.

Combining Acts 16:8, etc., with what Paul now states, we cannot agree that a church had already been established in Troas but conclude that a good opportunity was now offering itself. This occurred in the fall. Acts 20:6, etc., shows that a church had been founded in Troas before the next spring. Did Paul return from his meeting with Titus in Macedonia and enter the open door and found the church at Troas? It seems that he did although we have no information beyond the data stated save the perfect participle "having been opened (and thus continuing to stand open) in the Lord." Paul, too, was not the man to leave such an open door without entering it.

13) A good deal is implied in the fact that, after not finding Titus at Troas, Paul was so anxious that he passed that open door and hurried on into Macedonia. The dative infinitive (the only one in the New Testament that does not have a preposition) expresses cause (R. 966; B.-D. 401; 406, 3): "because I did not find," etc. Ἔσχηκα is a perfect, yet not one that is used in place of an aorist (B.-D. 343, 2) but a true perfect that describes the past continuation of his anxiety to the point when he at last found Titus. The aorist would not have shown this continuation, and the imperfect would not have indicated that it ceased (R. 901). Ἄνεσις = relaxing, and "for my spirit" is the *dativus commodi*. The tension for Paul's spirit was not relaxed. It is put negatively, but we may well say that the expression is like a litotes: the tension was increased. It soon grew so strong that Paul took leave of Troas and hurried into Macedonia.

Here we have the full revelation of Paul's anxiety regarding the outcome of affairs in Corinth. It drove him past that inviting, open door in Troas; it speeded him on into Macedonia to meet Titus at the earliest possible moment. Are we disappointed in not meeting a cool, calm, self-assured apostle, a spirit that nothing could perturb? Do we think that this would be the ideal Christian spirit? We shall have to revise our ideal. Stoics are thus insensible. Paul shed tears, felt grief, was in anxious tension, confesses it in v. 4 and here; let that comfort us. But all of this emotion concerned not his own person or his earthly welfare, it concerned the church. Ah, there is the point! Sad and dangerous conditions and situations in the church — do they draw tears, prayers, anxiety from our hearts?

Paul calls Titus, not "the brother," but "my brother." The connection leads us to think of Paul and Titus as two brothers who are deeply concerned about the same thing, and that one would not leave the other without information any longer than was absolutely necessary. We have another touch like this. Paul does not say only that he left Troas but that he left it "after taking my leave of them" ("them" is used *ad sensum*). This refers to the open door, to people who wanted Paul to stay, to work auspiciously begun in Troas. If we may read between the lines we think of Paul returning after his meeting with Titus, of his fully entering that open door, Timothy (1:1) at least, if not others, assisting him.

14) Now we see the relaxing that came at last. It is expressed in a jubilant way. **But to God thanks, to him who always causes us to triumph in Christ and who makes manifest the odor of the knowledge of him by means of us in every place!**

A new paragraph, some say section, does not begin here; nor is Paul introducing a digression which some make long, others longer. In v. 12, 13 Paul says: "So anxious have I been"; he now adds: "So grateful am I now," and two such statements are not divided between two paragraphs. But he now changes to "we."

He and his assistants share this joy and this gratitude, and they do so because of their office and their work. This is apostolic jubilation. Therefore it means so much to the Corinthians even as Paul also writes to them about it.

More than this. The victory which is being celebrated is the one that was just secured in Corinth. Paul sees Titus returning, and he, Paul, and Timothy are in a triumphal procession. Still more — Paul's view — which is always comprehensive — sees all of their victories: "always — in every place," the latest which occurred in Corinth being ranged among them, others are still to come as note the one in immediate prospect in Troas. What a grand triumphal procession! No; this is not a digression. How could Paul digress regarding the office of the ministry when it is here impossible to celebrate anything else?

We see, too, why he was so anxious. Was the great line of victories now to be marred at Corinth when a new one was ready to fall to his lot in Troas? All of those many previous victories increased the anxiety about the outcome of the battle that was pending in Corinth. And so that anxiety about Corinth now increases the joy of the triumphal procession which is now in Paul's mind since Titus has come with the great news of victory on the field at Corinth where Satan had staged a dangerous countercampaign.

The figure of a commander and his generals celebrating a grand triumphal procession is most apt. All that history tells us about these old Roman triumphs which were granted to a successful commander by the emperor is brought to mind by the first distinctive term employed by Paul: ὁ θριαμβεύων. He extends the imagery when he adds the words about the odor, for in these triumphal processions flowers were strewn, vessels burning incense were carried. That was sweet odor for the victors, but for the vanquished, who marched as captives in the procession, it meant execution at the end of the march. The entire imagery is magnificent.

Regarding the meaning of θριαμβεύω in Col. 2:15 see that passage. There is some discussion as to whether this verb can here mean "cause us to triumph," a meaning that has not as yet been found elsewhere although we have the analogy of other verbs in -εύω which mean "cause to" do or be something, viz., μαθητεύω, "cause to be a disciple." Aside from its reference to emasculations, when this verb has a personal object, the meaning is "to lead the vanquished in a triumphal procession," and some commentators introduce that meaning here: God leads Paul and his assistants as vanquished. But such captives were executed after the triumph was over. None of the softened meanings such as "to lead about publicly" are satisfactory. Criminals were thus made a spectacle. With the remark: "Picture here is of Paul as captive in God's triumphal procession," R's *W. P.* contradicts his *Grammar* 474.

There is no need to hesitate and to think of an impossible figure. God is conceived as the great emperor who grants to Paul, the commander, and to his generals, Paul's assistants, the high honor of a triumphal procession. And this one exceeds any that was ever granted by a human emperor, for the participle is present and durative and is modified by the adverb "always." Paul pictures the apostolic success from beginning to end as such a triumphal passage.

The fact that it is ἐν Χριστῷ, "in union or in connection with Christ" (see Rom. 6:11), is added although this is self-evident because Paul and his assistants are triumphing only in union with Christ. It is a strange idea to think of God or of Christ as the triumpher. The picture presents Paul and his helpers bowing before God for according them the high honor of the triumph. We should not overlook: "To God thanks!" What captives in a Roman triumph ever thanked their captor for leading them on display and to execution?

The companion figure is also taken from a triumph: "and who makes manifest the odor of the knowledge of him (Christ, objective genitive) by means of us in every place." The odor is the knowledge (appositional genitive, R. 498), and the genitive adds the reality to the figure in order to interpret it. Hence the participle is made to agree with both the figure and the reality: "making manifest," again durative. In military triumphs garlands and flowers and much incense furnished the odor. Even the pagan temples were filled with it. Paul compared the knowledge of Christ to such an odor of triumph. "In every place" whither the preachers of this knowledge come its blessed odor is spread. Paul thus combines "in every place" with "everywhere," and "by means of us" once more points to the high victors.

15) Boldly and in triumphant tone Paul advances the figure of the odor. **Because Christ's sweet odor are we for God among those who are being saved and among those who are perishing; to the one an odor from death for death, to the other an oder from life for life.**

The fact that the figure is changed is made very plain in two ways. In v. 14 the odor = the knowledge, and it spreads "through us," the preachers being the media just as the victorious commander and his generals cause the garlands, the flowers, and the incense to waft an odor along their course. Now the preachers themselves are the "sweet or pleasant odor," and this is Christ's (genitive of possession or of source), offered to God by Christ as a sacrifice much as Paul speaks about Christ in Eph. 5:2. The difference is that in Eph. 5:2 the odor is due to the sacrifice upon the cross while it is here due to the gospel which Christ's preachers preach among men. In Phil. 4:18 there is a different thought. The main thought is obscured by those who think of the Christian conduct and character of Paul and his assistants and then make the application that all Christians ought also to be Christ's sweet odor for God. The thought concerns only preachers, their being genuine, never chaffering or bargaining with the Word of God (v. 17), and inserting a little malodor of error.

Such a sweet odor Paul and his helpers are "among those being saved" and also "among those perishing," both are substantivized present participles: "those in process of being saved by Christ, grace, and the gospel; those in process of perishing in spite of Christ," etc. The thought is important: one participle is passive, for the Savior saves them; the other is active, for they are perishing by their own action. Neither is complete (present): those being saved may turn from their Savior and perish; those in the way of perishing may be reached by the Savior whom they are spurning. But the preachers are the same among both, the same sweet odor of Christ and the gospel Word comes from their lips.

16) With οἷς μέν — οἷς δέ both the power and the effect of this odor in the case of each class is tersely stated. The evidence of the manuscripts is in favor of retaining the two ἐκ; nor is anything gained, as far as the meaning is concerned, by cancelling them, for the genitives that are then left would have practically the same sense, and one that would vary only according to the conception of the genitives as to whether they are genitives of source, of quality, or of possession. What some regard as a difficulty will always remain a difficulty, namely how Christ's sweet odor for God can at one and the same time be for some "an odor from death for death," and for others "an odor from life for life."

The view that the two nouns "death" and "life" are repeated merely for the sake of emphasis, and that the function of the prepositions is to make possible this repetition, is untenable. It is because Christ is Christ, grace is grace, true gospel preachers preach only Christ's gospel, namely that we are saved by Christ alone, that this odor, which is so sweet for God, so full of life because of its very source, namely Christ, the Life, and so effective for life to all who believe, is and in its very nature must be the very opposite for all who do not believe. Since there is only one power and one source of life, when that is spurned it becomes for those who do spurn it a power and a source of death. This only appears to be an anomaly or a paradox; it is no more so than any positive and negative are.

Note the chiasm: those being saved and those perishing — the one (the latter), the other (the former). The analogy that certain odors destroy certain creatures while they delight other creatures, is really not an analogy, for in their original condition men are all alike. Nor is the thought correct that one class of men make Christ life for themselves while others make him death for themselves. He is what he is apart from all of us. So are his preachers through whom he operates. What is said regarding him and regarding them is also said by Paul concerning the law in Rom. 7:7, etc. Always good and holy and divine in itself, the law, nevertheless, and because it is thus, slays. The law, however, never makes alive, and in this it differs from the good, holy, divine gospel, which does bestow life while it also kills. Mark 16:16 states how it does both. Beyond that statement no human mind has ever penetrated.

Although the mystery lies in the human will, we never penetrate to the bottom of it. It is not a question as to how some are saved; Christ is the plain answer to that; it is the fact that others reject him, draw death from him, refuse the life he brings them. Determinism is as incorrect an answer as are Pelagianism and synergism, neither of which exists in actuality. No explanation is possible because the rejection is an unreasonable, we might even say insane, act, and no reasonable explanation can be given for what is unreasonable, not even by those who do the unreasonable act.

With a sudden turn Paul asks: **And for these things who** (is) **sufficient?** "Who" is placed after the phrase. The mind is to dwell on "these things," so mighty, saving many from death for life, sending many to death by death, making this tremendous division among men. Then two incisive words bring the startling question: "Who (is) sufficient?" The answer is not: "Christ." Paul is speaking about God's preachers. While "who" is singular it refers to preachers. The question calls on the Corinthians most closely to examine all who come to them as preachers and to weigh them as to their sufficiency. Paul demands that he and his helpers be thus weighed. Others had broken into the church at Corinth, and Paul will reckon fully with them. Here is his first crushing blow. If it were not for them, the present question would not be needed. The test which is to be applied to Paul and to his helpers must be applied equally to these false preachers.

17) "For" = I ask this vital question for the following reason. **For we are not as the many, haggling over the Word of God, but as from sincerity, but as from God, in the presence of God in Christ we do speak.**

The answer to the question asked in v. 16 is not to be negative: "No one is sufficient." In that case the question would have been worded: "Who is sufficient of himself?" and the answer would be: "God supplies the sufficiency." All this is presupposed. We see that

God has supplied his sufficiency to Paul and to his helpers. False men, who deny it, have entered Corinth. They claim this sufficiency for themselves and intend to oust Paul, to destroy his work, to capture the Corinthians for themselves. Paul places himself and his helpers beside these false apostles and shows the Corinthians the glaring contrast: "Not are we like the many," etc., a gulf lies between them and us. "The many" includes the whole class. We do not think that Paul intended to indicate that all of them were busy in Corinth, but that quite a number were running around in the churches, some of whom had come also to Corinth. Compared with Paul and his few assistants, they were a crowd. When did the devil ever lack tools?

"The many" is significant. So many Christians are still impressed by numbers. "All these other preachers say so, teach so, do so, etc.!" That convinces the superficial, they look no farther. The true preachers are so often rejected simply because they are few in number. In this world of sin truth is often in the minority. Paul lifts out the distinguishing mark of the many and contrasts it strongly by using two ἀλλά ὡς with the distinguishing marks of the true preachers.

He certainly chose a telling word when he describes the many as καπηλεύοντες τὸν λόγον τοῦ Θεοῦ. A κάπηλος is a huckster, which is suggestive in a number of directions. He peddles cheap wares, he haggles about the price, he is known to cheat because he does not expect to return, he is out for his own personal gain. The ancient hucksters, for instance, peddled wine and adulterated it so that the verb that is derived from this noun came to mean adulterating wine, food, and the like. Philosophers used it a few times in characterizing the sophists as spurious philosophers; Paul is thought to adopt this use here. "Huckstering" is too common for such a restriction; Paul is not speaking philosophically to philosophers. He is using a word which everybody understands, a homely figure. Nor does οἱ πολλοί refer to the common herd, the uneducated crowd upon whom the educated look with disdain.

We now see how we get the various translations: "which corrupt the Word of God" (A. V.), and "deal deceitfully with" (margin); "making merchandise of the Word of God" (R. V. margin). The Germans use *verschachern,* which is more apt because of its reminder of the Jew peddler. Probably, since the object is "the Word of God," "haggling over" is the idea, "chaffering with." They try to get what price they can and shape the Word of God accordingly. The genuine Word calls for contrition, faith, obedience. These hucksters take far less and, of course, make the Word less so as to match the price they take. They dicker and offer "something just as good," yea, "something far superior" and at a far lower price. How attractive to the buyer! They turn from the real Word, scorn it, are happy with the far better substitute; it costs so much less. So they sell the Word minus inspiration or say that it was inspired only as Shakespeare was inspired under the plea that "now the Bible is understood far better, and means ever so much more to us."

Who has not heard this huckster line of talk? They sell a Bible that has only the human Christ, a great "personality" but minus deity, not the bloody Christ who died as our substitute; a Christ whose righteousness is not imputed to us, who only inspires us to live more righteously by emulating his example. It is a far better Bible, for it is emptied of hell and the devil and damnation, of total human depravity and all such low views, and it is embellished with the universal Fatherhood of God and universal sonship, and that is all that one needs to believe. And certainly the price is so very cheap! Others huckster about this or that doctrine or group of doctrines, and they, too, sell, oh, so reasonably! But in the end the cheap diamonds turn out to be — glass!

When we are interpreting we should let what Paul says about himself and his assistants shed light on what he says about "the many" as hucksters. It has been well said that we should read slowly and pause for each item, each being so weighty. Both ἐκ phrases state the source, the one subjective, the other objective. Each has ὡς, not in the sense of "as it were," but in the sense of "as indeed."

"But as from sincerity" recalls 1:12 and states one opposite of huckstering and dickering about the Word. It surely requires complete sincerity and honesty to preach the real Word, which is not only life for some but also death for others. Could one chaffer about that? Could one be satisfied with less than true contrition, faith, obedience?

But are not false teachers just as sincere in their wrong dealings and doctrines? One answer is that godly sincerity is coupled with what follows. And that uncovers the other answer. The two sincerities may look alike, yet their sources differ. God never makes sincere in any wrong act, course, or dealing; all such sincerity is self-made. Often, too, it is only sincerity on the surface, for not a few of these many are ready to shift to another view when they see that it is advantageous to do so, when the public seems to want something else. When a true preacher makes a shift like that he demonstrates that he has lost his former true sincerity. This happens too often. Temptation is great and constant. Why not follow "the many"? To hold out in the old sincerity and to suffer accordingly do not seem to pay. No wonder that a book appeared with the title: *Kann auch ein Pastor selig werden?* Claim not Paul's sincerity of soul too hastily for yourself!

The repetition of ἀλλ' ὡς is impressive. Although each ἐκ is made to stand out separately, the two are never separate. No man can speak "as from God" without sincerity; and no man speaks "as from sincerity" unless he speaks also from God. To speak from God = as actually sent and commissioned by him and thus also as his mouthpiece. For this reason we have λαλοῦμεν, which means only "we make utterance" as one who lends mouth, lips, tongue, voice wholly to God so that he may use them. No man ever spoke "as indeed from God" unless he uttered God's own Word in truth and verity. Acts 20:20, 21, 27.

Even to this Paul adds: "in the presence of God in (in connection with) Christ," with his eyes resting upon us, he hearing our every utterance. The phrase recalls the pronouncement of Christ that we shall at last stand (Matt. 12:36) before God's judgment seat to give an account of every word we have spoken. In 12:19 as well as here we must combine "in the presence of God in Christ" and not, as is often done: "we speak (for one thing) in the presence of God and (for another) in connection with Christ" (we and our speaking being joined to him). If this were the intention, "in Christ" should follow the verb. Paul conceives his standing in God's presence as itself being connected with Christ. As he looks up and sees the witness to his speaking, namely God, it is "in Christ" that he sees him, i. e., as his gracious God. This is the God who commissioned him with his Word even as the center and the circumference of that Word are Christ. Here is the source of the sincerity that fills his soul, the impossibility of his dealing with that Word like a haggling, dickering huckster.

So little is all this a digression that its pertinency lies on the surface. Paul tells the Corinthians how he has dealt with them in regard to the Word. Many of them had not liked it, and other teachers had come in who were only too ready to deal otherwise, we might say, tried to undersell him. Now was the time to say these things. It was the hour of victory after what had threatened to be a serious defeat (v. 12-14). Thanks to God who had bestowed the triumph! The hucksters had not succeeded, the true ministers of God had won. And the Corinthians were to see that as such true ministers God had helped them to win in Corinth, and what a calamity it would have been, nothing less than defeating God's true servants, if because of folly on the part of the Corinthians they had not won. For when these ministers spoke to the Corinthians, these Corinthians, too, were "in the presence of God in Christ." We need not add the strong applications that offer themselves in regard to ministers and congregations of today, such as huckster and such as are true, such as heed the spurious sales talk and such as spurn it.

CHAPTER III

VIII. *"You Are Our Epistle!"*

1) For the restoration of the right relation between the Corinthians and Paul the right view of his office, work, and affliction is of essential importance, and when Paul now dwells on these different points in due order he neither digresses nor diverges into abstract, unletter-like discussion but writes most directly in line with his great aim and object, that of re-establishing the original, sound relation that existed between the Corinthians and himself. This, of course, includes also his assistants, hence he uses the plural "we."

He has just characterized himself and his assistants in a striking way in contrast with all false preachers, some of whom had invaded Corinth. Such entrance as they had found was due, as it seems, to letters of commendation which they had submitted in Corinth. Here again there is a mighty difference between Paul and his helpers and these false teachers. **Are we beginning again to recommend our own selves?** Will someone, perhaps, make this fling at us because of what I have just written in order to discredit us as though we were compelled to write our own letters of recommendation since nobody else was willing to do so for us? "Are we beginning" implies that Paul expects to write more on this subject; and "again" implies that he has written in this vein about himself and his helpers. He has done so in First Corinthians. Letters of recommendation were as common in Paul's time as they are in our own. Many of them are letters of introduction. We may note Acts 15:25, etc.; 18:27;

Rom. 16:1; less pertinent I Cor. 16:10, etc.; II Cor. 8:22, etc. It is in a way incongruous that a person should recommend himself, especially should write a letter recommending himself.

Paul adds a further, broader question; but he now uses the interrogative particle μή which implies the negative answer: "Certainly not!" **Or do we (really) need, as certain people do, recommendatory letters to you or from you?** The verbal adjective συστατικός is derived from the preceding verb συνίστημι. It is a little ridiculous to think that Paul and his helpers might be needing introductory and recommendatory letters to the Corinthians who knew them for so long a time and so well. The reason for adding this with an acknowledged negative answer lies in the point that such letters *from others* would be more valuable; but if they are not needed and thus are foolish when they are offered, why would Paul and his helpers offer less valuable *self*-recommendation? This is true also as far as others of Paul's congregations are concerned. Does anybody think that Paul needed recommendations from the Corinthians?

But there are, of course, τινές whom Paul does not deign it proper to characterize again (the hucksters mentioned in 2:17), who certainly need many letters in order to have people accept them, for they would have nothing in themselves to recommend them. These false teachers who broke into Corinth seem to have come with letters of recommendation. It is usually assumed that it was by this means that they obtained entrance in Corinth although Paul merely says that these people needed them. Paul and his assistants did not.

2) In a typically Pauline manner a startling turn is given to the idea of recommendatory letters. **Our letter are YOU, written in our hearts, known and read by all men, on public display because you are a letter of Christ, ministerially by us, written not**

with ink but with the living God's Spirit, not on stone slabs but on slabs that are fleshen hearts.

"A bold use of the figure of a letter of recommendation!" say some of the commentators, but they do not see how great and wonderful it is. Their "bold" is not intended as a compliment to Paul, for they think that he becomes too bold. All of them find an incongruity: at one time this letter, Paul says, is written in *our* hearts, and in the next breath he says it is written in fleshen hearts, meaning the *Corinthians*. This supposed incongruity disturbed even the ancient copyists; some changed the ἡμῶν in v. 2 into ὑμῶν: in *your* hearts; others changed the καρδίαις in v. 3 into the genitive singular καρδίας: on fleshen slabs *of heart*. The former change alters the sense so that all of the writing is done on the hearts of the Corinthians; the latter so that all of it is found on the hearts of Paul and his assistants. This letter *must be written on both sets of hearts*. And the moment we see this, not only other objections will disappear such as the question as to how all men can read a letter which is written in the hearts, but also the perfect mastery of Paul in the use of the figure and the perfection of what he expresses by means of this figure will move into our line of vision.

Some of the commentators think only about a *letter* and reason that, since the Corinthians are called "our letter," Paul means that he needs no other letter. But disconcertingly he says: "written in *our* hearts," which seems to make Paul and his helpers the letter and not the Corinthians as Paul has just so emphatically said. To cap all, he says that this letter which is written in our *hearts* is known and read *by all men*. "All men" cannot refer to the whole universe of men; "all men" means anybody and everybody, the public in general. But how can the public "know and read" writing that is in our hearts? If the *Corinthians* are the letter, how is it written in *our* hearts so that *all men* may read? That is the riddle, and many cannot solve it.

3) The solution lies in v. 3, a solution that is complete, for every angle is cleared up. The key to the interpretation lies in the fact that in v. 2 Paul has advanced from the idea of a letter as a *letter* (v. 1) to the idea of what a letter of recommendation actually does, namely *unites the hearts of those who are recommended to the hearts of those to whom they are recommended*. For this reason ἡμῶν ὑμεῖς are united, and for this reason Paul does not write: ὑμεῖς ἐστε ἡ ἐπιστολὴ ἡμῶν, separating the two significant words as our versions translate: "*Ye* are *our* letter."

But this is only the half of it. "All men" reading this uniting letter is yet to be considered. Paul is thinking of a vaster letter than one that is written on paper and transmitted to the elders of the Corinthians to be read to the congregation. He writes φανερούμενοι, which means public display, and he writes about "slabs" that are made of even grander material than stone. Paul has in mind a letter which is engraved on a public monument. He thinks of a grand unveiling of this monument, a displaying the writing to public gaze, all men being gathered about it and afterward passing by it and reading it, reading how indissolubly the Corinthian congregation is united in heart and in soul with the heart and the soul of Paul and of his assistants.

Extravagant? Not a bit. These are the public facts. The Corinthian congregation is a great public body in the city of Corinth. "A city that is set on a hill cannot be hid," Matt. 5:14. The congregation is greater than any public monument in Corinth. As men come and go in Corinth, this world-city, as hosts from many a land also come and go, they pause to look with interest. Here is a grand, new kind of monument that is not like common ones which are made of stone slabs. It is covered with writing. Not a writing with ink such as a mere letter that is made of parchment or papyrus would show, one that is simply submitted and thus read in a private gathering. "You are a letter of Christ," "a Christ-letter," you as a public body in Corinth. You are better than cold, dead "stone tablets" that are erected in a public place; "tablets that are hearts of flesh," living, pulsating, receptive flesh (καρδίαις σαρκίναις an apposition). Christ himself has inscribed you. And he used "God's living Spirit" who alone is able to indite plastic hearts. This does not make the Spirit a spiritual ink as some think but something that is vaster than any ink. For ink of any kind cannot be used to inscribe even stone slabs, and hearts of flesh are greater than the finest marble. Nor have these stone slabs anything to do with those that are mentioned in v. 7 as some suppose.

Διακονηθεῖσα ὑφ' ἡμῶν is the adverbial participle as is φανερούμενοι and means: "ministerially by us." The aorist is historical to indicate the ministration which made this letter what it was, ὑπό is the regular preposition to indicate the agent with passives. This word is beautifully chosen for its place. It was, indeed, διακονία that had made this monumental letter what it was, ministry rendered to the Corinthians for the sake of their benefit alone and for no selfish end. Paul and his helpers were the hands which Christ employed, for the Spirit always comes through the preached and taught Word. Some think of the Lord's pen, but this adheres too closely to the figure of a letter; and no diaconate of a pen is possible, and no personal agency of a pen such as ὑπό demands.

We now see why we twice have the perfect participle ἐγγεγραμμένη, once "having been written (the writing being still there) in *our* hearts," and again "having been written on slabs that are hearts of flesh," the hearts of the *Corinthians*. This writing, once made, stands forth so that all men may read it as it is recorded on *both* sets of hearts even as this writing has united them on the grand, living monument that is inscribed by Christ as his monument in Corinth, inscribed by the living God's Spirit. The "living" God matches the hearts of flesh which beat with life. Stone is dead.

What connects the two sets of hearts is the participle "ministerially by us," the success of *our* ministry for *you* and in *you*. By that ministry *you* were written in order to remain so (perfect participle) in *our* hearts when by *us* Christ wrote *us* in *your* hearts. Letters of recommendation join hearts, and here is the joining of your hearts and ours — our ministry united them in permanence. The great public of Corinth reads the inscription which Christ has set up in Corinth so that all may know and read it (present participles, durative, ever and again know and read); and when the public does this it cannot read *you* alone, it ever reads *you and us* together, *our* hearts that ministered to *yours, yours* for what they are by that ministry of *ours*. The union is insoluble. "This letter of *ours* YOU are." The perfected recommendation, not as it is *intended* to recommend, but, as already long ago being effected and made a permanent thing, is public before the eyes of all men who look at you, the Corinthian church in the capital of Achaia.

The whole thought simply overwhelms. Here come these deceivers who steal into a true church that was founded by Christ through the Spirit by the ministry of men sent out by him and try to worm their way in by recommendatory letters from foolish people whom they have previously deceived. These base proselyters have had many successors. Talk about Paul and his assistants needing such letters for the Corinthians or needing anything like self-recommendation! Look at what all men read and continue to read when they regard the Corinthian church! They read Paul and his assistants written all over that church. They read what Christ wrote. They read the writing of the Spirit of the living God. They read our ministry to you in the fruit of this ministry. They read it as having been written on a great, monumental, living heart tablet, the greatest ever erected in Corinth. Paper letters now at this late date? Here is perfected recommendation itself, the Corinthian church of our ministry.

Paul again presses the Corinthians to his heart. They belong together in their hearts, not merely secretly, but before the whole outside world. All glory of it is Christ's. He who wrought it was God's living Spirit. Paul's delight is based on the fact that the ministry of it was allotted to him. What a grand view of a true minister's and missionary's work in a congregation! Surely, when the Corinthians read this passage, their hearts were drawn mightily to Paul. No "I" appears, it is always "we," yet Paul was the apostle. We, of course, think of the founding of the church, but "we" certainly includes Titus and his recent work in Corinth.

This paragraph applies to the work of any pastor who has made and kept any congregation what it should be. The fact that grave faults had recently crept in and were not yet fully overcome, the fact that deceivers were still present in Corinth, changes nothing in regard to past accomplishment with all of it that still stood so that all men might see it. So often the recommendation of which Paul speaks is seen by men without the church but is by the church members themselves perceived too late, perhaps not until the faithful minister's eyes are closed in death. Here, too, one may think of the pitiful epistles which some produce by their "ministry." The invaders tried to wipe out and to rewrite Paul's epistle in Corinth.

IX. "Our Sufficiency Is from God"

4) Because the word "sufficient" occurs in 2:16 and is the key word in 3:4-6, the intervening paragraph (3:1-3) has been called "an insert." Such criticism substitutes words for the connection of thought. Without self-recommendation Paul has declared his and his assistants' sufficiency over against the hucksters (2:16b, 17), his recommendation to the Corinthians being the church at Corinth itself. Where did they get this sufficiency of which the church at Corinth was such a public attestation? Its source involves its genuineness even as its product does (3:1-3). Δέ adds this somewhat different point. **Moreover, such confidence** (as just expressed in 2:16b-3:3) **we have through Christ in regard to God.** It is the sure confidence which Paul and his assistants have in their office and thus in the genuineness of its product. It comes to us, and we have it, Paul says, "through Christ." He mediates this confidence; he is the channel through which it flows into them. Paul does not as yet name the source; this follows in v. 5. "Through Christ" connects with v. 3: "You are Christ's letter," one which he has written so that all men may see us, our office, and our work.

This confidence through Christ is "in regard to God," πρός, the face-to-face preposition especially when it is used with persons (R. 625): "when we face God, and he us." Many are confident enough in themselves and boldly assert their confidence in order to quash any doubts which men may have regarding their sufficiency. They often do this even when they are facing God, calling him to witness, claiming that they speak "as from God" (2:17), but the work which they do cries out against them. For this reason v. 1-3 precedes, the Corinthian church was a letter that had been signed, as it were, by Christ himself. Πρὸς τὸν Θεόν is easily said, but woe to him who says it lightly, in false self-assurance! It will not remain a mere word, such men will soon enough stand face to face with God, and Christ will disown them, and God's judgment will be against them.

5) What are the facts with regard to this sure confidence of ours? **Not that of our own selves we are sufficient so as to claim anything as** (emanating) **from our own selves, on the contrary, our sufficiency** (is one emanating) **from God** (alone). Οὐχ ὅτι is like the English abbreviation "not that" which means: "it is not that." This is simpler and better than the usual explanation of the Greek: "I do not say that"; and οὐχ ὅτι is not the same as ὅτι οὐκ: "because not," etc., R. 423.

There is, first of all, a denial that sufficiency is derived ἀπό, from our own selves. The sufficiency referred to is a sufficiency "for these things" (2:17), those implied in 2:14-17 and again in 3:2, 3, namely ability to achieve results such as have been described, results such as rightly fill us with the confidence we have. "We are not sufficient (with any sufficiency derived) from our own selves" to accomplish such work, such results that could lend us the confidence we have. As to the confidence, it is already stated that this comes to us solely "through Christ," which already declares that it and our sufficiency are from (ἀπό) a higher source than our own selves.

Denying this is therefore also denial that we can lay claim (aorist) to a single thing in the way of title, credit, praise, etc., as having its source in our own selves (ἐκ, source). The infinitive means "to reckon" and is used in its ordinary force as it is in 10:2; 12:6; I Cor. 4:1. The aorist refers to one act of reckoning, the mental act of accounting that anything, no matter what, originated or had its source in our own selves and thus came "out of" (ἐκ) our own selves. We translate: "so as to claim (by this reckoning in our own minds) anything (whatever) as from our own selves (originating from this source)." Our versions labor with this infinitive. The A. V. says that we cannot even think anything of and from ourselves; and although we let the context restrict this thinking to right thoughts in the work of the ministry, the point is, nevertheless, lost in the A. V's. translation. The R. V's.: "to account anything as from ourselves," leaves no clear impression unless one has obtained it in advance from the Greek.

The infinitive λογίσασθαι does not depend on the adjective ἱκανοί: "sufficient to think or to account" (our versions). This gives a wrong sense to the last clause by having it mean that God makes us sufficient to think or to account something although the clause does not say this. The infinitive modifies the whole clause "that of our own selves we are sufficient"; it states contemplated result and forms an infinitive clause: "so that as a result we may reckon or claim something" (no matter how little) as having originated from our own selves. No, Paul says with ἀλλά: we have no sufficiency whatever and hence can reckon and claim nothing as our own product. Cancel the very idea. All our sufficiency is derived from God. He is its one source (ἐκ). This agrees with ἐκ Θεοῦ in 2:17 and explains how our confidence comes "through Christ" and is thus confidence that dares to stand "before God" (v. 4). He supplies the sufficiency *in toto*, he does it through Christ; the results are apparent, our confidence is according. There is nothing about which to reckon, nothing on which to enter a claim to our own credit.

Do both phrases belong together: "sufficient of our own selves, as from our own selves"? They most emphatically do not; Paul even separates them as widely as possible. "To reckon as from our own selves" is likewise not to be construed together. God is not enabling Paul to reckon, think, account. Construe together: "anything as from our own selves."

In the *C. Tr.* 787, 885, 891 our passage is used as proof for the natural man's total inability in spiritual things, in fact, it has been generally used as such proof. This use is assailed on the plea that here Paul speaks only of his sufficiency for the ministry. We must, of course, correct the translation of Luther, which the A. V. followed, and which the R. V. has bettered only in part; but the pertinency of the passage as proof for the total inability of the natural man remains, in fact, is made clearer and stronger by the correct rendering. The basic sufficiency for the ministry is all that makes a genuine Christian, the special features needed in the office are only moderate additions that can and dare never be dissociated from their great basis.

Paul is *not* speaking about the whole of it. All of it is from God alone; ministers can claim not "anything as from themselves." All Christians must do the same. Paul has described the sufficiency of ministers in I Tim. 3:2-7, and Titus 1:6-9. The bulk of what he lists, the real basic requirements are Christian in general with only the teaching ability and the maturity added. All is from God alone, all the basic elements in particular; these no natural man ever possessed. This passage may, therefore, be used as proof. Christ and the apostles have used a large number of passages in the same way in which this passage is used in *C. Tr.*; take the striking instance recorded in Matt. 22:31, 32.

6) We are told what this divine sufficiency has made of Paul and of his assistants. We see how God's own act produced this confidence in "regard to God," how they are happy and assured when they face him. We further see how all their success is

fully explained, and that there is nothing they can claim or reckon to their credit. **He who also made us sufficient as new testament ministers, not** (a testament) **of letter, but of spirit, for the letter kills, but the spirit makes alive.**

Ὅς is here not the common relative, it is demonstrative, for it adds a strong, independent statement. See other examples in Rom. 1:25; 2:29; 3:8, 30, which are elucidated in the author's volume on Romans. We translate not "who," but "*he* who," "*he the One* who." Nothing as coming from our own selves is reckoned and claimed for our own account; everything is set down to God's account, to his credit.

As he does so often, Paul at once goes to the basis and does not stop at the intermediate points. Everything intermediate is covered, and that as it really ought to be when we at once go right to the bottom. Paul does not stop with his conversion, with his call to the ministry, with his personal spiritual equipment, he does not consider how God has made him zealous, courageous, faithful, etc. All these features of his sufficiency have a deep, rich, glorious, divine, objective source.

God "made us sufficient as ministers of a new testament," etc. Our boast concerns him alone. Note the turns on the same word: ἱκανοί (adjective) — ἱκανότης (noun) — ἱκάνωσεν (verb). This is not an affectation nor a mere play on words; it is natural, simple, and most effective. This is not false humility: Paul and his assistants do possess full sufficiency. They must also declare this fact when there is need for so doing; failure to do so would be denying credit to God. The point is not that God "sufficiented" (coining a verb to indicate the Greek) us "as ministers," as men who serve others for the sake of benefit to others, but "as new testament ministers." Like a fountain of life, this testament flows with life for all men, and God has let us drink from it and has bidden us to dispense its living waters to others. Here is our whole sufficiency. If it were not for this testament, we should be nothing and could accomplish nothing.

The R. V.'s translation "a new covenant" ("testament" in the margin) is not an advance on the A. V.'s "a new testament." Commentators also waver. See the author's exposition of I Cor. 11:25, from which we repeat only the main point: the Hebrew *berith* is "covenant," which is rendered διαθήκη, "testament," by the LXX which thus conserves the main idea of onesidedness: this covenant is like every testament that is made by God *to* Israel and is not a mutual agreement between equals. Its substance was promise, Christ fulfilled the promise, and this fulfillment is now laid down in a testament. All believers are named as the heirs who are to be paid out with all the gospel blessings. We may call the ministers of God the administrators (I Cor. 4:1), yet they themselves are heirs. So in the New Testament διαθήκη = "testament." And we should render, not "ministers of *a* new testament," but as one concept: "new testament ministers." The newness lies in the fulfillment of the former covenant promises by Christ.

Now the greatness of this testament is the fact that it is one, "not of letter, but of spirit," and what this means is at once briefly stated: "for the letter kills, but the spirit makes alive." The genitives are qualitative or descriptive, and the absence of the articles with the genitives makes prominent their qualitative force. When we remember that γράμμα = *Vorschrift*, law put into writing by the legislator, Paul's words become plain. Then we shall see the contrast with πνεῦμα and shall note that this is "spirit" and not, as is often argued, the Holy Spirit. We have the same contrast in Rom. 7:6. This new testament is not one whose characteristic quality is *Vorschrift*, law fixed in writing, external, with which to confront us to our undoing. Its great mark is "spirit," the opposite of the "letter" of the law, an inward, living force. The word γράμμα already reminds us of the two tables of stone on which God's finger wrote the ten holy demands; we shall have the plural γράμματα in a moment.

The difference is tremendous, as great as that between death and life. "The letter kills." It cannot help it because we are all sinners. Confronted with the letter of the law, our death warrant is sealed. "But the spirit makes alive." It enters the sinner's heart, quickens, regenerates, gives him life. The articles are anaphoric (second mention), R. 762: the letter and the spirit just mentioned. One may well compare Rom. 7:6 (see the author's exposition).

It is incorrect to assume that the Old Testament was entirely "letter," all law, and that not until Christ came did men have the gospel with its quickening "spirit." Hosts of Old Testament saints were saved, just as we are, by "the spirit" that makes alive and not by "the letter": "Ye could not be justified by the law of Moses," Acts 13:39. This is true, the old covenant was marked by the *gramma* of Sinai which was inscribed on stone tables; but the covenant consisted of promise. Abraham had it long before Sinai.

The *gramma* killed the Jews who were faithless to the covenant promise and tried to win life by the *gramma* and not by the covenant promise. Yet the promise always quickened and saved those who believed the covenant promise. Then came Christ who brought, not another *gramma*, but the complete fulfillment of the old promise. The old covenant was turned into a new testament. The *gramma* of Sinai still threatened death, but more mightily than ever the fulfilled gospel, which was all pure "spirit," bestowed life on all who fled from that death.

By some the whole written Word is made "letter," and "spirit" is made its opposite, something that is not bound to the written words but is a so-called inner, spiritual meaning at which one arrives by an immediate inward illumination of the Spirit. What the written Word *says* is thus set aside; to adhere to that as its real meaning "kills." What the Word is said to *mean* although it be contrary even to what its writing says, this alone "quickens." To this we answer that the meaning of Scripture is one. What the writing records, the Spirit means, that and that alone. No double or multiple meaning exists such as literal and spiritual, patent and occult, ordinary and allegorical, and the like. The writing is the one honest as well as adequate medium by which the Spirit speaks, and what he thus says is spirit and life. All else is imagination, self-delusion, deceit. Luther says in regard to the *Schwaermer* (fanatics): "They cry *Geist, Geist!* (spirit), but this *Geist* is the devil!"

X. *Our Ministry Exceeds in Glory*

7) Because Paul was at one time a Jew, this section (v. 7-18) has been called a *Midrash* (a little Jewish exegetical treatise) on Exod. 34:29-35. Others use the word "digression." The style is said to differ from the context. If this section is omitted, we are told, v. 6 could be joined to 4:1 without difficulty. But if we make this omission, a break in thought is at once felt; if we reject the omission, all is smooth and in order. The personal note is said to be absent, but in v. 12 "we" appears and in v. 18 "we all." Even the verbal connection is close. The four διακονία occurring in v. 7-9 continue the διακόνους used in v. 6. The other key word δόξα which is found in v. 7-11 is directly suggested by the contrast between "letter" and "spirit," "kills" and "makes alive" which occur in v. 6. When v. 7 begins: εἰ δὲ ἡ διακονία κτλ., the continuation with the preceding

is so close that even the R. V. does not make a new paragraph. In the case of any other writer these things would be reckoned with; we shall not treat Paul less fairly.

Others say that he speaks about Moses and becomes didactic; he "leaves the communicative letter style." But Paul has already dropped all reference to subjective excellence as this might appear in himself and in his assistants and has begun to tell about the office they have and what they have in it: "we have" in v. 4, "accordingly having" in v. 12. He impresses the Corinthians with a reference to the office "we have" and shows them that, having this office, we have confidence (v. 4), hope (v. 12), and do not faint (4:1, 16). How could Paul better show the glory of this office, aside from pointing to its results (v. 2, 3), than by contrasting it with the greatest Old Testament office, that which Moses had held? The fact that a polemical edge is intended by thus utilizing Moses, an edge that is turned against Judaistic invaders in Corinth, is not apparent. In order to cement anew the relation between himself and his assistants and the Corinthian church instruction such as this given in v. 7-18 is eminently in place.

Now if the ministry of the death, engraved in letters on stones, was in connection with glory so that the sons of Israel were not able to gaze upon the face of Moses because of the glory of his face although it was being done away with; how shall not rather the ministry of the spirit be in connection with glory?

Paul asks the Corinthians to consider the greatest minister of the Old Testament and to compare the ministry which Paul and his assistants now have in the New Testament with the ministry which he represented. Who will say that it is not rather the latter that must have glory? The whole Old Testament ministry is represented in Moses, and the very pinnacle of his ministry is selected, the incident when he brought from the mount, where he had been face to face with God, the tables of stone that were inscribed with the divine *grammata* of the law.

The Corinthians are reminded of the fact that Moses' face shone with a light of divine glory so that the sons of Israel (υἱοί, "sons," not "children," our versions) were unable to gaze upon that face of glory but were compelled to look away or to cover their eyes. That certainly was glory for that ministry, glory directly from God. The condition of reality, εἰ with the aorist, deals with the well-known historical facts. The Koine prefers the aorist passive ἐγενήθη to the middle and has it here in place of the aorist of εἶναι which was not formed; note ἔσται, the future of εἶναι, in the apodosis.

All this glory for Moses, yet his was only "the ministry of the death." This is not the subjective genitive (R., W. P.): death did no ministering. This genitive is objective: Moses' ministry caused death. His ministry is named according to its effect. "The ministry of the death" is that of the whole Old Testament. It had other ministers, but they were all second to Moses; he is the great representative of all of them, and his mighty ministry of death continues to this day. The writing inscribed on those tables of Moses still stands and deals death to all transgressors. For this reason the participle ἐντετυπωμένη is perfect: "having been engraved in letters on stones" and standing thus engraved forever.

It is striking to say that the ministry was graven in letters on stones (dative of place); yet these letters are the message of Moses' ministry, and so it is true that his ministry is graven in them. Because it brought death, how could it be glorious? Because these *grammata, Vorschriften,* graven laws, were God's own and voiced his judgment on all transgressors. God's judgment is glory, his righteousness and his justice are attributes of his glory. Its refulgent light blazed on the face of this great minister of God. The sons of Israel could not endure it to gaze at this glory-light even when it was transferred to Moses. How, then, shall sinners endure the glory-light that is on God's own face when he comes to judge them?

The glory on Moses' face was temporary. Paul adds the articulated present participle which has concessive force: "although (it had the quality of) being done away with," the Israelites could nevertheless not look upon it. The glory served its purpose in God's minister of the law by revealing the glory of the great Lawgiver. The record that it did this continues the revelation. In the Word Moses still stands before us with those *grammata* on stone tables as God first gave them by his glorified minister.

How soon the divine light faded from Moses' face, whether suddenly or gradually, is immaterial. The idea that the Israelites were not to see the fading, and that for this reason Moses covered his face, is fanciful. The participle must be passive; even when it is regarded as a middle it could not mean that the glory "was passing away," to obtain this sense the verb παράγω would be used. God was doing away with it, putting it out of effect, and so it was gone. Paul's addition of this statement is significant. God intends that the glory of the *grammata* of judgment and death shall disappear before another glory that is to abide forever, the glory of grace in Christ, the glory of pardon and life which is conveyed by the New Testament ministers, Christ's apostles. See v. 11.

In order to exclude a misunderstanding let us remember that the old covenant was established with Abraham 430 years before Moses (Gal. 3:17), and that it was into this covenant that the ministry of Moses was placed. The law entered in order fully to reveal sin (Rom. 5:20) and thus to lead to the knowledge of sin (Rom. 3:20) in true contrition so that faith in the gospel might follow. It would be incorrect to think that Moses and Israel had only the *grammata* of law; they had them in conjunction with the covenant. Every Israelite who was made contrite by the law found forgiveness and salvation in the covenant.

Now the covenant that was inherited from Abraham was entirely promise, simply promise. All that Moses added to it with his ministry was the law set in fixed *grammata*; he could not bring the fulfillment which those promises had to receive, the fulfillment on which all the saving power of the promises rested. Jesus had to bring that. John 1:17. But the bringing of the *grammata* gave Moses a distinct office for the world; it stands ever: "The law was given by Moses" (John 1:16); he and those stone tables, which still pronounce death on all sinners, ever belong together in one *diakonia*. We should misconceive God's intention if we should make Moses all law and only law or all law for Israel. God would never have added this engraved law if it were not for the sake of the far greater covenant with its promise and the future fulfillment of the promise. But it is ever Moses and his ministry that function to this day in the law that was divinely given to be our guardian slave (παιδαγωγός) to lead us to Christ, Gal. 3:24, 25.

8) So another "ministry" had to follow, "the ministry of the spirit," objective genitive, that bestowed the spirit which makes alive (v. 6; Jer. 31:33). It had to follow when the promise of the old covenant received its fulfillment in Christ, when what was at first covenant (promise) became "testament" (v. 5) by fulfillment. The supreme function of this ministry was to act as administrator of this testament by paying out to all the heirs according to the testamentary pro-

visions. This was the apostolic ministry. As Moses still ministers with his tables of law, so the apostles still minister with Christ's testament. The apostles still speak and minister, and all true believers still adhere steadfastly to the doctrine of the apostles (Acts 2:42), who with their doctrine (Christ's testament) are the foundation of the church (Eph. 2:20) on which we are built as living stones, a spiritual house (I Pet. 2:5, etc.).

As with the law which God introduced through his ministry Moses led the sons of Israel by faith to embrace the covenant of Abraham, which freed from death and gave life to all the Old Testament saints, so Moses now leads to Christ and the fulfilled promise, the great gospel testament, which dispenses life over all the world. For the sake of this vast dispensation of what is now far more than promise, of what is now actual fulfillment for "all nations" (Matt. 28:19; Mark 16:15) the apostolic ministry was established, its distinctive function being the administration of the fulfilled gospel. To all those who are still condemned to death by Moses' ministry this apostolic ministry brings life. As the minister of law pointed to the promised Christ (Deut. 18:15-19; John 5:46), so the gospel ministers point to Moses and the law (Rom. 3:20). Moses died, but his ministry went on; the apostles died, and their ministry goes on. All who ever proclaimed the law have been Moses' assistants as all who now proclaim the apostolic gospel are still assistants of the apostles (such as Timothy, Silas, Titus, Luke, etc.).

Two great ministries thus stand forth, one that is centered in Moses for death, the other that is centered in the apostles for life. They are only ministries, neither produces what it brings. The death brought by the one is God's judgment; the spirit of life brought by the other is God's gift of grace. The ministers are only God's "slave-stewards," his "underlings" (ὑπηρέται), I Cor. 4:1. He made the face of the one shine with his own glory, with the blinding, unendurable light that shows forth his holy righteousness. Paul asks how, having done this, God could leave the other, the great apostolic ministry, without glory. Does not this ministry minister God's love, grace, mercy; plant spirit and life in place of death? Is there no glory in these attributes of God that can reflect itself in the human ministers of these attributes? It will not be blinding glory light, which accompanies divine justice. It will not be a light that shines upon the sinners as judgment comes upon them but a light that "shines in our hearts" even as this ministry puts spirit and life in our hearts; it will match the love, mercy, and grace of God; it will be and is "the light of the knowledge of the glory of God in the face of Jesus Christ" (4:6). This light will never be "done away with." This light shines not only in the hearts of the ministers but likewise in the hearts of the New Testament believers.

Οὐχί is only the stronger οὐ; it is here the interrogative particle which implies an affirmative answer. "How shall not rather" (μᾶλλον) implies two things: first, the fitness of glory for the ministry of Moses, secondly, the even greater fitness of glory for the ministry of the apostles when this is compared with that of Moses.

9) "For" means: in order to explain. The explanation is a restatement in which other, namely explanatory, words are used. **For if the ministry of the condemnation** (is) **glory, by much more does the ministry of the righteousness abound with glory.**

From the self-answering question Paul advances to a direct assertion. Yet the "if" of a condition of reality is retained, which retains the idea of comparison of the two ministries. The elucidation lies in the two contrasted genitives: "of the condemnation" and "of the righteousness." All the Corinthians know from the Old Testament how glorious the ministry of Moses was and remains. Yet it is "the ministry of the condemnation," of that one well-known condemnation which needs only the article to bring it to mind.

Κατάκρισις is the act of condemning and not the result as some think; the suffix -σις indicates the act, -μα the result (R. 151). The act is here referred to; compare "the letter kills." It kills by an act of condemnation; it causes death in this way. It is, of course, God's act. Although they are ascribed to the letter (v. 6) and now to the ministry, these are only God's means of condemnation. The genitive is objective just as is the genitive in the phrases "the ministry of the death" and "the ministry of the spirit." They are blinded who see only the letter and the ministry and then scoff at these as being unable to kill by condemning; they overlook the fact that God acts in the letter and in the ministry. Every sinner has to deal with him. Heb. 4:12 states how the Word is like a sword; and I Cor. 2:4 how the ministry is a demonstration of divine power.

Paul does not reduce the glory which he ascribed to Moses' ministry in v. 7. When he says without a copula and thus more effectively that the ministry of the condemnation "(is) glory" he actually identifies that ministry with glory. It is all glory. It would be a mistake on the part of Paul to minimize the glory of Moses' ministry when his object is to show the full glory of the apostolic ministry: the less the one is, the less would be the other by comparison; but the greater that of Moses is, the greater is that of the apostles since the latter exceeds the former. Nor is there the least question in regard to Moses. God's righteousness and holiness are always most glorious when they execute eternal condemnation as the whole universe will see at the final day of judgment. And were not the thunders and the lightnings of Sinai, which were swathed in unearthly smoke, terrible in gloriousness?

Only one other glory exceeds this, it is again that which is found in God, his grace, which bestows the quality of righteousness on the sinner who repents and believes. It exceeds because it is a greater matter to acquit the condemned sinner than to condemn him; because it takes only the letter of the law on stones to condemn him but the blood of God's own Son and the Spirit's power that produce repentance and faith to acquit the already condemned. In regard to δικαιοσύνη study Rom. 1:17; Rom. 3:21, etc.

The explanatory point lies in these two, κατάκρισις and δικαιοσύνη, as *forensic terms* (see them in C.-K.). The latter is the quality produced by the divine verdict alone when by grace for Christ's sake it acquits the sinner and thus changes his status before God. In Romans it is called "God's righteousness," here it is connected with the apostolic ministry: "the ministry of the righteousness" (again objective genitive; again the article to indicate the one well-known and only righteousness). God conveys it through his Word by means of this ministry. This ministry preaches Christ and thus works faith and thus secures acquittal and righteousness for the sinner. "By much more then it abounds with glory," dative of means, of respect, R's (*W. P.*) instrumental, all are only grammatical terms.

10) Paul comes to the climax. **For even what has been glorified has not been glorified in this point** (or part): **on account of its transcendent glory**. It has been glorified (perfect tense, and forever remains so) in all other points; it is lacking only in this one, in which the ministry of the righteousness is not lacking. "What has been glorified" is the ministry of the condemnation, and the perfect tense has the same sense:

what has been and forever remains glorified. The subject and the verb are passive, but Paul is not the agent who has been doing this glorifying of Moses' ministry; God has done this, and therefore also the glory of that ministry remains.

In one μέρος, part, point, respect God has not glorified Moses' ministry, namely in this point of making its glory superlative, transcendent beyond the glory of all other ministry. Such superlative, all-transcending glory God bestowed on the apostolic ministry. What a mighty fact for all true ministers of Christ, the present assistants of the apostles, to contemplate! We all share in this superlative glory which outranks that of Moses. "On account of its (the) transcendent glory" is said from the point of view of the ministry which has this transcendent glory.

11) "For" explains the one point that is still left open although it was incidentally touched upon in v. 7: just why the ministry of Moses is not equally superlative with that of the apostles. **For if what is being done away with** (is being done away with) **despite glory, much more what remains** (remains) **with glory.**

The Greek needs no verbs; their omission makes the contrast all the sharper. Both participles are substantivized presents. Here is one thing the nature of which is that it is being done away with; here is another the nature of which is that it remains. In our comment on v. 7 we explained the first participle: the condemnation is to give way to the righteousness. The condemned sinner is to be pardoned. This does not merely happen, it is God's arrangement. He always and always wants to put out of commission the condemnation of the *grammata* by his grace and pardon, by the righteousness of faith in Christ Jesus. This righteousness is the thing that remains, which is never to be superseded by anything else.

The other contrast is between διὰ δόξης and ἐν δόξῃ. This is the use of διά which is not listed in grammars and in dictionaries. R. W. P., says "with glory — in glory" is a contrast between the phrases; in his *Grammar*, page 583 he states that the διά used in Rom. 2:27 is a shading off between means and manner. In regard to Rom. 2:27 B.-D. repeats the view of Winer, Kuehner-Gerth, etc.: *Umstaende*, circumstances, *Beziehung* is usually added. A late German commentator has διὰ δόξης = ἐν δόξῃ occurring in v. 7 with the remark that Paul loves to change prepositions without always wanting to express the finer nuances; he faults those who search for a difference in the two prepositions that are used here. Some suppose that διά = *with* and denotes a transient flash while ἐν = *in* and denotes permanence.

Διά = "despite glory" while ἐν, of course, is "in or with glory." And the difference is great and vital to the thought. We may add the two samples occurring in Rom. 2:27 and 4:11 where we have the same use of διά with the meaning "despite" or "in spite of." The original idea "between" is retained. The action is sometimes favorable and in harmony with an object; but when it is contrary and inharmonious, the resultant sense of διά is "despite." So here it means *despite* glory, in spite of all the glory with which the condemnation is done away with by God; but the righteousness remains *in* glory. In every justified believer the condemnation has been made to disappear *despite* its glory; righteousness, which abides for him, remains *in* all its glory.

What a glorious ministry, then, is that of the apostles which ministers this righteousness! Unbelievers, are, of course, left to the ministry of Moses, whose glory blinds and kills them with judgment and condemnation.

XI. *Our Ministry Bestows Glory*

12) The point of this paragraph is not the hope of Paul and of his assistants, not the openness of speech they use, not the liberty with which they operate; all these are subordinate. The point is that the glory inherent in their ministry (v. 7-11) is one that brings glory upon glory upon us all, upon those who are served by this ministry as well as upon those serving in it. Paul once more draws the Corinthians to his heart. By showing them the true exaltation of his ministry he is showing them the true exaltation of themselves as affected by that ministry, an exaltation that goes from glory to glory and cannot be obtained by any means other than this ministry.

Could Paul use a better way to heal the breach that had been made between himself and the Corinthians, a breach that was now almost healed? By turning from his ministry and by listening to voices that are hostile to it the Corinthians could only lose this glory; it would fade away instead of increasing. The loss would be fatal. Not, however, on this negative side does Paul dwell; he presents the positive side, which is most effective.

As he used Moses' ministry when he was showing the glory of his own ministry, so he again uses Moses when he is showing the glory which the Corinthians have by this ministry of his. He uses the very same feature of Moses' ministry, but now another point of that feature, namely the veil. Thus he adds the effect made upon the sons of Israel in contrast to the effect of his own ministry upon the Corinthians. It is so simple and so obvious. In v. 7-11 the two ministries, Paul's and Moses', suffice for the comparison; now the comparison is between the effects of these ministries as exhibited in the Jews and in the Christian Corinthians. To be sure, the effects are to be found in the people.

In v. 7 "the sons of Israel" are mentioned only incidentally and not for their own sakes but to show what the ministry of Moses is.

Paul has been criticized because of his treatment of the veil, nor has this criticism always been adequately met. An unwarranted canon has been set up, namely that Paul should not go beyond an exegesis of Exod. 34:29-35. Paul evidently goes beyond that canon; hence the criticism of him. It all depends on the commentator's mind as to how severe he makes this criticism. Some accuse him of falsification, of allegorizing, and the like. In fact, they serve Moses no better. He is called a hierophant who practiced deception upon the Israelites; Paul is called a mystagogue who initiates his adepts into his wisdom. Pagan ideas are the stock in trade of this exegesis.

Paul changes nothing in the account of Exodus in regard to Moses and the veil. He uses what is there said about the veil as being illustrative of the blindness of the Jews regarding their entire Old Testament and contrasts this with the effect of the gospel in "us all." Instead of remaining on the surface of the account in Exodus, Paul sees and uses the full illustrative possibilities in regard to the Jews and in regard to all of us Christians. He sees the veil shutting out the Jews from Christ by their refusal to use the glorious ministry of Moses as God intended them to use it. He sees the veil removed for the Christians by Christ and his ministry so that their faces now shine with ever-increasing glory that is reflected from Christ himself. The very glory of Moses' ministry is left far behind in the beneficiaries of the apostolic ministry who are transformed "from glory to glory." All this is done by using the great fact that the veil is to be done away with even as the glory of the ministry of Moses is to fade and to disappear during the apostolic gospel ministry. The key to the illustration is the significant verb "to be done away with." We have had it twice, in v. 7 and 11 (participles), and its opposite "that which remains" (v. 11); we now have it twice, in v. 13 and 14 (participle and finite verb) plus its synonym in v. 16, and in v. 18 the full unveiling with ever-increasing glory.

Having, therefore, such hope, we continue using full openness of speech and not as Moses kept putting a veil upon his face so that the sons of Israel should not get to gaze on the end of what was being done away with, but their considerations were made like stone.

In v. 7-11 Paul writes objectively about the two ministries, the Mosaic ending in the enduring apostolic. He is through with the comparison of the ministries as such. When he advances to their effects he speaks subjectively, first about us who are in the apostolic ministry and then about "us all" who receive its gift of glory (v. 18). We of the apostolic ministry, he says, "have such hope," namely that ours is the ministry with transcendent glory, never to be done away with, always to remain in glory (v. 10, 11). The condemnation brought by the ministry of law despite its glory ends when the righteousness of faith in Christ acquits the condemned sinner, and the glory of this ministry and its effect, this blessed righteousness, remain forever. We have this hope, Paul says, not as though we are yet uncertain but as being fully assured and certain. It is "hope" because the Parousia, the last great day, has not yet come with its full and final revelation of what our ministry is and brings to all believers.

Having this divinely assured hope in regard to our ministry, Paul says, "we continue using full openness of speech," παρρησία, which means speaking with full openness, withholding nothing, without reservation of any kind. Throughout our whole ministry we ever continue such openness. The verb is the durative present, the durative of constant continuation, and matches the iterative imperfect which is used when he is speaking about Moses. So the Corinthians have ever heard Paul and his assistants speak, so he speaks to them also in this letter. This is in contrast to the ministry of Moses.

We may go farther and include all the Old Testament prophets. Their message was preparatory even for Israel. Because of its nature it withheld much, for the fulfillment in Christ had not yet come. But the apostolic ministry had that fulfillment, the complete manifestation of grace and salvation for all men for all time. All reason for reserve or for withholding had disappeared. Moses and the prophets had to leave much to the future when Christ should finally come. Pagan religions had their esoteric doctrines which were at best to be communicated only to the initiated. The gospel of Christ ever speaks with "full openness" and dispenses all its blessings with utmost prodigality.

13) Paul makes the comparison with the distinctive feature of Moses' ministry, his bringing the law on tables of stone to Israel and telling them all the commandments of God. In the whole section, v. 7-18, the prophetic phase of Moses' ministry is not mentioned: "The law was given by Moses," John 1:17. Moses = the law. Our versions alter the construction, but the Greek is not elliptical. "And not as" simply adds the opposite, but it adds this in the form of a negative comparative clause. R. 1159 is obscure; B.-D. 482 says ellipsis.

There is considerable dispute in regard to just what Moses did, and still more in regard to the purpose of what he did (πρὸς τό κτλ.). The iterative imperfect states in accord with Exodus 34 that Moses repeatedly put a veil over his face. Exodus 34 states that Moses spoke the commandments to Israel with his face unveiled; that whenever he was done speaking he put on the veil; that when he spoke to God he again removed the veil. In v. 7 Paul says that the glory on Moses' face was so great that the Israelites could not gaze upon it, which means that they were compelled to cover their eyes. It is incorrect to say that Moses had his face covered and spoke to the Israelites only through a veil. All that both Exodus and Paul say is to the effect that the glory of Moses' face was to be seen by the Israelites, for this divine glory gave the effect to the divine commandments as they came from Moses' lips. The fact that the eyes could not endure this glory was due to the death, the killing power, the condemnation of the commandments which Moses spoke (v. 6-9). The glory on Moses' face was the glory of the divine law and the judgment that was reflected by God's minister of law.

All of this occurred at Sinai, and we hold that it ended there after the communications of the law to the Israelites were concluded. The opinion that this veiling and unveiling continued for the entire thirty-eight years of the journey until Moses died is unacceptable to us.

On the reluctance of the grammarians to admit that πρὸς τό with the infinitive means result and not always purpose see R. 1003, who here speaks of subjective purpose (1075). In spite of this stand of the grammars we confess that here result is better than purpose. This does not evade the issue involved in the idea that God had such a purpose, but we note that the positive ἀλλά clause, which is a counterpart to the negative πρὸς τὸ μή clause, states result, this clause also having an aorist. So we submit the question whether we do not here have result: "so that the sons of Israel did not get to look earnestly on the end of what was being done away with but got their thoughts hardened" (both verbs are ingressive aorists, ἀτενίσαι and ἐπωρώθη).

We have had this "being done away with" twice before (v. 7 and 11), in v. 11 it was substantivized as it is here. We have seen what "this thing being done away with" means and thus have no trouble regarding what "the τέλος or end" of it signifies. The *gramma* and the *grammata* which are death, which kill by their condemnation of the sinner, are done away with, their "end" is reached when the gospel brings "the righteousness" of justification by faith in Christ. The glory of the former, which is a glory of divine judgment and justice that was reflected on the face of Moses when he came from Sinai, yields to the greater glory which ever remains and shines in the pardoning righteousness of God, shines as gospel glory in the apostolic ministers and then in "us all," the gospel believers (v. 18). The condemnation which Moses brings is done away with and reaches its end (τέλος) when the righteousness of Christ comes. "End of law (τέλος νόμου) Christ for righteousness for everyone believing," Rom. 10:4.

If πρὸς τὸ μή = result, Paul says that the sons of Israel were not permitted to gaze upon this end, in fact, they never saw it at all because they remained in unbelief. This ending of the law or function of Moses and something of greater and ever-abiding glory that follows in the gospel and the function of Christ, Paul sees in the acts of Moses when, after speaking the legal commandments to Israel, he again and again covered his blazing face with a veil.

Ἐτίθει, Moses kept doing this until he had concluded this speaking of the commandments, the repetition emphasizing this coming to an end, this being done away with, so that another, who is greater than Moses, might come and speak as the covenant of Abraham promised, the covenant which Israel had, yea, to speak of salvation from the condemnation. A result clause would state the tragic fact that all this was lost upon the Israelites, the ἀλλά clause adds that they were hardened. To state the two historical facts as resultant facts does seem to be Paul's meaning.

If we regard the expression as indicating purpose, then the clause says that it was God's intention that the sons of Israel should not see this end, this would point to Christ and to righteousness. But how could God have such an intention regarding "the sons of Israel," this very name pointing to their covenant relation to him? Predestinarianism is not the answer, but the punitive justice and judgment of God are. They who will not believe shall finally not believe. Read Matt. 13:14, 15; Acts 28:26, 27; Rom. 11:8-10, and similar passages that refer to judgment. No Bible student will have difficulty with this divine intention. He will know, too, that God at all times had a believing remnant who were true sons of Israel.

14) So "their considerations were made like stone," petrified or hardened to stoniness because of unbelief. Regarding this verb see Rom. 11:7, and regarding the noun 11:25. The other verb which indicates a hardening like that of a branch or twig which is cut from a tree is seen in Rom. 9:18. The subject of self-hardening, which is followed by God's judicial hardening, is treated in connection with these passages in Romans. We need not hesitate to supply the agent for the passive ἐπωρώθη as though Paul purposely left the agent unnamed, or as though the passive is to be taken in the sense of the middle "became petrified." The Scriptures are too plain in regard to God's agency in judicial hardening; and we gain nothing by trying to evade it here.

However, instead of saying "they were hardened" or "their hearts were hardened," Paul predicates this hardening of their νοήματα, their thoughts with which their minds considered what Moses said and did. Their "considerations" did not respond in a proper way but grew obstinate like stone. Read Stephen's description in Acts 7:37-53 and note his significant reference to Sinai and to the Mosaic law in v. 38 and 53. The aorist is again ingressive: "got to be petrified," it at the same time states the historical fact. We note that we here certainly have result whether the infinitive clause with ἀτενίσαι also denotes result or only purpose.

"For" explains by pointing to what we see in the case of the Jews today. The marvel was great already in Paul's day, so many centuries after the Jews saw the end of each display of glory on the face of Moses with unbelief — they were still in the same unbelief. Now the marvel is still greater — after twenty centuries they retain the identical stoniness of unbelief. **For to this day on the reading of the old covenant the same veil remains unlifted because (only) in Christ is it (ever) done away with. Yea, till today, whenever Moses is read, a veil lies upon their heart. Yet whenever it turns to the Lord, the veil is removed all around.**

Paul might have stated all this with stark literalness. He uses rich figurative language instead because it conveys so much more both directly and indirectly. The Jewish unbelief of Paul's own day is exactly like that unbelief which was manifested at Sinai. The Moses of Sinai still appears to the Jews of today every time they gather in their synagogues where they regularly read "the old covenant," διαθήκη is here the Torah or Pentateuch. They have it divided into *parashas*, regular lections for their Sabbath services, so that it shall be duly read.

Paul does not say "the reading of the *gramma* or *grammata*" which was once engraved by God on stone tables (v. 6, 7), the divine law of commandments which is now in the Pentateuch. This law was also read when the respective *parashas* were reached; but the five books of Moses were "the (whole) old covenant" which was made with Abraham and was continued with the sons of Israel until Christ came. Here διαθήκη = "covenant," the Hebrew *berith*, because it refers to the unfulfilled promise that fills the Pentateuch; in v. 6 the word should be rendered "testament," for there it refers to the fulfilled promise. See v. 6 on the subject and the elucidation by C.-K.

Compared with the fulfillment, the covenant of promise was "old," antedating the fulfillment. It remained "old" until Christ came; then the "new" arrived, καινή, "new" as related to the old (not νέα or "new" as unrelated to anything old). The point to be noted is the fact that in the synagogues the Jews faced the *whole* Moses, not only as one who brought them the *law* of death that kills by the condemnation of all sinners (v. 6. 7), not only his ministry of death, but also the Moses who brought them the covenant promise of Abraham with its *gospel* deliverance from condemnation by faith in the promised Messiah. The whole Moses, the entire covenant together with the law that was added to it 430 years after Abraham (Gal. 3:17; Rom. 5:20), were constantly read to the Jews.

Paul means that what happened at Sinai is ever and ever repeated in the case of the Jews. There Moses spoke the law to the sons of Israel with glory on his face; here, after speaking it, he put a veil over his face to show that the condemnation of the law was to have an "end," was to be done away with (καταργούμενος, v. 7, 11, 13) by the righteousness of justification (v. 9) which ever does away with condemnation. This gospel righteousness was announced already in the old covenant of Abraham (Rom. 4) as a promise. At Sinai Moses ministered also this old covenant and this promise (gospel) although God there made him the minister of the law to serve as such for all time. So, Paul says, as the Jews had him at Sinai they have him at every reading in the synagogue to this very day.

And they ever respond in the same way. As they did at Sinai, so they have done through the centuries in the synagogue when Moses speaks to them. Their thoughts harden like stone with the opposition of unbelief. The thought is not that they discard the Pentateuch. They read it continually, revere it and laud Moses to the skies; but they do not believe him and his writings (John 5:46, 47) nor what the veil on his face tells them so effectively, what his whole ministry and his writings ever expound to them: condemnation done away with only by the righteousness of faith in the promised Redeemer. Paul states this figuratively by using the veil in an illustrative way just as God had Moses use it: "to this very day the veil remains unlifted," literally, "not being drawn up to reveal." The original idea of the veil is retained, for Paul says "the same veil."

The veil does not mean covering the eyes so as to prevent vision and to make people blind. The veil on Moses' face means the end of the glory of the law as it is condemnation for the sinner. The glory soon disappeared from Moses' face, and he discarded the veil. The abiding glory of righteousness is to extinguish (καταργεῖν) the glory of the judgment that condemns. But in the case of the unbelieving Jews it is as though the veil still hangs over Moses' face, as though the glory of the condemning judgment of the law still burns on Moses' face under that veil. For them his ministry lies altogether only in that glory of the law.

This glory and the veil ever go together; if it were not for the one, the other would not exist. By leaving the veil the glory is left. And that glory ever means condemnation. It is a glory of judgment, that alone. So if the veil "remains" (present, durative: ever remains), which means that the burning glory of condemnation continues to burn under it with a destructive light that no man can endure (v. 7), the Jews are lost. But that is the manner in which "up to this very day" they read Moses, with only "that same veil" and the glory of the law under it. Because they read in this way they never see "the end of what is intended to be done away with" (v. 13), the glory of righteousness which is to quench the glory of condemnation and is then to remain forever (v. 11). The wrong thing remains for them. They are adamant in these their perverted thoughts, νοήματα (v. 14a).

For the unbelieving Jews the veil remains unlifted "because (only) in Christ is it (ever) done away with." This is added for the sake of the Corinthians who know it. They also know how the unbelieving Jews hate Christ. "In Christ" = in union and connection with him, this ἐν always involves faith. The thought is perfectly plain, the construction simple, and ὅτι means "because."

Our versions and R. 729 prefer the reading ὅ τι, a relative: "which (veil) is done away with." The R. V. margin construes still more abstrusely: "remaineth, it not being revealed that in Christ it is done away." This makes μὴ ἀνακαλυπτόμενον an accusative absolute participle, a rare construction. The idea that otherwise the use of μή with the participle cannot be explained is answered by the fact that any participle whether it is predicative or not, is regularly negatived by μή.

15) Ἀλλά is not adversative, it is continuative and climacteric (R. 1186); it adds no opposite thought, no "but," "on the contrary." It carries the precious thought to its climax: "Yea, till today, whenever Moses is read, a veil lies (durative: continues to lie) upon their heart." To read Moses is the same as to read the old covenant, the Pentateuch. "Till today" is the same as the previous "to this day." These repetitions emphasize the fact that the old unbelief continues down

to the very present, continues when Moses is constantly read, is constantly before the Jews. Only here in the New Testament does the classic ἡνίκα ἄν appear, it is indefinite and has the note of repetition: "whenever," R. 971.

The climax is reached in the statement: "a veil keeps lying on their heart." In v. 14 "the same veil remains unlifted" leaves the thought unfinished. What must be added is the fact that this is meant subjectively with reference to Moses. The reader could have understood this without assistance, but it is better that Paul say it in so many words. Moses and the veil which he wore at Sinai have passed long since; the Pentateuch is fully clear as to how the law with its condemnation leads us to the gospel of righteousness in Christ. On the objective side all has been done.

But these unbelieving Jews disregard all that in their νοήματα or "considerations" (v. 14a). Subjectively and for themselves they are bound to have "a veil" (note, not "the veil"). They cannot veil Moses nor his Pentateuch (objectively) so they put a veil over their own heart (subjectively). What this veil is has been intimated, the stoniness of their unbelieving thoughts whenever they read the old covenant or Moses. They refuse to understand what Moses really was and what he really wrote; they are fixed in their own thoughts about him and also about all that he wrote. They keep, as it were, a veil of their own making wrapped around their hearts.

16) Paul adds, and we know that he does it with a happy heart: "Yet whenever it turns to the Lord, the veil," this self-imposed veil (article of previous reference), "is taken away all around." Not all the sons of Israel pass into hopeless hardness. Although they were reared as Jews with their ancient veil upon them, in all ages and even now not a few nevertheless come to conversion. Then the hand of divine grace

takes the veil away from around them. The present tense περιαιρεῖται is iterative.

Chiliasts refer this to the national conversion of the Jews at or in the millennium; but then we should have the future tense; and then, too, ἡνίκα ἄν does not fit with its indefinite note and its repetition: "whenever." See the author on Rom. 11:7, 25, 26. Paul has no subject with ἐπιστρέψῃ. Our versions supply "it" (R. V. margin: "a man"), others "their heart" or "Israel" as implied in the context. The singular is noteworthy after the plural αὐτῶν as though Paul indicates that this turning is an individual matter as it, indeed, always is. Since no subject is written out, the sense is: "whenever there is a turning to the Lord," the aorist to denote a definite, decisive turning.

Ἐπιστρέφειν is the regular verb to denote the act that is called conversion (Acts 9:25 and repeatedly). To turn "to the Lord" includes turning from sin, falsehood, etc. The turn includes contrition and faith. "Lord" needs no article in the Greek, it is like a personal name, here it denotes Christ. The expression "to turn to the Lord" with the veil taken completely away is a beautiful allusion to Exod. 34:34, where Moses faces the Lord with the veil removed.

17) The statements of this verse are transitional, preparatory to the climax which is reached in v. 18. **Now the Lord is the Spirit; and where the Spirit** (is, there is) **liberty.** In the phrase πρὸς Κύριον (v. 16) no article is needed, but when it is the subject of the sentence, and when it is mentioned a second time, the article is in place: ὁ Κύριος. This Lord is Christ. The Greek usually indicates the predicate by omitting the article; but πνεῦμα would then mean only that "the Lord is spirit," i. e., has spirit nature as this is said about God in John 4:24. Paul, however, means that "the Lord is the Spirit," the Holy Spirit, the third person of the Godhead.

The fact that Paul is not fusing the two persons of the deity into one is at once apparent when he writes "the Spirit of the Lord." They are two persons but of identical essence and do the same work. Where the Lord is, there is his Spirit, and where the Spirit is, there is the Lord. In the presence of the Spirit we see the glorification of the Lord, and in the presence and the glorification of the Lord we see the Spirit and his work, John 16:14. This is what Jesus told Philip about himself and about the Father: "He that hath seen me hath seen the Father," John 14:9-11; 12:45; or still stronger: "I and my Father are one," John 10:30. This is true also with regard to the Lord and the Spirit.

Now this about the Lord and the Spirit is said because "where the Spirit of the Lord is, there is liberty," liberty in the fullest sense of the word. Paul says this in order to show what turning to the Lord really means: it means turning to the Spirit, and this means "liberty." In v. 16 he speaks about Jews turning to the Lord. What do they leave behind when they thus turn? Gather the answer from v. 6, etc.: the *gramma* and *grammata* that bring death, that kill, that minister condemnation; gather the rest of it from the reading of the covenant and of Moses with a veil: hardened thoughts that are like dead stones and lack everything that Christ brings. Now we see what turning to the Lord is: it is the most blessed spiritual liberty.

But why mention the Spirit, why not ascribe this liberty to the Lord alone? We have the answer in John 14:16, 17, 26; 15:26, 27; 16:7. The Lord ever works through his Spirit. The graven letters of Moses have no power to convert and to give liberty, only the Lord's Spirit can do that. Those letters bind and condemn so that we may flee to Christ and to his Spirit and be freed. Therefore also there is this "ministry of the spirit" which is the opposite of the "ministry of the letter," which makes alive whereas the latter only condemns and kills. It is the ministry "of the spirit" because it is the Lord's gospel ministry, one that works with his Spirit in order to make men turn and be free.

18) We reach the climax of the entire paragraph: **But we all, with unveiled face reflecting as in a mirror the glory of the Lord, are ourselves being transformed into the same image from glory to glory as from the Lord** (who is) **the Spirit.** The apostolic ministry has abiding glory (v. 11). The incumbents and the beneficiaries of this ministry, "we all," have this glory, in fact, it transforms us from glory to glory.

Paul is not yet through with Moses. The wonderful presentation as it has followed Moses from v. 7 onward has Moses as the basis in the climax. From the glory which his face reflected on Sinai we reach the glory that is in us all. From his transient glory which was intended to yield to another we come to the fulness of this other that is glory upon glory. From the law of Moses which drives to Christ we come to Christ and his Spirit, to rest in glory forever.

These two paragraphs are a most marvelous structure of thought as they present the mighty facts of salvation. Paul shows his ministry as what it really is to the Corinthians. It ministers to the Corinthians, and they are shown what they are by means of this ministry. How this fact must draw them to this ministry, to it alone and to Paul, its chief minister, their apostle! Only an inspired apostle could offer a presentation like this that is so mighty and so glorious for its purpose. Lord, help us by thy Spirit to read it aright, and let no one dim the words for us in the least!

"We all" = Paul and his assistants and the Corinthians, those in the ministry and those beneficiaries of his ministry who are now entirely on the same level, for also the ministers are beneficiaries. We all are like Moses: "with unveiled face reflecting the glory of the

Lord," with a face that has been and that remains unveiled (perfect participle) and that, unlike Moses' face, we never veil. As Moses' face reflected the glory of God on Sinai, so our face now ever reflects the glory of the Lord. Note the turning "to the Lord," πρός, face to face, in v. 17. What was granted only to the highest minister of the old covenant and in a transient outward way is granted to all of us in the New Testament in a permanent, inward way. None of the sons of Israel had a reflected glory on their faces, they hid their eyes even from that which was reflected on Moses' face; we all shine with glory.

The dictionaries are unsatisfactory in regard to the middle participle κατοπτριζόμενοι. B.-P., for instance, leaves us with the idea of catching something or of beholding something in a mirror. The Latins have *speculantes* in the sense of "beholding" or *contemplantes*. The idea of the κάτοπτρον or mirror is retained: to behold in or by the help of a mirror, which the commentators frequently understand as a reference to Christ or the Word or the believer's heart. This idea lacks linguistic evidence, especially here where, if *"beholding"* is meant, we have had ἀτενίζειν twice already (v. 7 and 13); moreover, the dative "with unveiled face" points plainly, not to "the sons of Israel," but to Moses who faced God without a veil, and to believers who turn to the Lord by having the veil forever removed. The context as well as the original Greek usage compel us to discard these unsatisfactory views ("beholding as in a glass," A. V.; "beholding as in a mirror," R. V. margin) and to prefer the meaning *"reflecting* as in a mirror." On the face of Moses the glory of the judgment of God was *reflected*; on our face the Lord's gospel glory is to be reflected.

Already this is much, namely becoming a mirror which reflects the brilliant sunrays of Christ's glory of grace and salvation. But in all of us who have turned to the Lord there is vastly more. A mirror only reflects, Moses' face only reflected. His face, like the mirror, remained only what it was. Christ's glory of grace enters into us, transforms, metamorphoses us "into the same image from glory to glory." The passive μεταμορφούμεθα retains the accusative that is used in the active, τὴν αὐτὴν εἰκόνα, in loose fashion (R. 486). Paul speaks about this spiritual transformation in Rom. 12:2 without the use of a figure and thus furnishes us the best commentary.

This transformation consists in losing conformity to the world, in renewal of the mind to prove what is the good, acceptable, and complete will of God and thus ever to follow it. This is no less than a metamorphosis, an inward change of the very μορφή or "form" of our being. At one time it had a form that corresponded to the world, sin, flesh; now it is more and more receiving a form that corresponds to "the same image," that of the Lord. "That ye may become partakers of the divine nature," I Pet. 1:4; "until Christ be formed in you," Gal. 4:19 (where μορφωθῇ is the verb); "Christ liveth in me," Gal. 2:20.

Some commentators refer to pagan metamorphoses because Paul uses this word. But what did pagans know about a spiritual transformation? How can pagan darkness illuminate glorious gospel effects? The verb is passive: "we are being transformed," namely by the Lord's Spirit; it is present and durative: the transformation begins with regeneration and the new birth (John 3:3, 5) and continues in sanctification through life (John 17:17). It has been well said that this transformation is *spiritualis* and not *essentialis*. We remain we, the Lord remains the Lord. Hence Paul writes "into the same image," the image of the glory of the Lord which we reflect.

Εἰκών is *Abbild* which presupposes a *Vorbild*; the image is drawn from the original: a child is the image of its father, the head on a coin the image of the monarch, the reflection of the sun in a mirror the image of the sun. Ὁμοίωμα = likeness and does not connote derivation: one egg only resembles another, one person, one house, one object resemble a similar one. See Trench, *Synonyms*. The word is most fitting in the present connection. "The glory of the Lord" is the original; we are transformed into its image.

The glory of our Lord is so constituted that no one can in the least reflect it without first himself having become transformed into an image of that glory. Christ's glory shone fully upon the Jews; they reflected none of it. The reflection begins at the moment of transformation, and the transformation instantly results in the reflection. Paul writes: "we are being transformed into the *same* image," i. e., "into *that very* image," which is only stronger and more emphatic than "into *his image*" (the Lord's), and truer than "into *its* image" (that of the Lord's glory). C.-K. 401: "into the same form, *Gestalt*." "From glory to glory" = progressively as we become spiritually more Christlike and finally reach the heavenly glory. Some prefer: from the glory in this life to the glory of heaven; yet the tense is the progressive singular, and we do progress already in this life.

"As from the Lord (who is) the Spirit" = as one might expect from such a source or agent. The work corresponds to the workman. Καθάπερ = κατά + ἅ + πέρ: "fully in accord with what things" come from the Lord, ἀπό indicates derivation. The Lord is not called the agent (ὑπό) but rather the source and fountain of our transformation. To be sure, ἀπὸ Κυρίου Πνεύματος can be construed in several ways, but here only the construction indicated in v. 17 is proper, namely that of apposition: "from the Lord, the Spirit."

This phrase and its two nouns, together with v. 17, have produced a good deal of discussion. We need note only this, that here more is said than *das Geist-Sein Christi* (the Spirit-being of Christ), for then τὸ Πνεῦμα in v. 17 ought to be only πνεῦμα, and the third person would not be referred to; nor is dynamic union of Christ and the Spirit all that is here expressed, a union of their power and their work. Unless the union is one of the divine essence in the Trinity so that one divine person is *in* the other, the full import of Paul's brief expressions is not fully understood. We might, indeed, translate, "from the Lord's Spirit," yet we hesitate because in v. 17b, where this is said, Paul writes τὸ Πνεῦμα Κυρίου (the article, the nouns in reversed order from that found in the phrase). Our whole transformation is the work of the Lord in and by and through the Spirit. All Scripture agrees in regard to that.

CHAPTER IV

XII. *"We Faint Not"*

Though Our Gospel Remains Veiled in Many

1) Paul and Timothy have described the glory of their ministry and have ended with the glory which this ministry produces in its incumbents and its beneficiaries. This led to a mention of the hardened sons of Israel (3:13-15). The gospel ministry continues to meet such stoniness (4:3, 4). This, however, affects neither this ministry nor its incumbents. It is one of the great burdens which they accept and bear without being induced to change either the gospel or their way or presenting it.

For this reason, as having this ministry even as we received mercy, we faint not. It is the glorious nature of this ministry as set forth in chapter 3 that ever upholds its incumbents. "We" is not a literary plural (R., *W. P.*) but refers to Paul and Timothy (1:1) and other assistants. A significant clause is added to their having this ministry: "even as we received mercy." The Greek verb, being transitive, has the passive: "we were mercied." This mercy is not the granting of the ministry to them, for the word for that idea would be grace. The connotation in mercy is wretchedness and misery. We were only poor creatures, Paul says, until God's mercy reached us. He refers to their conversion. By calling it a reception of mercy he disclaims for himself and for his assistants any high standing or possessions that might make them able and worthy of being placed into this ministry. He thus reverts to 3:4: their whole sufficiency is from God. God took us, Paul says, who of ourselves were poor, miserable creatures and first of all raised us up with his mercy and then set us into this glorious ministry. Here is something which every true minister may well ponder.

It is thus, Paul says, that "we faint not" as men who were once nothing, whom God then blest doubly, first with his mercy, next with this office. "We faint not" = "we are not discouraged." This is said in view of the apparent failure of this ministry because so many reject the gospel which it brings (v. 3, 4). It is said also in view of the way in which Paul and his helpers conduct their ministry by refusing to stoop to such base means as men in office often employ, as Paul's rivals in Corinth also employed to attain what they imagine to be success.

Some think the verb means "we are not cowardly"; but it has this implication only where bravery is suggested as a virtue as in the case of soldiers. Here, where ministry is the subject, the verb implies worthlessness for the work of this ministry as when men lose heart and despair and resort to questionable means and thus become κακοί, unfit for their task. This negative implies the positive which is expressed so strongly in 1:14: "we feel triumphant," and in 2:4: "we have this confidence through Christ to God." We know that we cannot fail as long as we attend to our ministry with God.

2) We faint not; **but we have renounced** (aorist, once for all) **the hidden things of shame,** as a result **not walking in craftiness nor adulterating the Word of God,** by such means attempting to attain success, **but by the publishing of the truth,** and by that alone, **commending ourselves to every man's conscience in the sight of God,** placing it upon every man's own conscience if he does not heed the truth as he knows he should. The verb ἀπεῖπον has no present stem; ἀπειπάμεθα appears with the tense suffix α in the second

aorist and is an indirect middle: "we renounced for ourselves." It is not a timeless aorist but historical and states the decisive past fact.

"The hidden things of shame" are such as bring shame and disgrace when they are drawn out of hiding into public light. "Shame," too, is objective: "disgrace," and not merely subjective: "the feeling of shame." These are always things that are disgraceful no matter how those who practice them feel about them. The genitive is qualitative: "shameful or disgraceful hidden things," the genitive being stronger than the adjective. While "the hidden things of shame" is broad, Paul himself states what he means: "craftiness" and adulterating God's Word, over against which he sets "the publication of the truth" (hiding nothing) and an appeal to every man's conscience in the sight of God. So Paul and his helpers began to conduct their ministry, so they are continuing it to this day — not fainting in the least, on the contrary, full of confidence (2:4), thanking God, and triumphing (1:14).

Paul has already referred to the charge made in Corinth that he was not always upright and truthful (1:12, etc.), that his yea was not always yea (1:17, etc.). He again speaks about this point when he says "not walking in craftiness." But it is now not "I," and not a defense against personal slander; it is "we," Paul and his assistants who are presented as men who might avoid discouragement and might seek greater success by practicing "craftiness." The word means ability to do anything and in the New Testament is always used in an evil sense: trickiness, cunning deception to gain one's end by underhand and dishonest means and methods. Men of this type had come to Corinth; before Paul is through he will reckon with them (chapter 10, etc.).

Now in 12:16 Paul says regarding himself personally: "being crafty, I caught you with guile" (blame me for it if you will!); but we at once see how open and honest that craftiness was. Craftiness has often been employed by the clergy (let us not say "ministers"); they have played politics in their conventions; they have gained — or lost their ends, but always and always to their own great hurt and to that of the church.

Crafty conduct is paired with "adulterating the Word of God." These two ever go together. He who is not honest with himself will not be overhonest with the Word. The reverse is also true — and the writer may be permitted to say that he has witnessed it too often — he who is not really honest with the Word cannot be trusted very far with his conduct. Δολόω = to catch with bait, to fix up something so as to deceive and to catch somebody. It is used with regard to adulterating wine. So here: "adulterating the Word of God," not leaving it pure lest people reject it but falsifying it to catch the crowd. Of all the dastardly deeds done in the world this is the most dastardly. None is more criminal nor more challenging to God himself. Not adulterating the Word of God had its edge against the falsifiers who had come to Corinth, who also cast aspersions upon the genuineness of Paul's teaching.

Robertson 1128 is right when he says that it is easy to split hairs about the participles and their relation to the main verb. Used with the verb in the aorist, these present durative participles mean: having renounced once for all — we never walk — or adulterate — but ever commend ourselves, etc. We see why one might resort to crafty conduct and to adulteration of the Word, namely thereby to commend himself to people, to get their favor and following.

In 3:1-13 Paul has already touched the question of recommending himself and his fellow workers to the Corinthians, where he states that they need no recommendation, that the Corinthians themselves are Christ's own letter of recommendation for Paul and his helpers, published like a monumental inscription in Corinth so that all men may read. When he after all speaks about "recommending ourselves" Paul in no way contradicts the previous statement which repudiates all self-recommendation. For see what this self-recommendation is — the very thing that made the Corinthians such a wonderful recommendation for himself and his assistants: "the publication of the truth" with its appeal "to every man's conscience in the sight of God." All ordinary commendations and recommendations praise the person concerned for what that person himself is. Here is a recommendation that fixes all attention upon what these men, Paul and his helpers, bring, publish openly, letting all men's consciences judge before God himself. A self-recommendation, yes, but one that asks nothing for self, that asks everything for the truth and its publication.

Φανέρωσις, the action of making publicly manifest, "the publication," repeats the participles used in 1:14 and 2:3, repeats the idea of "speaking from God before God in Christ" stressed in 2:17, and of "using full openness of speech" stated in 3:12. "With the publication of the truth," the whole truth and nothing but the truth, with that alone Paul and his assistants expect to win, know they will win, ever feel triumphant with gratitude to God, ever undiscouraged, never fainting. It is the full divine truth of the Word of God, "the whole counsel of God" (Acts 20:20). Ἀλήθεια = the reality revealed by God for our salvation. Its publication constituted the office or work of the apostolic ministry in which all who assisted the apostles helped. All true ministers are still such assistants.

This work of publishing God's saving truth recommends those who truly do this work "to the conscience of every man in the sight of God." On conscience see 1:12. Paul says: We come with this truth to every man's conscience in a public proclamation, presenting it to him in God's sight (2:17). What any man thinks of us depends on how his conscience reacts in God's sight to this divine truth which we publish. We have nothing else to recommend us. The Greek idiom "every consience of men" is our "conscience of every man." Paul adds "in the sight of God" because conscience holds us accountable to God. Drop the idea of God, and the vitality of conscience is destroyed. Mere abstract ideas of "right" and "wrong" do not bind the conscience; the idea of God and of his judgment does. With their own conscience bound in the Word of God (Luther's expression at the Diet of Worms), Paul and his assistants in all their work came with this same Word to every man's conscience and dealt with every man as in the sight and presence of God, with God watching how each man's conscience reacted to the truth of his Word.

It is the same thought as that expressed in 2:17. Some preachers, like hucksters, are ready to dicker about the Word of God as though they can discount something to make a sale, as though the deal is between them and men alone. This is what Paul also means by adulterating the Word of God, mixing in unrealities to make the Word acceptable to men. In the case of Paul and his helpers all is pure truth, all is for conscience in God's sight. Truth ever recommends itself to conscience and thus recommends also those who publish this divine truth. Conscience must ever say that truth is right and must be accepted, and that falsehood is wrong and must be rejected. So conscience must speak with regard to the proclaimers of truth and the announcers of falsehood. Only when conscience is deceived so that it thinks truth is falsehood and falsehood truth, or when it suspects the truth in some way, does its commendation fail. Some hate truth because it is truth (John 8:45), hate the light because their evil deeds want darkness (John 3:19-21). These have seared consciences. Still others are indifferent, cynical, like Pilate: "Why bother about truth?" These have blighted consciences. Yet truth ever finds the conscience and there wins its victories.

Truth needs no aids. Nothing is as strong, as convincing, as sure, as good as the truth, any truth (reality), and thus supremely the saving truth or reality of the Word. If truth itself cannot win a conscience, what can you add to truth to make it win? Some of your craftiness, or some adulteration of the truth? Truth needs no outside argument, its mere presence is greater than all argument. The conscience binds us to the truth; the whole operation is not on the plane of the intellect, not one of argument. The issue only passes through the intellect; it lies ultimately in the conscience and the will. When the sun bathes the rose, its petals open; so conscience should respond to the truth. So many preachers have never fully realized the quality and the power of the truth. A lack of their own full conviction weakens their effort to aid the truth with other means. The one means is "the publication," the full, complete presentation, "the manifestation." All victories of the truth are 100 per cent its own.

The truth is the reality. No power is able to destroy it, and no man or no conscience can possibly escape it in the end. All lies soon explode. The truth is the Rock of Ages; let your conscience build on that. All else is sand; and woe to those who built on it, Matt. 7:24-29. Much more could be said. The truth either crowns or destroys you in the end.

3) Paul sets forth why the truth does not commend itself effectively to so many consciences. It is supposed that this fact was used against Paul in Corinth: "If you and your gospel are all you claim them to be, why do so many reject you, why do their consciences not respond?" Paul is thought to answer this objection: "This is not my fault or the fault of the

gospel I preach but the devil's fault!" But these suppositions are unsatisfactory for the obvious reason that the same objection could be hurled against any and all of Paul's enemies. Did *they* win everybody? They won even fewer than Paul won and had to break into his churches to do even that. So we take it that Paul is here not making a defense but is simply stating the facts as they are. He and his assistants do not faint in discouragement, do not resort to questionable means despite the fact that many are not won by the publication of the truth. This sad fact in regard to so many does not in the least shake confidence in the gospel. As it does not do so in the case of Paul and of his helpers, so it ought not in the case of the Corinthians. It will not when they once more consider why and how men perish in spite of the gospel truth.

But if our gospel is also veiled, (only) **in those perishing is it veiled.** The condition of reality considers the sad fact as a fact. Although the full proclamation of the gospel is brought to them, many refuse to accept it despite its appeal to their conscience as the divine and the saving truth. But these are only those who are perishing. The substantivized present participle describes them as being in the act of slowly perishing, i. e., going on into everlasting death. We shall see that this is not due to an eternal, irrevocable decree of God. He sends them the gospel in order to save them. It is the same gospel with the same power as that which saves the rest. Paul calls it "our gospel" as he at times speaks of "my gospel." He refers to no distinction from the gospel in general, to no special form or formulation of the gospel. "Our" = of which we, I and my associates, are the ministers.

He twice uses the perfect passive tense (its periphrastic form) "has been veiled" with its present connotation "and thus now remains veiled." The figure is taken from Moses who was mentioned in 3:7 as he utilized it for the unbelieving Jews mentioned in 3:14. But it is now carried still farther — the very thing we expect in Paul. From veiling the heart (3:15) we come to seeing the gospel itself veiled. The agent for the passive is indicated as Satan in v. 4. The gospel light and radiance are not altered or destroyed, are not veiled for believers but only for those who refuse to believe. How Satan succeeds in throwing a veil over the gospel in the case of these people is now told us.

4) Although it is only a relative clause, it is weighty with meaning: **in whom the god of this eon blinded the thoughts of the unbelievers so that the illumination of the gospel of the glory of Christ, who is the image of God, did not get to dawn.** In this way the gospel is veiled for many. Only here is Satan called "the god of the eon," *grandis et horribilis descriptio Satanae,* Bengel. Aἰών = eon, a vast length of time but one that is marked by what transpires in it. Hence "this eon" is opposed to "the eon about to come," this world age in contrast to the coming blessed eternity.

The Gnostics and the Arians misused the expression "the god of this eon," the former having it mean one of the inferior demiurges, the latter using it to support the idea of "God" in a lower sense and applying this to Christ. In order to meet this misuse the ancient fathers construed so as to read: "in whom God blinded the thoughts of the unbelieving of this eon," which is, of course, an impossible construction. "The god of this eon" says no more than "the ruler (ἄρχων) of this world," John 12:31; 14:30. Calov calls him *simia Dei,* "the ape of God," because of his aping God. "The god of this world" is apt in this connection, not because the unbelievers worship him, but because he is the embodiment of all wickedness and ungodliness in this world, the author and the propagator of hostility to God. He originated the perdition in which men perish. "The god of this eon" trenches on the idea of the true God no more that does the commoner expression "the gods of the heathen" and this or that "god."

One of his worst activities is mentioned: "he blinded the thoughts of the unbelievers." The aorist means "he got to blinding them." Τὰ νοήματα has the same force it had in 2:14: the products of the νοῦς by virtue of its νοεῖν, "the thoughts, considerations, conclusions" that arise in the mind on hearing the gospel. In 3:14 they are said to have been "stonified." But the figures are different. On hearing the truth of the gospel published all the mental reactions are blind. The mind is confronted with the divine reality, but instead of reacting as if it sees this reality, all its thinking and reasoning are as if it does not see it at all. The thoughts are blinded. To be shown God's grace, Christ's blood and righteousness, justification by faith, the new life and salvation in Christ, and to think of them as nothing is to have been blinded. Take a modern example: the gospel tells about the devil. He is treated as a joke, he the very one who so blinds these thoughts of men. Lying in his power, men see him not even when he is fully shown.

The addition of τῶν ἀπίστων is often called pleonastic: "in whom he blinded the thoughts of the unbelievers," and many of the commentators write as though the genitive is unnecessary. Some differentiate: all the unbelievers are blinded, but only some of them are perishing. But the opposite is evidently true, for if any are rescued from perishing they are *eo ipso* rescued also from blindness and from unbelief. This genitive is necessary for Paul's thought. "In whom" refers to "the perishing," and to say that Satan blinded their thoughts leaves a gap in the thought, for he does not blind all their thoughts so that they act senselessly in all respects. This blinding has to do with the gospel, it is the blindness of unbelief of the gospel. Satan "blinded the thoughts of the unbelievers"; the genitive fills the gap, does it simply and effectively. We need not ask as to the sequence of perishing, having been blinded, and being unbelievers; they all start together. To be sure, all men who are without the gospel are perishing; here, however, Paul speaks about the time when the gospel reaches them, and then the perishing becomes certain for those who reject it in unbelief while those who are in a perishing condition but believe it escape.

Εἰς τό with the infinitive is regarded by our versions and some of the commentators as expressing purpose, in this case Satan's purpose. Result alone is in place here. These unbelievers are perishing, our gospel is and remains veiled in them, and this is explained by the fact that Satan "blinded their thoughts." What is the result? The divine illumination of the gospel never dawned in them, αὐγάσαι, which is in all probability ingressive: "did not get to dawn." The emphasis is on the infinitive which is placed forward, but the subject, too, is made impressive because of its concatenation of genitives: "it did not get to dawn, namely this illumination of the gospel of the glory of Christ." Some think that "in them" should be added, the place where this dawning failed to occur; but the Greek feels no need of such a phrase.

Φωτισμός, like other words that have the suffix -μος, denotes action (R. 151): "the illumination," and the word used is not "light" (our versions), the term for which is φῶς. In the case of these unbelievers there is not only light but the full gospel activity of "illuminating," but despite all this effort and this action no dawning, no morning glow, no bright and beautiful sunrise results, the veil of black night remains.

Let us note well how the imagery has advanced from the idea of a veil over the face, a veil that first hides the light under it (Moses, 3:7), that then shuts out the light that comes from without (the Israelites, 3:14, 15), to the idea of no veil at all, yet the fullest sunlight of the gospel produces no sunrise, not even the first dawning (aorist) for unbelievers. These are things worth seeing in Paul.

A discussion is carried on as to whether αὐγάσαι is intransitive, *erglaenzen, strahlen,* "to dawn," with τὸν φωτισμόν as its subject; or transitive: *erhellen, den Augenstrahl auf etwas richten,* to direct the beam of the eye upon something, an expression which is used by poets to state what ordinary people mean by "to see," and "the illumination" is its object (R. V. margin). Those who do not accept the former meaning say that it would require ἐν αὐτοῖς: get to dawn "in them"; those who do not agree with the latter meaning say it would require the accusative subject αὐτούς with αὐγάσαι, which is true. But what is really decisive against the transitive sense is the fact that the very thoughts of the minds have been blinded, and in the case of blind thoughts even the greatest illuminating action is unable to effect a dawning. And if Paul intended to say "to see," why should he resort to the rare poetic use of a verb instead of using one of the verbs of seeing that mean just that in prose?

"The illumination of the gospel (which proceeds from the gospel, genitive of origin) of the glory (genitive of contents) of Christ (genitive of possession)," B.-D. 168, 2. The Greek frequently has such a series of genitives; they here make the subject stand out in all its grandness. The glory of Christ in the gospel is the sum of his divine and his human excellencies. It has been well said that this glory makes him the radiant point in the whole universe, the object of supreme admiration, adoration, and worship. There should be added that the word "glory" takes us back to 3:7-11, to the glory light of the law and the judgment which was reflected on Moses' face, and to the greater and abiding glory light of grace and the gospel in the gospel ministry. This is the Christ glory that fills the gospel. This glory and its illuminating radiance can, of course, never be dimmed; Satan cannot hurt the gospel itself or rob it of its glory substance or of its illuminating activity. All he can do is to blind men by unbelief so that this illuminating activity does not get to dawn in men's minds and hearts. They remain in darkness while the light plays around them and seeks to make them glorious with its power, "from glory to glory" (3:18).

The relative clause: "who is the image of God," reveals fully who Christ is. Its meaning appears in John 14:9: "He that hath seen me hath seen the Father"; in John 12:45: "He that beholdeth me beholdeth him that sent me." Then in Phil. 2:6: Christ in the form of God and equal with God; and in Heb.1:3: "the effulgence of his glory and the very image of his substance." Εἰκών has been explained in 3:18. It here refers to the exalted Christ: the God-man on the throne of glory is the essential image of the Father. In him now shines forth forever all God's love for us, and in him we are to behold all that this love has wrought for our salvation. To have the illumination of the gospel of his glory dawn in our hearts (by faith) is to be saved from perishing. God created man in his own image, after his likeness, but man lost this image. Christ is the image himself, is equal with the Father, and shines in the gospel for us in order that his grace may restore God's image in us.

5) "For" is not illative, it does not bring proof; it is explanatory: in this whole matter of the gospel light and of Satan's blinding so many against that light the part which Paul and his helpers play is entirely minor. "For" = remember that in the case of this antagonism between Christ and Satan we are nothing but δοῦλοι whom God had also to fill with

light. **For we are not engaged in preaching our own selves but Christ Jesus as Lord and ourselves** (only) **as slaves for you because of Jesus.**

To be sure, if we preached ourselves we might well faint and give up in discouragement (v. 1) and admit that we are beaten by Satan. If it were a case of getting as much as possible out of preaching for our own selves, we might well think of using craftiness and adulteration of the Word instead of publishing nothing but honest truth and by that commending ourselves to men's consciences (v. 2). That, in fact, is what "the many do who huckster the Word of God" (2:17), make it a matter about which to dicker, to get out of it as much as they can for themselves. But "we are not engaged in preaching ourselves" at all, in seeking any worldly advantage from our work of preaching. If anyone ever charges us with doing that he is wrong. Whoever listens to us will ever find us doing only one thing, namely preaching "Christ Jesus as Lord." Since our whole work is κηρύσσειν, "heralding," it is public (a φανέρωσις, 2:14; 3:3; 4:2), anyone can see it without effort.

Since the days of Paul the ministry has always had men who, in the last analysis, preached themselves. They offered their own thoughts and their own doctrines, reshaped the Word and what it says about Christ Jesus as Lord according to their own notions so as to gain favor, following, honor, emolument, and personal advantage for themselves. They tried to beat the devil by selling themselves into his hands although no one has ever cheated him in that way. The temptation to yield something in regard to Christ Jesus with an eye to ourselves is often subtile, and we must ever be on our guard.

The very wording Χριστὸν Ἰησοῦν Κύριον instead of τὸν Κύριον X. Ἰ., indicates that Paul means: "Christ Jesus as Lord" with "Lord" as a predicate apposition (R. V.)

and not "Christ Jesus, the Lord" (A. V.). The latter spreads the emphasis over the entire designation; the former centers it upon "Lord" (= that he is Lord). This is more pointed and thus weighty, exactly as it is in Acts 2:36; 10:36; I Cor. 12:3. "Lord" is to be taken in the full soteriological sense just as when we call him "our Lord" Jesus Christ, the one who redeemed, purchased, and won our salvation, bestows it by his gospel and his Spirit, makes us his own to live under him in his kingdom of grace and in his kingdom of glory. Far more is meant than majesty and rulership. For this reason "Christ Jesus" is modified by this predicate: the Jesus who walked on earth and was the Christ, the anointed Messiah, who worked out salvation.

The statement has a pregnant force like I Cor. 1: 23: "We preach Christ crucified," and I Cor. 2:2: "I determined not to know anything among you save Jesus Christ, and him crucified." Christ Jesus as Lord is not only the center but the entire sphere; not only the central doctrine but the sum of all doctrine, omitting none. Christ Jesus as Lord means every word he spoke or gave by his apostles, dropping not one. What a pitiful thing to be preaching ourselves in any manner or degree over against preaching nothing but Christ Jesus as Lord! To preach him as Lord means to serve his interests alone; and since this preaching is the preaching of the gospel it is serving only the interests of the gospel. To devote ourselves wholly to his interests and those of the gospel, that is blessedness indeed; to substitute our own little temporal interests is the height of folly. Are we all sure of this?

Δέ adds the other point: "and ourselves (only) as slaves for you because of Jesus." Since "we" are the preachers and are thus involved when the preaching of Jesus Christ as Lord is mentioned, it is unavoidable that something be said about just what our position and our interest are. "Well," Paul says, "in a way we *are* preaching ourselves, the thing really cannot be helped." In v. 2 he even says, "We are recommending ourselves." But now comes the astonishing predicate: we are preaching ourselves "as slaves for you."

Ὑμῶν is the objective genitive: not "slaves owned, commanded, ordered about as slaves to do your will"; compare I Cor. 7:23: "Be ye not slaves (δοῦλοι) of men!" "Slaves for you": you to receive the whole benefit of our slaving (preaching). This is the sense because the master of these preacher slaves is at once named in the significant phrase "because or on account of Jesus." Because of him, our heavenly Lord and Master, whose slaves we are, because of his will and gracious order, because of his interest in you, we are slaves for you and preach, advertise, commend ourselves as such. The variant that has the genitive "through Jesus" is less well attested and not so forceful.

In four little words the whole position and work of Christ's ministers are expressed by one who, because he was such a minister, knew all. No minister has ever improved on these four words; many a minister has not learned their full secret. We are slaves who do nothing but serve Christ's people. Unselfishly, never tiring, never complaining, seeking nothing, giving everything, listening to no allurements or threats, happy only when we heap up profit for others — so we slave. All "because of Jesus." Why did Paul say "Jesus" and not "the Lord"? The very word "Jesus" recalls that here on earth, where this was his ordinary name, he came, not to be ministered unto, but to minister, yea to give his life for many, Matt. 20:28. "Jesus" recalls his example; "Lord" would bring to mind the reward he has in store for us.

"Slaves for you" = not lords over you but helpers of your joy (1:24), debtors to both Greeks and barbarians (Rom. 1:14), never lording it over God's heritage (I Pet. 5:3). Never slaves *of* men, ever slaves *of* Christ (Rom. 1:1; Phil. 1:1; Tit. 1:1); without question or hesitation where he speaks and orders, deaf where others would give us orders. This word should have made all the Roman popes and the little Protestant popelets impossible; likewise all the man-pleasers in the ministry.

This word, coming from an apostle of the Lord himself, surely must have had a strong effect on the Corinthians. With it Paul once more mightily draws the Corinthians to himself and to his assistants; what else could they do but respond in the same spirit when they thought of Christ Jesus as the Lord in whom they believed?

6) With ὅτι Paul states the subjective, personal reason that he and his helpers preach Christ Jesus as Lord and themselves as slaves for the Corinthians because of Jesus. The reason is that the very thing which they seek to accomplish in others has been accomplished in their own hearts. After that experience how can they possibly preach themselves and not Christ and thus themselves only as slaves for the Corinthians because of Christ? The great subjective reason is: **because God, he who** (once) **said: Out of darkness light shall shine!** he (it is) **who shone in our hearts for the purpose of illumination** (by means) **of the knowledge of the glory of God on the face of Jesus Christ.**

He who himself created light "shone (or ingressive: came to shine) in our hearts for the purpose of illumination" (the same word that was used in v. 4, where the illumination did *not* dawn). There is no doubt about the strong emphasis on the subject ὁ Θεὸς ὁ εἰπών, ὅς, "the God, he who said, he (it is) who," etc. The effort to place the emphasis on the last phrase: "on the face of Jesus Christ," is not in accord with the wording of the Greek. The statement that ὅς is not οὗτος ("this One") says only that the emphasis would be still greater than it is. Nor is it ὅς alone that supplies the emphasis although it has demonstrative force. It is, first of all, the weighty apposition ὁ εἰπών κτλ.: "he who once said," etc.

Ὁ εἰπών is the aorist because it refers to the one act of speaking. On the first day God created light, and he did it by speaking the word: "Out of darkness light shall shine!" Paul's aim is not to reproduce the divine fiat with diplomatic exactness but to reproduce it so as to convey what he has in mind. The very first manifestation of God was his calling light out of darkness. In order to heighten the idea of "light," "darkness" is also mentioned; and this is done because all of the manifestations of "the god of this eon" are to the contrary, to blind, to prevent all illumination from dawning. The substantivized ὁ εἰπών is an apposition: "he who said."

The future λάμψει is like that which is used in legal commands and is highly peremptory: the thing *shall be,* and there can be no question about it. It is not the power of God that is described; so many think only of power. It is the nature of God, the fact that he is the God of light, that is stressed. He shattered the darkness of chaos by creating the cosmic light; that shows the kind of God he is. The universe has been bathed in light ever since. We incidentally note that Paul reproduces the account of Moses as it is written: light was created by a fiat in a timeless instant. And it is true, an evolution of light is unthinkable. Darkness cannot produce its absolute opposite; nor are stages in the coming into existence of light conceivable. The Scriptures testify that by his fiat God created light.

This is the One, Paul says, "who shone in our hearts," the aorist just indicates the past fact or in addition is also ingressive: "came to shine." The verb is intransitive; since no object is mentioned either time this verb occurs, λάμψει cannot be regarded as being intransitive and ἔλαμψεν as being transitive. God "shone" has the very same meaning as "to dawn" had in v. 4, but now it is God himself who is the subject. Note the advance of the thought: in v. 4 the illumination did not get to dawn, and now God shone successfully so as to bring about illumination. At one time an impersonal expression is used, and now one that is gloriously personal.

Some find only a parallel: God created natural light — he also created spiritual light. Some add another point: by his word he created the one light — by his Word also the other light. Then they are inclined to stress the idea of creation by power and say: the same power that created the natural light created also the spiritual light. But this is not true, for in the one instance the power was the word of absolute omnipotence, but in the other instance it was the Word of infinite grace. In the one case resistance even in thought is not possible, in the other case (as v. 4 shows) many actually do resist.

This is not a parallel, this is a climax: God himself entered our hearts, God himself shone there and, we may add, still shines there. The same climax appears in the means employed and in the manner in which Paul states the means: once the word of omnipotence: "Let there be light! and there was light"; but in the other case: grace "for the purpose of illumination (by means) of the knowledge," etc., the knowledge produced by the gospel Word. Once the inanimate, in the other case persons: God himself shines, shines in our hearts. Mere nature shines with light; our hearts, the center of our personal being, shine with the knowledge of the glory of God, with his living, gracious presence in Christ.

While πρός is usually regarded as expressing purpose, here, where an aorist of past fact precedes, we take it as indicating accomplished purpose: "for the purpose of illumination" (our versions circumscribe), φωτισμός is repeated from v. 4. We also have a repetition of three genitives like the three occurring in v. 4, which creates the same impression of majesty in thought, and it is the grander because this is the second set of such genitives: "of the knowledge of the glory of God." The effect is enhanced by using "the glory of God" instead of "the glory of Christ"; and instead of the relative clause with reference to Christ which occurs in v. 4, the significant phrase "on (ἐν) the face of Christ." This mastery in expression and in thought and carrying both to a climax are wonderful. One must take time to contemplate all that is so simply done in order to get the full effect. It is a joy to let the mind dwell in turn on all the details.

In English we cannot say "for illumination of the knowledge," for we do not use the genitive in this manner. This genitive is intended to indicate cause: the knowledge causes the illumination to take place. We only approximate the meaning by rendering this "for the purpose of illumination (by means) of the knowledge." Knowledge is the full realization which fills "our hearts." It is such knowledge "of the glory of God," and "the glory" denotes all God's blessed, saving attributes (these especially). See the counterpart: "the glory of Christ," in v. 4. In v. 4 the advance is from Christ to God: "Christ who is the image of God." Now we have the reverse which brings all the glory of God to rest in Christ: "of God on the face of Jesus Christ." This is the same word πρόσωπον which was used in 3:7, yet it is here employed with a mighty advance and contrast. Unless this is noted, the force of the repetition of the word is lost.

The glory of God was only reflected on the face of Moses, the mediator of the law; the glory of God is embodied in Jesus Christ, the Mediator of the gospel.

The former glory was that of the divine law and its judgment on sin and on sinners, and the face of Moses could only reflect it since he had been with God only for a few days. The other glory is that of the divine gospel and grace for sinners, and the face of Jesus Christ radiates this glory because he is its very embodiment, he who came from God, the very Son of God, and returned to God as our Savior-Lord forever.

"Face" means that Moses turned to the Israelites; Jesus Christ turns to us. But they could not endure to look even upon that reflected glory while we receive the light of this embodied glory into our very hearts. The glory of the law and the judgment kills (3:6), the glory of God on the face of Jesus Christ makes alive (3:6) and saves forever. So we might go on and mention further details, for all that has been said from 3:6 onward is involved and is brought to its final focus and climax.

This verse with its present plural "in our hearts" still speaks only about Paul and his helpers in Corinth. It speaks about them as being filled with the light of the glory of grace and the gospel. It speaks about them as being the opposite of those who are perishing and are unbelievers (v. 3, 4). Paul and his assistants are themselves true Christians. The application lies on the surface: all believers of all time are like Paul in all this. In connection with v. 5 ὅτι in v. 6 shows that, since they are true Christians, Paul and his helpers can do only one thing, namely preach Christ as Paul states. And again the application to all other true preachers is obvious. With that we must stop. Some have not done so but have generalized from v. 6: all who have God shining in their hearts have this knowledge; and this knowledge enables them likewise to preach as Paul preached. We decline to follow this generalization. The Christian ministry requires the special call in addition to this knowledge.

Some think that when Paul wrote "the glory of God on the face of Jesus Christ" he had in mind his vision on the road to Damascus. More should be said. That light struck Paul to the ground. It was the light of the law like the glory on Moses' face; for Jesus said to Paul: "Saul, Saul, why art thou persecuting me?" and confronted him with his sin and his crime. Like the sons of Israel, Paul could not endure that light (3:7).

Yet that light of the glory of God on the face of Jesus Christ was also the gospel light. Jesus called Saul to repentance. He did not there on the Damascus road preach the gospel to Saul, but he did send him to the man who would do that. Jesus still comes thus to sinners in his Word. However, in regard to this experience of Paul's we must distinguish what pertained to his personal conversion (law, contrition; gospel, faith) from what pertained to the Lord's qualifying him for the apostleship (actually seeing the risen and glorified Lord), placing Paul on a level with the Twelve, I Cor. 15:8, 9 in connection with 5-7. In the present connection this "we" (Timothy, Titus, etc.) must be restricted to the former.

XIII. *"The Treasure in Earthen Vessels"*

7) This paragraph still belongs under the caption of v. 1: "We faint not." This word is even repeated in v. 16. First, we do not faint in view of those who reject our gospel (v. 3, 4); secondly, we also do not faint in view of what we endure in preaching this gospel. Here again v. 12 and 15 draw the hearts of the Corinthians to the hearts of Paul and his assistants. "Slaves for you" (v. 5) is the underlying thought. We marvel at this man's valor which glows with such devotion and love.

But we have this treasure in earthen vessels in order that the exceeding greatness of the power may

be of God and not from us. The context indicates that "this treasure" is God's shining in our hearts by the knowledge of faith filling us with his glorious grace in Christ Jesus. Paul says that he and his associates in the work have this treasure "in earthen vessels," those made of baked clay.

'Οστράκινος is derived from ὄστρακον, anything that is made of burnt clay, it is also used to designate pieces of such vessels: potsherds, *ostraka,* so many of which have recently been discovered in Egypt. They are covered with Greek writing and, like the papyri, shed so much light on the Greek of the New Testament. Clay vessels are cheap, utterly common, the least valued, used with small care, bound to break sooner or later. All these ideas are touched in Paul's figure. If it be asked whether just our bodies are meant as being "earthy" (I Cor. 15:47), made of clay, the answer is yes, but not apart from our souls and as still being in this earthly life. In 5:1, etc., we hear about the soul's entrance into heaven, and already in 4:16 the resurrection of the body is mentioned.

The astonishing thing is that such a divine treasure, God's own presence of grace, the ultimate of what is heavenly, absolutely priceless, beyond the value of all rubies and diamonds of earth, should be placed into such wretched vessels and be kept in them so long. One would expect that this treasure would be entrusted only to vessels of the highest value, be placed where they and their treasure are only admired and are ever handled with utmost care and reverence. But see what God has done! Yet this is his way with this treasure as I Cor. 1:26-29 shows. He sent his own Son into our flesh, permitted him to be born in a stable, in a paltry village, in lowliest surroundings, him in whom all the Godhead dwelt bodily (Col. 1:15-19; 2:9). Astounding, yet a fact.

The explanation of this lies in God's purpose: "in order that the greatness of the power may be of God and not from us." This is more than saying "that it may be seen to be." This is reality and not only manifestation or appearance. The latter does not always match the former. Many things appear to be and are supposed to be "of God" while they are only "from us." But if a thing *is* of God though at first it may not be *seen* to be, it will soon enough be *seen* to be of him. The genitive "of God" is the ablative denoting source (R. 514), a possessive in the predicate, and it really belongs to the noun subject and is not affected by the copula (R. 497). "Of God" is the opposite of "from us"; but ἐκ = derivation while the simple genitive denotes possession. This is God's own power and not merely one that is derived from him: God and his power are one.

Ὑπερβολή may be comparative, excess over something else; but it is also superlative when, as here, no comparison is indicated. The R. V. conveys that idea better than the A. V. by rendering: "the exceeding greatness," i. e., the superlative power with which no comparison of any kind can be made. In this connection "the power" is not God's omnipotence but, as in Rom. 1:16 where it is attributed to the gospel, the power of God's grace. The superlative power of which Paul speaks is the one that is contained in the treasure. He is speaking only about God's ministers: they have this treasure, which is, of course, their personal blessing, which makes them rich for salvation. When Paul adds this statement about "power" he goes beyond what the ministers have from the treasure for their own benefit. They are ministers for others; the power that is contained in this treasure in their own hearts (v. 6) is thus to operate also in all its superlative greatness from them as ministers upon others, to bless also them with salvation. It is the power which works "life in you" (v. 12), to multiply "grace" in many (v. 15).

God's purpose and his arrangement are to have this saving power wholly as being his possessions and in no measure or degree as having their source in us. For this reason he placed the great treasure into such poor earthen vessels. It cannot possibly be true that the superlative power is generated or produced by these vessels. They are so worthless and fragile in themselves that, if he did not protect them during the many shocks they receive, they would at once be broken into potsherds. As it is, these poor vessels endure only for a time. To be sure, Paul says "we have this treasure," it is in us as vessels, and God uses us ministers for the operation of this wondrous power. The power comes "out of us" but only because it has been placed in us by God and is thus the power that is wholly of God and in no degree "from out of us ($ἐκ$)" as the source.

8) Such poor vessels holding so vast a treasure! Such superlative power using such fragile vessels! Will they not break at once when this treasure and its power attempt to operate among men? Yes, they are ever at the point of breaking, yet, marvelous to say, they are kept from breaking, and so the mighty power works its wonders and does so as the power that is "of God" and never "from us," the vessels, as the source. The drama is breath-taking, the greatest drama in the world; but it is glorious in what it ever and ever achieves. "Sheep among wolves" (Matt. 10:16), and yet the sheep win! Death all around, yet so many given life! There is no spectacle like it in all the world. "Of God" alone explains it; "not from us" again explains it.

Throughout (v. 8-11) there are no connectives but just the striking participles. In the Greek this means more than it would in English because the Greek loves to use connectives, and every asyndeton arrests. All the participles are iterative presents, all are descriptive of what constantly goes on in repetition after repetition. All but the last have their sharp contrast, the last has it in a ἵνα clause (v. 10) with a turn of the thought to conclude the series. The negation of the participles is indicated with οὐ (not the usual μή) R. 1138 says because the negation is thus clear-cut and decisive, B.-D. 430, 3 because the verb concept itself is negatived. B.-D. states the fact, Robertson only the effect.

Paul continues: **on every side pressed but not hemmed in; being at a loss but not having lost out; persecuted but not abandoned; thrown down but not destroyed; always bearing around with us in the body the putting to death of Jesus in order that also the life of Jesus may be made publicly manifest in connection with our body. For ever we, the living ones, are being delivered unto death because of Jesus in order that also the life of Jesus may be made publicly manifest in connection with our mortal flesh. So, then, the death keeps working in us, but the life in you.**

Note the gradation and the picture of a mortal chase and a flight: hard pressed — at a loss which way to flee — chased — caught and thrown down — ever carrying around this hostile action of being put to death. Why do they not at once receive the fatal blow? Not because Paul and his helpers are able to ward it off. We know why: "Lo, I am with you alway, even unto the end of the world," Matt. 28:20. This explains all of the negations. There are four, the usual number employed by good writers when they wish to sketch completeness. 1) Pressed on every side but not hemmed in — the Lord makes a way of escape. 2) Being at a loss what to do but not having lost out — the Lord helping us out. 3) Persecuted and chased but not abandoned, namely by the Lord. 4) Actually getting caught and thrown down but not perishing and done for. Paul is describing the experience which he and his assistants constantly undergo and not the end of it all. What that will eventually be does not need to be said. That this will happen only by the Lord's own will is likewise plain.

Θλίβω = to press, and the noun = affliction; στενοχωρέω = to get into a narrow place where the pressure cannot be evaded. So there is pressure, but it is not so intense as to close off all escape. The next two participles form an *annominatio*, the second participle having perfective ἐκ (R. 1201, and 596). We imitate this: "being at a loss but not having lost out," the Greek means "being at a loss but not being utterly at a loss."

9) Διώκω = to pursue and hence to persecute. Ἐγκαταλείπω = to abandon unto. It is well to note this meaning in connection with Acts 2:27, where our versions and many commentators translate: "thou *wilt not leave* my soul in hell"; but David's soul and Christ's were not *abandoned unto* hell at death. Not to be abandoned unto pursuers means that the Lord helps us out as he did Peter in Acts 12:7, etc. To be thrown down means to be at death's door, the enemy is over us in order to administer the last blow; yet not even then to perish is deliverance indeed. This reaches the climax.

But the gradation thus sketched is not intended to be one that follows these steps in order. No; sometimes only one of these four happens, sometimes the other. In Acts 14:5, etc., Paul fled from the danger; but in 14:19, etc., Paul was dragged out as dead and yet did not perish. Two or more of these four may happen in succession, again only one of them may occur.

10) Now all four of them are combined as the νέκρωσις of Jesus, which is best conceived, not as "the dying of Jesus" (our versions) with "Jesus" as the subject that is dying, but as "the putting to death of

Jesus" with "Jesus" as the object. Taken in either sense, νέκρωσις is active (contra C.-K. 746 who speaks of it as being passive), for words ending in -ις denote action. What v. 8, 9 picture is not something that Paul and his assistants are doing but what others are doing to them. "This putting to death of Jesus," Paul says, we are always bearing around with us in the body; it is like a load upon us every day of our ministerial lives. It is "in the body" for the simple reason that the attacks of the enemies are directed against our bodies; and these enemies are always after us, at least to hurt us if not also to kill us.

Much the same explanation is needed as was given in connection with 1:5 regarding "the sufferings of Christ." The expression is not mystical. The glorified Christ is not still dying in us, nor is he being put to death in our sufferings. His own being put to death has been completed; but what his enemies once did to him they continue to do to his ministers "for his name's sake" (John 15:18-21) even as Jesus foretold. The same hatred that pursued and killed Jesus now pursues his believers who are one with him by faith in his name. It is an advance of the thought to use "the putting to death," this point was not reached in v. 8, 9.

The point of the whole statement is in the ἵνα clause, in the great purpose which God has in thus letting us constantly carry around with us in our bodies this putting to death of Jesus; it is "that also the life of Jesus may get to be made publicly manifest in connection with our body." "The putting to death of Jesus," his νέκρωσις, and "the life of Jesus," his ζωή, are opposites. As the one, so the other is exhibited in our bodies; in fact, the one is so exhibited "in order to" exhibit also the other. We should also note that the verb is again φανεροῦν; this exhibition is *public* in every way. Note this meaning of the word in 2:14; 3:3; 4:2 (noun).

11) Paul himself explains just how this strange effect is accomplished, that by our being put to death the life of Jesus is publicly exhibited in us, yea in our very bodies that are so constantly harried almost to death. But not until v. 12 are we told just what this public exhibition of the life of Jesus is. Verse 11 is an explanatory restatement of v. 10. It repeats the same thought with one vital addition, namely ἡμεῖς οἱ ζῶντες; the rest is only a slight variation from v. 10, it is also explanatory but adds no essential point. Moreover, ἡμεῖς οἱ ζῶντες, "we, the living ones," is only a part of the explanation, the preliminary to the main point as to how this life of Jesus is brought to public manifestation in our bodies. This main point is stated in v. 12.

"We are ever being delivered unto death because of Jesus" thus restates "always bearing around with us the putting to death of Jesus"; and this restatement serves a twofold purpose: it makes Paul's meaning clearer and it emphasizes the thought as being exceedingly weighty in itself. "Being delivered unto death" is exactly what the Jewish leaders so long plotted for Jesus and then finally accomplished. We know that in Paul's case, too, he was finally killed. The very word παραδίδωμι is used in the Gospels with reference to Jesus, and the traitor is called ὁ παραδιδοὺς αὐτόν (Matt. 26:25; Mark 14:12; John 13:11). But the difference between Jesus and us is now marked by saying that we are delivered to death "because of Jesus," only because of our connection with him. "Because" is meant intensively and includes both faith in him and ministry for bringing others to faith. It is the latter especially for which Paul and his assistants, like all the apostles, were hated.

In the same manner the ἵνα clause restates the ἵνα clause of v. 10. "In order that also the life of Jesus may be made publicly manifest in connection with our mortal flesh" = v. 10: "in order that also the life of Jesus may be made publicly manifest in connection with our body." The restatement emphasizes the divine purpose as being weighty, indeed, and at the same time clarifies by the slight change. "Our body" = "our mortal flesh"; our body is nothing but mortal flesh and is so considered here. As mortal flesh it can be delivered unto death. Though because of our souls they hold the priceless treasure, our bodies are nothing but "earthen vessels" that are liable to be broken at any time (v. 7). Yet they hold "the life of Jesus," for this is "this treasure" (v. 7).

These are the emphasizing and the clarifying restatements. Now to a consideration of the main point. This lies in the twice repeated subject "the life of Jesus," in the apposition to ἡμεῖς, "the living ones," and then the twice repeated verb "may be made publicly manifest." It is essential to understand what is meant by "the life of Jesus," his ζωή; otherwise we cannot understand what is meant by "the living ones," οἱ ζῶντες, in which ζωή is repeated; nor can we then understand what the public manifestation of this life in connection with (this is the force of ἐν) our body, our mortal flesh, signifies.

The word used is ζωή and not, as in John 10:17, 18, ψυχή. Unfortunately, we have only one English word to translate the two, namely "life," although there is a vast difference between them. Jesus never laid down his ζωή or "life" for us in order to take it up again. Jesus is himself ἡ ζωή, "the life" (John 14:6), the fountain of life, the source of all spiritual life and of life eternal for us. How could he lay that down? His ψυχή is the "life" which animated his body. This could be taken from his body by death. This he laid down for us on the cross when he died; this he took back into his body when he arose from the tomb. This is also true with regard to us; our ζωή is our life everlasting which death cannot touch, but our ψυχή leaves our body at death in order to be returned to it at the time of our resurrection.

"The life of Jesus," this fountain of life which Jesus is, this source of salvation and life everlasting for men, this was to be made publicly manifest, grandly advertised. How? Through us, the ministers of Jesus. That is the first point. Paul and others are the called ministers to dispense publicly "this treasure" (v. 7) by publishing the gospel. Hence they are here called οἱ ζῶντες, "the living ones," they who have the ζωὴ αἰώνιος, "the life eternal" in their hearts by having received it from Jesus who is the life. "The living ones" has no reference to being physically alive, for οἱ ζῶντες = the ones spiritually alive. They are the ones whom Jesus appoints to manifest publicly "the life of Jesus."

Now the further answer as to how God intends that this shall be done. It is astounding indeed! The life of Jesus "is to be publicly manifested in connection with our body," writes Paul with regard to himself and his assistants, yea, "in connection with our mortal flesh" which is liable to death and thus is constantly attacked by our enemies "because of Jesus," they ever pursue us with the threat of delivering us unto death. As ministers of Jesus who have spiritual life in themselves from "the life of Jesus" they preach Jesus and the life publicly in city after city, and the hate that followed Jesus and brought him to death follows them in the same way "because of Jesus," so that they actually carry around with them "the putting to death of Jesus" (v. 10).

12) All that lies in the phrases "in connection with our body," "in connection with our mortal flesh," as well as all the persecution sketched in v. 8, 9, is now concentrated and also elucidated in the clause which is advanced from purpose (ἵνα) to result (ὥστε): "So, then, the death keeps working in us" (durative present

tense). "The death" that has been graphically described has hold of us, keeps at work hurting us in order, as soon as possible, to end our work. Its attacks are, of course, being made on our bodies which are only poor mortal flesh, "earthen vessels" (v. 7). This death cannot, of course, touch our ζωή or spiritual life.

One additional point is needed to show that the life of Jesus is thus brought to public manifestation. We twice have the passive φανερωθῇ, effective aorist: a manifestation that is actual. We have the medial point, namely God's ministers who are filled with spiritual life and pursued by death because of their work. We still need the terminal point where this public manifestation, this public advertisement, comes into full reality so that all men may see it (compare "read by all men," 3:2). This point has purposely not been touched thus far. Paul intends that it shall come as a surprise.

Some commentators think that "the life of Jesus" means his restoration to life through his resurrection from physical death and thus conclude that this life of Jesus manifests itself by keeping Paul and his assistants physically alive among so many deadly dangers. It is obvious that the death of which Paul has been speaking will sooner or later reach the prey it is stalking. This does not imply that all these ministers of Jesus will be killed as martyrs although some, like Paul himself, will end thus. They may die in other ways, yet they have been suffering martyrdom all along. But if this manifestation of "the life of Jesus" denotes only that the exalted Jesus keeps his ministers physically alive for a longer or a shorter time, what becomes of this public manifestation when they at last do die, whether in one way or in another? The manifestation is defeated. This death wins and not Jesus, not "the life of Jesus." Therefore such an interpretation is not acceptable.

"So, then, death keeps working in us," and sooner or later it will lay us in the grave with our mortal flesh, "but the life in you." Physical "life" or ψυχή? All of the Corinthians will die physically as did Paul and his helpers. "The life of Jesus," which is here called briefly "the life," has a grander goal than keeping us away from physical death, keeping our ψυχή in our mortal flesh. This is the divine, eternal ΖΩΗ, "the life of Jesus," of him who is "the LIFE" and fount of life for us, and this works spiritual life, eternal life in the Corinthians. The Corinthians are brought to regeneration; made spiritually alive as οἱ ζῶντες, "the living ones," like Paul and his helpers (v. 11); the Corinthians grow and develop in spiritual life until they at last enter the life of glory.

The Corinthians are delivered from the dead world. They stand out in Corinth as those who are alive in Christ Jesus. And that is a public manifestation for the whole city of Corinth and for all who come there. The Corinthian congregation is like a monumental letter that has been inscribed in gold characters and been set up in Corinth so that all men may read it (3:2, 3). The divine purpose (two ἵνα, v. 10, 11) is attained (ὥστε, result). "The life of Jesus" has reached public manifestation in Corinth and has worked all the blessed spiritual life in the Corinthian church. It is public indeed: "You are the light of the world. A city that is set on a hill cannot be hid," Matt. 5:14.

But the marvelous thing is that this public manifestation is accomplished through ministers who are hounded by death. This death of persecution "because of Jesus" (v. 12) is busy working in them and will, of course, kill their poor bodies; yet by means of these mortal bodies, which are earthen, fragile vessels, the miracle is accomplished, "the life of Jesus" works the true life in the Corinthian church, and the whole world may see the public manifestation. What an accomplishment of God! And what a glorious achievement, to which Paul and his helpers yield their bodies and mortal flesh in order to let death work its will in them while the life uses them to work such an eternal result in the Corinthians!

13) What holds Paul and his assistants to their ministry despite the fact that because of it they are constantly being delivered to death, what makes them think only of the life they are able thus to bring to the Corinthians is now stated: **But having the same spirit of the faith according to what has been written: I believed, therefore I spoke, also we on our part continue to believe, therefore also continue to speak, having come to know that he who raised up the Lord Jesus will raise up also us with Jesus and will present us together with you.**

Δέ is adversative and turns to the new thought. We have the same spirit, Paul says, that David had according to what he has written (perfect tense: and thus has left on record) in Ps. 116:10: "I believed, therefore I spoke." This is exactly our case. Paul says: "Also we on our part continue to believe, therefore also continue to speak." Nothing deters us. Even if we were tomorrow to be killed by the enemies who want to silence us we would go on speaking (preaching Christ) today. Read the entire psalm and see how it breathes the same spirit that is voiced by Paul. Death stalked David, too: "The sorrows of death compassed me, and the pains of hell got hold upon me: I found trouble and sorrow." So also in the verse quoted: "I believed, therefore have I spoken," David adds: "I was greatly afflicted."

Paul and David have "the same spirit of the faith," τῆς πίστεως, note the article. This is objective faith, *quae creditur*, "which is believed," not *qua creditur*, "by which one believes." "What we believe" contains a certain "spirit," and that spirit we "have" when we believe. "The faith" is identical in both testaments; both contain the same truth, the Old Testament in the form of promise, the New Testament in the form of fulfillment. Hence the spirit of both is identical in defying persecution and death.

We pass by the views that "the same spirit" refers back to v. 12 or to the spirit of the Corinthians. It is "the same according to what has been written" by David. Peter gloriouly voiced this spirit before the Sanhedrin in Acts 4:20: "We cannot but speak the things which we have seen and heard"; again 5:32: "We are his witnesses of these things."

14) It is not bravado that animates Paul's words. Men often laugh at death and imagine that they are heroes when they plunge into it. In the case of Paul and his assistants the resurrection of the blessed removes all fear of temporal death: "having come to know (aorist participle to indicate the point when this knowledge set in) that he who raised up the Lord Jesus will raise up also us with Jesus." The one fact is past, the other future, but they are connected at both ends: by the subject — by the object. It is the same God who did raise up, that will also raise up; and it is the same Lord Jesus who was raised up, with whom we shall be raised up.

The association expressed by σὺν Ἰησοῦ is far deeper than that expressed by the second phrase σὺν ὑμῖν. "With Jesus" because he is "the Lord Jesus," called "Lord" here for this reason. We are in living connection with Jesus, and that assures our blessed resurrection. For that reason, too, the name "Jesus" recurs in this paragraph and not "Christ." "Jesus" = the human person who walked on earth; he suffered, died, was raised up by the glory of the Father and by means of all this was made "the life" for us so that we shall be raised up with him: he the first fruits, then we the harvest at the last day (I Cor. 15:20).

Those who think that Paul changed his mind about the Parousia and now no longer expects to live until Christ's return overlook the fact that Paul faced just what we are facing today: total uncertainty regarding the arrival of the Parousia plus total uncertainty regarding the arrival of death. We, too, therefore, like Paul, still speak in two ways: at one time as if the Parousia may come tomorrow before we die, again as if it may delay long and come after we have died. Here Paul, of course, dwells on the imminence of death as far as he and his assistants are concerned.

The sure knowledge of Paul and of his assistants includes far more than their personal resurrection. They believe and therefore speak and work with all their heart to bring others to believe because these others will also attain the resurrection of the blessed. In Paul's heart a mighty faith is paired with an equally mighty love so that he adds: "and will present us together with you." The association expressed by σύν is whatever the context requires. Here it is not only that of fellow believers raised up together but of an apostle and of ministers of Christ raised up together with those whom they brought to Christ and kept with him.

Nor need we inquire what "shall present" means. The idea of the verb is complete in itself; so we do not think of presenting before the judgment seat, of presenting for victory or for glory. When God, he who raised up the Lord Jesus, presents us together with you as belonging together and does this by raising you and us from the dead, he presents you and us as what we are by virtue of his grace. It is the highest possible honor when God thus presents anyone. The first aorist of the verb is transitive, "to make stand beside." The opposite is to order away out of God's presence: "Depart from me."

15) With γάρ Paul unfolds what lies in "us together with you" at the resurrection. **For all these things are because of you in order that the grace, by being multiplied by means of the multiplied number, may cause the thanksgiving to abound for the glory of God.** Thus the divine purpose back of all our ministry will be fulfilled.

Paul says that we ministers must have all of you Corinthians and you Achaians with us (1:1) on the day of resurrection. God does not desire that on that day only we lone ministers shall stand glorified beside him and be full of thanksgiving for the glory of his grace. He wants all of you, a great host, to stand together with us, all to raise the everlasting psalm of thanksgiving for his glory.

His present purpose is to multiply his grace in Christ Jesus (see "grace" in 1:2). This multiplication is to be effected "by means of the multiplied number" of all the believers who are filled with his grace by our ministry. Grace cannot be multiplied in itself; it is multiplied by being put into more and more hearts by faith. A beautiful *paronomasia* appears in πλεονάσασα διὰ τῶν πλειόνων, literally, "by being made more through the more." When we and you stand forth glorified on resurrection day, a great symphony of thanksgiving will rise from our lips. God is now planning his work of grace toward this end.

Here Paul again draws all his readers into fullest union with himself. How sad if any of them would not be among the blessed number of those standing together at God's side at that day; how glorious that all of them and even still others with them should be in company with Paul and his fellow workers when the final thanksgiving for God's glory is raised!

It is thus that now "all these things are because of you," on your account, for your sakes. Τὰ πάντα is not the same as πάντα; the former is definite: "all the things" of which Paul speaks in v. 7-14, in particular all the persecutions and all the delivering over to death which Paul and his helpers endure. Πάντα, without the article, would be indefinite: "all things in general" (our versions) and would thus not be correct.

XIV. *"We Faint not"*

"We Look at the Things not Seen"

16) Paul once more writes "we faint not" (see v. 1), but now he does it in view of the resurrection and the glory it will bring. Let the present afflictions be what they will, not only do they appear as nothing when compared with that glory, they are even instrumental in working it out for us during our brief lives. **Therefore we faint not, on the contrary, even if our outer man is being destroyed, nevertheless our inner one is being renewed day by day.** We are not discouraged and thus inefficient in our ministry. The very opposite is true. Paul is not blind to what is happening to him and to his assistants because of their work. He has stated it at length in v. 8, 9 and now restates it with a condition of reality: "even if our outer man is being destroyed."

He contrasts "the outer man" with "the inner one." This is not merely the body over against the soul, or the flesh (sinful) over against the spirit (the new life), and similar distinctions offered by C.-K. 147. Too abstruse is the idea: "whatever man is able to think away from himself, having it for himself only as a means." The outer man is what Paul himself says can be and is being destroyed, and the inner man is what is being renewed day by day. The latter is our regenerate, spiritual existence which is renewed day by day (the two datives of time to indicate repetition, R. 522,

750) by divine grace in Word and Sacrament. This involves the body as well as the soul, for the renewal extends to the uses which we make of the body and its members in our new life. The outer man is the Christian's existence in the outer world, his natural life here on earth amid all the outer surroundings. This is subject to destruction, and the Christian's foes may expedite the destruction.

Paul's designations are quite plain; simple Christian readers have always understood them. As they are here used, the designations apply only to the Christian, for he alone has an inner, spiritual, renewable life. The debate as to what outer and inner man might mean when these terms are applied to a non-Christian is academic; the terms are not so used. I Pet. 3:4 speaks of "the hidden man of the heart." The old and the new man are a different distinction which is not to be introduced here.

The "being renewed" has the adjective καινός, "new" as compared with something old and discarded. With perfect calmness Paul can watch the destruction of his outer man. What if his enemies hasten the process, yea, bring it to a sudden end by means of a violent death! He loses nothing. The inner man blossoms into new youth, beauty, and strength day by day. This inner renewal is not hindered but is only helped by the tribulation that assails the outer man. These "bloody roses" have the sweetest odor. These enemies are only defeating their own end; instead of causing Paul to grow discouraged, his elation is increased.

The renewal is a process that proceeds "day by day" as long as the earthly life endures. Its completion comes with death. Paul was not a perfectionist. Luther writes: "Woe to him who is already completely renewed, that is, who imagines he is already renewed. Without doubt he has not yet begun to be renewed and has never yet tasted what it signifies to be a Christian.

For he who has begun to be a Christian does not consider himself that he is a Christian but longs greatly to be a Christian, and the more he grows and increases, the more he seeks to become one and the less he considers himself that he is one." Walch VII, 325. Paul is speaking only about himself and his assistants, but the application to all of us lies on the surface.

17) "For" explains by advancing the thought from a statement of the two opposites: being destroyed — being renewed, to the connection between these two. **For the momentary lightness of the affliction is working out for us beyond all measure an eternal weight of glory, we not keeping our eyes on the things seen but on the things not seen, for the things seen are transient while the things not seen are eternal.**

Here we have an application of Rom. 8:28 in a most exact statement. Note the exact opposites: momentary — eternal; lightness — weight; affliction — glory. Then the great paradox that something momentary — light — affliction are working out ($κατά$ perfective) something eternal — a great weight — and all glory. We, of course, know that the affliction is not the *causa efficiens, meritoria,* or *medians,* but the medium used by the efficient hand of God which thus accomplishes what he designs. It is like a sharp knife that cuts one cord after another that holds us to this earth and to its earthly glory.

The remarkable thing is that Paul should call all that he describes in v. 8, 9 nothing but feathery "lightness." We should be inclined to call it a dreadful load. But the severest tribulation and affliction are as nothing compared with the glory awaiting us. Everything is weighed by comparison. The articulated neuter adjective τὸ ἐλαφρόν is used in classic fashion like an abstract noun: "the lightness," and not Hebraistically or in place of an adjective: "our light affliction" (as in our versions), but to match the noun "weight."

The lightness as well as the weight are explained in great part by the adjectives that modify them: the former is so light because it is παραυτίκα, "for a moment," the latter so weighty because it is αἰώνιος, "eternal." Affliction is always felt only at the moment, for we live in the flux of time. Every moment and its pain are over in a moment; so the next. It is never anything but momentary. The moments keep flying away, they never amass and concentrate. Not one is able to continue even for a day.

Now eternity is the absolute opposite, it is not a *fluxum* but a *fixum*, a *simul tota*, an absolute altogether, timelessness, a concept of such vastness that our minds have only an indistinct impression of what it really means. Since our poor minds are tied to concepts of time, we use terms of time to express eternal and eternity, which is like describing *white* with words that mean *black*. Even so we may catch Paul's meaning. When ten years of affliction are spread out over all the seconds of the ten years, the spread becomes very thin and light; but if ten years of affliction were centered in one second, that would be weight indeed. But "the affliction" (the article referring to the one which Paul has been describing) is spread so light and thin while the "glory" (no article, a new concept) is one incomprehensibly weighty concentration, being timeless, eternal.

The double phrase modifies the verb "working out beyond all measure" and not the noun "weight of glory" (A. V.). *Gemaess Uebermass zu Uebermass* = according to excess or highest possible measure, for excess or highest measure; the English lacks this idiom. When we reach that glory we shall wonder why we ever even sighed during the tribulation; we shall say that, if the tribulation had been made a thousandfold greater and longer, it would even then have amounted to no more than lightness.

18) What Paul says about affliction and about glory applies both as a fact and as a conviction only to people like himself: "we not keeping our eyes on the things seen but on the things not seen." Instead of merely adding the participle in the dative to ἡμῶν Paul writes a genitive absolute with ἡμῶν and makes this a more independent statement with the emphasis on ἡμῶν. But this genitive absolute still leaves the connection undetermined. Our versions make it temporal: "while we look not," etc.; it has often been conceived as causal: "since," etc., also as conditional: "on condition that we look not," etc., or "provided that," etc. Only the general thought is left to guide us. With ἡμῶν drawing special attention to the persons involved, this genitive absolute describes the persons: "we being people who keep not our eyes on the things seen," who do not regard them but regard the things not seen. For us and for such as are like us this weight of glory is being worked out by affliction; for others who regard only the seen things such a thing could not be possible.

Σκοπεῖν means "to regard or to fix the eyes upon watchfully," while βλέπειν means only to see in general. "The things seen" are the ordinary, earthly ones, among them being those of the outer man (v. 16). In the case of the apostle they were painful and distressing enough, and anyone who regarded such things would flee from them and seek other things seen that appear more agreeable. "The things not seen" are the spiritual and heavenly, among them being those of the inner man. Ordinary eyes and unenlightened minds cannot see them and hence never regard them and, when they are told about them, imagine them to be folly.

But the things seen are "transient," πρόσκαιρα, for a brief, fleeting season. To regard them and to let them fill our eyes and our hearts is folly, for what when their brief season is over? But the things not seen, these are eternal and never pass away, our inner, spiritual man and the eternal weight of glory. To regard them so that they become ours, this is blessedness indeed. It sounds paradoxical, to keep the eyes fixed, not on the things seen but on the things not seen; but Paul is speaking about the spiritual eyes of faith, which ever do this very thing. "We walk by faith, not by appearance," 5:7.

CHAPTER V

XV. "A House not Made with Hands"

1) There is a close connection with the preceding. In 4:18 "we are keeping our eyes on the things that are not seen." How do we do this, and what are these things not seen? "For" explains. **For we know that, if our tent house here on earth is taken down, we have a building from God, a house not made with hands, eternal, in the heavens.** This is what we keep looking at, and it lifts us far above "the things that are seen," all the persecutions and the death we endure (4:7-15).

"We know" refers only to Paul and to his assistants in the ministry. The previous context as well as what follows in v. 11, etc., show who "we" are. "We know" is often used by Paul to introduce a piece of general Christian knowledge, but here this word is addressed *to* the Corinthians and does not combine their knowledge with Paul's. Yet the sense is not *"we know"* this that *you* do not know; no emphatic ἡμεῖς is written. The fact is that all true Christians know what is so comforting and strengthening for all of us, that our true home is in heaven. Yet it is only by way of an application that we can add this "we, too, know" to Paul's "we know."

Ἐάν with its subjunctive denotes expectancy and thus vividly visualizes what may occur at a future moment. It is significant here, for it does not say positively that Paul and his assistants will die before Christ's Parousia. Paul does not know when Christ will return and thus expresses himself accordingly. Those are unfair to him who charge him with at first being certain that he will live to see the Parousia and now with having given up this certainty for the opposite, the certainty that he will die long before the Parousia. See further remarks under 4:14.

In the expression "our tent house here on earth," ἐπίγειος = "here on earth" and denotes a place; its opposite is "in the heavens," which is again local. Our versions use "earthly," which may pass if it intends to refer to a place. The word is not equal to ὀστράκινος which occurs in 4:7, "earthen," made of earth. In ἡ οἰκία τοῦ σκήνους the genitive is appositional or definitional (R. 498) and is thus the main word: "the house of the tent" = the tent home. Its opposite is οἰκοδομή, a permanent "building," the permanence of which is fully stated by ἐκ Θεοῦ, "from God." This building has its whole source and origin (ἐκ) in God.

While it, too, is an οἰκία like the tent οἰκία, the latter is one that is constructed by ourselves, by our hands, while the one in heaven is "not made with hands," one that is vastly above any handiwork, any fashioning or constructing by ourselves. God's grace and glory create it. And thus it can, of course, never be taken down as a tent is always taken down. Καταλύειν corresponds exactly to σκῆνος or "tent"; our idiom is "to strike tent"; the Greek idiom is "to loose completely" (κατά perfective), to loose the ropes from the pegs so that the stretched canvas collapses and can be rolled up.

Here we again have a beautiful sentence in which all terms are exact and placed in exact contrast. "Our tent house here on earth," which may be taken down at any time, is our earthly existence, it is like living in a tent, simply that sort of a home or οἰκία (see "for a season" in 4:18). Its opposite is "a building from God, a house or home not made with (human) hands, eternal, in the heavens" with God and Christ: a permanent, glorious, infinitely blessed existence in heaven. Let the one form of existence or life come to an end, be folded up and put away like a tent; we have the other awaiting us, an existence and a life like an everlasting, great building, which were created for us by God himself in heaven. The sense of what Paul says (his metaphors are so carefully worded) is simple and easily understood.

The usual form of a condition of expectancy is ἐάν with the subjunctive (protasis) and future indicative (apodosis). But here the apodosis has ἔχομεν, a present indicative, "we have." R. 1019 regards this as a futuristic present or as expressing Paul's confidence. Now, Paul says, amid all our sufferings, in this our tentlike existence and earthly life, "we have and possess" the eternal, heavenly existence and life. It is "not seen" (4:18) as yet by our earthly eyes, it is regarded and looked upon (σκοπεῖν, 4:18) by the eyes of faith, but it is there in heaven awaiting us. The mansions for this existence are already built (John 14:2). In what manner we already have this coming glory life the Scriptures tell over and over again: as heirs, as coheirs of Christ. "An eternal weight of glory" (4:17) is already worked out for us. This is the "building from God, not made with hands, eternal, in the heavens."

The R. V. prints in its margin "bodily frame" as a translation for σκῆνος. Dictionaries follow the cue, B.-P. 1212; M.-M. 577: "the body as the dwelling place of the soul," and cite our passage. But this is a rare, semioccasional use of the word and is found in the writings of only a few philosophers. We cannot agree that Paul uses a philosophic word here and in v. 4 when he is addressing his readers who were for the most part ordinary people. Was Paul not a tentmaker? Had he not worked for a year and a half in the shop of Aquila making tents right in Corinth? When the Corinthians heard σκῆνος from this tentmaker's pen read to them, could they think that he meant "bodily frame" and not "tent"?

And this philosophic use of the word here nullifies Paul's contrast. If "our tent house here on earth" = our *bodily* frame, our house of the soul, then "a building from God," etc., must mean a corresponding heavenly *body*. At death the earthly body remains on earth, in the grave; the soul alone enters heaven. So the commentators and the makers of the dictionaries think that in heaven the soul receives some kind of body from God.

Some advance the inadequate idea that in place of our earthly body we get heaven, a mansion in the skies: the soul is here tented in "the bodily frame," it lives there in its eternal mansion. The soul does not carry a mansion around with it in heaven as it carries the body around with it here on earth. So others advance a view that is more consistent. In place of the body tent that is left in the grave the soul gets some kind of an ethereal body when it enters heaven at death. It would otherwise be "naked" (v. 3). Clothed thus with this ethereal body, the old earthly body is, of course, no longer needed, its resurrection is unnecessary. We are thus told that Paul has changed the opinion he so valiantly defended in I Cor. 15; conjecture seeks to supply what intervened so as to produce this change; at any rate, we are informed that Paul has discarded belief in the resurrection of the body.

The idea of ethereal bodies (some think of ether, others of a firelike substance) is theosophical and anti-Scriptural. It is frequently extended also to the angels; they, too, are invested with such bodies. Consistent reasoning along this line extends the idea even to God, and also he is given a body. We need not follow the argumentation which supports these ideas. Let us add that "we have" is sometimes extended to mean that these ethereal bodies are now ready, awaiting the coming of our naked souls. Still more is offered, for some hold that the souls of the dead, also of the godly dead, do not enter heaven at death but enter an intermediate place, the *Totenreich*. "The great problem," as it is called, is thus complicated still more.

Even a man like Besser is drawn into this current. We are glad to name Stosch, *Apostolische Sendschreiben* II, 147, as one who is more reliable. Left to the common run of commentaries, Field and the *Expositor's Greek New Testament* among them, our preachers are frequently led astray and are unclear in their sermons on this great Pauline text. For this reason we mention a few names. We may note also that Paul's words do not lend themselves to such an interpretation. Take the adjective "not made with hands." We are told that it is not used properly here since "the natural body is *also*, of course, not made with hands." This adjective is a warning that "the tent" does not mean "the body" or "bodily frame." But this adjective plainly implies that "our tent house here on earth" is made with (human) hands. So, preserving the idea of the body or bodily frame, it is thought to be made "by the hands of the *Erzeuger*," of the parents who beget the body (Windisch). It is not the physical body that is made with hands but our life here on earth as we live it in our earthly existence. It could not be without our hands and all that they make for us and do for us, all of which is not needed for the existence and the life to come, either before or after resurrection day. We have one of the essential distinctions between tent οἰκία and heavenly οἰκία.

2) **For, in addition** (καί)**, in this we continue to groan, longing** (constantly) **to put on our habitation, the one** (that is) **from heaven** (and bears the nature of its origin, ἐκ). Καί is not "verily" (R. V.), nor is it to be omitted (A. V.). It adds the subjective feeling (groaning and longing) to the objective fact (we know that we have); and "for" makes the new

statement explanatory. We need spend no time on determining the antecedent of ἐν τούτῳ, for in v. 4 its counterpart is "we who are in the tent"; so here "in this tent" (σκῆνος, v. 1) is the meaning. The sense is simple and clear: In our present life and existence, filled, as they are, with affliction (4:8-18), we can only groan and long to enter the blessed, heavenly existence which is prepared and awaiting us. The thought is the same as that found in Rom. 8:22, 23, and the same verb "to groan" is used. Both the verb and the participle are present and durative: continue to groan and to long. The groaning is due to the life here, the longing to the glory ("eternal weight of glory," 4:17) beyond.

Paul advances the idea of *"a building* from God" by now writing *"the habitation,* the one from heaven," ἐκ, with heaven as its origin, thus heavenly in its very nature. "Habitation" = occupancy and thus "building," and the two ἐκ phrases: "from God" and "from heaven," indicate the same source. When we remember that these metaphorical terms mean the heavenly life and existence we have no difficulty with regard to ἐπενδύσασθαι, "to put on ourselves," aorist middle.

Metaphors picture realities; their propriety and their excellence are governed by the realities they are intended to express. The heavenly existence and life awaiting us are put on by us at death. Paul has called them "an eternal weight of glory"; this envelops our soul at death, a divine, heavenly garment, indeed, "from God," "from heaven." The word "habitation" is the middle link: we inhabit a building and still more a garment. "Habitation" and the verb "inhabit" contain the very idea of "habit" or garment. "To put on" is thus perfectly proper as a figure, but it is, as is characteristic of Paul's method of writing, an advance of the idea, a fuller, more intense expression for the great reality to be pictured.

Nor should we forget that "the things not seen" (4:18) are ineffable. The Scriptures constantly resort to figurative language in an effort to convey some impression of them to us. The realities cannot be put into direct human language. Besides using figures to present the positive side they also employ negatives: not so as here on earth: no tears, no death, no sorrow, crying, or pain — all these have passed away (Rev. 21:4). Even so, as we catch dimly what is meant, the glory of it all overwhelms us. It is not easy to put divine and heavenly realities into a human, earthly medium.

The very verb "to put on ourselves" bars out the view that an exchange of bodies is referred to in v. 1. This earthly body was never "put on," from our conception onward we were never without it. The Scriptures know of no ethereal body that our soul puts on when it leaves the body of clay. The old earthly life and mode of existence are taken down and folded away like a tent; the new heavenly life and existence are put on like a glory garment. This is what the Scriptures teach.

But this is not all. The best of men may miss Paul's thought, and we should all pray that the Spirit may ever guide us. And the Analogy of Faith and the Analogy of Scripture will be valuable guides. Paul's thought is sometimes misunderstood because of the ἐπί found in the infinitive ἐπενδύσασθαι. In v. 3 Paul has ἐνδυσάμενοι without ἐπί. This is enough. In many instances the addition of a preposition only strengthens the idea of the verb, and in repetitions the preposition is dropped. The verb Paul uses is sometimes taken to mean "to put on *over*" the earthly body this heavenly garment, this ethereal (theosophic) body. And the following thought is constructed. Paul dreads to die; he is afflicted with *Todesscheu,* horror of death. Since he writes "we," Timothy, Titus, etc., also cringe before death. What they long for is Christ's Parousia so that they may be changed while they are still alive, which is conceived as putting on the ethereal body over (ἐπί) the physical body. Windisch suggests "that the *Himmelskleider* (heavenly robes) would be brought along by the angels who accompany the Messiah." But I Thess. 4:15 states, "Shall not *prevent* them who are asleep."

3) With strong assurance Paul adds: **since also** — and this is placed beyond all question — **after having put it on, we shall be found not naked,** no indeed! Εἴ γε = *siquidem* in the sense of "since" (Liddell and Scott, 426 ²), literally, "if indeed, which is assured." The aorist participle expresses the one act of putting on the habitation and precedes the future "shall be found": "after having put it on." In v. 2 the aorist infinitive likewise indicates the one act. The sense of οὐ γυμνοί, "not naked," is determined according to the context; "not naked" = fully and forever clothed, never found otherwise after this garment has once been put on, never destitute of a habitation like those who are cast into outer darkness.

The charge that this is too simple a thought is unwarranted. Throughout all his trials, with death constantly impending, the one comfort and stay of Paul and his assistants are "the things not seen" (4:18), "the eternal weight of glory" (4:17), this everlasting habitation, which, should death strike them down, will not let them be found naked as those will be found who look only to "the things seen." We do not read εἴ γε as an indirect question: "whether, indeed, we shall really be found as clothed and not naked," i. e., groaning with this question in mind. This turns Paul's assurance into doubt and negatives all that he has said (4:1-18), negatives also "we know" (5:1).

Few words of Paul's have been as variously interpreted as this little clause, and some say he should never have written it. Plato has been referred to as giving the word γυμνοί the meaning souls deprived of their bodies, poor wraiths in the nether world. Plummer regards them as souls in *sheol* "without form and void of all power and activity," and R., W. P. likewise. Not once does Paul use the word "souls," to say nothing of "naked souls" *à la* Plato or some paganized Jew. And would these naked souls be happy if they got back their bodies? Does the body constitute bliss for the soul in the nether world or in *sheol*?

The interpretation: "if so be that, being clothed (with the garment of Christ's righteousness), we shall not be found naked (destitute of the right to heaven)," which is offered by a few, would serve excellently for homiletical purposes and would keep fully to the Analogy of Faith, but it is not suggested by the text or the context. This interpretation is only a pious effort to put an orthodox meaning into Paul's words.

4) A little more (καί) must be said in explanation (γάρ) of the previous statement about our groaning. See καὶ γάρ in v. 2. **For also, as they that are in this tent we keep groaning as being weighted down for the reason, not that we want to put off, but to put on in order that the mortal may be swallowed up by the life.** We are not Stoics, we feel the burden and we groan; not because we are cowards and just want to escape our burden, but because we want to put on the heavenly life. So both the groaning and the longing mentioned in v. 2 are further elucidated.

By substantivizing and by writing οἱ ὄντες κτλ. Paul secures an apposition: "we, as being in the tent." This avoids an adverbial idea such as "while or because we are in the tent" and merely describes the subject: "we who are," etc. "The tent" with the article of previous reference is enough in the Greek; in the English we say "in this tent," i. e., in this transient, tentlike life and existence, which, like a tent, shall presently be taken down, no longer to be used. The wording is a little fuller than it was in v. 2: "in this (i. e., tent) we groan." An unmodified participle is now added adverbially: "we groan as weighted down," since we are under a constant, depressing burden.

What the heavy burden is Paul has described in 4:8, 9. It is surely enough to make anyone groan. The thought is not that we are womanish and always give way to our feelings in loud complaints; but we do feel the burden, and our hearts groan inwardly. There is a kind of paradox in the idea of a tent, which is light enough, and in being burdened, which implies something overheavy. In v. 2 the participle that is paired with groaning is "longing," which looks forward; here it is "burdened," which looks at the present.

Ἐφ' ᾧ, in the classics also the plural ἐφ' οἷς, here as well as in Rom. 5:12 and Phil. 3:12 = ἐπὶ τούτῳ ὅτι, B.-D. 294, 4; *darum dass, weil*, 235; see also R. 604; Abbott-Smith, Lexicon 166, etc.: "for the reason that, because"; B.-P. 447, and many others. This phrase amounts to a mere conjunction: "because." See further Rom. 5:12. Paul now restates and explains what he means by the longing mentioned in v. 2. It is not a longing to escape but a longing to attain. It is not cowardice but glorious hope.

There are many who tire of life and its excessive burdens; that is a morbid state which Christians should conquer. Some also quail at the thought of death, but this, too, is not the normal Christian feeling. Worldly men prefer anything to the great vicissitudes of this life and then simply throw life away with the thought that the hereafter cannot be worse. This negative motive is wholly foreign to Paul and to his assistants. When they groan under their heavy burden as ministers of Christ, the reason is (ἐφ' ᾧ), "not that we want to put off, but (that we want) to put on." The two infinitives are enough; they need no objects, especially not in the Greek. The Greek mind is always nimble enough to supply what the thought requires whereas the English mind is slow and often demands that the objects of verbs be written out. While it is a little terse for the English reader, yet even to him it is clear: "not do we want to put off but to put on." The emphasis is on these two infinitives which are aorists because the acts are momentary.

The ἵνα clause forms the climax of the entire statement. It states the real purpose, aim, and object of what we want when we groan under our burden in this tentlike existence. It states this object in language that overtops all the metaphors that were used in the preceding verses, for the two realities are now named outright: τὸ θνητόν and ἡ ζωή, and the verb climaxes the figure of putting on a garment and in this climax comes far nearer to the actual reality: "to swallow up." It is the identical verb that was used in I Cor. 15:54: "Swallowed up was the death in victory." In fact, in I Cor. 15:53, 54 the same advance is made from the idea of putting on to that of swallowing up; study the passage as Paul's own commentary on what he is now saying. None better has been written. "In order that swallowed up this mortal may be by the life" — that is the purpose which we so mightly desire to have fulfilled when we groan as we do.

Τὸ θνητόν, a substantivized neuter adjective, in classic Greek fashion is more than the abstract noun, for it is most concrete: our entire mortal existence. "The life" is not ἡ ψυχή, mortal life animating a body in its earthly existence, but Ἡ ΖΩΗ, "the life," spiritual, divine, heavenly, eternal, the existence in heavenly glory of which Paul has been speaking. This life shall swallow up the mortal one. Nothing shall be left of it just as death shall be swallowed up in victory (I Cor. 15:54). This life, born in regeneration, working in us now (4:12) so that we are already οἱ ζῶντες, "the ones really living" (4:11), at our death will swallow up our earthly existence and leave nothing but itself. Christ is "the life" (John 14:6), the source of the life for us, the life Paul has in mind. Amid this mortal with its heavy load — who would not groan for this that is life indeed? Indeed, we wish to die that we may live.

The ἐπί in ἐπενδύσασθαι is again stressed as it was in v. 2, and we are told that Paul was *kreuzesscheu* and *todesscheu*, shied at the cross and at death; and that what he wanted was the earliest possible return of Christ so that he would not need to undergo death but would be changed in the twinkling of the eye, the life thus swallowing up all that was mortal in him. But Paul contradicts this view in the very next words.

5) Now he who wrought us out for this very thing (is) God, he who gave us the pledge of the Spirit. The entire credit belongs to God. He made us what we are; he did it by giving us his Spirit. By the use of two substantivized participles instead of verbal modifiers, everything is centered most personally on Θεός, the predicate, which is hence without the article; the copula is omitted for the sake of greater emphasis. He is the One who wrought us "for this very thing," namely that the life is presently to swallow up all that is mortal. "This very thing" is God's aim and goal in all his previous work in us. Surely, then, we, too, should long for its consummation.

For this "he gave us the pledge of the Spirit" (see the explanation in 1:22), the great down payment as a full guarantee that all the rest would follow. This gift he made to us in baptism; it has ever been ours, always our ἀρραβών, which is even increased by hearing the Word and by partaking of the Lord's Supper. "He gave" makes the assurance objective and subjective in one: the gift — objective; we experiencing the giving and having the gift — subjective. Only a little while, and the consummation will follow.

XVI. *"We Are of Good Courage"*

6) Knowing what we do about the life that awaits us despite all our groaning in the present life and our longing for the life for which God himself has made us ready, "we are of good courage" and only too ready to be at home with the Lord and make it our aim to please him even as we must all appear before his judgment seat. Οὖν thus introduces the conduct that is in proper accord with the convictions which steady us amid our groaning while we are here in the body. All that is stated in the section from v. 1 to 10 is woven closely and compactly together so that we do not follow those who find a contradiction between the groaning (v. 2, 4) and the good courage.

Accordingly, being of good courage always and having come to know that while at home in the body we are away from home from the Lord — for by way of faith we walk, not by way of sight — we are then (δέ) of good courage and well-pleased rather to be away from home out of the body and to be at home with the Lord.

This is not an anacoluthon unless this term is made very broad. After the parenthesis Paul takes up θαρροῦντες with the finite θαρροῦμεν and marks that fact with δέ. We have no irregularity. The sentence is purposely constructed thus because it enables Paul to repeat the verb. He has twice written "we are groaning," so he now wishes to write twice that "we are of good courage," and by doing this in the same sentence, once with the participle and then with the finite verb, he makes this even stronger than the two "we are groaning," in which we have mere repetition. "Being of good courage, we are of good courage." So he said previously, and that also twice, in 4:1, 16: "we do not faint." That is the negative side of what is now stated positively, being of good courage. The groaning is, then, not a contradiction. Many a man has been in great hardship and even mortal danger and has yet not lost heart but has kept high courage to the last. In fact, groaning amid severe experiences shows that not fainting and keeping courage are genuine.

But the good courage of Paul and of his assistants is not like that of worldly men who face misfortunes and dangers with head erect and flying colors and march right into the jaws of death. They face eternity blindly and rush to their doom. Paul and his helpers are not like that. He has already shown us the solid ground on which their assurance and their courage rest. See 4:6, 14, 17; 5:1, 5. This does not call for further repetition; it is enough to say how they have come to view their present situation in the light of their assurance regarding death and eternity. Why should they grow faint and discouraged when in the body they are away from the Lord only for a little while and are soon to join him forever? Note the tenses: "being of good courage always," durative present; "having come to know," ingressive aorist. Once having reached the point of this knowledge, their courage goes on without a single misgiving.

Paul has not dropped the figure of the tent, house, building, and habitation which he used in v. 1 and 2. He advances it and makes it more personal when he speaks of putting on and putting off. And he does so still more when he uses "to be at home" and "to be away from home." This is typical of Paul's mind; he sees all the different angles and facets of the thought, all the ways in which he may turn and adapt a metaphor. One is at home in a house that really belongs to him. The body is a house that belongs to us in its present state only for the time being; the heavenly glory is our everlasting habitation and home.

In ἐνδημεῖν and ἐκδημεῖν we have δῆμος or "people" and thus "to be among one's own people," i. e., at home, and "to be away from one's own people," a pilgrim or stranger in alien surroundings, i. e., away from home. So Paul says that we have come to know "that while we are at home in the body," in this our distressful earthly existence, "we are away from home from the Lord," away from that blessed existence in the visible company of our Lord, the true home of all God's blessed children. The statement is perfectly clear. It prepares us for the coming one which reverses this our rather being away from home out of the body and at home with the Lord. The chiasm is beautiful to say nothing about thus using "at home" and "away from home."

7) The parenthesis explains (γάρ) by at once stating the reality: "for by way of faith we walk, not by way of sight." In this manner we now walk and live, altogether by way of faith and not by way of sight. This explains both what we have and what we lack while we are at home in the body and far from home from the Lord; it also states both what we shall not need and what we shall have when we get to be at home with the Lord. The thought evidently reverts to 4:18, "the things not seen." We now have only faith with regard to them; they shall be actual objects of sight anon. Διά expresses the medium, we may render it "by" or, as we here attempt, "by way of." Yet "faith" is not minimized as though it amounts to little or nothing. Heb. 11:1 should preserve us from that idea. For this life "faith" is everything, the all-sufficient substitute for "sight." It deals with the unseen as if it were the seen: "seeing it afar off" as strangers and pilgrims on the earth (read Heb. 11:13). By dealing with "the things not seen" in this way faith really has them, and sight will follow.

Even the world, in its worldly affairs, goes on faith or trust. If no man trusted another, earth would be an earthly hell. Let men mock at Christian faith, these very mockers have faith in handling their own affairs. The trouble with the world is that its faith is so often misplaced, it trusts where it is cheated, where it ought to mistrust; it mistrusts where it ought to trust and thus again cheats itself. Take these mockers at Christian faith: they will not trust Christ and cheat themselves in that way; they do trust in religious fakes and so cheat themselves once more. The faith by which we walk, as did Paul, rests on the Rock of Ages. Unseen, it holds Christ and salvation, and soon these shall be fully seen. They who demand sight too soon will also have to wait, but then they shall have more sight than they want, enough to terrify them forever.

Εἶδος is not ὄψις, "seeing," yet this need not cause difficulty as far as the contrast with πίστις or faith is concerned. The former is *species*, the visible appearance of the thing itself. Yet Trench adds regarding ἰδέα (= εἶδος): *species sub oculos cadens*, something that is seen with the connotation that there is one who does the seeing. As in connection with πίστις, the act of believing, we think also of him who is believed, so it is with regard to εἶδος, but the reverse: with the appearance we think of the act of seeing the appearance, for without this act appearance would be nothing. Our English "sight" is quite good; a sight is objective, yet it is called so only because it is subjectively seen.

In both "faith" and "sight," we should note, the *same* object is referred to, which, we may say, is here the Lord (mentioned twice), once not seen directly (faith), finally seen with direct vision (sight). Another point: heavenly sight will not end faith as such (see the author on I Cor. 13:13): trust goes right on in heaven; only this will be ended, that then faith will need to do without sight as it must now. Compare John 20:29 on faith and sight (Thomas) and I Cor. 13:12 on the sight "in part" that is possible now.

8) "We are, then (δέ), of good courage" as has already been stated by the participle. The point is

emphasized, and they are mistaken who think that the main statement is that "we are well-pleased rather to be away from home out of the body," etc. No; courageous, courageous are we — that is the main point, and to this καί adds another which lies in what is said about our now walking by way of faith and not yet also by sight, namely that we should prefer to have also sight. This is the explanation of the longing mentioned in v. 2. Our longing is to be satisfied by realization. What faith now embraces as being unseen it shall presently embrace as seen. "The things not seen" now (4:18) shall presently turn to things seen.

This must come, otherwise faith would trust in something that does not exist, it would be like the faith of the worldling who trusts in something that does not exist and that he will, therefore, never see. He is like a man who *thinks* that he has a million dollars in the bank, who goes on in this fatuous faith, and who, when he at last tries to draw out his million, finds that he never had a million, finds that he owes a million and cannot pay. We trust that our bank has a million dollars that were deposited for us by Christ; he has, indeed, deposited them for us, and when at death we come to draw them out, they will be handed out to us, we shall get sight of every penny of them, shall have them in our hands forever.

Certainly, then, we are of good courage as we go on here in the body, walking by faith. Why should we not be? And yet at the same time this, too (καί), is our feeling that we are pleased rather (i. e., that we prefer) "to be away from home out of the body and to be at home with the Lord." See the same thought in Phil. 1:21-23. The present existence in the body is like being at home (v. 6) but like living in a tent (v. 1, 4), in only a temporary home. What makes it temporary is the fact that we can now live only by faith,

faith that still has to wait for sight of him in whom it trusts. We are thus while we are at home here really away from home from the Lord, from the full, blessed sight of him (v. 6). So faith ever longs for and greatly prefers "to be at home with the Lord," everlastingly at home. That is being at home indeed. For this is the ultimate, the eternal goal. Nor could the soul attain or hold more even as more cannot be imagined.

Paul is speaking about death: "out of the body." He has been speaking about nothing else throughout, (5:1, etc.). The idea that he dreads to die, that he groans to escape dying by living to see the Parousia and then being transformed, is unwarranted. All that is true is that ἐάν in v. 1 leaves the possibility that the Parousia may come at any time. To be sure, "out of the body" means that the body will be left behind; it will go to the grave. To say that this will be the end of it, to deny the resurrection of the body on the strength of this phrase, is untenable. The proposal that we should believe that Paul has given up all that he wrote in I Cor. 15, the most magnificent presentation of the resurrection of the body in the entire Bible; that Paul has now come to believe that the body will *not* be raised up at the Parousia, is unacceptable to us. At one time we are to believe that Paul wanted his body to be transformed at the Parousia and then that, if he died, his body would never be raised and transformed. Yes, there is a separation from the body; but 4:11 has already told us that in due time the body will be made to share in the home with the Lord: "and will present us together with you."

It remains to note the prepositions. In v. 6 it is "away from home ἀπό the Lord," and in v. 8 "at home πρός the Lord." The latter = "face to face"; R. 625: "It is the face-to-face converse with the Lord that Paul has in mind." The other preposition means that we are still "away from" this. In v. 6 "in the body" =

"away from the Lord"; in v. 8 *"out of* the body" = *"face to face with* the Lord." The exactness of these prepositions ought not to escape our attention.

9) In v. 6-8 we see the feelings that stir in the hearts of Paul and of his assistants; we are now shown their corresponding conduct: **Therefore also we are making it our honor aim, whether at home or whether away from home, to be well-pleasing to him.** Those who have this hope purify themselves even as he is pure, I John 3:3. The thought of approaching nearer and nearer to the Lord and of soon seeing him face to face, makes us ashamed to do anything that is displeasing to him, spurs us on to do everything that is well-pleasing to him. Note how "we are well-pleased" corresponds with our being "well-pleasing" to the Lord.

Φιλοτιμούμεθα is a noble word, containing, as it does, both "affection" and "honor": "to act from love of honor," honor that the Lord bestows. R., W. P., points out that the Latin *ambitio,* from *ambire,* to go both ways to gain a point, has an ignoble flavor. The A. V.'s "we labor," margin "endeavor" is not good; the R. V.'s "we make it our aim," margin "are ambitious" is only a little better. "We love it as a point of honor" ever to be well-pleasing to the Lord, not only to do what he says, but to have him take pleasure in us and in all that we do.

And we do this "whether being at home or whether being away from home"; whether being in this life or in the next. "For whether we live, we live unto the Lord; or whether we die, we die unto the Lord: whether we live therefore or die, we are the Lord's," Rom. 14:8. "That, whether we wake or sleep, we may live together with him," I Thess. 5:10. In v. 6 and 8 the words are placed chiastically: at home — away from home; away from home — at home. But each is defined by the addition of a phrase. We now have only the two participles without phrases in the sense: no matter in which state we find ourselves, at home or away from home, all we want is to have the Lord pleased with us. It is most natural, however, to think of being in this bodily life and being out of it at death and not the reverse, of being with the Lord and still being away from him. The implication is also that it belongs wholly to the Lord into what condition he places is. Our supreme concern is that he ever be pleased with us.

How we may ever please him need not be said here; it has been indicated throughout. In the case of the Corinthians, however, the point to be noted is that they should understand and fully appreciate the motives of Paul and of his helpers, these motives and these aims in all that they have been doing with the situation in Corinth, yea, in all that they will yet do. Paul and his helpers are pleasing neither themselves nor men but ever only the Lord. Do the Corinthians want them to do that? Will they themselves not want to join Paul and his assistants in that? Paul is not saying all of this just for his own sake; in 4:15 he says plainly: "All these things are because of you."

10) The thought of being with the Lord and of being well-pleasing to him brings to mind the last judgment. **For we must all be made publicly manifest before the judgment seat of Christ in order that each one may get to carry away the things** (done) **by means of the body, according to what things he did, whether something good or something bad.**

This is the great fact that Paul and his helpers always keep in mind. Τοὺς πάντας ἡμᾶς = "the whole number of us" (R. 773) and takes them all together in their totality. Φανερωθῆναι is passive, hence it means more than "appear" (A. V.), it is rather "be made manifest" (R. V.), but with the idea of the greatest and completest publicity: before the whole world of angels and men so that all of them may see who and what we really have been. Christ will do this with us.

Δεῖ denotes all forms of necessity, here the one from which no man can escape. The βῆμα is the dais or platform on which the chair for the judge stands, from which he pronounces his verdict. The scene pictured is the final judgment with Christ (note that he is named according to his office: he who is our Savior will be our Judge) seated on the platform, all of us facing him, and all of us made public so that nothing shall be hid. Human courts and human judges try to achieve this, they often do so with poor success. Those who are being tried hide their guilt as much as they can, their lawyers help them in this, the prosecution often connives, is inefficient or even tries to invent guilt or to exaggerate such guilt as there is. The all-perfect judgment before the omniscient and all-righteous divine Judge awaits us all.

We are all judged now and in the instant of death. This judgment is secret. Many a man dies concerning whom we are wholly uncertain as to how Christ judges him. Even when we feel certain we know that we may be mistaken. The last judgment is public. All the verdicts are the same, but now they are not only made public, now they are also publicly substantiated and established before the universe as being just; see further Rom. 2:5. For this reason the Scriptures regularly state that the judgment at the last day will be based on our works: "in order that each one may get to carry away (aorist) the things (done) by means of the body" in his present existence.

This is not work-righteousness. Nor does this plural refer to isolated works, one here and one there. These things done by means of the body (τά makes a substantive of διὰ τοῦ σώματος) constitute the sum of each man's life, what his life truly amounts to in God's sight: πρὸς ἃ ἔπραξεν, "facing what he really did." And this will be one of two things: ἀγαθόν, a sum or unit that is "good" in God's sight or one that is φαῦλον, "bad," good for nothing. The one is the fruit of a life of faith that was marked and beautified by trust in Christ and thus revealed to all eyes who it was that produced this "good." The other is the product of a condition where faith was absent and reveals the unbeliever as what he truly was.

In no case will there be the least doubt. So, too, it will be faith or its absence on which the verdict will rest, but both as determined by the indisputable public evidence of the works. All the saving power of faith in Christ will appear, all the damning power of refusal to trust Christ. No balance will be struck for the believer between the sins he committed and the good works he did as though the latter offset the former. All his sins will be utterly wiped out by the blood of Christ, removed as far as the east is from the west (Ps. 103:12), cast into the depths of the sea (Micah 7:19), blotted out, yea, blotted out as a thick cloud (Isa. 43:25; 44:22), not to be found forever. All the imperfections of his good works will also be removed forever. No inquisition will or can be made into any believer's sins. In their place will be found only Christ's blood and righteousness.

But in the case of the unbeliever everything, even what the world was pleased to call good, will be marked by unbelief and insult to Christ. Yes, that will be a revelation indeed. Paul and his assistants ever keep it before their eyes so that they may please the Lord. And what is thus stated applies to "us all," to the Corinthians also, so that they may take it to heart in their treatment of Paul. These words are written to *them*.

Note how Paul varies the plural and the singular. First, "the whole number of us" in mass, next, "each one" as an individual; first, τά and πρὸς ἅ, all that each has done, next, singulars, unit sums, ἀγαθόν or φαῦλον.

On the latter see Trench, *Synonyms*. The verb κομίζω, here the aorist subjunctive middle, means more than "receive," it means "may carry away with or for himself." The thought is that all that each one has done in the body is decreed by the Judge to be his own so that he may take and carry it away together with all the consequences. Thus, when a murderer is sentenced by the judge, he carries his crime away with him to the gallows or to the electric chair; the innocent man, acquitted by the judge, carries his innocence away to freedom and to honor. The absolute justice of Christ is indicated in this verb.

XVII. *"The Love of Christ Constrains Us"*

11) In close connection with Christ, the Lord, whom they ever seek to please, and before whose judgment seat we all must appear, Paul and his assistants conduct their ministry and want to be judged and esteemed accordingly by the Corinthians. **Accordingly, having come to know the fear of the Lord, we are busy persuading men and have** (long already) **been made manifest to God, and I hope have** (long already) **been made manifest also in your consciences.**

Οὖν connects what is said about the fear of the Lord and its effect with what is said about the judgment in v. 10 and about the holy ambition to please the Lord in v. 9. The aorist εἰδότες is again (v. 6) ingressive: "having come to know." "The fear of the Lord" — why our versions translate this "the terror" we are unable to say — is the same in both the Old and the New Testament. Together with the love of God it controls the Christian during his whole life.

Only the godly have this holy fear. Its distinctive mark is that it is always combined with trust in God and love toward God and is thus differentiated from the fear and dread of God which at last overwhelms the ungodly. The fear of God ever shrinks from offending him, from calling forth his judgment and retribution. It ever feels and speaks as Paul does in v. 10. How it keeps from sin is shown by the fine example of Joseph, Gen. 39:9.

With fear ever before our eyes, Paul says, we do the work of our ministry, and he describes this ministry in two words: ἀνθρώπους πείθομεν. The present tense is not conative (R., W. P.): "try to persuade," but durative: "we are busy persuading men." Note the chiasm which places the emphasis on the two objects: come to know — the fear of the Lord; men — we are busy persuading. Our feeling toward *the Lord* controls all that we do in regard to *men*.

Paul is not alluding to slander that was uttered in Corinth to the effect that he and his helpers were just persuasive talkers, and those who uttered this slander claimed that they saw through them. Nor is the sense that Paul and his helpers seek to allay suspicion regarding themselves by persuading people in regard to their good and honest intentions. No such ideas are developed here. "Men we are engaged in persuading" is broad and general and signifies: bringing them to faith. Persuasion is still the great task of the gospel ministry. It is not done with human argument, with "persuasive wisdom words" (ἐν πειθοῖς σοφίας λόγοις), I Cor. 2:4, but with the greatest persuasive force which men have ever used, the gospel.

The two δέ are adversative, but each adds another point, δέ noting that it is different; καί would mean that it is very similar. The English cannot indicate this distinction, the sense alone must show it. "And we have (long already) been made manifest to God," or, to reproduce the emphasis, "as far as God is concerned, to him we have long been fully manifest." The perfect passive reaches far back into the past and extends to the present. Πεφανερώμεθα refers back to φανερωθῆναι in v. 10: on judgment day all will be brought to public manifestation before the whole universe; Paul and his helpers have long been manifest to God in this way. He has known and still knows as something that is lying fully open before him how these ministers of Christ are ever conducting their work of persuading men in the true fear of the Lord.

"And I hope," Paul adds with another δέ, "have been made manifest (this long while) also in your consciences." The singular "I hope" amid the many "we" is only incidental. Our work, Paul says, and the way in which we do it have certainly been before your eyes long enough so that we have been fully manifest to you Corinthians, and you have been able to see who we really are. "I hope so," Paul says; not, "I know it." There has been opposition to Paul, and this has caused him great worry in regard to Corinth. He is writing in order to remove the last of it. "I hope" is just the right touch. So he also does not say "have been made manifest also to *you*," but far more searchingly, "in your *consciences.*" Regarding conscience see 1:12, and Rom. 2:15.

Next to God, conscience is the most honest judge. It tells us what it thinks is right or wrong irrespective of what we may desire or men say. So Paul appeals to this unbiased and honest judgment of the consciences of the Corinthians. He cannot look into their consciences, hence also for this reason he says "I hope." Conscience is often also misled; so one cannot be too certain about what the conscience of another person may tell him. "In your consciences" touches another point, one that is brought out in v. 12, namely the treatment which Paul has of late received from the Corinthians when some of them thought ill of him; Paul says, "in your consciences you certainly, I hope, have seen how wrong this is." Just as Paul knows how to appeal to his own conscience (1:12), so he knows how to touch the consciences of others (4:2 and here).

12) What he is saying about the way in which he and his helpers do their work among men in the fear of the Lord and have long ago become manifest to God, is, as the reference to the consciences of the Corinthians shows, not intended as self-praise and self-commendation, it is not intended to help the standing of Paul and of his helpers among the Corinthians: **Not again are we recommending our own selves to you.** It is intended as something that is quite different, namely as furnishing the Corinthians themselves with a good starting point (ἀφορμή) for their praise of Paul and his assistants, the men who, in the fear of the Lord, have done so much in Corinth. With this praise they are to stop the mouths of the fellows who have invaded Corinth, who try to ruin the reputation of Paul and of his assistants, whose own praise is nothing but their face and the show they make and not at all their heart and what God sees there: **but as giving you a starting point for glorying on our behalf in order that you may have** (something) **against those who glorify themselves** (by what is) **on their face and not** (by what is) **in their heart.**

Paul once more refers to this matter of self-recommendation. In 3:1, etc., he has already said most emphatically that he and his assistants need no letters of commendation and recommendation to the Corinthians or from the Corinthians since the Corinthians themselves constitute the grandest letter of recommendation which Paul could wish, one that is inscribed as on a public monument so that all men in Corinth may read it. We founded your congregation; it stands as a public monument in Corinth; whoever passes by can read upon it the fact that we have reared it. What are little letters of papyrus or parchment which are secured from persons far away compared with a monumental letter like this which is open to the eyes of all men in all Corinth?

This is Paul's answer to the slanders that he has no letters of recommendation, that he does no more than to recommend and to glorify himself. In 4:2 he adds that he and his helpers do recommend themselves, do it by putting away all tricks and all falsifications of the Word, by publishing the truth, and by thus recommending themselves to every man's conscience. If that is not genuine recommendation, what is? So he again says: "We are certainly not again trying to recommend ourselves to you." We read the present tense as being conative. After founding the Corinthian church, after building it up so strongly, does Paul still dream of recommending himself to the Corinthians? Is he not as yet manifest in their consciences as what he really is?

What he is saying about himself and his assistants, their work and their way of working, is intended to give the Corinthians the information which they need so they may praise Paul and his helpers and by this praise stop the mouths of these false slanderers of Paul. The Corinthians should really have no need of being given such ammunition against such men. The moment they came to Corinth and began their attacks upon Paul, the Corinthians should have hushed them up with their own loud boasts of what Paul was and what he had done for them. Not even one ear should have taken in one slanderous word against Paul.

But that is the way church members often act. Instead of defending the best pastors that God ever gave them they are often inclined to listen to evil-minded men who want to destroy the work of such pastors. It is the devil's cunning: he cannot stop the work, so he inspires men to tear it down and finds that those who ought to prevent that tearing down let it proceed, perhaps even lend a hand. This occurs so often after a good pastor has left a charge. Paul had been absent from Corinth about three years.

The grammarians regard συνιστάνομεν, ἀλλὰ διδόντες as an anacoluthon and supply something before the participle: "we do not recommend but (say or write these things) as giving you," etc. R. 439; B.-D. 468, 1. In the writer's opinion this is pedantic, especially with reference to the Greek which is noted for its flexibility and for its varied use of the participle. By using the participle instead of the finite verb Paul subordinates the giving, that is the reason for the participle. This is not an oversight or an irregularity, it is intentional, it says something, and language and construction are intended to do just that.

As we have said repeatedly, the subject of the so-called anacoluthon still awaits adequate treatment. This treatment has begun in part by regarding many passages that were formerly so regarded as not being anacolutha (R. 439); it ought to advance to the full recognition of the anacoluthon as a legitimate use of language, which is not to be listed as grammatically improper but is to be set forth as a means for conveying what would otherwise not be conveyed. Here the participle avoids the direct assertion: "we give to you," and only intimates: "as giving to you."

This accords with ἀφορμήν, which is even emphatic by being placed before the participle. Paul reduces his intimation: the Corinthians may use what he is saying as such "a starting point," as something that furnishes an impetus. The idea of "basis" is too strong. The genitive is objective: "a starting point (impetus) for glorying on our behalf." And καύχημα is not the activity as such, the word for which idea would be καύχησις, but *what* the Corinthians may say in behalf of their great teachers, Paul and his helpers. Starting with what Paul indicates in v. 11 as the right starting point, he intimates that the Corinthians, who truly know him in their consciences, will want to say much more, but it will all be in line with this starting point: persuading men in the fear of the Lord and as ever manifest to God and thus also manifest in the conscience of right-thinking and truly conscientious men. Paul wants no false praise from anyone; but he does want true recognition. As he strives to obtain it from God, so he strives to have it in men's consciences. It is spurious humility to regard the conscientious recognition which we receive as true ministers of Christ as nothing. Our very success in the ministry depends on securing proper recognition in men's consciences (4:2).

This was vital in Corinth because of the opponents who had been busy trying to turn the church against Paul and against his work. The way in which he characterizes these opponents shows that they were not Corinthians but had come to Corinth and had been trying to attain leadership. They had letters of recommendation. From whom they had received them we do not know; they had certainly not received them from any of the other churches. It is always an easy matter to get such letters; men who ought to be more careful often sign them without due thought.

These letters seem to have impressed the Corinthians, who thus foolishly listened to these strangers. Paul calls them "those who make a business of glorifying themselves" (durative present to indicate a standard characterization and middle reflexive); and this they do ἐν προσώπῳ, καὶ μὴ ἐν καρδίᾳ, which is too terse for the English, hence we expand: "(by what is) on (their) face and not (by what is) in (their) heart." Face and heart, appearance and real inner purpose do not agree. On the surface these opponents look like good and reliable men, but if the Corinthians would compel them to manifest what is really in their hearts they would be shocked and horrified.

Paul stops with this brief characterization. The commentators at times supply more. On their face these invaders are said to be born Jews, advocates of legalism and law observance, eloquent, boasting of Scripture knowledge, of acquaintance with the other apostles, perhaps even of acquaintance with Jesus. But it seems more important to ask how Paul can speak so confidently of what is in the hearts of these men when he had not been in Corinth and had not himself seen them.

Is Paul guilty of *Herzensrichterei*, this dangerous business of judging men's hearts? Paul had received full accounts from Titus who had just returned from Corinth (2:13; 7:6, 13). It was no longer a question as to what was in the hearts of these invaders; they had exposed that from the beginning by using even foul means (slander, etc.) to break down what Paul had built up at such cost of labor. The sin of judging the heart consists in imputing base motives to another person's heart even when he does what is right. These men were tearing down the true work of God under cover of praising themselves by an outward display as reliable men. The Corinthians looked at the latter and became impressed thereby and failed to note the former which revealed what was really in the hearts of these men. Paul bids the Corinthians to look at what has come out of their hearts. Was that something by which these men could glorify themselves?

Paul wants to be judged and can properly be judged only in the same way that he judges these men. The Corinthians must look at Paul's heart through the window of what he has wrought among them and is still trying to work as he states in 4:2 and, in fact, throughout, also in the rest of this chapter where he once more enters into the very heart of the gospel and of his own ministry. This entire epistle more than the others bares Paul's inmost heart, all his deepest motives and inner purposes, and does all this by means of what he has done and is still doing. When in chapters 10 to 12 he is compelled to compare himself with others in an outward way he says that he feels like a fool for doing so. His glorying was in his infirmities, for which men would despise him. It is his glorying to be nothing but a clay vessel in order to make the treasure of the supreme power of God stand out the more by contrast (4:7, etc.). He thus indicates to the Corinthians what they may use in regard to himself and his assistants for silencing and for getting rid of the imposters who had come to trouble them.

13) The γάρ introduces a point on which he and his assistants had evidently been attacked; its force is "for example." **For whether we have lost our wits, (it was) for God; whether we are keeping our wits, (it is) for you.** First an aorist and then a present tense: ever lost our wits — have them now. We note that the plural "we" continues, and it refers to Paul and to his assistants throughout the chapter. R., W. P., finds a literary plural in v. 13 among all the ordinary plurals. He and others apply the two verbs (especially the first) only to Paul. They apply also to Timothy (1:1), to Titus, to Silvanus, and to other assistants of Paul.

We also note that ἐξίστημι is never employed in the technical sense of being in ecstasy in either profane or Biblical Greek (C.-K. 532). This bars out all ecstatic conditions such as the one described in the case of Peter in Acts 10:9, and such as the visions and the revelations of Paul mentioned in II Cor. 12:1, etc., or the speaking with tongues referred to in I Cor. 14:18.

Finally, the two datives "for God" and "for you" are not in opposition, do not exclude each other as though "for God" = for him and not for you, and "for you" = for you and not for God. All that Paul and his assistants did and do is for God and for you.

Ἐξίστημι has two meanings: 1) being dumbfounded because of something miraculous (often); 2) being touched with lunacy as in Mark 3:21. The latter is the meaning here. The reference is to instances such as that recorded in Acts 26:24, when Festus cried out excitedly to Paul: "Thou art mad!" Paul, however, assured him that he was far from being mad. We thus see what both the plural and the aorist mean: actual instances in the past when Paul or one of his assistants spoke about the great things of the gospel with such fire and fervor as to astonish people so that they thought the speaker was mentally unbalanced. Also Paul's assistants on occasion spoke like men who were carried beyond themselves by what they uttered. It is fortunate that we have Luke's full account of such an instance in Acts 26:24, when, not Paul, but Festus lost his equilibrium (see the author's exposition of the scene in his *Interpretation of Acts*), for it helps us to understand just what Paul means by the charge of having lost his wits.

Before the days of Festus, men who had as little sense as he, and men who were like the relatives of Jesus himself in Mark 3:21, saw nothing but unbalanced minds when they watched the burning zeal and fervent speech of these ministers of Christ. When these opponents of Paul's invaded Corinth they very likely caught up the charge and sought to make the Corinthians believe that Paul and his assistants were mentally somewhat unbalanced. The Greek uses the aorist whereas the English employs the perfect: "have lost our wits" (R. 845).

It is Paul himself who adds the counterpart: "whether we are keeping our wits"; he naturally does this with a present tense, an aorist would be improper. This has been understood as being another charge. To some, we are told, Paul was too extravagant in his language and his zeal, to others too sober in both; or, to some incomprehensible, to others too calculating. But these opinions are not in accord with the terms here used. Nobody would advance as a charge against a man the fact that he is sober-minded; and sober-minded is never used in an evil sense like calculating. Paul adds this so that he can make his answer complete.

And he does this with two words: Θεῷ — ὑμῖν, *dativi commodi*. Their ministry has two sides: "for God" who called them; "for you" whom we serve. Neither excludes the other, yet the two cannot be reversed. The first means: If in our zeal and our fervor of speech anything ever seemed beyond some of you, let them remember that we serve *God* who is higher than you are. The second means: When any of you find us sober-minded in word and in act you surely see that we are serving *you*. In other words: If some of you have not always been able to keep peace with us and to understand all our fiery devotion, God understands it well enough, and there has always been a great amount that you could well understand as certainly being most beneficial for you.

14) **For the love of Christ constrains us,** his love for us (subjective genitive) as the following establishes. On ἀγάπη see 2:4, the love of fullest comprehension and of corresponding purpose and action. Paul does not say that our love for Christ holds us to our ministry in such a way that men sometimes wonder whether we have lost our mental balance when they see us going beyond what they imagine to be reasonable. That would be stopping at the halfway station. Our love for Christ is kindled and constantly fed by his love for us. Paul goes at once to the supreme source of motivation in his and in his assistants' ministry. "Christ's love" — that ought to make plain how they above all serve God and thus also serve the Corinthians. If this love's constraining power now and then impels Paul and his assistants to go beyond what ordi-

nary men are able to grasp, it is not strange at all just as it is not strange that the Corinthians should find themselves so abundantly served by the sober wits of these ministers. For the constraining power, Christ's love, is active even in the latter.

Paul is speaking about his ministry, about how the love of Christ constrains him and his helpers in their ministry, συνέχει, holds them tightly together with their task so that nothing can keep them from it. It is because Christ died for all men with two mighty results: the one that all died; the other that all who live should live for him. This love that made him die constrains his ministers to bring the knowledge and the power of this love to all men everywhere so that they, too, may be made alive by it and may ever live unto him. The mainspring of all energy in the Christian ministry is the love of Christ as evidenced by the death of Christ for all men with its automatic universal effect ("therefore they all died") and its saving purpose ("in order that they who live," etc.). If his love died with this effect and this purpose, how can we do anything but live for him in devotion to this purpose?

Paul continues with the ingressive aorist of purpose: **having come to judge this: One died for all, therefore they all died; and he died for all in order that those living may no longer live unto themselves but unto him who for them died and was raised up.** We have arrived at this judgment, Paul says; the aorist participle states its finality. This is not a mere theoretical, logical conclusion or just a subjective opinion; it is the judgment which finds this a fact and so accepts and declares it as a fact. As a judge declares what the fact in the case is, so Paul does, so do his assistants with him. When they first came to this judgment need not be said; it was when the whole significance of Christ's death dawned upon them. "Christ" is also the proper name because it designates him according to his Messianic office. We regard ὅτι as *recitativum* so that what follows is direct and not indirect discourse. The judgment is pronounced directly: "*One* — for all — died, therefore *they all* died," and the emphasis is on the two subjects. In v. 15 the emphasis is on the verb: "For all he *died* in order that they who *live* may *live*," etc. Note how "one" and "for all" are abutted in order to indicate contrast and emphasis. "He died" = he did no less, he sacrificed his very life for them on the cross.

He did this for "all." The Calvinistic efforts to limit this word to "all the elect" constitute one of the saddest chapters in exegesis. The Scriptures shine with the "all" of universality, but Calvinists do not see it. Their one effort is to find something that would justify them to reduce "all" to "some." Calvin himself says that all = all kinds, all classes, rich and poor, high and low, rejecting no class, taking *some* of each, but *not all* in the sense of every individual. Hodge has the statement: "therefore all died," refer to the death of the old nature in conversion; and since this occurs only in some, the preceding statement is likewise said to refer to "some." The real assurance for me that Christ died *for me* is this alone, that he died for absolutely *all*. If he omitted any, then, knowing what a fearful sinner I am, I must come to the judgment that he surely passed by also me. In regard even to the lost II Pet. 2:1 declares: They deny "the Lord that bought them and bring upon themselves swift destruction."

Ὑπέρ = over and is used in many connections, in particular where substitution is to be expressed. This was formerly denied on the score that ἀντί should be used as it, indeed, also is in Matt. 20:28, and Mark 10:45. But the papyri have disclosed the fact that ὑπέρ is the favorite preposition for expressing substitution, much more so than ἀντί or πρό or any other (R., *W. P.*). The overwhelming evidence for this Robertson presents in part in *The Minister and His Greek New Testament*, 35, in the chapter on "The use of ὑπέρ in business documents in the papyri." His verdict is that in our passage "substitution must be understood" (R. 631).

The church has always held this conviction, nor has it ever been uncertain regarding the force of the preposition. Our present advantage is the mass of purely secular linguistic evidence for the correctness of this meaning of the preposition. In large numbers of instances an act could not be "for," "in behalf of," "for the advantage of," if it is not "instead of," in substitution for another person. See also Trench, *Synonyms*, and his quotation from Tischendorf.

The matter is of supreme importance because the vicarious, substitutionary death of Christ has ever been and is still the main point of attack on the part of rationalism and modernism that mock at this "blood theology." The so-called "theories of the atonement" (the Scriptures know of no "theory," they know only the fact, just as they know only the fact of inspiration and no "theory") also dispense with the substitution.

"Therefore all died," ἀπέθανεν and ἀπέθανον, ἄρα being placed between them: when Christ bowed his head on the cross, in perfect correspondence with (ἄρα) his death all men died then and there. All who had ever lived, all who will yet live until time ends, died in Christ's death, died in Christ, their Substitute. One mere man may substitute for one other man; when equivalence is more inexact, one man might substitute for several. But one mere man could not substitute his death and have it equal the death of the universe of men in all ages. Only the God-man could be this Substitute. Without Christ's deity his effective substitution becomes fiction. If Christ is not true God he might die a thousand times, and despite all the deaths it could never be said: "therefore they all died." Οἱ πάντες, "they

Second Corinthians 5:14

all,' the article taking up πάντων = these very all instead of whom Christ died.

In what sense did they all die? The answer lies in ὑπέρ, in Christ's substitution. It is indicated in Matt. 20:28 and Mark 10:45: he gave his life as a ransom in the stead of many. He laid down the price, and that price was reckoned as though we had laid it down. Each of us might die a thousand times, and this would amount to nothing even for those who did this: we are sinners who are damned to die. The death of the sinless Son, the Lamb without spot or blemish, this, and this death alone, equals the death of all for whom he died.

Erase the substitution, and Paul's judgment becomes fiction, ceases to be fact. Christ's death ransomed all, atoned for all, satisfied for all, made sacrificial expiation for all, paid for all. All these are statements of the same fact, all define ὑπέρ to the same effect. The death of Christ, in which they all died, changed the relation of all to God. All of them are now redeemed and ransomed, their sin and guilt being expiated by Christ's death. They all died, not by a death of theirs, but by Christ's death which he died in their stead. Cancel his death by altering it in some way, and our relation to God remains unchanged; then we are all unredeemed, lost beyond hope.

"They all died," yet by this alone none obtained life, the life that lives forever. How we now as the result of Christ's death by which we died also obtain this life, will be told presently. But this must be noted: Christ died 1900 years ago, on a certain day, at a certain hour in time. But this counts for all time: for the entire future time, for all the prior time. For by Christ's death "all died," Adam and all his descendants. The effect covered all. It is literally true: "the Lamb slain from the foundation of the world." His death availed for Adam. All in the Old Testament who believed were saved by that death just as all are in the New Testament who believe.

15) First the objective effect (v. 14) and now the purpose with the intended subjective result. This, too, rests on the fact that Christ died in the stead of all. Hence we have the important repetition: "and for all he died." It is difficult to understand how this can be regarded as an unnecessary repetition. The fact stated is so tremendous that it cannot be stated too often. Repetition emphasizes, and if emphasis is ever in place, it is so here. Yet this is more than emphasis of the fact alone. Εἰs is omitted. The contrast: "One — they all," is dropped. A new one enters: "He *died* — that they who *live* may *live*," etc. Although Christ died "for all," not all live, only some do.

Paul is writing to Christians who know how all this is to be understood. Out of the whole plan of salvation he is taking what he needs to show how the love of Christ constrains us, namely his ministers in their work, but these only as belonging to all others who have the life that comes out of Christ's death. So Paul at once advances from Christ's death to our living. See how οἱ ζῶντες appears already in 4:11, there it is also applied to Paul and to his helpers, there, too, it is connected with Christ's death and with his life. We connect all that is there said with what is here said.

"They that live" are they that have the ζωή, the spiritual, deathless life, and the divine purpose in Christ's death for all men is that, having been brought to this life, the living ones should live this life, namely live no longer unto themselves as they once lived before they were reborn but unto him who died for them and rose again. Living thus defines what it means that the love of Christ constrains us. Our whole life's interest should center in Christ, and no interest should center in ourselves apart from Christ. The statement of this purpose is general and is predicated of all who have this life although it applies in particular to Paul and to his fellow ministers. In their holy office their spiritual life is to have a special field of manifestation (φανερώμεθα in v. 11). The datives are *commodi* (R. 539).

Instead of saying: "should live for Christ," the death of Christ is mentioned for the third time (it deserves to be), but it is now joined with his resurrection: "should live for him who for them died and was raised up." We regard ἐγερθέντι as a passive; our versions regard it as a middle: "rose again." Some passive forms are middle in sense; that question arises repeatedly in regard to this verb. The point itself is not material since the Scriptures say both that Christ arose and that he was raised up by God. R. 799 says regarding ἠγέρθη: "usually transitive," but in 817 he reduces this to "sometimes passive" although he quotes Moulton who says "often."

We see no reason for any force but the passive in the present connection. After twice saying in regard to Christ: "for all he died," with the phrase being placed before the verb, Paul once more writes in the same way: "he who for them died," i. e., for those who are spiritually alive. This is sufficient to settle the point as to whether the phrase modifies both participles or only the one. It modifies only the one. Although one article unites the two participles, if the phrase is to modify both of them it should be placed after the first participle (although this would still leave doubt) or after both participles (which would leave no doubt).

This matter has become important. It has been taken for granted that the phrase modifies both participles, and from this assumption the deduction is drawn that ὑπέρ cannot mean "instead of" in this phrase or in the other two but in all three must mean only "for the sake of," "in behalf of." It cannot be said that Christ was raised up instead of anybody. To be sure, this cannot be said, and for this reason Paul places this last phrase exactly as he does the other two so that no one should assume that he intends to have it modify both participles. Moreover, although the death and the resurrection of Christ always go together, and although the apostles generally emphasize the resurrection (this already involves the death since only one who died can be raised up), here, where the great point is the love of Christ, it is his death "in our stead" that must be emphasized, for this is the great proof of his love. And Paul does that very thing.

Furthermore, when he speaks about all men, it is enough to mention the death, for by it Christ made a bloody atonement for all. When he now speaks about believers, among whom are Paul and his assistants, all of whom respond to Christ's love, he adds to the great fact that Christ died in their stead also the other fact that he rose again. No modifier is needed in the case of this second fact, and Paul adds none. In the case of believers, who are to live unto Christ, it is in place to add Christ's resurrection: they are to live unto him as their ever-living Lord.

One of the unacceptable interpretations is the view that ὑπέρ has a mystic meaning. But it never has and cannot have. The mystic union is expressed by ἐν: I *in* you, and you *in* me; or by σύν: we died, were entombed, rose again *with* Christ. This is the true mystic union. It is predicated only of believers and never of all men. When a mystic sense is attributed to ὑπέρ, the meaning of the preposition is changed, and the force of the first two ὑπέρ phrases is altered by the idea that all men were in mystic union with Christ when he died, and so all died in his death (but why did they not all also rise in his resurrection?); or by the idea of Calvin that "all" does not mean *all* but only some. This mystic phase seems to appeal to a good many, but they seem to lack a clear conception of what "mystical" signifies and so find mystic statements where none exist and thus are led into other errors. See Rom. 6:4, etc., on mystic language. But note that what is Biblically mystic has nothing to do with the so-called mystics like Tauler, Boehme, etc.

16) The Lord's purpose that we who have the spiritual life should live unto him alone has been realized in the case of Paul and in the case of his assistants. Paul says so, not, however, merely in order to place himself and his conduct toward the Corinthians into the right light for the Corinthians, but also to induce them to reciprocate fully so that they, too, may think and do everything only as unto Christ who died for them and was raised up again. **Wherefore we on our part from now on know no one in a fleshly way. If also we have known Christ in a fleshly way, yet now we know him so no longer.**

Ἡμεῖς has the emphasis: "we on our part among those who are living unto Christ." "From now on" = "henceforth" (our versions) with less of the temporal than the resultant idea: "we in consequence." Our whole way of looking at people has undergone a change: "we know no man in a fleshly way." "Flesh" has ceased to be the norm of our thinking and judging in regard to anybody; carnal ideas no longer control us, but the high and holy considerations which center in Christ do. We neither approve nor disapprove, love nor hate any person from motives and with purposes such as rule people who have not experienced the love of Christ in their hearts. This love alone constrains us; we live unto him (v. 14, 15). Here we have an exposition of v. 14, 15 as far as the contact of Paul and his assistants with other persons is concerned.

In both statements κατὰ σάρκα belongs to the verb and needs no article in the Greek. It is like so many other phrases in this respect. The phrases are purely adverbial, each is placed immediately after its verb where it naturally belongs. The supposition that the phrases modify the objects or both the verbs and the objects is untenable. It is doubly so in regard to Christ, for the phrase precedes "Christ"; if it were intended to modify "Christ," we should have τὸν κατὰ σάρκα Χριστόν. When the phrases are referred to the objects, abstruse ideas result that are out of line with Paul's thought. "According to flesh" means that in our knowing anyone, no matter who he is, we follow no norm of flesh whether it be flesh as sinful flesh or flesh as mere natural flesh, i. e., whether it be sinful or mere natural, human thought.

The Corinthians are to apply what Paul says about the way in which he and his assistants know anyone to the way in which they have dealt with the Corinthians throughout and during the difficulties which the Corinthians have been causing. The treatment which Paul and his assistants accorded and still accord the Corinthians in no way smacks of anything like flesh. Would that every minister could say that to his congregation!

The Corinthians may also think of themselves, of the way in which they have been acting toward Paul and toward his assistants. Has only the love of Christ always constrained them? Have they always been living not unto themselves but only unto Christ? Has flesh been the norm of their treatment of Paul? Would that every congregation and every member of a congregation could say what Paul says about himself and his fellow workers!

The thought is carried to its climax by being extended to Christ. Him, too, we no longer know in a fleshly way. This was the wrong way, Paul says, in which we once knew him, but it has changed completely, changed since we came to be constrained by this love, came to live unto him as the One who died for us and was raised up again. R. 1026 says regarding εἰ καί, "if also," that the protasis is treated as a matter of indifference. "If there is a conflict, it makes no real difficulty. There is sometimes a tone of contempt in εἰ καί. The matter is belittled." The sense is: "What if we have once done so," i. e., known Christ in a fleshly way? The asyndeton tends toward emphasis. The condition is one of reality, and the perfect tense of the verb indicates that Paul and his assistants have for a long while known Christ only in this wrong way. We now have γινώσκω, to know by observation and experience; in the preceding clause οἶδα means to know through mental reflection. So the idea of knowing is now intensified; it should be, for Christ is not just "anyone." Any knowledge of Christ that a person obtains affects him far more deeply than knowledge of any other person would.

Consider the case of Paul alone. At one time he knew Christ with a carnal mind, in a carnal way. He was offended in Christ, considered him opposed to Jewish interests, saw him only with fleshly eyes. To his fleshly, pharisaical mind Christ was a false Messiah. We know how this affected Paul. He looked at other men in the same blind, fleshly way; but when he looked thus at Christ he raged like a wild beast (Acts 8:3; 9:1) that was full of fury. It is still so today. Many know Christ only "according to flesh" and are filled with foolish, pernicious, vicious thoughts about him, which, when they have come to know his love, fill them with utter shame in deepest repentance.

By construing "Christ according to flesh" a few commentators think that Paul means that he was acquainted with Jesus while the latter lived on earth. This introduces an irrelevant and a wrong thought. For in the preceding sentence "no one according to flesh" would then have to mean the same thing. Paul does not write "Jesus," the name by which the Master was known when he lived among men. Whether Paul ever saw Jesus while Jesus was on earth has no bearing whatever on what he here says to the Corinthians. Besides, Paul says "we," which includes Timothy (1:1), Titus, Silas, Luke, etc. As far as evidence goes, Paul never met the Savior during his earthly sojourn as little as did young Timothy or Luke.

When the love of Christ constrains us, Christ becomes the chief object of our knowing and realization, and we know all other men only as Christ bids us know them. But this has an obverse side, and the Corinthians may well think of that. When we begin to look at men in a fleshly way, the love of Christ is slipping from its control, we are beginning again to live to ourselves and thus are in the greatest danger of again knowing Christ only in a fleshly way. Unless the fleshly treatment which the Corinthians had accorded Paul and his assistants is checked, it will develop into a similar treatment of Christ himself. He and his Word ever try to stop us from knowing anyone only according to flesh; when we persist to the contrary we can do so only by thrusting him and his Word aside, i. e., by treating him according to flesh. For this reason Paul has written the two statements, one in regard to any person, the other in regard to Christ himself.

17) A second ὥστε mentions a second result, and the asyndeton calls for attention. We are shown what underlies the first result. Knowing and realizing depend on what we are. The love of Christ controls us only when we are new creatures; we live unto Christ only in the new spiritual life as new creatures. Paul ever follows the facts to the very end. **Wherefore, if anyone (is) in Christ, a new creation (is he). The old things have passed away. Lo, things have become new!**

Three short, incisive statements, and the third is exclamatory. There are no connectives; this makes the statements sharper in the Greek, for the Greek loves to join everything so that, when he omits connectives, he feels a jolt. "Wherefore" presents what we find when we trace things to their source. In v. 16 "wherefore" = when we follow forward and note the effects. Both ὥστε = results, but as indicated.

To be constrained by Christ's love and to live unto him alone evidently involves an inner connection with Christ. One must then be "in Christ." This is the phrase which is used a large number of times by Paul in many varied connections and has called forth monographs as has also the phrase "through Christ." Ἐν = in union or in communion with or in connection with. The picture is that of a sphere or a circle. Christ fills that circle as Christ, as our Savior, our Lord, etc., with all his love for us (v. 14), with his life (4:10), the fount of life for us. We, too, are placed into this sphere. How? By the objective means of his Word and his Sacrament, by the subjective means of faith which is wrought in us by the Word and the Sacrament. Thus we are in living, spiritual connection with Christ, ἐν Χριστῷ. Christ "in us" is merely viewing this in the other way. We and our emptiness, need, etc., are viewed as the sphere into which Christ and all that he is and has enter by his blessed means. The condition "if" and the indefinite "anyone" include all individuals who are thus joined to Christ spiritually.

The predicate, which is without a copula, καινὴ κτίσις, is pointed, incisive: "a new creation," no less! This is no mere mending or improvement but an actual "creation." This word means the act of creating and is then applied also to what the act creates. A Creator is implied, and we may take him to be God or the Holy Spirit. "Creation" leads us to think of what God did when he created the world. The two acts are comparable. See 4:6. This comparableness has at times been drawn too closely, especially when the δύναμις Θεοῦ is mentioned, or when the figure of resurrection is employed. We are not made a new creation by omnipotence but by grace. The two are distinct and are never confused in Scripture. The one is God's power as much as the other, the other creates spiritually. We are "a new creation" ("creature" is less exact) by virtue of the spiritual life created in us, the life by which we live not to ourselves but to Christ (v. 15). This is καινός, "new," in contrast with something "old," here "flesh," our former sinful being and state. "A new creation" — if only we would always think of ourselves in this way and not try to hold fast to the old!

A new creation means that "the old things have passed away," have gone παρά, have been cast "aside." These are "the old things" of the flesh, in which we at one time lived, which at one time were our love and our delight, which at one time filled our whole being. Paul is a master in using the singular and the plural: "a new creation" — now "the old things." A new unit — the entire mass of old things discarded. What would a new creation have to do with these good-for-nothing old things of the old life? The Greek uses the aorist: "did pass away," our idiom the perfect: "have passed away." The aorist denotes one decisive past act by which the grand severance was made and the new creation was wrought. That is, of course, conversion or regeneration. And "passed away" is correct despite the fact that some of the old things still cling to us in this life. They only cling to the new creation; they are now "old things" and not really any longer a part of us.

So wonderful is this that Paul exclaims because of it by using the opposite: "Lo, things have become new!" "All things" in the A. V. is an importation from Rev. 21:5. But the R. V. is also mistaken with its rendering: "*they* are become new," i. e., the old things. They could not possibly become new; they had to be cast entirely away; other things had to take their place, things that were newly created. The subject of γέγονε is not drawn from παρῆλθεν; "have become new" contains its own subject, one that is implied in καινά: "things have become new." The perfect tense signifies: became new in the past constantly to remain so. In these new things we live unto Christ.

In conclusion a few remarks regarding 16b, about no longer knowing Christ κατὰ σάρκα. Something like nine different opinions are offered, and a tenth that a choice cannot be made. The details need not be offered the reader. Yet this may be added. Paul's "we" is made an "I." A "Paul and Jesus problem" is said to arise. Paul is thought to be writing polemically. He does not have all the material about Jesus which the other apostles possessed, he knew only the death and the resurrection of Jesus. He does not know the contents of our four Gospels save for the two points mentioned. He feels this lack keenly in serving his congregations. So in "an act of desperation" he here rejects "the authority of the earthly Jesus." He has his own "Christ conception," the "death to life" idea, which is offered to him in the cult doctrines and the mystery religions of Hellenistic paganism. The cult god dies and comes to life again. The "Jesus and Paul problem" is thus solved. It is needless to state that we find none of this in Paul's statement regarding knowing "Christ according to flesh."

XVIII. *"The Ministry of the Reconciliation"*

18) This change in us is due to what God has done for us. Paul has already described the expiation: "instead of all Christ died and was raised up again." He now goes still farther: "God reconciled us to himself through Christ," and this brings him back to the ministry which connected him with the Corinthians. Δέ is merely metabatic, it passes on to the new thought.

Now all these things (are) from God, him who reconciled us to himself through Christ and gave to

us the ministry of this reconciliation — how God was in Christ reconciling the world to himself, not reckoning to them their transgressions, also having deposited in our charge the statement of this reconciliation.

Τὰ πάντα are not "all things" (general) but all the things just mentioned (specific), these that have become new, by which we are a new creation, men who live unto Christ, who are constrained by his love (v. 14-17). All these things without an exception have their ultimate source in *God* (ἐκ); but again specifically God as he "who did reconcile us to himself through Christ." From him who effected our reconciliation we (Paul and his assistants) have obtained all these new things. They go with reconciliation as its essential products.

It is imperative to note the tenses used in v. 18, 19; next, to note "us" in connection with which the tense is an aorist to indicate an act that is finished, and "the world" and "them" (all the individuals in the world) in reference to whom the participles are present to indicate actions that continue. The difference is this. For Paul and for his assistants God's reconciliation had been accomplished both objectively and subjectively: through Christ's death and expiation God had removed their guilt, which had separated them from God; and by making them a new creation so that they were now living unto Christ and were constrained by his love, God had transformed them also subjectively from enemies into friends, which is exactly as Rom. 5:10 states both of these acts of reconciliation. It is vital to note that this is the sense of the aorist. *God* did this, he alone.

It is unwarranted to think of only the objective fact; or to have the pronoun "us" include all Christians much as it is true that, like Paul and his helpers, all Christians can say also in regard to themselves what this aorist says. But in the case of the world the tenses must be open, must be continuous. True, Christ died for all (aorist, v. 14, 15, three times), and in that sense the whole world has been reconciled to God; if that were all that is here meant, we should have had another aorist. But Paul means more. He has in mind especially the subjective fact of the reconciliation as he does in v. 18 where he speaks only about "us." God is ever busy with this feature, namely transforming enemies into friends. Hence we have the present participles: "engaged in reconciling to himself, engaged in not reckoning to them their transgressions." This work goes right on, it is now in progress.

For this reason, and in sharp distinction from the two present participles, the third is an aorist: "also having deposited in our charge (ἐν ἡμῖν, Paul and his helpers) the statement (τὸν λόγον, declaration) of reconciliation." By means of this ministry which has been placed into our hands by God, Paul says, God is doing this wondrous work, bringing reconciliation and pardon from sin to the world, i. e., "to them," the individuals in the world. This θέμενος is a historical aorist and even a middle: God placed this *logos* in our hands for himself. *He* called and appointed us ministers, made me an apostle to do this work for him. In these chapters which are so full of "we" forms ἐν ἡμῖν is not an exception that in this one phrase refers to all Christians in general.

Verily, as Robertson has said (*The Minister and His Greek New Testament*, 88), there are "sermons in Greek tenses." Entire doctrines pivot on the tenses that are here used.

The usual exegesis has sometimes failed to see what these tenses convey. "He who reconciled us to himself through Christ," v. 18, is referred only to the objective reconciliation which was effected through or by means of (διά) the death of Christ. How God could then give to men who were reconciled only objectively "the ministry of this reconciliation," is not made clear. The gap is ignored, but Paul filled it. "Reconciled us to himself" includes also the subjective side, what Rom. 5:11 states thus: "we received (into personal possession) the reconciliation" (effected by Christ's death). Only to such men could "the ministry of this reconciliation" be given by God. The very task of this διακονία is to bring to the world this objective reconciliation for subjective appropriation by faith (v. 20). The genitive in "the ministry of this reconciliation" is objective: to serve this reconciliation by bringing "the word of this reconciliation" unto men (v. 19).

19) The same truth is restated in v. 19: "also having deposited ἐν ἡμῖν, in our charge, the word (statement, declaration) of this reconciliation." The genitive is again objective as it is in "the word of this salvation" (Acts 13:26); "the word of the cross" (I Cor. 1:18); "word of life" (Phil 2:16): the word which tells about this reconciliation, salvation, cross, life. Both δόντος and θέμενος are properly aorists. Note also "gave" *to us* as a gift but "deposited *for himself*" (middle) with us. How could God deposit this "word" with anyone whom he had not yet brought to personal reconciliation? Τοῦ καταλλάξαντος emphasizes the subjective reconciliation.

Some of the current exegesis asks: Does Paul not write "world" and "them"? Then he refers to only objective reconciliation. We ought to have three aorist forms *if* objective acts are referred to; we ought to have God *did* reconcile the world, *did* not reckon, also (καί) *did* deposit. But Paul writes an imperfect ἦν and two present participles and only *one* aorist. There is some discussion about ἦν καταλλάσσων being a periphrastic imperfect, but should this not include also μὴ λογιζόμενος? Since it is assumed that this is objective reconciliation and thus a historic *past* act on the part of God, this ἦν, whether it is made periphrastic or not, whether it is construed with one or with both participles, is regarded as if it were an aorist, as if it expressed *an aorist past* act, one that God did when Christ died. Some date this act at the time when Christ was raised up on Easter morning.

What does Paul say? That what God has finished for him and for his helpers (aorist καταλλάξαντος) he is still busy with (durative present participles) in regard to the world, namely the individuals in it; that in steadily working at this reconciling and not reckoning to men their transgressions God employed Paul and his helpers in the ministry which he gave them with the word of reconciliation that he deposited with them. This work began when Christ died, when "God was in Christ," when he wrought the objective reconciliation "through Christ" (v. 18). That objective reconciliation includes the whole world. But it must be brought to the world, to be made a personal possession by faith, a personal, individual reconciliation by means of the ministry of the reconciliation and the word of the reconciliation.

The ἦν cannot be construed periphrastically. It has its own modifier "in Christ" and thus states a separate and a continuous past fact: "God was in Christ." This statement of fact is modified by two present, durative participles: "engaged in reconciling the world to himself, (doing this by) not reckoning to them (the plural in a *constructio ad sensum*, B.-D. 282) their trespasses." Καί in the sense of "also" adds in further explanation: "also (by) having placed in our charge the word of this reconciliation." Καταλλάσσων cannot be read periphrastically because it has its own object. Moreover, this participle is separated from ἦν by both "in Christ" and "the world" (κόσμον needs no article, being a word for an object only one of which exists).

Our versions translate correctly. R. 891 calls καταλλάσσων descriptive, which is helpful, but the tense expresses continuousness. The present participle is also used to express purpose (B.-D. 418, 4; 339, 2c; R. 991, 1115). May we then not translate: "God was in Christ *in order* to be reconciling the world by not reckoning," etc.? Since μὴ λογιζόμενος has no connective it explains how the reconciling is to be effected, namely by no longer reckoning to men (αὐτοῖς) their trespasses, by no longer charging their sins against them. The position of κόσμον before its participle renders it emphatic: God's continuous work of reconciling extends to the whole world, to no less than that; God is now operating so.

"There is no doubt of the use of ὡς ὅτι in the declarative sense = 'that'" (R. 1033); B.-D. 396 says only: "ὡς ὅτι = ὅτι apparently three times with Paul." But it is so used in the LXX and in the papyri. The debate about this connective may thus be concluded. Our versions are quite satisfactory: "to wit, that," etc. The Greek uses παράπτωμα, the result of falling off to a side, away from the right road, whereas the English has the conception of going across (contrary to): "transgression," or of going where one is forbidden to go: "trespass."

"To reckon" is to impute, to charge against. Here we have "not reckoning." All these sinners have transgressions, but God does not charge them against sinners. This is a litotes, a negative expression for a positive idea: God remits the sins, cancels the debit in his ledger, blots out the handwriting with Christ's blood. Instead of reckoning unto them their sins he reckons unto them their faith (i. e., Christ embraced by faith); in regard to this positive reckoning see Rom. 4:3 *in extenso*. God continues to do this again and again, always when sinners are brought to faith, καταλλάσσων and μὴ λογιζόμενος are iteratively durative.

Regarding καταλλάσσω and καταλλαγή see Rom. 5:10, 11. There, as here, it is not *God* who is changed but God who changes *men*. God always loved the world (John 3:16). *He* was "in Christ" when Christ died for all (v. 14, 15). *He* gave his Son to die for the world. *He* needed no reconciling, nothing to change him, for he is love — why should *he* change? The trouble is with the world, with us, with what our transgressions have made us. The conception is wrong that, what happens so often in the case of men also occurred between God and us, that we had mutually fallen out with each other, and that reconciliation had to be a mutual change. No; this reconciliation was one-sided, completely so, even doubly so: we were wrong, we alone; moreover, it was impossible to change ourselves, *God* alone could effect a change in us. That required the death of his Son. *God* reconciled us to himself "through Christ" (διά, Christ became the Mediator by his death for all, v. 14, 15). In καταλλάσσειν κατά is perfective, and the root is ἄλλος (G. K. 252): "to make thoroughly other." God is always the agent, men are always the object. It is never said that *we* reconcile God; never that Christ reconciled *God*. We, we have to be made thoroughly other, and God has to do this if it is to be done at all.

And this must be done in a double way. First, the trespasses we accumulate have to be removed. Christ removed them by dying in our stead, by expiating them with his blood. This changed the whole world of men in its objective relation to God. It was then and there a redeemed world, every sinner from Adam onward to the end of time was redeemed, in this sense made thoroughly other by God himself through Christ. But these transgressors (Rom. 5:10 calls them ἐχθροί, active enemies) had to undergo a subjective change, had to be personally changed in their hearts. Individually they had to be brought to contrition, faith, and new obedience. God has to do this by means of the word of the reconciliation as this is preached to the world by his ministers. Men had to be changed from enemies into friends. We have to be reconciled to God also in this sense.

In the proposition: "God was in Christ," the phrase "in Christ" is according to the persons involved and thus goes beyond v. 17: "anyone in Christ." We are twice emphatically told: "God reconciled and is reconciling *to himself*." Christ is named twice: "through" and "in Christ." Christ is the Mediator, Christ, the sphere in the whole reconciliation. As far as the objective side is concerned, this underlies the whole of v. 19, and on this objective rests the subjective, the forgiving of sins αὐτοῖς, i. e., to the individuals reconciled, for which also the ministry is instituted (καὶ θέμενος κτλ.).

We do not find the idea that Paul here says that when Christ died, when in and by his death God reconciled the world objectively, he then and there (or at the time of Christ's resurrection) forgave all sins to the whole world. Αὐτοῖς = individuals and refers to their subjective reconciliation. The use so often made of this passage should be modified. On the question of universal and personal justification consult the author's *Interpretation of Romans*, 5:10, also 1:17.

20) **Accordingly, for Christ we are ambassadors, God, as it were, admonishing you through us. We keep begging for Christ: Be reconciled to God!**

The point of all that Paul says is his own and his assistants' connection with all this continuous reconciling work of God. The reason for stressing this point is to show the Corinthians his own and his assistants' right relation to them. So in v. 19 Paul ended with God's depositing with himself and with his assistants "the word of the reconciliation." The very term θέμενος is weighty: for himself God officially invested them with this word. "Accordingly," Paul now adds, you Corinthians can see what our position is because of our office, first in regard to Christ and God, secondly, in regard to you and to men generally. "We are acting as ambassadors of Christ," as no less.

Πρεσβεύω and its noun πρεσβύτης are derived from πρέσβυς, "old," since old and experienced men were usually sent as ambassadors of emperors and of kings. This word is a noble one and conveys a great deal. An ambassador represents his government also in all its dignity. To scorn an ambassador or to mistreat him is to scorn and to mistreat the government which sent him. To send him away is to break off relations with the government and the ruler whom he represents. An ambassador speaks wholly for his ruler, he is his ruler's mouthpiece. He never utters his own thoughts, offers, promises, demands, but only those of his ruler. An ambassador's person lends no weight to what he says. They to whom he is sent see and hear in him only the king who sent him.

We now see how much is conveyed by the statement "deposited for himself" in v. 19. Here there is food for thought for all ambassadors today. How dare we alter, change, reduce the word committed to us? How dare we act as if *we* were dealing with men or let men think they are dealing only with *us*? How can we ever lower our high office? No potentate is as high as is he who commissioned us. An ambassador is absolutely responsible to his king. Woe to him if he forgets that!

Here, too, ὑπέρ = "instead of" and only in this sense "for" and "in behalf of." It is unwarranted to stress the point that God sent us, that he deposited his word with us, and that he admonishes men through us as though this means that as ambassadors we represent God and not Christ. For v. 19 states in so many words: "God was in Christ." No distinction such as indicated can be made between Christ and God. We must take both together: "for Christ" = as representing Christ, as speaking to men in his stead; and "God admonishing through us" = the same thing. The force of ὡς is "as it were."

Without a connective and hence with emphasis Paul adds in brief how as ambassadors in Christ's stead he and his assistants speak in Christ's name, or, which is the same, how God speaks through them: "We keep begging for Christ (again the significant ὑπέρ): 'Be reconciled to God!'" Note that no "you" is added, there is no reference to the Corinthians. They were already so reconciled. Paul is speaking of his office in general and how it is being executed in the world among men everywhere (αὐτοῖς in v. 19). Παρακαλέω may have various implications: to admonish, to encourage, to comfort. Here the former meaning is best: God admonishes men. Our versions have "beseech," which is less good. For δέομαι, which follows, means even more: "to beg."

This word is remarkable in every way in this connection. Here is the God of heaven and of earth and Christ, his Son who by his death (v. 14, 15) reconciled all to God, and here are their high ambassadors representing God in Christ. On the other hand are transgressors (v. 19). And lo, these ambassadors are sent by God and Christ to *beg* these transgressors: "Be reconciled!" Yet here there is a secret. In Rom. 5:10 they are called "enemies." It is love, condescending love alone that wins enemies, overcomes their enmity and hostility and thus works reconciliation in them. No threats of law can do that, no demands but only the gospel voice that admonishes and begs.

Note that καταλλάγητε is the second aorist passive imperative: "be once for all reconciled." It is not a middle: "become reconciled." God is the agent who is named as the agent no less than twice in v. 18, 19.

This is subjective reconciliation. No man can produce it in himself even to the least fraction. God must do so by his word of the reconciliation (v. 19). The dative τῷ Θεῷ is the ἑαυτῷ, "to himself," which was used twice in v. 18, 19: "God reconciles to himself." The synergistic reasoning is fallacious that, since God tells men to be reconciled, men must have the ability to obey. The imperative is passive; it does not say: "Reconcile yourselves to God!" "Turn *thou* me, and I shall be turned!" Jer. 31:18. Reconcile *thou* me, and I shall be reconciled! Every gospel imperative is full of the divine power of grace to effect what it demands. If it counted on even the least power in the sinner it would never secure the least effect. Jesus calls this the Father's drawing (John 6:44; 6:65; 12:32). Every reconciled sinner *was* reconciled by God to God in Christ — by God alone. "Be reconciled to God" = "the word of the reconciliation" (v. 19). Thank God for this passive verb.

21) It is part of the ambassadors' word, which has been deposited with them by God so that they may convey it to the transgressors: **Him who did not know sin, for us he made sin in order that we on our part may become God's righteousness in connection with him.** This is one of the most tremendous statements written by Paul's pen. It is so tremendous because it so completely and in such a striking form reveals what God has done for us. Therefore, too, no connective joins it to the foregoing. Here is the objective ground of our reconciliation and together with it the definition of our personal reconciliation which is expressed as God's purpose.

The object and the verb are reversed, hence both are strongly emphatic: "him who knew no sin — he made sin." Even the predicate accusative is placed before the verb: "sin he made." He who knew no sin = "a Lamb without blemish and without spot," I Pet.

1:19. "Which of you convinceth me of sin?" John 8:46. "Who did no sin," I Pet. 2:22. The aorist τὸν μὴ γνόντα is constative; it covers the whole life of Jesus. Γινώσκω has its intensive meaning: *nosse cum affectu et effectu*. Jesus never knew sin as we do by sinning, by in any degree realizing sin in himself. Tempted to sin, he did not, even could not, sin. No sinful motive or desire ever entered his soul. The Son of God was made flesh, but "without sin" (Heb. 4:15), ever "separate from sinners" (Heb. 7:26), so that those who were closest to him ever beheld his sinless glory, glory as of the only-begotten, glory as of the Father (the testimony of John 1:14). Attacks on the perfect sinlessness of Christ will continue to be made by the sinners who want no such Savior from sin; they continue like other blasphemous sins.

The older grammatical supposition that the negative μή is subjective still creates confusion by raising the question in whose thought or consciousness Jesus is called sinless. But μή is the regular negative with the participle and does not concern itself with such questions. "Who knew no sin" states a negative fact, and it makes no difference to whose thought or consciousness this fact is present.

So also the discussion about anarthrous ἁμαρτία, its being abstract and its relation to the concrete, is misleading. Jesus did not know "sin," anything that is so named and designated throughout Scripture. Ἁμαρτία, "that which misses the mark," is the commonest, broadest, most general term and is used here on that account. Moreover, the ideas of sin and guilt go together, and this is the connotation of "sin" in the present connection.

Now the astounding thing is that this sinless One God "made sin for us." "Sin" is to be taken in the same comprehensive sense. God did not make him "a sinner." God did less, and he did more. God left Jesus as sinless as he was. The idea of God making anyone a sinner, to say nothing of his own Son, is unthinkable. God did something else entirely: he laid on him the iniquity of us all (Isa. 53:6) so that he bore our sins in his own body on the tree (I Pet. 2:24), so that he was made a curse for us (Gal. 3:13, ὑπέρ, "in our stead"), so that he died for all (v. 14, 15, again ὑπέρ, "instead of all"). God made Christ sin ὑπὲρ ἡμῶν by charging all that is "sin" in us against him, by letting him bear all this burden with all its guilt and penalty "in our stead" in order to deliver us. It sounds incredible that God should have done this with his own *sinless* Son. Because it is so astounding Paul puts it in this astounding way. But it is fact, God *did* this.

To the three ὑπέρ occurring in v. 14, 15 there are added three in v. 20, 21; all are used in the same sense: "instead of." Four times Christ "instead of" all (us); twice God's ambassadors acting "instead of" Christ. Each of the six is so plain when the persons involved are considered, that its meaning cannot be mistaken. Note also that the first two phrases cover "all" (v. 14, 15), the next covers "them," those who live for Christ (v. 15), while the last in v. 21 mentions "us," Paul and his fellow workers. In the first two "all," "them" and "us" are embraced. As Paul has something to say about "them" in particular, so he now has much to say about "us." Hence we have the particular mention of the smaller groups. But all that is said about them is due to what the universal phrase "instead of all" contains.

God made the sinless One sin instead of us "in order that we on our part may become God's righteousness in connection with him." Let us get the relation of the tenses. This was God's purpose when he "made" Christ sin for us (historical aorist). This purpose was fulfilled in Paul and in his assistants when Paul dictated these lines. He has just said that "we are acting as ambassadors for Christ." He is now dictating as such an ambassador. Because it is written out in the Greek, ἡμεῖς is emphatic. Paul says: God wanted me and my assistants to be justified when he made his Son sin for us. God certainly wanted the same thing for all men even as he gave his Son into death for all. But ὑπὲρ ἡμῶν and ἡμεῖς speak about Paul and his assistants alone. They are so specifically singled out because God is using them to bring the reconciliation (v. 19) and this righteousness of God in connection with Christ's death to others. This causes no difficulty whatever, especially after all that precedes from v. 14 onward. Note that γενώμεθα is an aorist and punctiliar: "get to be" or "become" in one decisive act. "Might" in our versions should not be regarded as being only potential, and "become" does not denote a process. The sense is: be justified, declared righteous by God in connection with Christ's sacrifice for the sin of all men.

Regarding "God's righteousness" see Rom. 1:17 and 3:21, 22 where Paul expounds this great theme of Romans: δικαιοσύνη Θεοῦ. God's righteousness, in brief, is the quality that is stamped upon us by God himself when in heaven, on his judgment seat, he renders the judicial verdict that acquits us of all sin and guilt "gratuitously, by his grace, by means of the ransoming that is in Christ Jesus," Rom. 3:24, which see at length. The genitive is that of source and origin. No sinner can possibly secure the quality, status, and standing of righteousness before God except by God's own verdict of acquittal. The instant that verdict is pronounced he is δίκαιος, "righteous." And this verdict God pronounces upon no sinner except ἐν αὐτῷ, "in connection with him," Christ, whom he made sin for us, who died instead of all (v. 14, 15). The connection is faith as Rom. 3:21, etc., sets forth so fully and so completely.

What makes this statement of Paul's so remarkable is the fact that he does not say: be given, get, receive, have God's righteousness, but "become." It is identifying us with God's righteousness in Christ. The expression constitutes a climax. Justification has never been put into stronger or intenser terms. Yet the fact that God made Christ sin is equally strong and intense. The two expressions also properly go together in their contrast: Christ all *sin* for our sakes and in our stead; all of us God's *righteousness* in connection with Christ. Sin — righteousness, true opposites. For this reason, after speaking of reconciliation, not "reconciliation," but "righteousness" is the most exact word.

Moreover, only righteousness, this righteousness that God's verdict declares, can accomplish our personal reconciliation to God. God can embrace only those who are righteous as being subjectively reconciled to him; and only they who let go their sin and accept God's righteousness by faith in Christ are personally reconciled and as such return to him. And "God's" is in place, "*God's* righteousness," with the same emphasis it has in v. 18: "These things all from *God,*" and "*God* was in Christ." God, the Reconciler, and we reconciled when we become God's righteousness. Let us dwell on these points and thus enter into the fulness and the blessedness of Paul's thought. These are the wondrous realities that are here stated for us in perfect language; we only stammer when we try to repeat them in words of our own. They are the realities for you and for me personally. What an incentive for apprehending them!

CHAPTER VI

XIX. *Working Jointly with God*

1) Δέ, "moreover," adds the other, somewhat different point. Παρακαλοῦμεν is parallel with δέομαι in 5:21: first "we beg" all to be reconciled; next "we admonish" those who are reconciled. At the same time παρακαλοῦμεν continues God's παρακαλεῖν mentioned in 5:20: God admonishes through us; in the same way, but now expressed differently, the ἡμεῖς of 5:21 work jointly with God and also admonish. The connection with the foregoing is linguistically perfect and is made in the simplest manner.

The chapter division of the A. V. is quite correct and in place. The R. V. makes a break at 5:20, which is not correct since 5:20, 21 belongs to the preceding. These two verses still speak about reconciliation as does 5:18, 19.

This is not all. When Paul is describing "the ministry of the reconciliation" (called so in 5:18) with its begging: "Be reconciled to God!" no pronominal object is added. Paul does not say: "we are begging *you*," nor does he add *whom* we thus beg to be reconciled. The Corinthians were already reconciled; the call mentioned in 5:20 cannot be addressed to them. We need not be told to whom it is addressed, for it lies on the surface that Paul and his assistants are ever calling on those who are not yet reconciled to God, whether they be located in Corinth or in any other place, to be thus reconciled. But in 6:1 we now have the pronoun "you": you Corinthians who have long ago heard the call to be reconciled and have accepted the grace of God, do *you* not receive this heavenly grace in vain; we and you are now living in the acceptable time, in the blessed day of salvation. This absence of "you" or other persons in 5:20 and the presence of "you" (ὑμᾶς) in 6:1, are most important for understanding the connection and the progress of thought.

As ambassadors of Christ (5:20) Paul and his assistants keep doing two things: calling on men everywhere to be reconciled and then admonishing those who heed and have heeded this call (here the Corinthians to whom this is written) to receive God's grace "not in vain." It is this double work of the ambassadorship, of the ministry of the reconciliation (5:18) with the word of the reconciliation (5:19), which is executed by Paul and his assistants in the way which he describes at length in 6:3-10. This description exhibits Paul and his assistants to the Corinthians as living examples of what it means to receive the grace of God not in vain. This is the pattern that the Corinthians should copy. To be sure, the pattern is that of ambassadors, of Christ's ministers, and the Corinthians are not such ministers. But "like priest, like people." "Brethren, be followers together of me, and mark them which walk so as ye have us for an example," Phil. 3:17; also II Thess. 3:9; I Pet. 5:3. When the Corinthians, each in his station of life, emulate Paul and his assistants in the spirit with which they exhibit God's grace in their lives, they will indeed not have received that grace in vain.

But Paul's purpose in writing this letter is to complete the work of winning back the Corinthians to himself. The breach recently caused by opponents of Paul's who invaded Corinth (which Titus reported to be healing) is to be completely healed. The old, sound relation between the Corinthians and Paul is to be fully re-established. For this reason Paul again expands on the way in which he and his assistants conduct their ambassadorship (compare 4:7-15). How can the Corinthians hold aloof from such ministers as these? How can they at all listen to men who deviate from the true doctrine in so many respects and who in their lives showed a spirit which was so unlike that of Paul?

The Corinthians knew only to well that every word of 6:3-10 was true in regard to Paul. No polemics against the invaders are inserted. Here is something that was stronger (and it dominates the entire first part of the epistle, chapters 1 to 7), namely drawing the Corinthians into Paul's own spirit of complete devotion to the Lord. When this knits the Corinthians and Paul together as it should, they will be proof against all enemies of Paul who may appear in Corinth, against all vicious influence which seeks to separate them from Paul and his blessed teaching.

Moreover, as jointly working (with God) we also keep admonishing for you not in vain to accept the grace of God. For the word is:

> **At an acceptable season I gave thee favorable hearing,**
>
> **And in salvation's day I came to thy aid.**

Lo, now is a season highly acceptable; lo, now (is) **salvation's day!**

"Jointly working" has its ample explanation in the ministry God gave us (5:18), in the word he deposited with us (5:19), and in our being ambassadors for Christ. As such "we keep working together with God"; the implication of σύν cannot be "together with you Corinthians" or just "we in association with each other." In addition (καί) to our other work we continue with this admonition (on παρακαλέω see 5:20) and urging: "for you not in vain to accept the grace of God." The emphasis is first on "not in vain" and next on the object which is placed before the verb, "the grace of God," finally on the subject "you" which is placed after the verb. The insertion of ὑμᾶς into this infinitive clause and not immediately after the main verb "we keep admonishing" yields the following sense: we so admonish all who have been reconciled to God, and this our admonition applies in particular also to you Corinthians.

On "the grace of God" see 1:2. Here, however, the unmerited *favor Dei* is specifically the reconciliation which God has effected both for and in us as described in 5:18-21. This is "grace" indeed, yea "the grace," grand and specific. Δέχομαι is "to accept," which is a little more precise than "to receive." The aorist infinitive denotes the one act of our acceptance, that comprised in faith.

"In vain," εἰς κενόν, means "in an empty, hollow way," the commentary on which is James 1:22: "doers of the Word, and not hearers only," also James 2:17, 20: "dead" faith, "inactive" faith (ἀργός). Matt. 13:20, 21. "The grace of God" sounds good to not a few, and they readily accept it; but they do not let it penetrate them so that the power of this grace works in them. When the tests come, tribulation, etc., the emptiness of the acceptance appears. This blight of emptiness at times also sets in later. God's minister-ambassadors must thus keep on admonishing just as Paul does here.

2) With γάρ and utilizing Isa. 49:8, and re-enforcing it by exclamations Paul's admonition reminds the Corinthians of the blessed καιρός or time period that God has sent them. Paul has in mind the present time in which the rich grace of God is brought to the Corinthians. What a pity if they accepted it only in an empty way! The formula of quotation λέγει is usually explained by supplying "God" or "the Scripture" (B.-D. 130, 3), but it is better to regard the verb as impersonal: *es heisst* (B.-P. 736), which the

English cannot duplicate except by the passive "it is stated" or the active "the word is."

The two poetic lines cited from Isaiah are synonymous, and Paul merely adopts them because they express what he wants to impress upon the Corinthians. "The acceptable time" = "salvation's day," the latter defines the former. Καιρός is a definite period which is always marked as such, here by its being "acceptable," i. e., accepted by God as the proper time for bringing his grace in Christ also to the Corinthians. "Salvation's day" is practically a compound and hence is decidedly definite because of the genitive. The A. V. renders this: *"the* day of salvation," while the R. V. loses the force of the word by translating it: "*a* day of salvation." This καιρός, this ἡμέρα, is the accepted one so that God may bring "salvation," rescue and deliverance and the consequent secure condition. Hence we have the aorist form of the verbs, the one explaining and intensifying the other: "I gave thee favorable hearing" (I listened favorably to thy cries of distress, σού genitive: hearing a person speak) — "I came to thy aid."

Paul adds the emphatic exclamations: "Lo, now is a season highly acceptable; lo, now is salvation's day!" Isaiah's word fits most exactly the "now," this time period, this day. "Lo — lo!" you Corinthians, do not fail to note it well! Instead of δεκτός Paul uses the intenser εὐπρόσδεκτος, "highly or well acceptable." A more acceptable time will not come. How tragic if, while we are living at this time and getting into contact with God's grace and salvation, it would finally become manifest that we had done so only in a superficial, empty way!

The time and day which Paul has in mind is that in which God is sending out the gospel into the whole world. We still live in this blessed time. See all those whom he has already heard so favorably with his grace, to whose aid he has come with his salvation! But there is also a more specific sense in the terms. Luther pointed it out to the German nation of his day when the pure gospel ran through all of Germany and beat down upon the land like a great shower of rain. He bade the Germans prize the gospel while they had it and warned them that the day might come when it could no longer be had. He bade the Germans look at the lands and the cities of Asia Minor where the gospel once flowed so freely, where the Turk now ruled and the gospel has disappeared.

The lives of individuals pass through a similar experience. Salvation's day comes, God's accepted time. Make fullest use of it, despise is not as though it might continue forever and wait on our pleasure. A time may also come when it may be too late. The disposition of these καιροί and these ἡμέραι in the case of the world, the individual nations, and the individual persons, rests in God's hands alone, in his providence which is always inscrutable to finite minds in these its workings.

3) Paul continues with two nominative participles which are followed by many phrases until in v. 9, 10 he again uses both nominative adjectives and participles. Especially in the Greek, which distinguishes the nominatives from accusatives (which is not the case in English), the construction is perfectly clear, it is a sort of duplicate to the nominative participles used in 4:8-10. There is no reason for making a parenthesis of v. 2 as our versions do and also B.-D. 465, R., and others. Others let these participles modify the "we" in "we keep admonishing" in v. 1. But this, too, is insufficient, for this "we" reaches back through the intervening verses to "us" in 5:18. Paul *used* grammar, used it for what it is intended: a flexible and a beautiful medium for expressing thought. He

was alive to all the flexibility for which the Greek is especially noted.

Every reader and every hearer without the least effort understood Paul's smooth transition to participles and all that follows even to v. 10. The surmise "that the text is not in order," that a pause in dictation intervenes, perhaps also a "sleepless night," that something has dropped out between v. 2 and 3, is unfounded. We have already (third and fourth paragraph introductory to v. 1) set forth the connection between v. 3-10 and v. 1, 2 and hence need not do so again. We act as ambassadors, etc. (5:20), and thus also admonish (6:1) and exemplify our admonition in ourselves and thus draw you Corinthians to our hearts: **giving no reason for stumbling in anything in order that the ministry be not blamed; on the contrary, as God's ministers commending ourselves in everything, in, etc., etc.** The negative and the corresponding positive are placed side by side for the sake of stronger effect.

The two words have μή because they are used with the participle. Προσκοπή occurs only here in the New Testament: "cause for stumbling," "offense" in this sense (A. V.). It is to be distinguished from σκάνδαλον, the trigger stick in a trap, to which the bait is fixed and by which the trap is sprung. This is fatal and kills whereas the other causes only the foot to strike and the person to stumble, at the most to fall and suffer only a slight hurt. These ministers of God cause no one even a slight moral or spiritual hurt in anything. So carefully they guard themselves at every point. Here is a sermon for preachers, to say nothing of church members! Offenses of preachers are especially offensive and damaging. We know how Paul acted in the domain of the adiaphora and of Christian liberty, Rom. 14:21; I Cor. 8:13.

Paul's purpose was "that the ministry be not blamed"; the subject and the verb are transposed in order to emphasize both. When the ministry is blamed because of thoughtlessness, lack of love, and lack of devotion on the part of its incumbents, men's hearts are closed to its appeal, and the cause of the gospel and of Christ suffers. Paul was blamed often enough, but wrongfully, never for a cause that he gave but only for a cause that was invented by the enemies of the gospel. As a man is known by the friends he has, so he is known by those who blame him. Get friends of whose praise you can be proud and thus enemies whose blame of you is equal to a compliment, of which you can be proud.

4) We must reverse the order of the Greek words in order to convey Paul's meaning because διάκονοι is nominative and is to be construed with the subject and not accusative and predicative to the object "ourselves." It is not "commending ourselves as God's ministers" but "as God's ministers commending ourselves," etc. We do this, Paul says, as being no less and as such men ought to do. On the question of self-recommendation Paul has already expressed himself in 3:1, etc.; 4:2; 5:12. He and his helpers had been slandered as merely recommending themselves. That slander is answered, and there is no special sting in the present connection when Paul says that we keep commending ourselves in everything. The sense is: we want people always to see in us true ministers of God, whose one recommendation it is that they act as such in every respect. They recommend themselves by letting their entire conduct as God's ministers speak for them. It always does that, and people always listen to what that conduct says. Ministers often fool themselves on that point, and some people are also fooled by them. But true spirituality and devotion to

Christ, the gospel, and the ministry are hard to imitate. An example: be a companion at cards with a man, and when he is on his deathbed he will not really want you. "Commend ourselves" is the direct opposite of "be blamed," i. e., by others; so also "in everything" matches "in nothing."

What Paul says about himself and his assistants as being "God's ministers" can easily be applied to God's people whom this ministry serves. The genitive is possessive: ministers who belong to God; he is mentioned because in 5:18 he gave the ministry of the reconciliation to us. The beautiful word "ministry," διακονία, must be noted: rendering service to others freely so that the benefit may be wholly theirs. The Corinthians had abundantly enjoyed these benefits through Paul and through his assistants.

Paul is saying a great deal here; just how much he is saying the following shows. It is not a boast but a catalog of concentrated facts, an elaboration of "in everything." Each item could be elaborated by many details. We should get an entire biography of the ministerial life of Paul and of his assistants, a wonderful volume, indeed. Some incidents, but all too few, we shall, indeed, get in chapter 11, etc.

Those who find a loose array of phrases, etc., in the following do Paul an injustice. Paul never writes loosely. His series of items is most carefully arranged. His rapid mind has often been noted, generally to prove that he outruns his expressions and his language whereas a rapid mind never does that but sees in advance and has the end present to the mind when the mind begins a thought or a list of items. This is evident here.

"Commending ourselves in everything, **in much perseverance, in tribulations, in necessities, in anxieties, in strifes, in prisons, in tumults, in labors, in sleeplessnesses, in fastings.**

Let us stop with these ten — ten to express completeness (like the Ten Commandments, the ten virgins, the ten servants, the ten talents, etc.). Ten is the grand number to indicate completeness; four, which is used three times here, is the common rhetorical number to express completeness and is so used by all good writers. Paul's ten is here composed of $1 + 3 + 3 + 3 = 10$. We at once see the principle that underlies this first list. The first phrase governs all the rest, and therefore it alone is distinguished by an adjective: "in much perseverance."

Why does "perseverance," literally, "remaining under," head the list? And why is "much" added? Ask one more question: "Why is this one alone singular while the remaining nine are plurals?" Yes, Paul has a keen mind — here is beautiful proof. "Perseverance" runs through this entire list of nine. And who will say that to endure all of those nine which, as the plurals indicate, are repeated over and over again does not require "much," yes, very much "perseverance"? All of these nine are hard to endure, not only when each is repeated, but when all nine heap up their repetitions like a mountain.

The three threes are as they should be: 1) three abstract terms to denote what must be perseveringly endured: "tribulations — necessities — anxieties," and these are not mere synonyms; 2) three concrete terms to denote heavy inflictions that are most painful to endure: "stripes — prisons — tumults," and again they are not merely synonyms; 3) three added abstract terms, one to denote exertions and two to denote deprivations. That fills the great measure to the very brim. Five additional groups await us, but none is like this one.

Now each item: "afflictions" is the most general and is derived from $θλίβω$, to press. Next, "necessities," forcings, compulsions against one's will. Third, "anxieties," the effect of the other two; the word is derived from στενός, "narrow" (4:8), as when one is in a tight place, hemmed in, full of anxiety in regard to getting out where he can breathe again. Yes, these three beautiful situations go together. To Paul and to his companions they came delightfully often. They certainly required much perseverance so that these men, facing such situations, did not grow faint (4:1, 16) and give up the ministry that was so full of such distressing experiences. If they could endure them with brave perseverance, could not the Corinthians hold out in what little share of them fell to their lot?

5) Do you wish for something that is a little more concrete and definite? Take these three which form a climax: "stripes" (like those which Paul and Silas received at Philippi, Acts 16:23, and the eight scourgings mentioned in II Cor. 11:24, 25); worse than stripes, "prisons" (thrown into jail as at Philippi; and in the case of the apostles this began early, Acts 4:3); worse than both of these, "tumults" as when the mob stoned Paul and dragged him out of the city as being dead, Acts 14:19. A few experiences of flogging by Jews or by Roman lictors, a taste of abominable jails, and a riot or two about one's house or one's person would alone be enough to take the heart out of any man. Even in Corinth itself the Jews started a riot, Acts 18:12

Another trio follows the preceding two: "labors," the word denotes what is hard, tiring, severe, without saying anything about what is accomplished as does "works." Now two negatives: "sleeplessnesses" and "fastings." In return for all the heavy labors many a sleepless night, many a foodless day and night. Since "labors" precede, loss of sleep and lack of food refer to ordinary experiences and not just to whippings, prisons, and tumults. Nor should we think only of Paul and thus perhaps of some ailment of his that caused insomnia or indigestion. These plurals refer also to all of Paul's helpers. When they took some of those long, hard journeys afoot and by boat, sleeping and eating were problems that were often not solved. Their ministry was not fitted out with parsonages, salary, perquisites, donations, comfort, and even luxuries but was graced by hardships such as the three mentioned in this group.

These are the men who tell the Corinthians not to accept God's grace in vain. The admonition comes from them with peculiar force, and the hearts of the Corinthians surely must respond to men who cling to their gospel work with wonderful perseverance "in" all these trying experiences.

6) **In purity, in knowledge, in longsuffering, in kindliness.** Two pairs and a rhetorical group of four. The A. V. lists six in this verse; but six do not constitute a unit group. One could regard the six as three pairs, which would be good; here, however, the eight ἐν are best divided into two groups of four. And this ἐν differs from the ἐν found with the preceding plurals which = "in the midst of" the experience of tribulations, etc. The present eight ἐν = "in connection with" purity, etc. They speak about what is in the hearts of Paul and of his helpers.

First "purity" of motive in all that they do and suffer. But motive, when it is ill informed though it be ever so pure in itself, leads to many a wrong deed as Jesus himself says in John 16:2. So "knowledge" is joined with purity in motive. These two constitute a pair. We at once see what a lack of either of these two would mean, and often enough one or both are lacking even in ministers. The insertion of "knowledge" has puzzled some, yet this is done only because the right motive must have also the right information.

"Longsuffering" and "kindliness" are the companion pair. Equipped with pure motive and full knowledge, the heart will exercise patience with men, will not be hasty to give up, to turn away, to cast off. Trench defines: "A long holding out of the mind before it gives room to action or passion." So also the heart will exercise *benignitas* or *bonitas*. This characterized the ministry of Jesus; it was one of kind, mild, gentle, helpful treatment of poor sinners.

These four should exhibit the effect of God's grace in the heart of every minister, who should be an example to all his flock so that grace might work the same effects in them.

Now another rhetorical four which is again in pairs: **in the Holy Spirit, in love unhypocritical, in truth's Word, in God's power.** It puzzles some to find the Holy Spirit inserted into this long list of ἐν phrases. If we group Paul's statements into six in v. 6 as the A. V. does, we cannot see why the Holy Spirit is put into fifth place, between kindliness and love. But when we group into fours, we get the last ἐν group of four, and in this group the Spirit is first. We at once see how the other three fall properly into line, each attesting the Spirit's presence in the clearest way. Rhetorically beautiful is the use of double terms after so many single terms with ἐν. "Spirit Holy — love unhypocritical" (adjectives); "Word of truth — power of God" (genitives) — all beautifully perfect in wording.

These four rise far above the fourteen that precede. The upward sweep is not a glide upward that ends with the mention of the Spirit but a leap upward that begins with him. The reader feels that the Spirit is involved in the entire fourteen that precede; now that the last, greatest, and highest are named he must be mentioned. As in the case of the first ten perseverance is not one of the ten but the one exhibited in the nine, so the Spirit is not one of these last four but the One who is back of the three. We drop mere mechanical counting. Even when the count is made correctly: 10 — 4 — 4, etc., this is not all. In each group each item is significantly placed in just its proper place. The list is perfect down to the last word.

We thus see why this group contains not only the three: Spirit — Word — power, which obviously go together, but includes love, genuine, "unfeigned" love, love without a trace of hypocrisy. The Spirit's Word with its power of God is conceived as being used ἐν or in the ministry of the reconciliation (v. 19), and thus this love must fill the minister's heart so that he may, indeed, wield this Word and this power. For this reason this love is placed before the Word and the power. Regarding ἀγάπη as the love of full understanding and corresponding purpose see 2:4. The ancient actors wore masks; "hypocrite" = one under a mask. Love is not to be a mere mask. I Cor. 13 is Paul's own wonderful description of genuine love that is wrought by the Spirit. Should not this love fill the hearts of the Corinthians as it filled these ministers who ministered to them?

7) It would be trivial to refer the weighty concept "truth's Word" to only the Christian virtue of truthfulness. We could not even consider such a meaning since "God's power" (Rom. 1:16 predicates this of the gospel) follows. Regarding "truth" see 4:2, ἀλήθεια, all the saving realities centering in God and Christ, revealed by the Spirit, embodied in the λόγος (see word in v. 19) or Word in order to be conveyed to men. The whole ministry is "in truth's Word" even as are the faith and the life of all Christians. And thus "God's power," all the saving power of God, is next. His love gave the Word with this power, and our love is to promulgate that Word and to bring its power of love to work on and in men. Wonderful, indeed, is this third group of four!

Why the A. V. and those who originally divided this chapter into verses did not make one verse of the three διά phrases seems strange. These three go together so markedly: **between the aids of the (true) righteousness on the right and on the left; between acknowledgment and despising, between bad report and good report.** Διά worries some interpreters. It need not, for its root idea is "between," and this shows what is meant here. We first have aids to the right and to the left, the ministers are "between"; we next have acknowledgment and dishonorable treatment, and again they are διά, "between"; finally, bad report and good report, "between" which the ministers go on. "Between" fits exactly.

Some regard ὅπλα as meaning "weapons," and then the right hand wields the sword and the spear, the left hand the shield, and Paul is said to be using the favorite figure of a soldier armed for fight. But the whole list is literal, and to insert a strong metaphor is unlike Paul. The figure of war, too, clashes with the rest of the list; it would be out of the line of thought. In Rom. 6:13 we have the same expressions: "present your members as ὅπλα δικαιοσύνης to God," and we are told that "weapons of righteousness" is the sense. But God does not use our bodily members as "weapons" or "arms."

Ὅπλα are any kind of equipment that aids one in his work; thus arms or weapons is the meaning only when we have a military connection. Ὅπλα alone do not refer to a soldier; not this word but the context does that. In the present connection the sense is: "the aids of the righteousness," both terms are articulated and definite: all the aids that this specific righteousness (see 5:21) which we preach by the Holy Spirit's help, with unfeigned love, in the Word of truth as the saving power of God, affords us in our work.

What these aids are calls for no elaboration. Since the three "between" phrases are synonymous, we may say that these aids are "acknowledgment" and "good report" and on the left "despising" and "bad report." God's righteousness, as this is brought by the Word with the power of grace, is not helpless and weak. It has its aids for its own effective and successful presentation. The genitive is possessive: the aids which belong to this righteousness. Paul says that we have them on both sides of us. "Right" and "left" are neuter plurals in the Greek and modify ὅπλων, literally, "the right hand and the left hand aids of the righteousness." These help us on both sides as our most adequate equipment for the ministry. Note the natural transition from "God's power" to these "aids."

8) With the first διά we have the two terms right and left; so with the next two διά we also have double terms, but these are opposites and not coordinates: "between acknowledgment and despising; between bad report and good report." It is an interesting question whether the bad as well as the good aids the ministry. The meaning of δόξα is not "glory" but, as its derivation from δοκέω shows, *Anerkennung*, favorable opinion; and its opposite is thus ἀτιμία, withholding credit, honor, or acknowledgment. We may translate "between credit and discredit." These are judgments that are based on contact. To these are added chiastically reports that are based on hearsay: "between bad report and good report." In I Tim. 3:7 Paul writes μαρτυρία καλή, "an excellent testimony from those outside," which is an entirely different matter from a report or a rumor about a minister. The bad reports of which Paul speaks are the slanders that are spread by enemies and repeated by those who hear them.

These three "between" mark the path also of faithful church members, should mark that of the Corinthians when they faithfully follow their illustrious teachers.

9) From ἐν and διά Paul advances to seven ὡς, "as." These are divided into three and four, and in the case of the third the formulation marks a break. In these seven the grouping into pairs continues, and we have striking opposites in each pair. Why this part of the list should be admired and not the preceding part and thus the whole strikes one as being strange: **as deceivers and yet true; as unknown and yet well known; as dying and yet, lo, we go on living.** All are paradoxes and yet simple facts. Decried and by so many treated "as deceivers" whose teaching leads astray, Paul and his assistants are ever found *wahrhaftig*, speaking nothing but what is true, the actual fact and reality. We have adjectives; ὡς indicates the appearance that catches the superficial eye, and καί has adversative force: "and yet."

"As unknown," men of no standing in the world, upstarts, unworthy of attention in the opinion of so many; and yet in reality "well known" wherever believers are found, their names even being written in heaven on the pages which do not show the names of so many who are admired and praised by the world. This is climaxed: "as dying," soon to disappear and to be forgotten, "and yet, lo," the astonishing thing is "we go on living." The interjection and the finite verb indicate that a break has occurred, and that the three statements form a unit. Men pointed at these ministers and considered them imposters, unknown upstarts, bound soon to die because of the way in which they worked. But look at the other side! They were content to be so looked upon — how could the world really understand them? On the dying see 4:10, etc.

Again: **as being chastised and yet not made to die; as grieved but always rejoicing; as poor but making many rich; as having nothing and yet thor-**

oughly having everything. Our versions regard the first of these four as a part of v. 9, probably because in Ps. 118:17, 18 living and not dying, being chastised and not given over to die, are combined, and because Paul apparently makes use of the thoughts of this psalm. On chastisement see Heb. 12:5-11. The constant afflictions which these ministers bore seem even to Christians as though, to say the least, God was constantly chastising them for all kinds of faults. Ἀποθνῄσκω is intransitive, "to die," θανατόω transitive, "to make to die." Always appearing to men as dying, we yet keep on living by God's grace; always as if God is chastening us in his displeasure and yet is never putting us to death.

10) "As being grieved" by being treated so "but always rejoicing." In fact, Paul writes: "Let us also glory in our tribulations," Rom. 5:3, etc. Here we have δέ and not καί as if to say that we are really not grieved, we ever rejoice, "ever," ἀεί, being added. Being chastised and grieved are a pair; so are "poor" and "having nothing." Πτωχός is "poor" in the sense of crouching and cringing as a beggar when asking for alms. The word is expressive of what one sees everywhere in the Orient, whining beggars. So we are considered, Paul says, "but" (another δέ) we are "making many rich," rich beyond all earthly wealth.

Yes, "as having nothing and yet thoroughly having everything," κατέχειν with perfective κατά, to hold fast. Matt. 5:5, the meek inherit the earth; "the kingdom ours remaineth," Luther. It is no loss to have nothing and no gain to have everything in the way in which the world has and has not; but to have as Christians have is to have everything, no matter how little they have according to the world's way of having. For "all things" work together for our good, Rom. 8:28, as if we owned them, and were our slaves.

11) All that Paul has been saying about himself and his assistants in regard to the way in which they conduct themselves in their office (from 3:1 onward), about their inner feelings, motives, purposes, spirit, experiences, etc., all that climaxes in this last admonition not to accept the grace of God in an empty way and then reveals how they themselves act under this grace (6:1-10), now comes to a head in a fervent appeal to the Corinthians which names them and speaks even as a father to his children. **Our mouth has opened to you, Corinthians; our heart has been expanded wide.**

Note the effect of the asyndeton. The two perfect tenses refer to all that Paul has been saying; they do not refer to what follows in v. 14, etc. All these personal, intimate things which Paul has been saying are such as he would be reticent about under all ordinary circumstances; but to you Corinthians, Paul says, we have opened our mouth, we have said them all. "Our heart has been expanded wide." We have let you see our very feelings, our inner motives, our deepest expriences, all for love of you. The passive "has been expanded" means by you, by our desire that you may reciprocate with like love and confidence. The effect of the perfect tenses is: our mouth is still open toward you in what we have said; our heart is still expanded to take you in with all its love.

We have continually noted this reaching out to enfold the Corinthians. It is now expressed openly and without restraint. It is for this reason that Paul is writing and writing in the way he has done. As we dwell on what he has written we see that he has laid bare his heart in this letter as in no other. Such a man, such men in their hard, hard ministry! How could the Corinthians help responding? Men had come to Corinth to make the Corinthians disaffected toward Paul and his assistants. Here is his answer; he lets his inner heart speak for himself. The Corinthians cannot resist that.

12) **You are suffering no restraint in us, you are suffering restraint only (δέ) in your own feelings.** The verb means to narrow in, to crowd, and the passive to be crowded in, "to suffer restraint." No, no, Paul says, there is nothing in us to hold you aloof, to put you under restraint; nothing in us to make you hold back as though you could not be free toward us as friend is free with friend, one heart toward another. And with the same open heart of love Paul adds: "you are suffering restraint only in your own feelings," and that should certainly not be the case.

The σπλάγχνα (always plural) are the nobler viscera, heart, lungs, liver, which are conceived by the Greek as the seat of the feelings and affections and are so translated here; "bowels" in the A. V. is misleading since it is generally used with reference to the intestines; "affections" in the R. V. is too narrow. Any restraint on the part of the Corinthians is due entirely to their own wrong "feelings" toward Paul and his assistants. Nothing stands between them but these feelings, which have no justification whatever. In order to remove them Paul has bared his whole heart to show the Corinthians all that is there.

13) **Now for the same reciprocation — as to children do I speak — do you, too, be expanded wide!** Paul asks that the Corinthians reciprocate by expanding their hearts wide in the same way as he and his assistants are expanding theirs. Then nothing will remain between them to cause restraint, a feeling of not being considered and treated aright. Wide open is the heart of Paul to embrace the Corinthians, will they not in the same way reciprocate and open theirs wide again to embrace him with the old warmth?

The accusative τὴν αὐτὴν ἀντιμισθίαν has received various explanations: adverbial accusative R. 487 ("as to the same reciprocity"), remote accusative with a passive (R. 486), or pregnant for "the same expansion as reciprocation" (B.-D. 154), which would be the cognate accusative with the passive. Take your choice. "The *same* reciprocation" is one "in like kind" (as the R. V. circumscribes), "in the same" (as the A. V. prefers). But "recompense" scarcely brings out Paul's idea. The aorist imperative is urgent but with the urgency of a great desire and love; moreover, it calls for one act of being fully expanded and not for only a gradual expanding. The passive is significant: "be expanded," i. e., by us whose heart has so expanded toward you. Love creates reciprocating love. The parenthesis: "as to children do I speak," inserts the note of great tenderness. The Corinthians are to hear a father's paternal voice, are to respond and to reciprocate as τέκνα, the word for "children" when the connotation is that of dearness.

The criticism that these three appealing verses are not in their proper place, do not fit here, come in without preparation is unfounded. Such criticism, to say only one thing, has failed to feel the heartthrobs, the expansion and the reaching out of a heart of love that are manifested in all of the preceding. For that reason, too, so much of what Paul says in the foregoing about his office, experiences, and conduct is regarded as being merely didactic and not in keeping with the style of a letter, as being parts that could well be omitted, which would improve the letter. But all such comment does not appreciate the spirit, the inner motive, and the purpose of Paul.

XX. *"Come out from Their Midst and Be Separate!"*

14) The call to reciprocate, to expand wide their hearts, and to take into them their old teachers, the founders of their congregation, includes complete, final separation from all others who are ranged on the op-

posite side. The positive ever stands opposed to its negative.

These others are here set forth in their fullest, sharpest opposition. Let us catch the full spirit of this chapter! Following the great reconciliation with God through Christ's death with its ministry of this reconciliation (5:18-21) there comes the admonition not to accept this grace of God in an empty way (6:1). Already here there is the cue for the opposites which are now presented together with the call for separation. It is an empty grasping at God's reconciliation and grace not to see the impossibility of trying to avoid this separation. Now is the acceptable time, now is salvation's day (6:2).

All this is intensified by the personal example of Paul and his fellow workers which is presented in the grand section 6:3-13. Here there is full devotion to God, to his reconciliation and grace; here are God's ministers who are leading the way. And here they open wide their hearts to take the Corinthians into this fellowship of God's grace (v. 11-13). Will the Corinthians not reciprocate, in the same way open their hearts wide to these their ministers? Then they will, indeed, break every contrary connection; they, too, will become wholly separate. It could not be otherwise.

This new paragraph matches v. 3-10 in rhetorical beauty; Paul intends that it should. The fervor of his utterance continues in the same flow. See the conclusion at the end of 7:1 for contrary opinions.

Do not try to be heterogeneously yoked up with unbelievers! The very idea should appear monstrous to you. Μὴ γίνεσθε with the present participle is a periphrastic present imperative (R. 375) and is conative in this connection: do not try, do not ever incline or begin to be so yoked up. This verb has been found only here, the adjective ἑτερόζυγος appears in Lev. 19:19, LXX. The idea expressed by ἕτερος, "different," is intense: a yoke that is utterly alien and foreign to you Corinthians who have accepted the grace and reconciliation of God and the blessed yoke of Christ (Matt. 11:29).

The dative is associative (R. 529): "with or in association with unbelievers." There is no article and thus their quality is emphasized, and at the same time all, whoever they may be, that have this quality are included. The reference is to Deut. 22:10 which forbade harnessing an ox and an ass, a clean and an unclean beast, together to a plow. Paul uses this passage in a figurative way: the believer has been cleansed, the unbeliever has refused to be cleansed. What business have they under the same yoke? It will always be the unbeliever's yoke, namely his unbelief. For never would the unbeliever take the believer's yoke of faith; it is always the other way. The unbeliever would laugh at the suggestion of his taking on faith's yoke; yet, strange to say, instead of equally scorning unbelief's yoke, many a believer accepts it upon his neck and even imagines that he can still retain faith's yoke.

Here again Paul employs just a few words; but they speak volumes, they contain an overwhelming argument, they strike at the heart of the whole danger that is threatening believers, they drive home a conquering appeal. What a picture: a believer with his neck under the unbeliever's yoke! What business has he in such an unnatural, self-contradictory association? What is he, the believer, doing by helping to pull the plow or the wagon of the unbeliever's unbelief? That yoke breaks the necks of those who bear it. God delivered us from it; can we possibly think of going back to that frightful yoke? See what Paul and his helpers are doing (v. 3-10); read this admonition in that light.

Ἄπιστοι is exactly the proper word; the Corinthians, then, are πιστοί. These trust God's grace, those refuse such trust. To be yoked together means that these are joined with those in their refusal to trust. For the association referred to is this very one of faith joining hands with unbelief. Contacts outside of this domain, as long as they do not lead to this contact and association, come under Paul's word written in I Cor. 5:10.

"With unbelievers" mentions the extreme. Some read this and the following like the Pharisees read the commandments: Thou shalt not kill, shalt not commit adultery! as if this forbids *only* the extreme. Did Jesus, then, expound in vain in Matt. 5:21, etc., by showing that every extreme includes everything of the same nature that has not yet reached that extreme? To be sure, the extremes murder and adultery must be named, for many go that far; but this forbids even the very first step in that direction. This is true with regard to total unbelief which makes open mock of Christ. It includes every bit of unbelief, every repudiation of Christ's doctrine, every little yoke that is not of the true faith. Besser is right when in these yokes he finds a reference to unionism with those who repudiate any part of the Word.

It ought not to be necessary to warn against this unnatural yoking together. Paul's elaboration and our constant experience show that it is only too necessary in fact. The Corinthians had been going back to the evil yoke. When invaders arrived, they had listened to them, had begun to believe their false teachings, had begun to turn from the apostle. These things have been repeated. Paul's words are not an academic discussion. These imperatives are personal. His elucidations ($\gamma\acute{\alpha}\rho$) are pertinent to the Corinthians in the highest degree. **For what partnership (is there) for righteousness and lawlessness?**

Five self-answering questions shed their penetrating light on Paul's admonition. What is as wide apart as Lazarus in Abraham's bosom and Dives in the torments of hell cannot be joined in a union in Christ or elsewhere. In this first question *the inner quality* of believers and of unbelievers is placed side by side. The copula is omitted for the sake of greater emphasis; we have two common Greek datives with ἐστί (εἶναι): "is for," i. e., belongs to. Μετοχή (μετά + ἔχειν, to have together) = partnership, sharing together.

The fact that "lawlessness" is the second dative does not imply that both datives refer only to conduct: the believer's righteous life and the unbelievers unrighteous, lawless life, so that the question would be: "What partnership is there between good works and evil works?" It is "righteousness" that determines its opposite "lawlessness," and not the reverse. Paul's progression is orderly: faith and unbelief and now righteousness and its opposite. The righteousness of the believer is that which he has by faith, the imputed righteousness of Christ which is so pertinently mentioned in 5:21 in connection with the reconciliation: "that we may become God's righteousness in him (Christ)." Due to God's verdict of acquittal, this quality belongs to the believer.

The unbeliever has no such acquittal, his quality is entirely "lawlessness." That is God's verdict in regard to him. "Thou hatest all workers of iniquity," Ps. 5:5. Rom. 8:7, 8. All the unbeliever's righteousnesses are filthy rags, Isa. 64:6. "Without fear of God, without trust in him, and with fleshly appetite," *Augsb. Conf.* II. In Rom. 2 Paul convicts all of the moralists, both pagan and Jewish, by means of the very law which they use to reform men; that law condemns even the moralists as being full of lawlessness (study the author's exposition of Rom. 2). The point to be noted here is that both δικαιοσύνη and ἀνομία refer to God's judgment: he pronounces righteous, and the believer thus has God's righteousness in Christ (5:21);

his law pronounces every unbeliever lawless; his law condemns that lawlessness.

"Or" marks the second question as being an alternative to the first. So these two are a pair. This is the conjunctive "or" which is to be distinguished from the disjunctive. The third question and the fifth are introduced by δέ, "moreover," and thus turn to a different angle; but a second "or" unites the third and the fourth. All this means that Paul is not using five coordinates, which would be unrhetorical, but three, namely two pairs and a single term. In such a succession the third and last is often the longest and the most ample. When, as here, it is but a single term after two doubles, this produces a kind of sharp halt and arrests attention. That is exactly what Paul desires. Many a man might go to school to Paul and learn even fine Greek style, not for style's sake, indeed, but for perfect transmission of thought and thought effect.

Or, what communion (is there) **for light with darkness?** From the attributes righteousness and lawlessness we are taken back to *the powers which produce* them. The synonyms are most carefully chosen. If righteousness and lawlessness could exist in the same persons, there would be a μετοχή or partnership; but if light and darkness operated together, they would be in κοινωνία, in "communion" or fellowship. But, like the attributes, they exclude each other by their very nature; where the one is, it drives out the other. The dative φωτί is the same as the previous two datives after ἐστί understood. R. 1051 has the idea that the substantive κοινωνία "has enough verbal consciousness left to govern" a dative. Here it does not need to have.

God himself is "light," and in him is no darkness at all, I John 1:5. Christ is the true light, John 1:9, the light of the world, John 8:12, and his Word is the light of life. This light power has entered the believer and makes him a child of light, Matt. 5:14; John 12:36; Eph. 5:8, and so the believer walks in the light, John 12:35, 36; I John 1:7, although there is still some darkness in him because his old nature has not been entirely put off. He is also a "partaker of the inheritance of light," Col. 1:12. Light = the divine, saving truth, concrete and full reality in God, Christ, the Word; but always active, powerful, streaming out.

Its opposite is "darkness," lie, falsehood, which are concreted in Satan, demons, the world; it is also always active, powerful, seeking to envelope and to penetrate. In the beginning God separated light from darkness (Gen. 1:4), and this separation is typical also of light and darkness in the spiritual sense. "Ye were once darkness but are now light in the Lord," Eph. 5:8. "Have no fellowship with the unfruitful works of darkness," Eph. 5:11. The devil and his angels are "the rulers of the darkness of this world," Eph. 6:12. All his followers walk in darkness, John 3:19, and shall be cast into outer darkness, Matt. 22:13; 25:30; II Pet. 2:17. Out of this spiritual darkness God has called the believers, I Pet. 2:9; from it he delivered them, Col. 1:13. Light brings life, darkness is death.

15) Moreover, what agreeing of Christ (is there) **with Beliar?** In what word, thought, purpose, work do these two agree? This question advances to the opposite *personal rulers* that are back of the qualities and of the powers. Συμφώνησις, act of agreeing, occurs only here and in ecclesiastical writers, συμφώνημα, the result, is a later word (M.-M. 599). The question is: Do these two ever agree? The fact that light and darkness are to be understood in a soteriological sense is clear from the mention of the σωτήρ and of the destroyer in this question.

"Christ" has obtained our righteousness for us (5:21), was made unto us righteousness (I Cor. 1:30), and is our everlasting light (Rev. 21:23). As "Christ," the Anointed, he is our Prophet, High Priest, and King. We prefer the reading "Beliar" to "Belial" (our versions). The former = "lord of the forest," the latter "worthlessness," Stellhorn, *Woerterbuch*, Abbott-Smith, *Lexicon*. The latter, namely Belial, is used as a common noun and is translated by the LXX as transgressor, impious, foolish, pest, and Milton describes Belial as a sensual profligate. The Jews used Beliar as a title for Satan. Christ came to destroy the works of the devil; that is his act of agreement with him.

The companion question is: **Or what portion** (is there) **for a believer together with an unbeliever?** This advances us to the *personal subjects* involved. In fact, all these questions focus in these persons and are intended for *us*.

The believer is one who is justified by faith (Rom. 3:28), the bearer of the highest blessing (Rom. 4:6, 7), at peace with God (Rom. 5:1), assured of eternal salvation (Mark 16:16). The light of the glory of God in the face of Jesus Christ has shined in his heart (II Cor. 4:6); he walks no longer as the Gentiles in the vanity of his mind, with an understanding darkened (Eph. 4:17), but presses forward toward the prize of high calling in Christ Jesus (Phil. 3:14). The unbeliever ("infidel," A. V., but not in the special sense of a disbeliever in the existence of God) has the very opposite of all this. He has been judged already, and he "shall not see life" (John 3:18); he is not of Christ's sheep (John 10:26); he shall not enter into God's rest (Heb. 3:18, 19); yea, he shall be damned (Mark 16:16) and be cast into the lake of fire (Rev. 20:15).

As subjects of their respective lords, what "portion" have they together? What the one has, the other has not: righteousness, pardon, spiritual light and life, peace, hope of salvation, a place in heaven. The portions of these two diverge at every point. The words πιστός and ἄπιστος without the article refer to any and every believer, any and every unbeliever. The proofpoint of this question brings the whole matter down into the very experience of each individual Christian. He must realize that not only righteousness, light, and Christ as such are utterly at variance and contradictory to lawlessness, darkness, and Beliar, but that this contradiction comes to an issue in his own heart and bars him completely from a yoke fellowship with an unbeliever.

16) We reach the climax in this final question. The others are pairs. In each pair the point of the question is divided into two, which makes the one question a double one. Qualities (righteousness, lawlessness) go with the powers that produce them (light, darkness); so these make up one question. Again, to ask about Christ and Beliar with reference to us is also to ask about believer and unbeliever, which again makes one question that has two parts. But in the final question no division into two members is necessary, for in reaching the climax the question is about us as being united with God and is thus complete in itself: **Moreover, what accord** (is there) **for God's sanctuary with idols?** All that is needed is to point out: **for we on our part are the living God's sanctuary even as God said, etc.** In the preceding pair of questions we had persons, but the doubling divided them into two: Christ — believer. Now the final, highest question unites and asks about us as "God's sanctuary." God and we are joined in this term; we have *the persons in their ultimate relation.*

The point of the question is misunderstood when it is said that nothing can be asked beyond God because he is supreme. The subject is not God. The question is not one about God and idols. We have what is more than that already in Christ and Satan (Beliar). This question is one about "God's sanctuary," God *united* with us. It rises above Christ and the believer, one who embraces the Savior by faith. To such a one God himself descends and dwells in him. This is the ultimate. "God's sanctuary" is absolutely for God alone. "I am the Lord thy God; thou shalt have no other gods before me." The word used is not ἱερόν, a temple including its courts and auxiliary buildings; it is ναός, the inner sanctuary. In Jerusalem it was the Holy and the Holy of Holies and not the courts and the other structures. In Solomon's Temple the presence of God filled the Sanctuary with a cloud.

Now consider "together with idols" and συγκατάθεσις, "depositing votes together." False gods, idols, and everything for which they stand, all their lies, all their false worships, are like a company that is able to sit together, talk together, vote together. They have no difficulty about it at all. They do not even clash. They combine in a pantheon. One may add a new god and idol at any time. Athens was full of gods, and the Athenians at first thought Paul was bringing only another god of this kind. A pagan has room in his heart for many goods. A whole mass of them dwells on Olympus. The German Walhalla has them feasting together. Their mark is unionism, syncretism. Thus also is everything for which they stand. Can God's sanctuary be placed in this company? Paul's question does not ask about God's sanctuary and the sanctuaries of idols; this is not an ellipsis as some think. The question goes beyond that. It does not inquire whether one can go into God's sanctuary and then also go into the sanctuaries of various idols. It asks whether an idol or idols can be carried into God's sanctuary there to speak and to vote in concord with God. This was the crime of Ahaz and of other kings of Juda. The whole idea is monstrous.

Some feel that Paul is thinking only of actual idols as he does in I Cor. 8 where he speaks about attending idols' feasts, etc. But Paul has started with "unbelievers," and his last question was about "believer" and "unbeliever." In his final admonition (7:1) he tells us that he is speaking of "all defilement of flesh and spirit" and of its opposite, "holiness in God's fear." "Idols" is a concrete expression for this double defilement; this expression at the same time indicates the extreme of such defilement. And again the extreme includes all lesser types and forms. All pagan gods can sit and vote harmoniously together; all the lies they represent, all the defilements of body, and all the defilements of spirit, all immoralities and moral filth, and all lying doctrines and errors of mind and spirit, since all agree in falseness and are fathered by Beliar, are in basic accord. But are *we*, we who are God's sanctuary? Can we admit into ourselves (flesh or spirit) even one of these idols or defilements, one immorality, one religious lie?

"For" explains: "*We* (emphatic ἡμεῖς: we on our part; we are the ones who) are the living God's sanctuary." We need not pause to consider the reading "you" which is found in some texts; for in 7:1 Paul writes, "Let us cleanse *ourselves*," and this follows immediately after the address "beloved," which shows that "we" includes the Corinthians and Paul and his assistants: we Christians all. Paul adds the participle: "the living God." All the idols are dead. The hearts that embrace them embrace what is devoid of life. In all these defilements of flesh and of spirit there is no life but only death.

"The living God's sanctuary" is a mystic expression: "Ye in me, and I in you . . . If a man love me, he will keep my Word: and my Father will love him, and we will come unto him, and make our abode with him," John 14:20, 23. What the old Jewish sanctuary foreshadowed is in the most blessed way fulfilled in every Christian heart: the living God dwells in him as in a sanctuary. There is no difference whether the individual Christian is named or the whole body of believers, "the church of the living God" (I Tim. 3:15), "an holy sanctuary (ναός) in the Lord — an habitation of God in the Spirit" (Eph. 2:21), "a spiritual house" (I Pet. 2:5).

Even as God said: I will dwell in them and will walk about in them and will be their God, and they shall be my people. The subject and the verb are reversed: "as said God," thus both are emphasized. This formula of quotation occurs only here. That is due to the fact that Paul uses a catena of Biblical expressions and not an exact quotation from any one Old Testament passage. But note well that Paul calls what Moses and the prophets wrote God's own Word: "God said it." He is the real speaker and none other. This is one of the strong incidental proofs for verbal inspiration, and they are scattered throughout the Scriptures. The citation draws upon Lev. 26:11, 12: "And I will set my tabernacle among you . . . and I will walk among you, and I will be your God, and ye shall be my people." Also upon Ezek. 27:27: "My tabernacle also shall be with them: yea, and I will be their God, and they shall be my people." The latter statement occurs often: Hos. 2:23; Jer. 24:7; 30:22; 31:33; 32:38; etc.

The blessedness of this union is not understood until we see it as God's intention from the beginning and note how it realized itself step by step when God dwelt with the patriarchs of old, travelled with his people through the desert in the pillar of fire and in the cloud, manifested his presence in the Tabernacle and in the Temple, in the words of all the prophets, finally in his own Son incarnate (who calls himself ναός in John 2:19) and in the Spirit who was shed abroad at Pentecost. All this shall reach its climax when John's vision shall be fulfilled: "And I saw a new heaven and a new earth. ... And I heard a great voice out of the throne, saying: 'Behold, the tabernacle of God is with men, and he shall dwell with them, and they shall be his people, and God himself shall be with them, and be their God.'"

17) On the foundation thus laid Paul makes his appeal. He puts it into the form of a deduction: **Wherefore.** But in a most striking manner he clothes it in words that are gathered from the Old Testament as though God himself is addressing the readers, Paul "doing this according to the riches of his spirit, melting together many passages into one heap and forming from them a text furnished by the entire Scriptures and one in which the sense of the entire Scriptures appears" (Luther).

Come out from their midst and be separated! says the Lord (Κύριος = *Yahweh*),

And stop touching anything unclean!

And I myself will receive you,

And I will be to you a Father,

And you shall be to me sons and daughters, **says the Lord Almighty.**

This is, first of all, an adaptation of Isa. 52:11: "Depart ye, depart ye, go out from thence, touch no unclean thing; go ye out of the midst of her; be ye clean, that bear the vessels of the Lord!" Verse 12 adds: "And the God of Israel will be your rereward," or exactly: "will gather you," hence Paul says, "will receive you." "Rereward" = rearward = rear warden, rear guard, as God in the pillar of cloud and of fire guarded the rear of the Israelites at the Red Sea. Compare also Ezek. 20:34: "And I will bring you out from the people and will gather you," etc.

Separation runs through the entire Old Testament and equally through the New. God's children are ever a separated and a separate people. Note how the active and the passive are combined: "come out from their midst — be separated." We come out when God separates us. The verbs are aorist imperatives, peremptory and indicate decisive acts. In the second line the negative imperative is present, and this often means to stop an action already begun, which is correct here: "stop touching" (R. 853), this verb is construed with the genitive ἀκαθάρτου (no article: "anything unclean"). God's sanctuary would be defiled and could not remain his sanctuary if we touched anything unclean. First, complete separation; next, no return as much as even to touch. Here we have the commentary on "idols" occurring in v. 16: "anything unclean."

The old Pharisees and the lawyers quibbled about "who is my neighbor," but only in order to restrict the term as much as possible. So some ask in this connection: "Just what is unclean?" and reduce the term so as to leave as many contacts as possible quite clean, quite proper for Christians to touch, yea, to embrace. In fact, some think that a certain amount of uncleanness in a Christian and in a Christian congregation is really normal. Some people get so "broad" and so "liberal" and so "modern" that the tainted pleasures of an evil generation, worldly business methods, godless and Christless associations and practices of all kinds no longer appear unclean to them. The worst is the unclean in the so-called learning, religious ideas and teaching, Christless altars, prayers, religious ceremonies, Christless brotherhoods and organizations.

The Scriptures nowhere make a list of what is "unclean" but they define most perfectly: everything in body and in spirit that is contrary to our righteousness in Christ, to the light (Word), to Christ, to our faith, to ourselves as the living God's sanctuary — these, everyone and all, are "unclean," from these be so separated by God as not even to touch them. Ever anew and in ever new variation we must preach separation and not unionism. We must accept the stigma of being "separatists." The danger is seldom of doing too much in this respect but always too little. Read I Cor. 6:9, and then 3:16, 17.

18) The promises are great indeed. Ἐγώ is most emphatic: "I myself will receive you." What this implies is stated in part: "I will be to you a Father" (εἰς is predicative, R. 595). And this is amplified: "You on your part (ὑμεῖς to match ἐγώ) shall be to me sons and daughters." This means more than "children" who are dear to me. "Sons" connotes all the high rights of sonship, and "daughters" does the same. Paul seemingly refers to II Sam. 7:14 (Father and son); Jer. 31:9 (Father); Isa. 43:6 (sons and daughters). In order to magnify the greatness of these promises Paul adds from II Sam. 7:8 (see Amos 3:13; Rev. 1:8): "says the Lord Almighty." The LXX render "the Lord of hosts" Κύριος παντοκράτωρ: Yahweh who has all in his power. *Ex hac appellatione perspicitur magnitudo promissionum* (Bengel). Who would jeopardize the promises by touching anything unclean and not remaining entirely separated?

7:1) This verse so evidently belongs to the preceding that we append it here. **Accordingly, having these promises, beloved, let us cleanse ourselves from every stain of flesh and spirit, bringing to its goal holiness in God's fear!** The fervency of 6:11-13 appears in the address "beloved," the verbal of ἀγαπᾶν (on ἀγάπη see 2:4). This is not a mere term of affection since on Paul's part it implies the love of true understanding and of purpose according therewith. The great promises, all of which are pure gospel, are the motivation to which Paul appeals.

The subjunctive καθαρίσωμεν is hortative: "let us cleanse," and is properly the aorist to express a cleansing that actually cleanses. Call it the effective aorist. This aorist does not denote a single act as some suppose who then stress the idea of its being single and compare it with the single act when God cleanses in baptism and in justification. We see the force of this aorist when we note what the present subjunctive or imperative would say, namely enjoin a constant cleansing, a working at it all the time, which would rather imply that the filth is never removed or that it multiplies as fast as we cleanse it.

Some also express surprise that Paul includes himself; but this is unwarranted. Paul writes plainly about himself in Phil. 3:12-14, compare I John 1:8-10. Neither Paul nor John were perfectionists. Believers cooperate with God, and one of the activities in which they do this is in keeping themselves clean, "keeping themselves unspotted from the world" (James 1:27). They refuse to touch anything unclean (6:17). They resist temptation. It is about this self-cleansing that Paul speaks. With it goes repentance for sin that we still commit, which brings God's cleansing, who is "faithful and righteous to forgive us our sins and to cleanse us from all iniquity" (I John 1:9). We are, indeed, clean (John 13:10; 15:3; I Cor. 6:11), and yet we need to wash our feet (John 13:10); every branch must be purged to bear more fruit (John 15:2), we must fight sin and temptation.

"From every stain of flesh and spirit" = from everything that would defile either body or soul. The question is raised whether Paul could write this phrase, and the answer given is negative. First, there is the rare word (found only here in the New Testament) μολυσμός; but in I Cor. 8:7 Paul has the verb μολύνω, and the noun appears in the LXX, in Plutarch, and in Josephus. It may happen to any writer that even in a large volume he uses a certain word only once.

Next, here is stain "of flesh and of spirit," and it is asked how flesh can still be stained, and how it is possible to stain the spirit. The matter is almost elementary: σάρξ = the body in its material substance of flesh; πνεῦμα = the immaterial part as distinguished from the material (see C.-K. 946, at the bottom, where our passage just precedes). In English we usually say "soul" to refer to man's immaterial part; our "soul" approaches the Greek πνεῦμα and rises considerably above ψυχή, which is often used to designate only the "life" that animates the body.

The genitives may be regarded as objective; there are sins that stain our bodily flesh, all those that need our bodily members for their commission, and there are sins that stain the spirit or soul such as thoughts, wrong ideas, philosophies, false doctrines, etc. Away with all of them! The latter are worse than the former, less readily regarded as sins, less easily cleansed away.

The fact that the aorist subjunctive, while it is effective, denotes a process appears from the present participle: "bringing to its goal holiness in God's fear." Ἁγιωσύνη, which is one of those words that are derived from an adjective by means of the suffix -σύνη in order to express quality, is not the action of sanctifying: *Heiligung*, but the resultant quality of holiness: *Heiligkeit*. "In God's fear" (see 5:11) = in this ethical sphere. The objective genitive names God as the one who is feared.

Although it is called a low motive, one that is no longer used by Christians today, it is not only found throughout Scripture but belongs to the highest Christian motivation even as Paul uses it here. It goes hand in hand with love: love is the positive side, fear the negative; love prompts one to do what pleases God, fear prompts one to refrain from what displeases God.

Neither can dispense with the other; neither functions alone. Fear in the sense of "terror" is quite another matter. This could not be called the beginning of wisdom, Prov. 9:10; Ps. 111:10; it is the deadly dismay which the wicked experience when God's judgment finds them out.

Ἐπιτελεῖν = ἐπί plus τέλος, "to bring to a goal." The durative tense is iterative, and the participle modifies the main verb in the aorist. Thus: we cleanse ourselves effectively when in every instance that presents itself we turn from the stain of flesh and spirit and thereby ever and again reach the goal, which is holiness in God's fear. In each case the holiness is the one attained in that case. The durative participle excludes sanctification that is attained by one act; moreover, *our* actions are here stated and not an action by which God totally sanctifies us in one instant.

Now a word regarding the "criticism" which would remove 6:14-7:1 from its place in this epistle irrespective of the suggestions that are offered as to what to do with this paragraph. Every known text has this paragraph where it is. The style and the substance are Pauline. The rare words that occur offer no basis for doubt. The question raised can be based only on the idea that this paragraph does not fit properly into the connection. But this doubt is raised by the critics already in regard to 6:11-13, yes, and 6:3-13. But this raising of doubt should raise another question, namely whether these critics have followed Paul's thought in its whole connection with 6:1, 2. We have seen how 6:3-10 is exactly in line with what precedes, and how 6:11-13 is due to 6:3-10. This is true also with regard to 6:14-7:1, a paragraph that is beautifully wrought in detail and exactly in place.

Opening their hearts wide to Paul and to his assistants in reciprocity for the way in which Paul has opened his own and his assistants' hearts for them can mean only one thing, namely separation from all cooperation with unbelievers no matter who they may be. This is not merely stated, it is elaborated, and exactly as Paul would elaborate it, namely by going to the bottom of what such cooperation would mean and by casting also the full light of Scripture upon what it means. Those are mistaken who think that this paragraph repeats I Cor. 8 and is aimed only at idols, or that it is aimed only at Judaizers and opponents of Paul. Since they are believers, indeed, who have become God's righteousness in Christ (5:21), who have not received God's grace in an empty way (6:1), who recognize the day of salvation (6:3), who appreciate Paul's example (6:3-10) and thus reciprocate his appeal to them (6:11-14), the Corinthians will drop and shun all wrong connections and embrace God's great promises with Paul and his assistants and will cleanse themselves and in every instance bring their holiness to its goal. In this whole letter we find what 7:1 again reveals: Paul joins the Corinthians to himself: "let us cleanse ourselves." He does not pose as a saint who rebukes them because they are unclean. He wins them by doing what he asks them to do. See the full beauty of this mutuality and appreciate its effect on the Corinthians themselves when they read these words.

CHAPTER VII

XXI. *"Died Together and Living Together"*

1) We attach v. 1 to the preceding chapter.

2) With the call: **Make room for us!** Paul repeats 6:13: "Do you also in reciprocity expand wide!" But "make room for us" connects also with 6:14, etc., not to be yoked up heterogeneously with people from whom they ought to keep entirely aloof. These go together as do positive and negative. Note the distinction which is so characteristic of Paul: in 6:14 the Corinthians are not to put their necks under the yoke of unbelievers; now, however, Paul does not add: "Put your necks under our yoke, come and join us!" No; he delicately states it the other way: "Make room for us — let us come to you, be received in your hearts!" Paul assumes that the Corinthians repudiate the foreign yoke, shun the stain of flesh and spirit which he has pointed out (v. 1). So the Corinthians will, indeed, make room, most expansive room in their hearts for him and for his fellow workers. "Make room" is not said with a doubt on Paul's part but with the assurance that the Corinthians will answer: "We certainly will!"

With the same assurance Paul adds: **To no one did we do injustice; no one did we damage; of no one did we take advantage.** He knows the Corinthians will respond: "We know it — you did not." Note the asyndeton, the object placed forward for emphasis; the aorists to express the simple facts (the English would prefer perfects: "no one have we done injustice," etc.). These are not charges that had been made against Paul and his assistants in Corinth; Paul refers to feelings and thoughts that some of the Corinthians may have cherished during the recent past, while his opponents tried to undermine his influence in Corinth. In particular these statements refer also to the case of incest in Corinth (I Cor. 5), to Paul's orders regarding action in that case, and to what Timothy and Titus had done in Corinth in supporting those orders. As in this case, so in all that Paul had written in First Corinthians and in all that his messengers had done the Corinthians, Paul was convinced, now saw that Paul, Timothy, and Titus had done no injustice to anyone, had damaged no one, had taken advantage of no one. Paul again uses the rhetorical three.

The assurance with which Paul states this he has derived from the report that Titus has just brought to him. The first verb means that no one has suffered injustice or wrong at our hands; the second, that as a result no one has experienced damage at our hands, anything that corrupts or destroys him in his faith; the third, that Paul as an apostle, Timothy and Titus as Paul's assistants, in no way took advantage of the congregation or of any person in it since these were only simple Christians and ordinary church members.

Alas, these things have often been done by preachers and by high church officials who have domineered, overridden, tyrannized congregations and church members like κύριοι instead of being συνεργοί (1:24). We get the full force of these three statements when we keep in mind all that Paul has already written about the way in which he and his assistants conduct their office and reveal all their inmost motives and purposes, how their one aim is always "you — you": "all these things because of you" (4:15), your joy (1:25), abounding grace, a greater volume of thanks for God's glory (4:15).

None of these three statements should be considered apart from the connection in which Paul utters them. They are not self-defense, not self-justification, and certainly not a touch of "joking self-irony." Even to mention such a thing as taking *financial* advantage of any of the Corinthians is unfair to Paul.

3) When Paul adds: **I am not saying** (this) **by way of condemnation,** he guards against an assumption of a wrong implication as though he is now in a covert way condemning anyone for having thought evil things about him and his assistants. Nothing is farther from his mind. Why, he is right here asking the Corinthians to make room for them in their hearts, to make room because the Corinthians know that Paul and his assistants have been full of the purest devotion to their true spiritual interests.

So he adds: **for I have just said that you are in our hearts so that** (you and we) **died together and are living together.** Προείρηκα, "I have said before" = "I have just said," namely in 4:10-15; and what I have said thus stands. Paul dictates for both himself and Timothy (1:1) and hence uses the singular. Paul lays stress on the strongest expression that he has thus far employed in order to indicate his feeling toward the Corinthians and to designate the bond that unites them. "You are in our hearts" — how could we ever think of doing any of you a wrong or damage or seek advantage of you? "In our hearts" = in the bosom of our love — how could we thus now utter covert accusation or condemnation? We see how penetrating Paul's mind is, how he anticipates even unfair assumptions in regard to his meaning and removes them.

The εἰς τό with its two infinitives denotes result, the more so since one is an aorist and the other a present tense. When the subject of an infinitive is not written out, the subject is the same as that of the main clause: here: "so that you died and are living together with us," i. e., you and we are having the same experience. The meaning is not that *we* are joined to *you* in this experience, but that *you* are joined to *us*, in whose hearts you are. By expressing this in regard to the *Corinthians,* Paul recalls all their blessed experience to them and thereby draws them into his heart. One marvels at Paul when one notes how he thus brings the strongest appeals to bear upon his readers. Censoriousness does not draw, love does. And Paul's love never strikes a wrong note. Having died and sharing the same life, this is union and fellowship indeed!

It is not difficult to see the difference between this and being yoked together with unbelievers, under a yoke that is alien to Christians (6:14). Yet we are told that 6:14-7:1 does not harmonize with 7:2-4. The harmony is perfect; the expressions used in each section shed light on each other. The wrong fellowship Paul can describe only as a being harnessed to an alien yoke like a clean beast (ox) with an unclean (ass), where the former does not belong. How can believers and unbelievers be in each other's hearts as having died together and as now, on the basis of that death, living together?

By our unity with Christ and in the love which he has implanted in us we are, indeed, spiritually bound together (John 13:34, 35): we are in each other's hearts. We died the same death to sin (aorist infinitive), and we are living the same spiritual life (present infinitive, durative). If Paul intended to reproduce 4:10, etc., exactly, both infinitives would have to be present: "so that we are dying together and living together." It is enough for his purpose to speak of having died and thereby to express the one decisive severance of which he speaks in the preceding paragraph.

In 4:11 οἱ ζῶντες, "those living," expresses the same duration as συζῆν in the present connection.

The striking feature is the order: death first and then life. The meaning is not "so that we are together in life and death." Even if the thought were considered ideally, this cannot be the sense. Confusion results when εἰς τό is regarded as expressing purpose: "in order to die together." To think of a physical death which is followed by the heavenly life disjoints the terms. Because it is followed by a present, the aorist infinitive excludes the thought of a constant dying that is parallel to a constant living; this is a death that is followed by life and living. R. W. P., makes the aorist infinitive ingressive: starting to die; he might as well make it constative. But the punctiliar idea of the aorist is emphasized by the contrast with the durative idea of the present. Moreover, the sense is plain: you died with us when you were severed from sin, the world, etc., in repentance and faith; you have ever since been living together with us in the true spiritual life. This is what makes you and us one. This should keep you from every alien yoke.

4) What Paul has said before excludes every idea that he is now writing to condemn them. And this adequately portrays his feeling in writing this letter. **Great is my outspokenness toward you, great my glory about you! I have been filled with the consolation, I have been made to abound with the joy in all our tribulation!** With these feelings Paul is writing this epistle. The Corinthians find great outspokenness in this letter, no reserve behind which this or that is concealed. The copulas are wanting: "is for me" = I have; and here: I use. We see why Paul uses the singular; it reappears in v. 8, 9: these are personal statements that apply to him in particular. It is he who is dictating. On the one hand he is maintaining no reserve or reticence, on the other he is

manifesting great glorying and boasting about the Corinthians. He is so happy about them. Πρὸς ὑμᾶς indicates what he says *to* them, ὑπὲρ ὑμῶν what he says to others *about* them, "in your behalf," *zu Gunsten* (B.-P. 1341), ὑπέρ is repeatedly used in this sense in this epistle.

"I have been filled with the consolation" and am thus still filled; the dative indicates means, a genitive would state what fills. Companion to this is: "I have been made to abound or superabound with the joy," the same dative of means. Consolation results in joy. The passives imply that someone has so filled Paul and made him overflow. The Corinthians have done this, Titus has just brought a report regarding them. The articles "with *the* consolation, *the* joy" = the one you well know as caused by you. The ἐπί phrase may be taken with both statements in the sense that the consolation and the joy have come "on top of all our tribulation," all that has been afflicting us as worry about you. Paul includes his assistants who had shared this feeling. Now it is entirely erased by the consolation and the joy.

Whether it is retained in the little paragraph v. 2-4 or drawn to the following, v. 4 is transitional. Paul tells how Titus changed his worry into joy.

5) For even when we came to Macedonia, no relief has our flesh had but — in every way afflicted: from outside fightings, from inside fears. Paul is now indeed full of consolation and overflowing with joy in the midst of all tribulation. Both sensations are intensified because of the feelings that preceded them, which place them into bold relief because of the contrast. Already in 2:12, 13 Paul has stated that he had no rest in Troas, that his anxiety to meet Titus made him press forward from Troas past the open door for work in that city into Macedonia in order the sooner to meet Titus or to get some word from him.

Paul now states what his situation was when he got to Macedonia and there continued his wait for Titus. Things were even worse for him than they had been in Troas. There a door had been opened to him to found a congregation and to do some effective work and thus in a measure to take his mind off his worries about Corinth and what he would get to hear when Titus did arrive. But in Macedonia Paul and Timothy (1:1) and whoever else was with him encountered a mass of trouble in addition to all the worry about Corinth and the anxiety about the return of Titus.

Paul uses the same expression which he employed in 2:13: ἔσχηκα ἄνεσιν, and retains the same perfect tense (see 2:13). In the former passage Paul writes, "I have had no relief for my spirit"; while here he says, "No relief has our flesh had." In Troas only Paul's own spirit was worried with anxious thoughts; here in Macedonia both he and Timothy and whoever else was with him had troubles that affected them bodily. "Our flesh" uses the word flesh in the neutral sense, the weak stuff of which our bodies are made (it is so used also in v. 1).

We get a glimpse and only a glimpse of what the trouble was when Paul adds "in every way afflicted: from outside fightings, from inside fears." Here in Macedonia everything caused trouble. It grew to tremendous proportions outside and inside, there was pressure in both directions. In Troas at least the outside was favorable, there was an open door for work. Here in Macedonia they encountered nothing but μάχαι, "clashes," "fightings," and to the fears which they already had about Corinth and Titus there were added others that were connected with these Macedonian fightings — "in every way afflicted: outside fightings, inside fears," no relief anywhere. As it often happens, it is darkest just before the dawn.

Paul's feeling of distress is reflected in the way in which he writes about it. He intends merely to indicate the miserable situation and not to tell about it at length. He paints the picture with only three strokes: a participle and two nouns, just three nominatives: "but — in everything afflicted (pressed): outside clashes, inside fears." These nominatives merely sketch, there are three flashes, that is all. One catches the feeling to be conveyed. Paul intends that we shall catch it and uses nominatives for that very reason, detached nominatives that are not included in the construction. Others have used such detailed nominatives for the same purpose. R. 439 is right, this is not an anacoluthon; 415 he is again right: "one must not be a slavish martinet." B.-D. 468 is wrong with his complaint of "harshness and lack of exact connection." All is smooth and exact. These nominatives express Paul's feeling perfectly so that the reader catches it.

6) Over against the dark background of what Paul, Timothy, etc., encountered in Macedonia there is set the glory of the coming of Titus and what he brought. **But he who comforts the lowly did comfort us, (even) God, with the arrival of Titus; and not only with his arrival but also with the comfort with which he was comforted in regard to you, (he) reporting to us your longing, your lamentation, your zeal on my own behalf, so that I rejoiced even more.**

This is one of God's wonderful names: "he who comforts the lowly." How could he comfort the proud, the self-satisfied? While they were in Macedonia, Paul and his assistants had certainly descended among the lowly. But, *wenn die Not am groessten, ist Gott am naechsten.* When the need of comfort was greatest, God brought the comfort: Titus arrived and was there (both ideas are contained in παρουσία). Παρακαλέω may mean to admonish, encourage, or comfort as the context indicates. The apposition ὁ Θεός is effectively placed after the verb.

7) It is the arrival of Titus as such that is stressed as being a comfort for Paul and for those with him. Note that "with the arrival of Titus" is repeated: "not only with his arrival." Paul had been worried about the safety of Titus. When he did not find Titus at Troas, when after waiting he then went on into Macedonia and still waited, the fear grew that perhaps something had happened to Titus. Things were either in a terrible condition in Corinth so that Titus dared not leave, or he had left and had been injured on the way (robbers, thieves, some accident) or had taken sick or had even lost his life. The last appeared the more probable, for surely, when Titus could not get back in proper time as had been agreed, he would, if he were alive, have sent some message, and he would have done this the more since he knew Paul's great concern. The death of Titus would have been a calamity indeed. And now he was at last here! Talk about being comforted? This was a vast load off Paul's heart.

Titus brought a load of comfort with him. Paul calls it "the comfort with which he (Titus) was comforted in regard to you." Note that the word is repeated four times: He who comforts — comforted us — with the comfort — with which he was comforted. Yes, this is Paul's way of ringing the changes on a word; but it has its purpose. It conveys the thought that a flood of comfort poured in on those who so much needed it. As to Titus, he did not only bring comfort, he brought it out of a heart that had drunk in all the comfort right in Corinth. He conveyed all of it like a full vessel.

Note that the plurals "we" include all of Paul's assistants. All these men are of one mind and one heart. These are not "literary plurals"; no writer says "we" and "I" in regard to himself in the same sentence. No literary plural occurs in this epistle; and none is found elsewhere in Paul's epistles. By designating the comfort as he does Paul means this: You Corinthians saw how you had filled Titus with comfort when he left; well, that is exactly how we were comforted when he poured out this comfort on his arrival.

There is no issue as to the relation of the present participle ἀναγγέλλων with the aorist παρεκλήθη. Titus "was comforted" in Corinth, his "reporting" takes place later in Macedonia. The relative clause does not include the participial statement. Nor is this an anacoluthon. The force of this participle would not be altered if it were a genitive absolute. It is construed *ad sensum* and in the most natural way. How Titus had been comforted in Corinth became evident to Paul, Timothy, etc., when he began "reporting to us" on his arrival.

And now Paul states the three main points of this comforting report in detail. "Your longing" is the desire of the Corinthians to have Paul arrive in their midst and to hear his approval of the way in which their hearts had opened to him and to his assistants. "Your lamentation (mourning)," Luther: *Weinen*, is the sorrow of the Corinthians for ever having become disaffected and for having called forth Paul's reproof. "Your zeal on my own behalf" is the zealous effort on the part of the Corinthians to meet the Christian requirements which Paul had laid upon them, had had to lay upon them. These three terms convey volumes. Note the three ὑμῶν (subjective genitives), all are emphatic. You — you — you are sending us all this comfort! The phrase "on my own behalf" is significant. Paul, the apostle, was the one for whom the Corinthians were now so zealous to defend him against any derogations, to obey him as their true leader and guide.

Paul was not like some preachers who attach their congregations mainly to their own persons. The restored devotion of the Corinthians to Paul rested altogether on the gospel of which Paul was the great exponent. They were faithful to him because they now fully recognized that he labored for Christ in the most disinterested way. Woe to the preacher who thrusts his person ahead of Christ and gets people to cling to him and not above all to Christ!

"So that I even more rejoiced," ὥστε with the infinitive is used in the Koine to express actual result (R. 1000). Μᾶλλον = that Paul even had joy beyond all the comfort. The aorist infinitive has the force: I positively got to rejoice. Comfort was precious indeed; but to be able to rejoice was like comfort being crowned. Forget not that all this came just when Paul was deepest in worry and in other troubles.

XXII. *"You Were Grieved unto Repentance"*

8) In the R. V. the American Committee translates v. 8, 9a as one sentence by making βλέπω κτλ. a parenthesis. This is not a gain. Since γάρ is textually sound, especially when it is regarded as explanatory, no parenthesis is needed. Paul has come to a rejoicing although the news from Corinth reported the lamentation of the Corinthians (v. 7). Already in 2:2 Paul refers to the fact that he had grieved the Corinthians. With ὅτι he now explains how he comes to rejoice although he had grieved the Corinthians. We now have a fuller exposition of 2:1-4 (which read). Paul did not want to come to Corinth in grief and delayed his coming for that very reason. Now he indeed rejoices and can go to Corinth in joy. What had so deeply grieved him was what compelled him to grieve the Corinthians, to grieve them in love. In 2:2 he says that only he who grieved him could remove that grief and rejoice him again. That is what happened, he is now voicing that joy.

For though I grieved you in my letter I am not regretting it though (for a while, I confess) **I was regretting it, for I see that that letter, though** (only) **for a time, did grieve you. Now I am rejoicing, not** (indeed) **that you were grieved, but that you were grieved unto repentance, for you were grieved according to God's way so that you were made to suffer loss from us in no way.**

The condition is one of reality. It is a fact, and Paul speaks of it as a fact that he, indeed, grieved the Corinthians in his letter. And he says: "I am not regretting it." Yet he admits and confesses: "Though I was regretting it." The imperfect tense states that this regret continued for a time, and that it then ceased, a different feeling took its place. This tense is open; it says that something lasted temporarily and then gave way to something else that closed the matter.

In this connection the question is raised: "If Paul wrote by inspiration as he did, under the very influence and the guidance of the Holy Spirit, how could such regrets later enter into his mind?" This is not the question of skeptics but the puzzling consideration of true believers in inspiration. They feel a difficulty here that other men do not feel. They then seek to explain away Paul's regret. That is not right. Their difficulty is self-made, imagined, not real. Paul's inspiration did not extend to his thoughts and anxieties in the trying situations in which he was placed. In these he felt distressed and perplexed and often greatly worried just as is the case with us.

We may say that Paul was in the position in which many a true pastor is today who has rebuked and chastised some member and has done this in perfect accord with God's Word and Spirit and knows that he has, and yet, when the effect hangs long in the balance, when, as here in the case of Paul, he cannot even see the effect, his poor human nature asserts itself in the form of useless worries, misgivings, even regrets. Paul's admission may serve as a great comfort to us. Neither revelation nor inspiration lifted the apostles above their poor σάρξ or human nature (here mentioned twice: 7:1, 5) which asserted itself in hours of weakness and depression in the form of even doubts and regrets.

The textual evidence against the reading with γάρ is so slight that the R. V. margin does not even note it. It is also not intended for proof, it merely explains: "for I see (by the report which Titus brings) that that letter (of mine) did grieve you although (as I am glad to hear from him, only) for a time" (ὥρα, "hour," in the sense of a short time). Paul thus explains how he can say "though I grieved you in my letter"; he has the facts from Titus.

9) All of that temporary regret which was due to being so far away from Corinth, so completely in the dark until Titus came, so plagued with uncertainty in regard to the manner in which his letter would be received, has now entirely disappeared. The asyndeton makes the statement emphatic: "Now I am rejoicing." It parallels the previous: "I am not regretting it." Both are markedly durative, the one states negatively what the other puts positively. Paul, of course, rejoices, "not that you were grieved," not that I merely hurt you deeply — how could he rejoice because of that? — "but that you were grieved unto repentance." The fullest stress is on this phrase. A surgeon may cause severe pain; he rejoices when he sees the cure that this pain has produced. It is not the pain as such but the pain as being productive of the cure that rejoices him.

The way to true repentance even in the case of Christians who have sinned and erred is the way of deep grief and sorrow. The mistake made by many a preacher is the endeavor to induce a painless, griefless repentance. Such repentance does not exist. Peter had to weep bitterly. A broken and a contrite heart is not a pleasant sensation. The *terrores conscientiae* will always be "terrors." Much repentance presses out tears. The peaceable fruit of righteousness grows from the pain of chastisement, Heb. 12:11.

Μετάνοια is one of the great concepts of Scripture. It means: "To change the mind afterward," when it is too late. This is deepened in the New Testament beyond everything secular writers conceived, this word expresses the vital inner change that is wrought by the law in conjunction with the gospel when the heart turns from its sin and guilt to God and his pardon in Christ Jesus. When it is used alone as it is here it denotes the whole act (contrition plus faith); when it is used together with faith it denotes contrition alone. R., W. P., laments that we have no better word for it than "repentance." A good preacher will always expound it. Repentance = conversion. When it is predicated of Christians it signifies a renewal of the heart's inner change: our daily contrition and repentance. In Corinth the congregation as a whole in a great change of heart turned back from the wrong and sinful course which it had followed.

Grieved "unto repentance," with this as the outcome (εἰς), should be distinguished from being grieved otherwise. So Paul elucidates with γάρ: "you were grieved κατὰ Θεόν," *gottgemaess*, which it is difficult to reproduce in English. We have the suggestions: "after a godly manner (sort)," our versions; "according to God," A. V. margin, which is literal; in a way that accords with God. This phrase explains "unto repentance." But it is not enough. One usually grieves over some grave loss; this grief which led to a repentance that was in harmony with God is the very opposite: the Corinthians were not thereby made to suffer loss in any way.

We confess that the ἵνα of purpose does not fit here, not even the ἵνα of contemplated result; we therefore regard it as indicating actual result: "so that you were made to suffer loss from us in no way," not the least loss. We may say: *eine Busse ohne Einbusse.* This was certainly the result in the case of the Corinthians. Why should Paul speak of it only as being God's purpose when that purpose was already actually accomplished in the Corinthians?

The passive accords with the preceding passives: were grieved — were made to suffer loss; the agent is expressed by ἐξ ἡμῶν, "from us." R. 997-9 regards this as the consecutive ἵνα; B.-D. 391, 5 still shrinks from making it actual result. Those who have not experienced true repentance might conceive of it as a great loss; it is always the very opposite, the greatest spiritual gain. The grief of repentance is never loss in any way; not to experience this grief, that is loss indeed.

10) **For the grief according to God's way works an unregrettable repentance for salvation; but the grief of the world works out death.** The two kinds of grief are contrasted as to their results. This confirms us in the opinion that also the preceding ἵνα clause speaks about result. Here is the great gain beside the great loss. Over against the grief κατὰ Θεόν, "according to God," stands the grief τοῦ κόσμου, "of the world." It is not God who experiences the grief, but the world does experience the grief, and the fact that its grief is κατὰ κόσμον, *weltgemaess*, "according to the world," need certainly not be stated. Note the difference: the one grief bears a relation to God (κατά); the other bears a relation only to itself (simple genitive).

So the one "works repentance for salvation," the other "works out death." Every word is exact. Present tenses are used regularly in doctrinal statements; they state what is always true. Ἐργάζεται εἰς = "works toward"; κατεργάζεται (with its perfective κατά) = "works out," actually produces. Godly grief does not "work" and mush less "work out or produce" salvation. It "works" only repentance "toward" salvation. God alone works salvation, and by producing repentance this sorrow aids in working the subjective means, namely repentance. Salvation and death are to be understood in their ultimate form.

The world's sorrow, however, "works out" and produces death. This sorrow is remorse, often despair, the direct forerunner of death. The world is full of it. How fearfully it "works out" we see in the suicide of Judas Iscariot. Where it does not end in open tragedy it is still of the same kind. The sins find the sinner out, judgment comes marching on inexorably, hope dies, i. e., all false hope, death waits. There is nothing "according to God" in this grief, nothing according to his good and gracious will, no outcome that in any way tends toward salvation; everything about this grief points directly to death. The world's grief is already death's shadow closing down.

The godly grief is wrought by God, by his law and his gospel. It is impossible without these. So the immediate outcome is repentance, and this leads to final salvation. The Bible furnishes many fine examples of such repentance: David, whose great sins Nathan reproved; Peter, who denied Christ and went out and wept bitterly; the malefactor on the cross, who was brought to his first repentance and received pardon. In the very first of his famous 95 Theses Luther declares that when our Lord and Master Jesus Christ says that we are to repent he desires that the entire life of believers should be a repentance. The grief of repentance may be painful, humiliating, crushing, and all that, but who will exchange it for the grief that brings on the pain and the terror of death? Who wants to exchange with impenitent Cain, King

Saul, Judas, the impenitent malefactor, Caiaphas, Pilate, Herod, or any of their class?

The verbal adjective ἀμεταμέλητον is to be construed with μετάνοιαν and not with σωτηρίαν. It is inconceivable that one should regret final salvation; "unregrettable salvation" is an impossible combination. "Unregrettable repentance" — that is, indeed, a proper idea here where the grief of such repentance is discussed: no one can ever regret his true repentance because of any grief that went with its production. The adjective is placed last because it is to modify the whole of μετάνοιαν εἰς σωτηρίαν and not merely the noun "repentance." The repentance is so unregrettable because it is "unto salvation."

The verbal adjective "unregrettable" is used because Paul has just said: "I am not regretting though (for a while) I was regretting." Paul used both verbs in regard to the grief which he caused the Corinthians, which also shows how "unregrettable" is to be construed. The A. V. translates as though the word were ἀμετανόητον, and some say that this ought to be the word: "unrepentable repentance." This view simply exchanges Paul's thought for one it deems better. Paul retains the idea of regretting and not-regretting from v. 8. He wants no pun on repenting and not repenting; that would not only run off on a different track, it would run off where Paul does not want to go, for the world is unrepenting, and "unrepentable" is even stronger.

11) All the blessed results of the godly sorrow that works repentance for salvation have now been stated, all the results that show how this repentance is "for salvation" and thus in the highest degree "unregrettable." These results have been actually accomplished in the Corinthians; κατειργάσατο is the same verb as κατεργάζεται but an aorist to designate the past fact. Paul exclaims because of these results and lists each

one separately as though he would hold it up with great delight. His grieving the Corinthians has actually done this. He was foolish for regretting at all that he had done this grieving. The Corinthians do not need to wait until their heavenly salvation arrives; all these results are evidence of the most blessed kind as to what their grief really produces.

For lo, this very thing that you were grieved according to God's way, what earnestness it worked out for you, yea defense, yea indignation, yea fear, yea longing, yea zeal, yea action of justice! In everything you did commend yourselves as being pure with regard to this case. All of these results have been actually produced by your having been grieved, nothing else could have produced them. All of them show your repentance to be genuine and truly "for salvation." We may regard αὐτὸ τοῦτο as modifying τὸ λυπηθῆναι which is then regarded as a noun or regard the substantivized infinitive as an apposition to αὐτὸ τοῦτο (R. 1078).

Πόσος = "how much, how great" (R. 740), and should be construed with the entire seven nouns. Paul holds up each one in order to look at it separately, to admire it: "Lo, how great each one is!" Ἀλλά is not adversative. B.-D. 448, 6, and B.-P. 59 retain this idea: "not only this *but* also." Read R. 1185, etc.; the sense is: "here is *another* thing," and the repetition is climacteric. B.-P. 59 has this idea in "yea even" this, that, etc. The seven nouns are thus stated in progressive order. The πρᾶγμα or "case" to which they refer is the case of incest (I Cor. 5). The Corinthians treated it with careless indifference, just let it pass and did nothing, considered neither the sin nor the sinner involved, disregarded what this sin did to his soul, and considered not themselves, and what this indifference and inaction did to them as a congregation. Then Paul took them to task in I Cor. 5. He even thought it necessary to send Titus. Finally there came the σπουδή, which means that the Corinthians dropped their indifference and got thoroughly busy and in earnest.

The first thing that resulted was ἀπολογία, "defense," clearing themselves. That was certainly the main and the immediate thing to effect. They could not go on when such a smirch was resting on their whole church. The next thing was "indignation" in regard to the sin committed and the man who had committed it. They indignantly expelled him (see 2:6, etc.). These three belong together and followed in close succession. Then came another thing, namely "fear" as to whether everything had been done that ought to be done; and another, namely "longing" to have Paul himself present in Corinth to direct everything; and still another, namely "zeal" to leave nothing undone that they might do ere Paul arrived. These three again belong together and are closely connected and properly follow the first three.

This makes six to which Paul adds a comprehensive seventh and thereby secures also for all these good results a group of (sacred) seven. This is ἐκδίκησις: "right or just action." "Revenge" (A. V.), "vengeance" (R. V.) is not the meaning. Those who hold this opinion refer the word only to the sinner in this case; but the preceding nouns show that all the Corinthians were equally involved with him. Then, too, this is the final term, and it cannot be one-sided where two sides are involved. This "action of justice" which so delights Paul was one of justice and right in both directions, in regard to the sinner and in regard to the Corinthians who themselves were so guilty because of their past indifference and callousness in regard to a crime in their midst which was unheard of even among pagans (I Cor. 5:1).

"In everything you did commend yourselves as being pure in regard to this case" (τῷ, the one concerned). "In everything" sums up the seven points. "You did commend yourselves" is aorist and contemporaneous with the aorist occurring in v. 11, "worked out for you." The English would use the perfect: "you have commended." The verb is significantly "commend yourselves," and we should know what Paul has had to say in 3:1 and 5:11 about the slur that he simply commends and recommends himself and his assistants, and in 4:2 where he shows how he indeed and in the truest way does recommend himself and them. He must tell this about himself and his helpers to the Corinthians, but joyfully and most generously he calls what he now sees manifested in the Corinthians the finest self-recommendation they can offer. So he gladly accepts it although they have not done equally well with regard to him.

There is some difference of opinion in regard to the time indicated by εἶναι as though it might mean that in this case the Corinthians had never been pure and blameless. But the context does not support that thought; they had repented. The time of this infinitive is present with respect to the aorists of this verse and not prior to them. The Corinthians are *now* pure in this case since the grief "wrought out" these blessed results. The very tense says so. Little needs to be added in regard to what πρᾶγμα, "affair" or "case," Paul has in mind, and to what letter he twice refers in v. 8. See 2:9, 11. Every word fits the case mentioned in I Cor. 5.

12) **So, though I wrote to you, (it was) not (just) on account of him who did the injustice, nor (just) on account of him who suffered the injustice, but on account of this that your earnestness in behalf of us should be publicly manifested to yourselves in the sight of God.**

Paul is speaking about the letter referred to in v. 8 and in 2:3. In the latter passage he mentions one purpose for writing that letter, the personal one of not wanting to have grief from those who ought to furnish him joy. What he now says about the primary reason for writing that letter agrees with that. The letter is First Corinthians, and the chapter to which reference is made is the fifth. That was not written on account of the ἀδικήσας or on account of the ἀδικηθείς, the man who committed the crime (incest) or the man against whom it was committed, who suffered as a result of the crime (the criminal's father). The Greek "not — nor" is not exclusive in the sense of "not at all — nor at all," but is equivalent to our English "not just — nor just." Paul was only in a minor way concerned about these two persons, his main concern was a far greater one, namely the whole congregation, that its earnestness "in behalf of us" (Paul and his assistants, two of whom he had sent to Corinth, Timothy and Titus, representatives of Paul) should be made publicly manifest to the Corinthians themselves in the sight of God by the way in which they applied Christian discipline to this criminal man as they had learned it from Paul and as his letter to them once more urged them.

This is the same σπουδή, "earnestness," that was mentioned in v. 11, where six other terms followed it. Φανεροῦν again (2:14; 3:3; 4:2) has the idea of being *publicly* displayed. The case was such as to require such a display, not simply in order that Paul might see it and be impressed by it but also in order that the Corinthians themselves might behold it. By way of their earnest action they were to become fully conscious of their earnestness in behalf of their former teachers. Yet this was to be done as "in the sight of God," under God's eyes, who even more than Paul and his assistants expected no less of them.

Paul uses ἀδικήσας and ἀδικηθείς in order to match the preceding ἐκδίκησις. This is merely verbal. In both words there is the idea of ἀδικία, that which runs counter to the δίκη or norm of right and has the divine judgment against it. It is unwarranted to say that these participles are mild, too mild for the case of incest. This idea is fostered by the dictionaries. C.-K. 39 mentions a social, mild meaning: "to do wrong," and says nothing more but lists our passage; then he lists a religious meaning, a severe one: incurring the divine judgment. In nonreligious connections the only mildness is that human verdicts condemn the act. But the word always has a forensic basis: ἀδικεῖν, "to do what justice (divine or human) condemns." In our passage it is certainly more than social justice that is involved. This case of incest was under the condemnation of the divine Judge himself. See Lev. 18:8.

Who is this ἀδικηθείς? Objections are offered to the supposition that he is the father of the incestuous son. But all suggestions as to who this man might otherwise be are open to challenge. The opinion that this ἀδικηθείς is the congregation itself is unsatisfactory because of the singular whereas Paul writes "you" to the congregation. The widespread critical opinion that this is Paul himself who was insulted by some Corinthian member while on his flying visit to Corinth, insulted in the public congregational meeting is unacceptable on several counts: the words Paul uses should then be ὑβρίσας and ὑβρισθείς, the insulter and the insulted; ἀδικεῖν does *not* mean "to insult." Paul uses "we" and not "I," and he cannot refer to himself by an unmodified singular participle. More may be added, but we let this suffice.

The father is not considered because he is mentioned only incidentally in I Cor. 5. But when Paul formulates the resolution which the Corinthians are to pass on the case (I Cor. 5:3-5, see the exegesis), the Corinthians are to do all that is in their power in the father's interest. Is the father not mentioned only incidentally also here in 7:12? Both he and his son are treated as side issues.

Some think that the passive participle refers to the woman; but the participle is masculine. Nor was she wronged, she did as much wrong as her paramour. It is urged that, if this is a reference to the case of incest, the woman ought to be mentioned. We agree, but only if she was not a pagan, only if she was a Christian; and then she should be named as a fellow criminal and not as a woman who was criminally treated.

13) **For this reason we have been comforted** because this earnestness on the part of the Corinthians became publicly manifest to themselves in God's sight. It meant so exceedingly much to Paul and to his helpers. The action expressed by the perfect tense started when the news reached Paul through Titus and still continues.

Titus has just come from Corinth, and he is to bear this letter back to the Corinthians. Paul very fittingly speaks of the part he had in bringing the comfort and the joy. **Moreover, in addition to ($ἐπί$) this comfort of ours we rejoiced the more exceedingly at the joy of Titus, that his spirit has received rest from you all.**

The two $ἐπί$ are alike. Titus made a joyful report. What the content of his joy was the epexegetical $ὅτι$ clause states: "that his spirit (we should say his soul) has been given rest," this joy of his came "from you all." 'Aπό is not exactly "by you all" (agent with the passive) but "from" (derivation). All of the uncertainty and the uneasiness with which Titus had gone to Corinth changed to rest for his spirit because of what he experienced "from" the Corinthians. No wonder Titus came to Paul with joy! And this joy of his caused Paul and Timothy (1:1) and any others who may have been with Paul to rejoice beyond the comfort and the satisfaction which were contained in the report of Titus. We take it that Paul is practically quoting Titus as to how his uneasiness was put to rest (perfect, to stay so) and how glad he was in consequence.

14) But the Corinthians are not to harbor the suspicion that Paul had perhaps filled the mind of Titus with uncertainty and grave misgivings when he had dispatched Titus to them. For that reason we now have the singular. **For if I have gloried somewhat to him concerning you I was** (certainly) **not put to shame; but as we** (in the past) **spoke to you all things in truth, so also this our glorying before Titus turned out to be truth.**

The condition is one of reality: Paul had boasted somewhat (τι) to Titus concerning the Corinthians, yes, he had boasted, not, indeed, extravagantly, but only "somewhat." Paul had encouraged Titus. Paul would have been foolish to discourage him when he was to go on Paul's own mission.

The perfect "I have gloried" says more than an aorist would; it brings out the fact that Paul kept up this boasting about the Corinthians when he was speaking to Titus. The implication is that it was necessary for Paul to do so because Titus had his serious doubts as to whether Paul was right. Now Paul is very happy to register the great fact: in all that I boasted about you to Titus "I was not put to shame." That is really a litotes, stating negatively what is intended positively: you Corinthians more than verified my words to Titus.

It is a reflection on the honesty of the apostle to comment in regard to Paul: In order to bolster up the courage of Titus, Paul in all likelihood said more than his knowledge of the situation in Corinth warranted; and this reflection is repeated when it is said in regard to Titus that he did not trust the truth of Paul's praise of the Corinthians. Paul says plainly "somewhat." He told Titus what was true, and Titus believed and knew that what was thus said was true. Some good things may still be most true in a bad situation. It would be folly not to note them well and to count on them.

Paul also says: "I was not put to shame." When he spoke to Titus about the good that he could count on in the Corinthians, Paul reckoned with the possibility of being put to shame; he did not send Titus away with the assurance that the Corinthians would and could not put him to shame. That would have been folly in the opposite direction.

Note that when Paul refers to himself alone he uses the singular "I" endings of the verb; yet some think that the "we"s used here and there are the literary "I." What "I was not put to shame" states negatively is now also joyfully repeated in positive form, but with amplifications: "this glorying of *ours* before Titus turned out to be truth." So others besides Paul had gloried about the Corinthians. Ἐπί with the genitive = "before" (Acts 23:30; I Cor. 6:1; and often). And this praise of the Corinthians proved to be the truth because the Corinthians more than lived up to the expectations entertained regarding them.

Nor was this so very strange as the ὡς clause emphasizes. The Corinthians know from their own past experience with Paul and his assistants that they are most careful to keep within the bounds of truth when they speak about any matter: "as we spoke to you all things in truth," i. e., in the past in all our dealings with you. We never tried to make or to leave a false impression. The supposition that Paul is proving his truthfulness by the truth of what he said to Titus about the Corinthians misunderstands what Paul does say, namely that the past, proven truthfulness received another item: as true in the past, so now in this case too. The Corinthians might have proved hostile and thus have given the lie to what was said of them in praise and put Paul to shame because of his praise. And this would have proved only that the Corinthians had become baser than their best friends thought possible.

15) Paul adds the effect which the action of the Corinthians has had on Titus: **And his feelings are** (now) **more intensely toward you when he remembers the obedience of you all, how with fear and trembling you received him.** On σπλάγχνα see 6:12. The predicate is εἰς ὑμᾶς, "toward you." Our versions translate interpretatively "his affection." The sense is: Titus now loves you more than ever. We construe the participle as a genitive absolute: "he remembering" (αὐτοῦ understood) and not as modifying the αὐτοῦ which is used with σπλάγχνα as R., W. P., suggests. Already the first reception impressed Titus. He had evidently not expected to be received "with fear and trembling" on the part of the Corinthians, i. e., with such readiness to obey the Word of God which he brought from Paul. There is a good deal back of this "fear and trembling," namely the fact that the Corinthians had returned to their allegiance to Paul, that they felt deeply that they had deserved the severest rebuke, and that they expected to receive chastisement when Titus came from Paul. How this change had come about we are unable to state; it is idle to speculate.

16) And now, in closing the first main part of his letter, Paul says regarding himself personally: **I rejoiced that in everything I am of good cheer in regard to you.** Paul is happy that he can be of good courage in regard to Corinth. The dark clouds have been dispersed. To be of good cheer implies that some things still need adjustment, but also that all misgivings have disappeared in regard to such adjustments as are yet to be made.

This conclusion of the first part of the epistle is said to be incompatible with what follows in the third part (chapters 10-13). We are told that these two cannot be parts of one and the same letter. Hence we have the hypotheses about the last four chapters, namely that they constitute a separate earlier letter, etc. We shall see what foundation such an assertion has when we consider those chapters. No text is extant in which Second Corinthians is without the last chapters. This alone is most decisive; but we shall see much more besides.

CHAPTER VIII

The Second Part of the Epistle

Chapters Eight and Nine

Expediting the Matter of the Collection in Corinth

I. *The Great Example of Macedonia*

Our first information regarding the great collection is stated in I Cor. 16:1, etc. In their letter to Paul the Corinthians had requested directions regarding it, and Paul sends these in I Cor. 16. We learned that the Galatian churches were already following the method proposed to the Corinthians, namely that on each Sunday each person lay by what he could. When Paul wrote First Corinthians he expected to get to Corinth eight or nine months later and so asked that the whole collection be completed by that time so that men who were approved by the church might then carry the funds to Jerusalem. Just when, where, and how this movement toward a collection started we cannot say, for all we have is the remark made in Gal. 2:10 about remembering the poor, which Paul promised to do.

The next information we have is found in these two chapters of this epistle. In 9:2 we see that the collection was started in Corinth a year before Second Corinthians was written, and that means five or six months before First Corinthians was written. Paul boasts to the Macedonians about the early start that was made in Corinth and in Achaia; but he now boasts to the Corinthians about the wonderful response he had found in Macedonia and writes in detail about the Macedonians in order to enthuse also the Corinthians. The danger is that the Corinthians will fall behind, that when representatives from Macedonia come to Corinth to join the party that is to convey the collection to Jerusalem, they will find Corinth unready although here in Second Corinthians Paul is boasting that Corinth began already a year ago. So Paul tries to speed up the collection in Corinth by sending back Titus to help direct matters. Paul himself will get to Corinth in two or three months, the Macedonian representatives will accompany him.

We can follow the main events from Luke's report in Acts 20:4, where he names the whole party which started from Corinth in the spring of the next year and carried the collection from the European churches to Jerusalem. Luke describes the whole journey. How the funds gathered in Asia and in Galatia were combined with those which had been collected in Europe we are not told. They were perhaps brought when the Ephesian elders met Paul and his party at Miletus (Acts 20:17). The collection must have been turned over to James and to the elders at Jerusalem when these received Paul and his party (Acts 21:17, etc.). In his defense before Felix in Acts 24:17 Paul mentions the fact that he had come to Jerusalem to bring alms to his nation.

We now go back to the six months that intervened between First and Second Corinthians. The relation between the Corinthians and Paul had become severely strained. All that we know about this is what we are able to gather from the two epistles themselves. We have this much in the way of facts. First Corinthians is filled with rebuke and corrections in every chapter. Conditions were bad, very bad in Corinth: party factions; the whole wisdom-folly; the case of incest; litigations; harlotry not considered wrong; wrong notions regarding marriage and celibacy; attending idol feasts; ruining the apage and the celebration of the Lord's Supper; the folly concerning gifts, forgetting love; capping this list the denial of the bodily resurrection. No wonder Paul shed tears while he was writing this letter (2:5).

Just consider this array of evils, all of which were found in one congregation. Timothy arrived in Corinth after this letter had been received. We know that after he returned to Paul in Ephesus, Paul sent Titus to Corinth. From Second Corinthians we gather that things had, indeed, looked bad in Corinth, and that Paul had feared even the worst. Judaizers had come in, and a movement to disown Paul was started. But the Corinthians thoroughly righted themselves with the help of Titus. Titus so reported to Paul in Macedonia, and Paul then wrote Second Corinthians.

But we see that because of all this disturbance the collection had fared illy. We may well suppose that it had gone by the board for the time being. It is with this background that Paul writes about it in order to set it going again. Paul had perhaps been attacked also on the score of this collection. We shall see how he guards his expressions. These two chapters regarding the collection are again a sample of how in a situation that is by no means simple Paul knows exactly the right thing to say, to touch only the purest motives, to avert every wrong implication, and to deprive every hostile mind of the least opening for an attack. The new part of the letter proceeds with transitional δέ.

1) **Now we inform you, brethren, about the grace of God which has been bestowed in the churches of Macedonia, (namely) that in a great test of affliction the excess of their joy and their down to depth poverty exceeded in the riches of their single-mindedness.**

Paul does not write: "I hear that the matter of the collection has stopped in Corinth; you must start it again." He does not put this matter into diplomatic language by sugar-coating it with smooth words. Paul issues no command of authority. He knows only one principle for giving, and that is the giver's own free will. He takes it for granted that the Corinthians, who have now returned to their true allegiance and love, will join in the movement of the collection (9:1). His aim in writing these two chapters on the subject is to make their participation pure and true in every respect, a product of the gospel spirit in every way, a delightful task that is performed in the fullest gospel consciousness. For this reason he starts with the Macedonians, who are now busy gathering their contributions in the finest Christian spirit.

It is Paul's delight to praise where praise is due. He cannot write on this subject without glorying in what the Macedonians are doing. He would glory thus no matter to whom he might write. Invidious comparisons do not enter his mind. Legalistic promptings are impossible to him. All these beautiful fruits are pure "grace of God." As far as the Corinthians are concerned, the only stimulation which Paul knows is that of rich gospel grace. He wants nothing from the Corinthians but a repetition of the delight which he is now experiencing among the Macedonians.

That he secured it we see from Rom. 15:26-28 which was written later in Corinth just before he and the selected delegates started for Jerusalem with the collection. The secret of Paul's success in this field is still hidden from so many who now manage the finances of the church. A little law, often just law, seems to them to be much more promising than pure gospel. When they do try to use the gospel they do it awkwardly because down in their hearts they do not trust it for complete effectiveness with Paul's full trust. Therefore their gospel appeals so often fail to ring true, and the results are, of course, according, which is not the gospel's fault but the fault of those who do not trust it sufficiently.

Nor is it the fault of our people, for they would respond to Paul as the Macedonians and the Achaians once responded, if Paul could come to them. We stand in Paul's place, we preachers and we church leaders. Would that his gospel trust and spirit radiated from us as we see it radiate in these two chapters and in all of Paul's work!

"We inform you," Timothy and I (1:1) and other assistants of mine. This is not an editorial "we"; there is none in the entire epistle. It is glorious news that "we" are able to send you Corinthians. The address "brethren" marks a new part of the letter and makes this part very personal for the Corinthians. The collection of the Macedonians should not be called "the grace of God." On χάρις see 2:1; it is the undeserved favor of God with all that it bestows. "The grace of God, the one that has been bestowed (and is thus remaining) in the churches of Macedonia," is something the Macedonians have received (and thus possess) *from* God, not something they bestow *on God* or on the poor in Jerusalem and thus on God.

Right here we have the full depth of Paul's view. All our fruit of good works, all our beneficence and contributions of money, are God's unmerited favor *to us*, his undeserved gift *to us*. How so? Every good work is the fruit of God's operative grace. It is a treasure that he and his grace deposit in our basket. Blessed is he who has his basket overflowingly full of such gifts of God! Those who refuse to give turn their basket away when God wants to place another gift into it. Ah, they keep their gift and lose the gift to themselves which their gift might have been. Poor where grace would make them rich in good works to come with rejoicing, bearing their full sheaves (Ps. 126:6), to stand among those whom the King shall call "the blessed of my Father" (Matt. 25:34-40).

2) Epexegetical ὅτι describes this grace which was vouchsafed to the Macedonians. This was grace indeed, "that in a great test of affliction the excess of their joy and their down to depth poverty exceeded in the riches of their single-mindedness." As the metal of coins was tested as to its genuineness, so the Macedonians have just undergone a severe "test of affliction" (genitive of cause). Was it persecution? Had the Macedonian province as such been "lacerated" by the Romans (R. W. P.)? No matter; it left these churches with two effects: 1) excess of joy, 2) poverty down to the very depths (R. 607). See the clashing terms: affliction producing excess of joy — joy and poverty — excess of the one, and the other "down to depth," κατὰ βάθους. What an eye Paul has to see all these angles, these contrasting correspondences!

This *excess* of joy in so severe a test of affliction which brought them so great poverty *exceeded* "for the riches of their single-mindedness." This excess did its exceeding in this direction (εἰς); it just bubbled over into this beautiful channel, namely "the wealth of their single-mindedness." "Riches or wealth" is placed in contrast with the deep "poverty." So deep was the poverty that you could not dip it out; so great their joy that it poured itself out in a tide of wealth. This is astonishing when it is put this way, but Paul labels all of the facts with exact terms. Every term states a fact, and Paul is able to put all the facts into one clause. Could you do that?

It is the moral, spiritual quality which Paul sees in the contribution which these Macedonians were making with such joy despite the affliction of poverty which had struck them. This quality stood the great test and was proven genuine. Paul calls it ἁπλότης, sincerity or "singleness" of heart, "single-mindedness." See also 9:11. This word does not mean "liberality" (our versions), and it does not intend to. No; Paul says that the Macedonians fixed their minds on a single thing. And we know what that is: to let God's grace give them its gift, namely this blessed work of helping in the collection. There was no doubleness in their minds; no one stood up and said: "Why, we are so poor that somebody ought to take up a collection for us instead of asking us to give to others!" That crooked "single-mindedness," I fear, would appear in many a church today that has members who are not nearly as poor as these Macedonians were. So the grace of God would be wasted by them. Despite the poverty which the affliction had brought to the Macedonians they had kept, yea increased, their greatest wealth and their joy with it. Grace of God, indeed!

3) Ὅτι is paratactic and not a continuation of the hypotactic ὅτι of v. 2. **For according to ability, I testify, yea, beyond ability, voluntarily, begging of us with much urging this grace and this fellowship of the ministry for the saints and not (merely), as we hoped, but their own selves they gave in the first place to the Lord and to us through God's will, so that we urged Titus that, as he had already begun, thus also he should complete for you, too, this grace.**

That is the actual story of what the Macedonians have done, the inwardness of which is stated so effectively in v. 1, 2. Paul personally (note the singular) testifies that they contributed "beyond ability," and that they did this "voluntarily," of their own choice. Despite their deep poverty they insisted on giving far more than anyone could even think they could give. They made a joy of robbing themselves.

4) Paul and Timothy evidently tried to restrain them, at least those who were in the direst poverty; but they literally begged with insistent urging. The Greek is like the English: "begging of us (genitive of the person) this grace and this fellowship of the ministry for the saints" (accusative of the object). The nouns have the articles. They wanted "the grace," i. e., "the grace of God" mentioned in v. 1. "And" is explicative, it adds what they considered a grace of God to themselves, namely "this fellowship" in giving, being in one communion with all the many other churches who were being vouchsafed the same grace. As has already been explained, they considered their gift a grace and a gift of God to themselves. They gave to the very limit in order to get into the communion of giving to the fullest possible extent. Paul calls it "the fellowship" (communion) of the ministry, the one for the saints," διακονία, service rendered for the sake of service, for the benefit of others, namely the poor saints in Jerusalem.

"The grace" is not a favor from Paul, nor a favor from the Macedonians to the saints, but God's favor to the Macedonians. They beg "us" for it because Paul and his assistants are managing the collection and the participation in it. "Grace and fellowship" are not a hendiadys, two words to denote one idea. Nor is κοινωνία anything but "fellowship" or "communion." "The ministry for the saints" does not read like a technical expression, nor is οἱ ἅγιοι a specific term for the Jewish Christians in Jerusalem; both Paul and Luke use it with regard to Christians as such, the ἡγιασμένοι whom God has sanctified as believers in Christ. The reason that Paul does not add "the saints in Jerusalem" is due to the fact that this is not necessary for his readers in Corinth.

5) The construction is perfectly simple, and all the modifiers of ἔδωκαν are heterogeneous: they gave

1) according to and above ability — phrase; 2) as people acting of their own accord — adjective; 3) begging of us, etc. — participle; 4) "and" in addition to all these points: "not (merely), as we hoped, but their own selves" — a clause. All these modifiers describe *how* the Macedonians gave, but the last introduces also the unexpected object, namely *what* they gave, "themselves first of all to the Lord and to us by God's will." "Not as we hoped" just contributions of money = they went beyond our hopes, they literally made a gift of themselves because of the way in which they gave. To give oneself when one gives a gift is the highest form of Christian giving. The idea is not, however, that of giving themselves for the work of the gospel but of a giving like that of the widow whom Jesus commended so highly. When she dropped her last coin, all her living, she gave herself into God's hands in absolute dependence on his care. For her living she then had God alone. And no gift can please God as much as that.

When Paul writes that the Macedonians "gave themselves first of all to the Lord" and then adds "and to us by God's will" he means that they did both "first of all" ($\pi\rho\tilde{\omega}\tau o\nu$), before they gave any money. Paul does not say first to the Lord and *then* to us. "To the Lord" and "to us" are not to be taken in the same way as some suppose, and the plea that this is a bold way for Paul to combine himself with the Lord is met by the obvious reply that this is not what Paul intends to say. Besides, "to us" is plural and does *not* mean to Paul alone; none of these "we" do. For this reason Paul says "to us through or by ($\delta\iota\acute{a}$) God's will" ($\theta\acute{\epsilon}\lambda\eta\mu a$, not the act of willing but the result of the act as recorded in the Word). The phrase belongs only to the pronoun. It is superfluous to say that it is God's will that anyone give himself to the Lord. But when we give ourselves to any man we, indeed, need the expressed will of God for that.

It was by one act that the Macedonians "gave themselves" to both "the Lord and to us." This act had two sides, one was directed "to the Lord," the other was directed "to us" (Paul and his assistants) — to the Lord who was their Master, who purchased and won them — to us who are this Lord's ministers; thus to the Lord to take care of his own but to us, the Lord's ministers, in full devotion, in complete attachment. And the latter was "God's will." In other words, Paul and his helpers understood what the Macedonians intended and did by so liberally contributing to the collection as far as they (Paul, etc.) were concerned. As the Lord's ministers they were making this collection, and these Macedonians were showing their complete devotion to them as such ministers.

This is said to the Corinthians who had of late turned away from devotion to these ministers. What a contrast the Macedonians are affording! Here is the example which the Corinthians should follow. Let them, too, first of all in this matter of the collection give themselves to the Lord in utter trust and to the Lord's ministers in devoted adherence. Then whatever money they would give would be acceptable to God.

6) As a result (εἰς τό, R. 1090), Paul adds, we urged Titus (the aorist implies: successfully) that, as he had already begun, so also he should finish for you also this grace. Ἵνα is subfinal and states what was urged upon Titus. The Greek is satisfied with the mere aorist "as he did begin"; in English we want the time relation "had (already) begun." Begun what? Evidently the work of collecting, which had lagged badly, which Titus had set in motion again; not all that Titus had begun in Corinth toward righting all the bad conditions. The context deals with only the matter of the collection.

We see that Titus is to return to Corinth at once. He is to finish what he began. Paul writes significantly:

he is to finish "for you also this grace," i. e., "grace of God" (v. 1). As for the Macedonians, so for the Corinthians the whole matter of the collection is to be a bestowal of God's unmerited grace, is to be their own spiritual enrichment. Paul implies that this bestowal had begun in the case of the Corinthians and wants it fully completed.

We need not look askance at the statements that Titus began and is to finish this divine grace and then change the word χάρις into something human, namely the favor which the Corinthians extend by their contributions of money. Even God's saving grace is extended through means, the Word and the ministry. As God's minister Titus "began," as such he is to "finish" this grace from God to the great enrichment of the Corinthians.

Here we have the right view of the work of the ministry in collecting money for the church. When we induce the congregations to give as these Macedonians gave, and as the Corinthians had begun to give and were to finish giving, we act as God's means for bestowing additional measures of God's grace upon them, we are helping them to new measures of priceless grace. In other words, we are enriching *them* and not impoverishing them. As to more and more bestowals of God's grace, read the salutations to the epistles, in which the writers wish for their Christian readers "grace from God, our Father," etc. (see 1:2). Grace does not exhaust itself in the one gift of righteousness when faith is kindled. Ever greater measures of grace are to become ours. But in this work of helping a congregation to be thus enriched by God's grace the minister who does not first of all secure this enrichment for himself by the right kind of giving with his own heart and his own hand will be but a poor helper if he is a helper to any degree.

II. *How the Corinthians Should Follow the Example of the Macedonians*

7) Now, as in everything you abound — faith and doctrine and knowledge and all earnestness and love from you to us — continue to abound also in this grace!

This is the continuative ἀλλά which adds the other side. In v. 6 Titus is urged in addition to the fact that the Corinthians themselves are urged. Something similar is done in both cases: Titus is urged on the basis of what he had begun; the Corinthians on the basis of that in which they already abound; each is to crown past achievement, the one his work, the others their possessions. Ἀλλά is not adversative, nor does this connective break off as it sometimes does by dropping a subject to take up a more vital point, for what Titus and the Corinthians are to do is most closely related.

Paul is happy to acknowledge what the Corinthians have in abundance. "In everything" is not absolute as though their possessions cannot be augmented. This is indicated by five datives which are added only appositionally and without ἐν: "in everything — faith, doctrine, knowledge, earnestness, love." Five is rhetorically the half of ten (fullest completeness), and thus this five calls for additions, one of which is named, "this grace." The Corinthians have faith and are believers. They have λόγος, which is not "utterance" (our versions), *Rede*, or speech (λαλία or ῥήματα). The *logos* refers to the substance of what is said; it is not διδαχή, "teaching," but more general, we may say "doctrine," what the Corinthians believe and confess. Hence "knowledge" follows. These three thus belong together in the order in which they appear. They constitute a wonderful possession, especially when they are had in abundance (see the noun and the verb in v. 2): true faith resting on true doctrine and apprehended by true knowledge.

Added to these are the moral virtues: "all earnestness" that is inspired by faith, doctrine, and knowledge; and then love for the Lord's ministers who have helped the Corinthians to attain this spiritual abundance or riches. The Greek has two expressive phrases: ἐξ ὑμῶν ἐν ἡμῖν; they are verbal opposites and yet belong together: the love that originates *"from* you" and rests *"in* us." We say *"from* you *to* us" since our idiom does not use "in" as the Greek does.

The poorly attested reading which is unnecessarily preserved in the R. V. margin: "our love to you," which reverses the pronouns, deserves no attention. It overlooks the close correspondence with v. 5, the fact that the Macedonians gave themselves "to us by God's will." Paul does not say: we gave ourselves to the Macedonians; so he does not here say: our love to the Corinthians. In both instances he says the reverse. Paul is now calling on the Corinthians to exercise their love to the Lord's ministers in the collection which these ministers have gotten under way. This their love for them is not the only motive, yet it is a motive. In the case of the Corinthians it is to be a most important one which demonstrates their fully renewed loyalty to these ministers.

We have the imperatival ἵνα with its subjunctive. This ἵνα is a mere expletive (R. 933) and very much in place with the present tense, thus placing the imperative meaning beyond doubt: ἵνα περισσεύητε, "continue to abound!" Περισσεύετε could be either indicative or imperative and hence ambiguous; ἵνα makes it imperative. "In the grace" is again "the grace of God" as explained in v. 1. Note how this word runs through v. 1, 4, 6, 7. It has the same meaning throughout, and this is not the favor which the human givers bestow on the poor saints in Jerusalem.

8) Paul's imperative is a sweet gospel command. "Abound in this grace!" means: "Let yourselves be made rich in God's favor and grace!" This imperative is not like a military order (ἐπιταγή). **Not by way of order do I speak** (Paul dictates this letter) **but as testing by means of others the genuineness of your love.**

Τὸ γνήσιον, the articulated neuter adjective, is used by Paul in the classic fashion instead of the abstract noun, here "the genuineness." Δοκιμάζω is explained in v. 2 ("test"). Paul is not issuing orders to the Corinthians as a commander who is simply to be obeyed; he is doing a far deeper thing, he is using the loving earnestness of others (the Macedonians) as a simple means for testing the genuineness of the love of the Corinthians. He is giving the Corinthians an opportunity to compare their love with the love the Macedonians manifested in their great earnestness. The genuineness of what the Macedonians are showing is beyond question; it is, then, a good means (διά) for testing the Corinthians.

Paul means for testing the love of the Corinthians to him and to his assistants as God's ministers. The context shows clearly that this love is referred to and not just love in general or love for the needy in Jerusalem. In v. 7 Paul acknowledges this love toward him and his helpers; it had declined but had revived and would now be tested by being asked to do something that would call it fully into action, namely this collection. In v. 5 he states that the Macedonians gave themselves to him and to his helpers in completest devotion by the way in which they responded in the matter of this collection.

We should not be surprised that Paul makes this collection a test of love toward himself. Love for Paul and for his assistants was love for the great work in which they were engaged. Through the collection the

Corinthians would participate in this work; their hearts would be knit together in purest love with the ministers who lived in this work. Coldness and indifference in the matter of the collection would show how little they loved these ministers. Paul has no fear that contributions might be made *only* for his sake. He ever conducted his work so that this could not be done. He so completely merged himself and his work in the Lord that one could show genuine love to him only by loving the Lord and genuine love to the Lord only by loving also Paul and those who helped Paul.

9) "For" makes this plain. **For you know the grace of our Lord Jesus Christ, that because of you he became poor while being rich in order that you by means of his poverty may become rich.** Who would not love the Lord's ministers who brought them to this Lord, through him to become so rich? This is not an isolated statement about the Lord's grace. It is embedded in a significant context which deals with Paul and his assistants, and deals with them in an effort to enlist all their congregations in the great collection as a work of love. All of the motives which the Corinthians are to follow are twined together: love for the Lord, love for his ministers, love for their work, love for the needy saints. It is a harp of many strings on which one melody is to be played, and every string is to give its concordant note.

You know the Lord's grace, Paul says, we have told you about that long ago and ever again. He restates this grace in a brief but extremely pertinent way. It is χάρις or "grace" in the fullest sense of the word, wholly undeserved favor. The full soteriological name is used: our Lord (his relation to us whom he purchased and won) Jesus (his personal name, which itself means Savior) Christ (his official name, the Anointed One sent us by God and anointed as our

Prophet, High Priest, and King). It is *his* grace that Paul recalls to the mind of the Corinthians.

Ὅτι is epexegetical and defines this grace: "You know that he wants you to become rich." Γινώσκετε = you realize. The Corinthians had experienced this enriching grace, had had some of these riches. Paul wants them to have much more. This verb often expresses the personal relation of the subject to its object (C.-K. 388), here the personal relation of the Corinthians to this grace of which they had had and were having rich experience.

How some can regard this passage as a reference to the mere example which Christ sets for the Corinthians passes understanding. In no way whatever is Paul pointing the Corinthians to Christ's example and asking them to follow it. The very idea of comparing God's (v. 1) or Christ's *grace* (mark the word!) with the contributions we make for poor Christians is out of place. Unworthy sinners who ought to be punished may receive grace from God or Christ, but saints who are sinners can never receive grace from other saints who are also sinners. That thought never entered Paul's mind. Four times we have had χάρις (v. 1, 4, 6, 7), four times as receiving God's grace, i. e., a new measure of favor from God, each time in the sense that, when we respond to God by bestowing gifts of charity, this is a new measure of his grace to us. Now Paul calls it "the grace of our Lord Jesus Christ," his unmerited favor to us, and describes it. The Corinthians had this grace but are to desire and to receive a new measure of it just as did the Macedonians even as it is the purpose of Jesus to make us literally rich in this grace of his. This is the sense of what Paul says and never that we are to copy Christ's example of grace.

"Because of you he became poor while being rich," — because of *you*, "in order that *you* by means of his poverty may become rich." Both aorists are ingressive, a common force of aoristic verbs that express state or condition (R. 834; B.-D. 331). It was not the incarnation by which Christ became poor although this idea is often expressed. He is incarnate now and certainly not poor in his glorified incarnate state. He became poor by entering the state of humiliation. He entered this state simultaneously with his incarnation, but the two should not be confused or made identical. Christ entered the state of humiliation in order to be able to work out our redemption.

In what sense did he become poor? He laid aside the use of his divine attributes, their constant use and not their possession, their χρῆσις and not their κτῆσις. In his ministry he made some use of his omnipotence and his omniscience, namely in the miracles, which shows that he retained the possession. It likewise shows that he laid aside the use only in so far as this was necessary for his redemptive work. He emptied himself (ἐκένωσε, Phil. 2:7) of the use and not, as the Kenoticists claim, of the possession. Christ was and remained God, blessed forever (Rom. 9:5) during the entire state of his humiliation. This state pertained only to his human nature and ended at the time of the vivification in the tomb, Christ's human nature then entered the state of eternal exaltation.

It makes little difference whether we translate πλούσιος ὤν: "while he was rich" or "though he was rich." The latter cannot and does not mean that Christ ceased to be God, ceased to possess the attributes of his deity. To speak about ὤν serving in lieu of an imperfect participle is no gain since the imperfect is just as durative in meaning as is the present. It is unwarranted to say that, unless Christ gave up the riches, he did not really become poor as if being infinitely rich and not using the riches but walking in the form of a servant and being made in the likeness of men (Phil.

2:7, etc.) is not a case of becoming poor. Yet, this is the ordinary way: a millionaire loses all his millions for good and all and then is poor. But does this ordinary experience in the unique case of the God-man when the figures of being rich and being poor are applied, not to outward possession of money, but to his own infinite attributes, change the realities of Christ's case into the same sort of ordinary experience? Figurative language is illustrative of the realities, each figure of only one feature of the reality. Figures are helps and never more than that.

Christ, so rich, became so poor in order that we may become infinitely rich. In literal language: He who possessed all exaltation also in his human nature used such lowly humiliation in order that we, who were in utter abasement in our sin, may become exalted by his grace. The dative "by means of his poverty" is a dative of means. The aorist should be rendered "may become" ("might" in our versions is too potential). This ingressive aorist = may actually become; it is effective as well as ingressive, an aorist for that reason. "May become rich" is not only justification, not only this fundamental reception of grace for our enrichment, but also all that flows from justification. Romans 5 to 8 describe these results at length.

Here Paul has in mind the grace of Christ for our enrichment when by his grace we give to the needy. In 1:16 John writes: χάριν ἀντὶ χάριτος, "grace for grace," grace in ever-new measure, in an endless stream. Do the Corinthians want this new and additional grace? Has all of the grace which they have already received been so sweet to them that they would delight in more of it? They need only to let Christ open their hearts to help these saints in Jerusalem. What a gift of grace that would be to the Corinthians themselves!

10) Still speaking for himself alone, Paul adds to the blessed purpose of Christ: **And I am offering a**

judgment in this matter, for this is of advantage to you, you being such as began a year ago not only the doing but the willing. However, now finish also the doing in order that, as (there is) **the readiness of willing, so also** (there may be) **the finishing from** (the resources you) **have.**

All that he is saying is "a judgment in this" (matter or thing), γνώμη ἐν τούτῳ; Paul is giving it to the Corinthians as such (δίδωμι). The word γνώμη does not mean a mere personal opinion but much more; nor a formal resolution which the Corinthians are to adopt in a meeting similar to the one he formulated for them in I Cor. 5:3-5; it is less than such a resolution, namely a well-considered judgment which will have great and decisive weight with the Corinthians.

With γάρ Paul points out a special additional reason that this judgment of his should have special weight. Of course, this fact should have decisive weight that our giving is really a grace and an undeserved gift (χάρις) bestowed upon us givers by God and by our Lord Jesus Christ. But in addition to this general consideration there is the special advantage that will accrue to the Corinthians (ὑμῖν συμφέρει) since they are such as had already begun this work a year ago; οἵτινες, as so often, has causal force: "because you are such as began."

The Corinthians are not just beginning; they began a year ago, but they had allowed the collecting to lag during recent months. It was good for them to take a new look at this blessed work, to see it with Paul's eyes, to note that it was not merely a work of doing something for other people but really a bestowal of a new measure of grace upon themselves by God and by Christ. Their great desire for this grace will now move them mightily after the delay to finish this work, to finish it so that it will be grace and enrichment for themselves from God and from their Lord Jesus Christ.

For this reason Paul states it in this significant way: you began a year ago "not only the doing but the willing" (substantivized object infinitives). He places the willing in the second place because this is the essential thing. No mere doing, even if it were completed (ποιῆσαι, effective aorist), would make the work a grace from Christ, for one might do the giving only outwardly, only because others were also giving, etc. No, Paul says, you also began the willing, the essential thing in this matter; and the infinitive θέλειν is present and thus durative, a willing that remains operative all the time. To have such willing is to have grace and enrichment from God, the giver of all grace, and from Christ, the mediator of all grace in having become poor for our enrichment.

11) So Paul says: "Now finish also the doing" (aorist, the complete doing). And do this "in order that, as (there is) the readiness of willing, thus also (there may be) the completed finish." In "the readiness of the willing" the genitive infinitive may be regarded as appositional: the readiness which consists in willing. Καθάπερ denotes correspondence. Paul does not make the completed finish the measure for the readiness of willing but does the reverse. Most properly. Let our completed deed measure up to our readiness and our will! For so often we will, we say we are ready, and we also mean it; but alas, when the deed is finished it falls far below our well-intentioned readiness. Many a measure is passed in a congregational meeting, in a church convention. It is voted with zest, unanimity, enthusiasm, and then, when we look at the final deed (τὸ ποιῆσαι, τὸ ἐπιτελέσαι), it turns out to be but half a job. So the individual starts with high resolve and often ends with only partial execution.

Now God looks at the willing (τὸ θέλειν, durative), for this is in the heart, this is decisive for grace and enrichment for ourselves. On the willing also depend the doing and the completing. But if these do not follow, it is due to the fact that the willing has not been genuine, true, deep, effective. The doing to completion is the evidence and the proof of the right willing. You may will with a loud voice, unless your will produces the corresponding deed, it is hollow, no grace of God and of Christ to you whatever, no enrichment for your spiritual life. Read I John 3:17, 18.

Paul's conception of true Christian giving as being a grace of God and of Christ which enriches us would, if it filled our preachers and our people, mightily stimulate their readiness to will and their fully completing what they thus will. The final phrase, which uses another infinitive as a noun: ἐκ τοῦ ἔχειν, leads over to the next thought. The six substantivized infinitives, three aorists, three presents, all placed so close together, are striking and exhibit Paul's linguistic skill, the more so when we note how exactly they are used to express Paul's thought. Note even the arrangement: one present infinitive between two aorists (first three), then one aorist between two presents (the second three). The last could easily be some other form of expression, but it completes the six. Literally: the completion "from or out of the having" = out of the resources you continue to have. Give as you have, i. e., as God's goodness lets you have of his beneficent abundance.

12) Paul elaborates this: **For if the readiness is there** — and Paul assumes that it is — (it is) **fully acceptable** (to God) **according as one may have, not according as one does not have.** This is said for the comfort of the poor. Let no poor man who is eager to give grieve because he has little, perhaps even nothing, to give; let him not think that, because he has

nothing to give, he is deprived of the grace of God and the enrichment which his giving would be to him. His readiness to give is fully acceptable (εὐπρόσδεκτος, which is stronger than δεκτός) to God as though he had much and gave accordingly instead of not having and not being able to give. For the grace and the enrichment lie in this readiness which God bestows and which is so acceptable to him and not merely in the size of the gift.

When a man has something he may give, God measures his readiness to give according to what he may have. That is the first point. If one should have much and yet gives little, his readiness is according; it is small, its acceptability on the part of God is equally small. If one has whatever he has and gives in full accord with that, his readiness is according, and the acceptability on the part of God is also according. In other words, the willing is measured by the deed. But this cannot be applied to the man who actually has nothing at all that he can give. The standard (καθό) applied in the one case cannot be and thus is not applied in the other (οὐ καθό). God looks at his readiness alone, regards that alone as acceptable. We say he accepts the will for the deed. Moreover, he is able to know fully without a deed on our part what genuineness there is in our willing and our readiness. The thought is as clear as it can be, and the words state the thought exactly. The man who cannot give a thing will, because of his readiness, have the same enrichment in proportion to his readiness. The enrichment is always in the degree of readiness in the heart.

13) We must understand this whole matter of giving to the saints aright as "for" now explains. It is not at all a matter of giving as much as possible to others even to the point of impoverishing ourselves — as though the virtue of giving lay in that. Then he who is too poor to give anything would, indeed, be

entirely excluded. But this is entirely a matter of ἰσότης (the word is even repeated), of "equity" or "equalization." In Christian giving the matter of the giver and those to whom he gives is always made even, we may say is balanced. All that Paul has been saying from v. 1 onward has been stating that, and it comes to a point here where "the willing" and "the readiness" are measured by the rule "as one may have" but not in the case of him who has readiness (perhaps great) but has nothing besides that, no actual gift that he can give. He is by no means excluded from this blessed equalization.

For (it is) not that others may have relief, you distress; but (it is a matter) **due to equalization — just at present your abundance for their deficiency in order that also their abundance may redound for your deficiency in order that there may get to be equalization, even as it has been written** (and is thus still on record) : **He having much did not get to have more, and he having little did not get to have less.**

The two datives ἄλλοις and ὑμῖν are merely the common idiom with the forms of εἶναι: "to be for," i. e., "others have — you have." Note "I have had ἄνεσιν" in 2:12 and 7:5, the noun meaning "relief," its opposite θλῖψις thus denoting "distress." This matter of Christian giving is not one of furnishing all possible relief to others even to the point of leaving ourselves in distress. The perfection of giving does not aim at (ἵνα, purpose) providing relief for others at the price of distressing destitution for ourselves. We should not so understand v. 4, the Macedonian giving "beyond ability." For one thing, that would be stopping up one hole by opening another, relieving paupers by just making new ones. But this is not Paul's point although some commentators think it is and then praise Paul for being "sensible."

14) Paul's point is that Christian giving is *not a one-sided* matter. If it were, relief for others and distress for ourselves would constitute its perfection. And then the man who has nothing (v. 12) is in this distress to start with and could get no grace or blessing from this matter at all, for he could not join in this one-sided operation. No, ἀλλά, Paul says, it is something ἐξ ἰσότητος, entirely. He, of course, uses the Greek idiom "out of, due to equalization"; we should say "based on equalization or equality." The Greek conception is: drawn "from" equality; and the noun means "sameness," two sides are even, alike, balanced. In true Christian giving the ledger is always balanced. There is never a debit; never so much to our credit for so much we have done. God conducts all of it on the principle of a perfect ἰσότης or balance. We are always even.

We construe ἐν with the rest of the verse as an explicative apposition to ἐξ ἰσότητος (as we have translated above). Here is the evenness in every account relative to giving as it appears in the case of the saints at Jerusalem: "just at present (ἐν τῷ νῦν καιρῷ) your abundance for their deficiency," that is the one side. But its purpose (ἵνα) is "that also their abundance may get to be (ingressive aorist) for your deficiency," that is the other perfectly balanced side. And the purpose of the whole is (ὅπως is now used in order to avoid another ἵνα, R. 986) "that there may get to be (again ingressive) equalization."

There is an exegesis which states that these two "abundance" (that of the Corinthians and that of the saints in Jerusalem), and the two "deficiency" (that of the saints and that of the Corinthians) are alike, are entirely financial: you help them now, times may change, and when you get to be as poor as they now are, and they get to be as prosperous as you now are, they will help you. Did a Christian giver ever give from such a motive, with such a purpose? Then Paul has written all that precedes in vain. And what about the poor man who can send no gift to the saints in Jerusalem! He can send only his readiness — and that will be all that he can expect in return!

Others state that Paul wants to re-establish what is called the Jerusalem communism (Acts 2:44, 45; 4:32), but it is now to be a communism between Corinth and Jerusalem. Paul's ideal is said to be a communism in which all Christians have *equal* financial means. Still others think that what Paul says about a return to be made to the Corinthians will come to pass when the national conversion of the Jews takes place, when Jerusalem will flourish above all other cities of the world and will dispense its wealth to poor Gentile Christians in the world (von Hofmann).

Others think that "at this present time" implies a future time, and thus introduce Luke 16:9: the saints at Jerusalem will receive the Corinthians into everlasting habitations, will testify before the Lord about the *Opferfreudigkeit* of the Corinthians. The Catholic Church adds: *Locus hic apostoli contra nostrae aetatis haereticus ostendit, posse Christianos minus sanctos meritis sanctorum adjuvari etiam in futuro saeculo.* Esthius. Christians of insufficient sanctity can in the future world be helped by the merits of the saints, i. e., by the merits of their works of supererogation. Finally, the return which the saints at Jerusalem will make is thought to be their intercession for the Corinthians, their admonition, example, and the like. This is to make things equal in return for the financial help which they have received; Rom. 15:27 is referred to.

This last view is on the right track, for it sees that the terms "abundance" and "deficiency" are not entirely material, but it misunderstands the immaterial. "Just at present" is not in contrast with a future date; "just at present" refers to all that is said. There is a play on the terms: "your abundance" — "your deficiency"; "their deficiency" — "their abundance." The key to the double meaning is the word "equalization" as stating the purpose to be achieved. According to all that precedes this key fits only the spiritual abundance and deficiency on the one side (Corinth) and the material or financial deficiency and abundance on the other side (Jerusalem). The idea is unwarranted: You Corinthians can help poor Jerusalem so that *if ever* you become poor, and *if ever* Jerusalem becomes rich, and *if ever* these contingencies happen to synchronize, Jerusalem may then help you; you Corinthians together with all the Gentile churches take out this financial insurance and place it in Jerusalem!

A double equalization is the purpose (ὅπως): one in Corinth which is spiritual; the other in Jerusalem which is material; and the greater is the first. Physical aid is to wipe out and thus to equalize the physical need obtaining in Jerusalem; the material deficiency is to become material abundance. This part is simple. But note that this requires τὸ ποιῆσαι and τὸ ἐπιτελέσαι, deed and completion of deed on the part of the Corinthians (v. 10, 11). Exactly. The Corinthians have an abundance, but they also have a deficiency. Their abundance is their readiness and their willingness; their deficiency is the grace and the enrichment which God and Christ want them to have (v. 1-10). The equalization is accomplished the moment the Corinthian readiness and willingness become finished action by relieving the Jerusalem deficiency and raising it to abundance, for by this action that grace and that spiritual enrichment will be the Corinthians' as God and Christ purpose. The ἰσότης will be effected. This finishing of the deed will make the grace of God and of Christ, the enrichment intended for them, actually and factually as abundant as are their readiness and their willingness. Wonderful — by effecting an evening-up in

Jerusalem (material) a far greater and more blessed evening-up (spiritual) will be achieved in Corinth. This, all of it in its double interaction, is the divine purpose.

15) It is like the equalization that is recorded in Exod. 16:17, 18, an evening-up that was also purposed by God and was also effected by him. The LXX and the Hebrew agree, and Paul quotes the LXX, but he places the subject first in the first clause and uses τὸ ὀλίγον in place of τὸ ἔλαττον. With ὁ τὸ πολύ we supply ἔχων, also with the next subject (R. 1202). The man who went out and gathered a lot of manna had no more than he needed; and the man who gathered only a little did not have less than he needed. This is a simple historical illustration. In every illustration the point of the illustration should be noted, and we should not stress anything beyond this point. An illustration is never an allegory. Here the one point is to show a divinely arranged equalization.

This illustration is not intended to illustrate *how* the equalization in Jerusalem, in Corinth, or between the two is to be effected. This illustration of the manna is not to illustrate *in what* the equalization of which Paul is speaking is to be made, namely in food, in material things. The man who had more manna did not give of his abundance to the man who had less manna and in this way produce equality. The giving on the part of the Corinthians to the saints is *not* illustrated. In the illustration only manna (food for the body) appears. The spiritual benefit accruing to the Corinthians is thus *not* illustrated. An illustration confines itself to only one point and hence is always much less than the reality which it illustrates. In the illustration the large amount of manna strangely shrank. Nothing that is similar to this appears in Paul's reality. Vice versa, the small quantity proved ample, just as ample as the large quantity. It is not so in the case of Paul's reality. If all these things were so, we should have an allegory and not just an illustration. But out in the desert there was a divinely intended equalization, yet it was neither socialistic nor communistic. In a double way a similar and much more blessed equalization is God's purpose and intention for the Corinthians in connection with the saints at Jerusalem.

Who in Corinth would not respond and eagerly, enthusiastically fall in line with the gracious intention of God and of Christ?

III. Sending Titus and Two Other Brethren

16) Transitional δέ introduces the new subject. **Now thanks to God for giving the same earnestness regarding you into the heart of Titus!** The exclamation needs no copula although the optative of wish or the imperative is usually supplied. The participle: "to him who is giving" states for what Paul is thanking God, and we so translate. "The same earnestness regarding you" = the same as my own; this is a case of ἐν used in the sense of εἰς as explained by R. 585 and B.-D. 218, it is a remnant of the old use of ἐν with the accusative. Paul thanks God for filling Titus with such earnestness for the Corinthians because he is sending Titus back to Corinth, whence he had just come (v. 6).

17) **For he accepted the urging though, being the more earnest, went forth of his own will to you.** Both aorists present the action from the standpoint of the Corinthian readers; they are usually called epistolary aorists. When the Corinthians read these verbs, the verbs will express the past actions indicated. Ὅτι may be explicative: "the earnestness that, etc." (as in v. 2); or may be "for" at the head of a new statement (as in v. 3, which see). The urging is noted in v. 6, its acceptance by Titus is now being noted. Μέν

and δέ balance this with Titus' own willingness to go. Αὐθαίρετος is the same word that was used in v. 3, the Greek idiom uses an adjective whereas we prefer an adverb.

There is no need of puzzling about the durative "giving" of God when the actions of receiving and going forth are punctiliar, about this earnestness from God and yet the going forth of one's own will. God was giving Titus this earnestness through Paul; Paul even says that it is the same as his own. Titus grew more earnest under Paul's urging ("we urged Titus," v. 6). "The same" is not one of degree but earnestness of the same quality; the degree lies in the comparative "more earnest." So we have this picture: God filling Titus with the same kind of earnestness as Paul's regarding the Corinthians, doing this under the urging of Paul and others until Titus accepted; and, his earnestness growing still more in intensity when he now went forth to Corinth, he really went of his own will. "Being the more earnest" explains "of his own will." Verse 6 would leave the impression that Titus went only because he was urged, thus with at least some reluctance. But his own earnestness, which was put into his heart by God, soon grew so that he went wholly of his own will. It was important for his work in Corinth that the Corinthians should know this. It was the best recommendation which Paul could send along with Titus. When one notes what Paul writes, all is clear.

18) Two others are to accompany Titus; we hear about the first of these two. **Moreover, we sent with him** (again the epistolary aorist) **the brother whose praise in connection with the gospel** (is) **throughout all the churches, and not only** (this), **but who also was voted as our travel companion in this grace which is being ministered by us to show** (πρός) **the Lord's glory and our own readiness,** (there-

by) avoiding that anyone blame us in this bounty which is being ministered by us.

The question is raised as to why Paul does not mention the name of this brother, and the answer is given that he must later on have turned out badly, and that his name was deleted when this epistle was published in Corinth. But that conclusion is unwarranted. Paul does not give the name of the third brother (v. 22). Did both of them turn out badly so that both names were suppressed? These two brethren arrived with Titus and the letter; it was not necessary to mention their names.

The supposition that "whose praise in connection with the gospel (is) throughout all the churches" describes this brother as an evangelist who was highly esteemed in the Macedonian churches, is extremely probable. But as the clause reads, he was not one of Paul's own assistants like Timothy, Titus, Silas, and Luke but an evangelist on his own account. The development of the church was proceeding independently.

19) In addition to mentioning the personal excellence of this gospel worker Paul in an emphatic way with οὐ μόνον δέ, ἀλλὰ καί, "moreover not only (this), but also," points to the fact that this evangelist was officially appointed by vote of the churches to be "our travelling companion." This refers to the journey by which the great collection is finally to be carried to Jerusalem. Acts 20:4 names seven men, and no doubt all of them were appointed by vote. This evangelist was one of these seven. Being from Macedonia, he was either Sopater of Berea, or Aristarchus, or Secundus of Thessalonica.

Χειροτονέω means to vote by holding up the hand. The supposition that a number of churches could not thus vote for a man is unwarranted. His name was proposed in church after church, and because of his splendid reputation all voted for him to be their representative.

Paul therefore used him to help with the work at Corinth already at this time. It was six months later, the following spring, when the whole delegation left for Jerusalem.

When Paul writes: our travel companion "in this grace which is being ministered by us," we take this to mean "the grace of God" mentioned in v. 1. See the exegesis of that verse and follow χάρις through v. 4, 6, 9. The whole movement of the collection is a grace of God and of Christ to those engaged in it, a part of the enrichment (v. 9) which Christ wants the givers to have. "Being administered by us" (by Paul and his helpers) means administered for God.

Commentators and dictionaries refer χάρις to the grace and favor which the givers bestow on the poor saints at Jerusalem and hence say that Paul and his helpers administer this kind human favor for these givers. How they can do so we cannot understand since the word "grace" is used five times in succession in the same sense, and two of those times (v. 1 and 9) so decisively, once with reference to God, once with reference to Christ. In the consciousness that he and his helpers are ministering this grace as a gift from God and Christ to the givers Paul twice writes this plain passive: "being administered by us," which means that God and Christ were employing them to minister and not that the givers were employing them. The brother about whom Paul writes had the high honor of being elected by the churches as Paul's fellow traveller in this divine work which administered such grace of God to all these churches.

"Being ministered by us πρός the Lord's glory and our own readiness" means "for" this glory and this readiness, i. e., "to show" both. Paul and his helpers are doing this ministering for the Lord's glory as his ministers who are bringing all his grace and riches (v. 9) to the churches and thus also this grace. And when they show his glory they at the same time show their own readiness as his ministers.

Προθυμία is the same word that was used in v. 11 and 12, where it denotes the "readiness to will" and thus by the act of giving receiving the Lord's grace; here it denotes the readiness of Paul and of his assistants to minister this grace to the churches by moving their willingness to action. There is not the least incongruity but the fullest harmony between "the Lord's glory" and "our own readiness" when it is a matter of divine grace that is ministered. The combination seems strange only when it is referred to human grace that is ministered, for then "for the Lord's glory" ought to suffice.

20) Paul continues with a plural participle in the nominative: στελλόμενοι. This brings up the question regarding the aorist passive singular participle χειροτονηθείς after "not only, but also" in v. 19. Both participles are regarded as anacolutha by some grammarians (R. 431, 433, 439, 1134). B.-D. 468, 1 makes the anacoluthon in στελλόμενοι greater by connecting this participle with the preceding ἡμῶν and not, as others do, with the subject of συνεπέμψαμεν in v. 18. R. 1136 even calls the construction of these participles a "volcanic eruption."

But Paul makes v. 18-20 one grand statement in one full sentence. The participles are not anacoluthic. We do not need the explanation of R. 1134 that στελλόμενοι is the Greek use of the participle as the finite indicative. We should remember that in the Greek the participles have number, gender, and case, which is not the case in the English; hence the Greek can use participles with precision and with a freedom that is not possible in other languages. And that is done here. That singular nominative participle in v. 19 is grammatically exact and is perfectly understood by the Greek reader as further describing the brother; the plural participle in v. 20 is equally exact and clear to the Greek reader. Robertson says that we must let the Greek have his standpoint. Most certainly.

This middle participle with μή means: we "arranging this lest anyone blame us" which = "avoiding that anyone blame us." Paul adds: "in connection with this bounty which is being ministered by us." "Bounty" is the proper word where there is a reference to possible blame. It is "bounty" for the saints at Jerusalem. The blame which Paul intends to avoid is by no means that he and his personal assistants might be charged with stealing some of this bounty. He is speaking about something else. The arrangement which he is making is that he is asking the congregations in the different provinces to elect "traveling companions," a delegation to carry the bounty to Jerusalem. This delegation and not Paul and an assistant or two of his is to make the presentation of the bounty in Jerusalem. Since it is made by elected representatives from all the churches, *these churches* will receive the credit for the bounty and not Paul. The money comes from the churches and not from Paul. The credit belongs to them, and Paul's arrangements are made so that it will be given to them.

The entire delegation is named in Acts 20:4. These representatives made the presentation. When Paul wrote I Cor. 16:3, 4 he had this plan of a delegation in mind. At that time he had not yet decided as to whether he himself would accompany the delegates; he might only give them letters that would accredit them to Christians with whom they might stop en route, accredit them also in Jerusalem. Paul eventually went with the delegates. No one is to cast the reproach on Paul that he is stealing honor or credit from the churches. This is the proper place to say that, in connection with this delegate who had already been duly elected.

21) For we are taking advance thought for things honorable not only in the Lord's sight but also in the sight of men. This recalls the LXX of Prov. 3:4 and not the Hebrew; compare Rom. 12:17b. We have the same thought in Phil. 4:8; I Pet. 2:12, and elsewhere. Καλά are "things excellent," often in the sense of "honorable." This is not a reference to "financial accounts" as if Paul and his assistants were handling the money as it was being collected. I Cor. 16:2 is sufficient in regard to that. "We are taking advance thought," as is explained in v. 20, refers to the delivery of the money and arranging in advance for a delegation so that even in the sight of men no question could be raised as to Paul's appropriating special credit to himself.

22) Moreover, we sent along with them our brother whom we have tested out often in many things as being earnest and now much more earnest with much confidence in you.

"*Our* brother," as distinguished from "*the* brother" referred to in v. 18, means that this is one of Paul's associates while the other man is not. The use of "our brother" shows that those are mistaken who in v. 18 translate τὸν ἀδελφόν "*his* brother," namely a physical brother of Titus'. Some regard "our brother" as containing the literary "our" and thus referring to Paul's physical brother. Others think of Luke, Apollos, etc. We know that this is not a man who was elected as a delegate for the journey to Jerusalem as the other is (v. 19). This is a man who was tested out often and in many things in the past and was always found "earnest." B.-D. 416 makes ὄντα complementary to the verb; R. 1123 has it predicative to the adjective. "Being earnest" states the result of past tests: "that he is (indeed) earnest." Let us note that "earnestness" (σπουδή) occurs in v. 8 and 16; then the comparative adjective "more earnest" in regard to Titus in v. 17, and now both the positive and the comparative in regard to this third brother.

Always found "earnest" in all of Paul's past experience with him, Paul is now sending him along to Corinth, not only for this reason, but also because, like Titus, he is now, after having heard the entire report of Titus and having seen Titus become "more earnest" (v. 17) for the work in Corinth, "much more earnest with great confidence in you." His confidence toward or in (εἰς) you makes him "much more earnest" about the task in Corinth than he has been in other tasks that were assigned to him by Paul. The Corinthians will certainly be eager to justify this brother's confidence in them.

23) But Paul makes a difference. Titus is the main character among the three men who were sent to Corinth, the other two are his aids. Call them a committee with Titus appointed as the chairman by Paul. The idea is not that Paul endorses Titus "up to the hilt," the other two not up to the hilt. Paul makes no difference on that score; but the Corinthians are to regard Titus as the leader of the little commission. The supposition of their "handling funds" and being "financial agents" is wide of the mark. These are not collectors.

Whether (anything comes up) **about Titus,** (he is) **my own associate, for you a fellow worker; whether our brethren** (be discussed, they are) **commissioners of churches, Christ's glory.** Εἴτε — εἴτε without verbs is classic; we supply whatever the connection requires. But note the distinction: on the one hand ὑπὲρ Τίτου, on the other just the nominative. So also in harmony with this distinction Titus is with you in *my* interest and in yours as *"my own* associate and *for you* a fellow worker"; but "our brethren" are with you in the interest of the *churches,* in the interest of Christ.

"About Titus" the matter is clear: as Paul's special associate he has been working together with the Corinthians and continues in this status. But the third brother is also an associate of Paul's as v. 22 shows; only the second has been voted as a delegate to Jerusalem. This means that "our brethren" are not, as is generally assumed, the two in addition to Titus, but all three, Titus included. Questions may be raised about the leader Titus or about all three, the entire committee. When Titus proceeds with his two aids, and it is asked how he comes to do so, the answer is: as Paul's own representative who is working for the Corinthians with his aids. If all three are discussed as being outsiders and not Corinthians they are representatives of "churches" (no article: quite a few of them), for a lot of churches are engaged in this collection.

Ἀπόστολοι is generally regarded as "men sent by the churches." But none were thus sent to Corinth; even the second was not thus "sent" to Corinth. He was sent to Corinth by Paul just as Titus and the third were sent by Paul. He was voted only a travel companion for the transfer of the collection to Jerusalem like six others (Acts 20:4). It was too early for him to start on that journey; six months later the start was made, and in the meanwhile Paul is using him in Corinth.

This explains δόξα Χριστοῦ which could not exclude Titus and apply only to the other two. In I Thess. 2:20 Paul says to the Thessalonians: "Ye are our glory"; so here these brethren are "Christ's glory." One person is another person's glory when he exhibits the glorious work of that person. So these three were Christ's glory because they were representatives of many churches who were busy with the work which these three had come to further in Corinth.

24) And thus the admonition is added: **Accordingly, display to them in the sight of the**

churches the display of your love and of your glorying about you! The emphasis is on the last phrase. These men (all three) are "apostles of churches" (v. 23) who were sent by Paul, but by him as connected with all these churches. Whatever treatment the Corinthians accord these three men will thus be "in the sight of the churches." This is said in order to awaken the full consciousness in the Corinthians that they are one church among all these their sister churches.

Today this unity and this fellowship between the congregations or churches are often ignored and set aside. One church cares little or nothing as to how its action affects its sister churches. It boldly outrages not only the feelings but the confessional convictions of its sister churches that are, perhaps, located in the same city. Inner unity is destroyed. Such disregard exhibits a low moral condition, a deep decline in spirituality. How can he love God, whom he has not seen, who does not love his brother, whom he sees? I John 4:20. Does this not apply also to the relation between churches?

"Display the display," like "die the death," is a case of the cognate object, the object intensifying the idea of the verb. Some texts have the present participle instead of the aorist imperative; but no one knows what to do with such a reading except to guess at a corrupted text. "The display of your love and of our glorying about you" is one display: by showing their love in the matter of the collection the Corinthians are to justify all the boasting which Paul and Timothy (1:1) and other assistants have made about the sort of people the Corinthians are. Note the neat little chiasm: nouns outside and ὑμῶν καὶ ἡμῶν, the pronouns, brought significantly together inside. This appeal surely met responsive ears.

CHAPTER IX

IV. *The Purpose for Which the Brethren Are Sent*

1) The admonition expressed in 8:24 to the effect that the Corinthians display their love and thereby justify the boasts that have been made regarding them does not make it necessary that at this late date they should still be told about the need obtaining in Jerusalem and what this collection means for the saints; that has long ago been attended to by Paul. What the Corinthians need is stimulation to speed up the collection itself. It has lagged due to the disturbance of the relation existing between the congregation and Paul. Since these difficulties have been practically removed, energy must be put forth lest, when Paul arrives and, what is most likely, some of the Macedonians with him, the Corinthians will still be found far behind and thus put all the good things which Paul has said to the Macedonian churches about them to shame. For this reason Paul sends not only Titus but as many as three able brethren to assist the Corinthians.

Titus will have some other things besides the collection to occupy his time. We must also remember, as the word "Achaia" intimates, that these three brethren are to look after the work also in other congregations in Greece even as this letter is to be communicated to the saints in Achaia (1:1). Some of the things said in this chapter have a wider scope.

Μέν is not the *solitarium* (regarding which see R. 1151); it includes v. 1, 2, and δέ follows in due order in v. 3. **For** (to explain further) **concerning the min-**

istration for the saints (the same expression that was used in 8:4) **it is superfluous for me to write to you.** You Corinthians know all about the need that is found among these saints at Jerusalem. Paul uses the singular "for me to write" because the idea of having all of his congregations help the poor in Jerusalem and thereby cement all his Gentile congregations into closest personal unity with the old Jewish mother church, originated in his heart.

2) Another "for" adds the fact that, when the need obtaining in Jerusalem was first presented to the Corinthians and the Achaians, it met a ready response: **for I know your readiness, of which I am (still) boasting concerning you to Macedonians, that Achaia has been prepared a year ago. And your zeal incited the majority.**

Paul is speaking about the readiness with which his first proposal of a grand collection for the relief of the poor in Jerusalem met, not only in Corinth, but in all the churches in Achaia. This readiness was such that he still boasts of it "to Macedonians" (no article: to such Macedonians as he meets). Paul even quotes what he tells these Macedonians: "Achaia has been prepared a year ago!" Ἀπὸ πέρυσι is repeated from 8:10

Several points must be noted here. First, "Achaia" and not merely Corinth, the latter being, of course, included. "Has been prepared a year ago" speaks only about the beginning that was made, of course, as a beginning that proceeded forward (perfect tense); but in this case the tense really says nothing about the present outcome of the start. "A year ago" limits us to that past time. A year ago Achaia "has been prepared" is passive: *Paul* prepared Achaia, *Paul* presented the needs obtaining at Jerusalem, *Paul* awakened readiness and zeal in Achaia a year previously. We should not convert this perfect passive

Second Corinthians 9:2 1161

into a present active: "stands prepared" now (R., W. P.), because that would leave a false impression.

Because they fail to note voice, tense, and phrase, all of which refer to what *Paul* has done in *Achaia* at the beginning a *year ago*, namely inaugurated *the preparation*, which was all that could be done then, some tell us that all had practically been completed in Corinth as long as a year ago. Then Paul seems to contradict himself. His boast about Achaia becomes unwarranted. He is now worrying about that. Some of the Macedonians may go to Corinth with him and find out that he has deceived them when he said that everything had been completed in Achaia. Paul will be compelled to hang his head in shame. The Corinthians, too, will look at him with surprise. Everybody will discover that Paul's word cannot be trusted. First he stirs up the Macedonians by what he falsely tells them about Achaia and then uses the zeal thus stirred up among the Macedonians to set the Corinthians going at a rather late date in order to save his double dealing from exposure.

But there is a gap in this picture. Even if Paul succeeded in now whipping things up in Corinth, would not the Macedonians who would go to Corinth with Paul soon find out that in Corinth things had not been as Paul had represented them months ago, that only recently by sending three good men Paul had brought things in Corinth up to the point where he had said they were a year ago? What a fool Paul would be to suppose that he could escape discovery in this way! Trickery has a way of always coming to light at last. Paul quotes exactly what he is telling the Macedonians. It is that he has prepared Achaia a year ago. That is exactly what he did a year ago. He was able to prepare the Macedonians much later. Last spring, only some months ago when he sent Timothy through Macedonia to Corinth (I Cor. 16:10), Paul began preparing the Macedonians. The Achaians thus had an early start as far as preparation for the collection is concerned.

When Paul began preparations in Achaia he met with great readiness. There was no reason that he should not. He told and still tells the Macedonians about that. This was the readiness on the part of all the Achaians and not merely on the part of the Corinthians. Can anyone suppose that now, after Paul himself came to Macedonia greatly worried about Corinth, he hid his worries from all the Macedonians? Compare 2:12, 13. He certainly did not. So the Macedonians knew that despite all the fine preparation made by Paul in Achaia a year ago, as far as Corinth was concerned, a serious slackening of effort had intervened. But this occurred only in Corinth. The Macedonians were vying not only with Corinth but with Achaia, throughout which Paul had made preparation as long as a year ago. The Macedonians, of course, knew also as a result of Timothy's visit that Galatia and the Asian province were busy with the collection (Galatia, I Cor. 16:1; Gaius and Timothy, Galatian collection bearers, and Tychicus and Trophimus, Asian collection bearers, Acts 20:4). Although this is not mentioned by Paul — naturally not — it yet completes the picture.

The zeal of the Macedonians was stirred up by what Paul told them about the preparation that had been made by him a year ago in Achaia and about the response of readiness to go to work, which his efforts toward preparation had then met with. Besides all this, let it be understood that the character of Paul is beyond reproach.

3) Paul continues: **yet I sent the brethren lest our boast concerning you be made empty in this (very) part that, as I was (just) saying, you have been** (indeed) **prepared, lest, perhaps, if Macedonians come with me and find you unprepared, we**

(that we say not you) be put to shame in this assurance.

Here Paul's purpose in sending Titus and the two other brethren is stated: when Paul and some of his Macedonian friends come to Corinth in a few months and find that nothing worth-while has been done during all this time, they would, of necessity, conclude that Paul had not rightly prepared the Corinthians in the first place, namely, as he said, already a year ago. Paul wants them to see from the results which they find when they get to Corinth that he had, indeed, made excellent preparation. There is still time enough left so that the results may catch up with the preparation which Paul certainly made; but, of course, that time must be diligently used to put speed into the attainment of the results. In an honest and yet most considerate way Paul indicates this to the Corinthians. His very considerateness will help to bring the fullest response.

Καύχημα is the substance of Paul's boasting, namely his statement to the Macedonians "that Achaia (of which Corinth was the very capital and had the main congregation) has (already) been prepared (by me) a year ago" (v. 2). This boast Paul does not want to see "made empty (κενός, made to appear as having nothing in it) in this very part" which Paul carefully restates. His boast contained various laudatory implications for the Achaians, but the essential part of it is the one that is now restated with subfinal ἵνα: "that, as I was just saying (in v. 2), you have been prepared," prepared, indeed, by me a whole year ago.

This is *not* the final ἵνα, and this perfect passive periphrastic subjunctive is *not* present; Paul does not write "in order that you may (now) be prepared." This is the same perfect passive as the one found in v. 2. Ἵνα is epexegetical, in apposition to "this part"; it states that part of the boast which Paul has in mind. He even adds "as I was (just) saying," saying in v. 2.

But this plain and most exact wording is not properly understood. Paul is speaking about the preparation which *he* made a year ago and not about a preparation which *the Corinthians* have made recently or are now making. The voice and the tense of the verb form will not permit the latter sense, which is also not in keeping with the context. The preparation made by Paul a year ago was thorough and effective. Verse 1 states that it would be superfluous to make it anew; v. 2 adds that, when Paul made this preparation. it produced "readiness." The finest results should have followed during the past year. We know what interfered in Corinth, namely disturbances which called forth First Corinthians with its rebukes, and even more disturbances which Titus then helped to allay. The fruits of Paul's preparation were accordingly rather scant. The past year had largely been wasted. Even six months previously, in I Cor. 16:1-4, upon inquiry from Corinth, Paul had felt constrained to give directions and information. Something had been done, but not all that could and should have been done.

4) Unless things were now greatly speeded up in Corinth, even upon Paul's coming to Corinth to spend the winter there (I Cor. 16:6) any Macedonians (no article) coming with him would find the Corinthians "unprepared," which discovery would certainly put Paul and his assistants to shame. The verbal adjective ἀπαρασκευάστους is derived from the two verbs that have already been used and is passive just as much as these two verbs are. On seeing such poor results after the passing of more than a year the Macedonians could conclude only that the Corinthians had never been properly prepared by Paul, that they still lacked this preparation in regard to which Paul had boasted that he had made it at the very beginning.

What could Paul say in face of the poor results? Even if he asserted anew what he had done, the Macedonians would have their doubts. Should Paul chide the Corinthians in the presence of these Macedonians and say that the fault for this lack of proper results was theirs? Would the Corinthians want Paul to do that? Then let them remember that whatever preparation Paul had made in Macedonia had yielded the very greatest results (8:1-5). That would certainly justify the conclusion that similar preparation made by Paul in Corinth should have produced somewhat similar results, the other alternative being that Paul had not made the preparation as he claimed he had.

Paul writes: "lest perhaps *we* be put to shame — not to say *you.*" This is *paraleipsis* (B.-D. 491, 1; R. 1199); Paul would place the blame on himself and his assistants although he intimates that he is doing this without being blameworthy, the real blameworthy people being the Corinthians. Certainly, Paul says, I and my assistants would be ashamed — what about you Corinthians yourselves? The phrase "in this assurance" modifies only "we" and not "you," for the little parenthesis regarding "you" is attached only to "we."

The word ὑπόστασις has many meanings so that its precise meaning is largely determined by the context. This naturally causes differences of opinion. C.-K. 541 propose *Standhaftigkeit, Mut,* (steadfastness, courage) which B.-P. 1359 support. Others take the word to have the same meaning as μέρος in v. 3, but without justifiable reason. "In this steadfastness or courage" is not nearly as fitting as "in this confidence" (R. V.) and as our choice: "in this assurance," which is probably the most common meaning of this word. All the "assurance" to which Paul and his assistants are clinging would be put to shame because it had not been rightly placed — ὑπόστασις, literally, "a placing under."

5) Accordingly, I considered it necessary to urge the brethren to go to you in advance and to fix up in advance the blessing you promised in advance, this to be ready thus as a (true) blessing, not as (an exhibit of) covetousness.

There was still sufficient time though none to lose. The ἵνα clause states what Paul urged. He takes the responsibility: "I considered it necessary," singular; in 8:18, 22 he writes: "we sent," plural. The aorist is epistolary as it was in 8:17, 18, 22. Note the three compounds with πρό, "in advance." The third is passive: your blessing "promised in advance" (by you). This is a gentle reminder. In their enthusiastic προθυμία (v. 2) the Corinthians had a yeear ago made these advance promises, but they still lack a good deal of being fulfilled. Note our word "artisan" in the verb καταρτίζω, which is here used in the rare compound with πρό, "to fix up in advance."

Paul calls the contributions to be made in fulfillment of the advance promises the εὐλογία or "blessing" of the Corinthians and wants this to be ready ὡς εὐλογία, "as, indeed, a blessing." This word is to be understood in the active sense: the Corinthians blessed the saints with their contributions, made them like a benediction, filled them with that kind of a spirit. "Bounty" in our versions is not the proper word. Whatever one wants to make "a blessing" will, of course, be bountiful in quantity, but in this connection the word means more than quantity, namely generosity from a deep desire to help.

Thus the opposite is quite correctly πλεονεξία, which is again active, *amor sceleratus habendi*, from πλέον and ἔχειν (Stellhorn, *Woerterbuch*): the desire to have more and more for self. This is our "covetousness," the German *Geiz*. We aid the English a little by translating "not as (an exhibition of) covetousness." The worst feature of this vice is not the niggardly quantity given but the mean spirit which wants more for self and cares nothing for others, however needy the latter may be.

The infinitive is not an epexegetical complement of the ἵνα clause, nor does this ἵνα clause denote purpose. This accusative with the infinitive is in apposition with "your blessing" — "this (your blessing) to be ready," etc. Already in I Cor. 16:2 Paul wrote "that there may be no gatherings when I come," i. e., do not delay, have everything complete and ready. His urgency is now due to even higher considerations.

V. *The Giver Whom God Loves*

6) The infinitive clause occurring in v. 5 forms the transition to the new paragraph. We are shown at length how our giving can, indeed, be "a blessing," a blessing all around, a blessing also to ourselves. Of course, there dare then be no "covetousness" about it. Here there is an exposition of giving that every preacher needs for himself as well as for his congregation.

Now this — he who keeps sowing sparingly, sparingly shall he also reap; and he who keeps sowing on the basis of blessings, on the basis of blessings shall he also reap.

Transitional δέ and a simple τοῦτο turn to the general subject of making Christian giving what it ought always to be in fullest measure, a great fountain of blessing. Review what Paul calls it in 8:1, "the grace of God," i. e., grace and thus a great blessing to the giver himself. Here this is extended by the significant word "blessing" — others are blessed, by means of their thanks God is blessed, and thus we ourselves are blessed most of all. If every Christian giver knew what a shower of blessings he starts through his giving he would be like the Macedonians referred to in 8:4, begging to let him give.

We supply nothing with τοῦτο; we regard it as a nominative absolute or as an advance apposition to the double sentence. The thought is similar to that expressed in Prov. 11:24: "There is that scattereth and yet increaseth; and there is that withholdeth more than is meet, but it tendeth to poverty." We have two beautiful chiasms which bring together "sparingly, sparingly" and "on the basis of blessings, on the basis of blessings" and thereby lift these words into prominence. Ὁ σπείρων = he who keeps sowing, makes it his regular business of sowing either in the one or in the other way. We are shown two classes of sowers; and the question is to which of the two do we belong, do we want to belong.

"He who keeps sowing." This is Paul's picture of the Christian giver. How simple, how illuminating, how true! Ὁ σπείρων is the exact designation which Jesus used in his wonderful parable in Matt. 13:3: "The sower," the one whose business it is to sow, "went out to sow." Here we have another parable about another "sower." Indeed, all Christian giving is sowing, sowing, all sowing. We are all farmers, our great business is this sowing and the resultant reaping. It looks like throwing good grain away when the sower takes it by the handful and just scatters it, happy to have as big a field as possible, to be able to scatter as much as possible. It looks like throwing away when we give. But Christian giving is always a throwing away that is sowing. The very word implies that a harvest is coming. So all our good works are a sowing; ever and ever a harvest is coming. It is foolish to say that this makes for a selfish motive. God designed grain to be sown and to yield its return; God arranged Christian life in good works and in giving in the same way. It is he who wants us to have the blessing of the harvest. This is his beautiful way of bestowing his blessing.

He has created the wonder of the grain as seed in order to fill our granaries with harvests. He gives us the grain in the first place, we could not make it. So he gives us the harvest from that grain which we do not make. He fills our hearts and our hands in the Christian life; all that we are and have is from him in Christ Jesus. All that he thus gives us is intended for great increase. It is like grain that is soon used up, soon disappears unless it is sown; but when it is scattered and sown, oh, how it multiplies! As he enriched us in the first place, so he wants this riches to multiply for us. Actually, we cannot become too rich for God, yea, for him we cannot become rich enough. He multiplies our seed, assigns us ever wider, newer fields to be sown, to reap ever vaster harvests. Loaded with sheaves, we are to come at last, rejoicing with harvest songs. Ps. 126:6.

Why is it so hard for us to catch this vision? Every farm and every garden reveal it every spring, summer, and fall. God is a God of showers of harvest riches. He is the same God of showers of blessings in the Christian life. He does not intend that we shall be poor; all his arrangements are designed to fill us with riches. It is not because of his lack of generosity that so many of us remain poor. Yet he correlates the two, sowing and harvesting. If he is to give us much, we must want much. How can God pour 1,000 bushels into a receptacle that holds no more than one? If, in spite of all that God wants to give us, we insist on taking only a little, perhaps nothing at all, shall he upset the entire generous arrangement which he has made in letting sowings produce rich harvests in order to give us abundance in some other way? What other way that accords with God's generosity could you suggest? The only other way which the world has ever found is to enrich oneself by robbing others, by grinding the face of the poor, by withholding the workman's wages, etc.

So it remains ever true: what a man sows he shall reap. By the way in which you sow, God lets you yourself say in advance in what way, what kind of harvest, and how much you want to reap. Sow "sparingly" if you will, just a few grains — what a pity to throw more into the ground! "Sparingly you will also reap." You certainly do not expect a few grains to produce barnfuls. You certainly know at sowing time for what size of harvest you are sowing.

Here is the proper way to sow: ἐπ' εὐλογίας, which does not mean "bountifully" (our versions), scattering much grain over wide fields; nor "with blessing" (R. V. margin); nor does the phrase waver between occasion and time (R. 604). The plural is real, it pluralizes the singular ὡς εὐλογίαν used in v. 5. He who sows "on the basis of, on the principle of blessings," he shall reap on this basis and this principle. Ἐπί is to be taken in its natural sense "upon" and makes the meaning rich. This sowing is ever done on one idea alone, on the idea of blessings — blessings, praises to God; blessings, benefactions to men; return blessings to ourselves. On no other basis or principle does this sower operate. On this basis he reaps. He reaps all the blessings to God and all those to men, and he reaps the return blessings that God pours out on him.

It is all very wonderful, yet all most true. The Catholic exegesis finds work-righteousness here, namely the harvest as a reward of merit. But no man ever earned a harvest. God makes seed, soil, sunshine, growth, ripening, and even the brain and the hand to place the seed into the soil and to bring the increase home.

7) Without a verb and with none to be supplied Paul adds: **Each one just as he has chosen for**

himself in advance in his heart, not from grief or from compulsion. The verb is the perfect middle, its voice brings out the idea that the person chooses freely what he wants and would like to have for himself, whether he wants a sparing return or one that is running over with all kinds of blessings. Πρό, "in advance," fits the idea of sowing which is always in advance of the harvest.

The two ἐκ phrases point to source. In the whole matter of Christian giving nothing is ever to be done "from grief"; no one is to be sorry about letting anything pass out of his hands, no one is ever to say: "I am sorry I gave or gave so much." These negatives imply their corresponding positives. Thus the first implies: "I am glad I gave; I wish I could give more." Nothing is ever to be given "from compulsion," from a feeling that one is forced to give, that he is being robbed. No one is to think: "They took advantage of me; they shall not do it again." The feeling is ever to be: "I am happy I gave; I really should have given more."

Paul wants nothing but voluntary gifts for his great collection. He here sets forth *voluntariness* as being the only true motive and principle of Christian giving. It actuated the apostolic church (Acts 2:44, 45; 4:22); it has ever distinguished true Christian giving. A large amount of giving has been vitiated by not being free and voluntary. A large number have had no faith or too little faith in complete voluntariness. They fear that this will not bring the needed and the desired sums. So they devise substitutes, all kinds of systems, schemes, and methods that seem to promise more than the giver's own entirely free volition. Instead of depending wholly on such volition and stimulating it by means of pure gospel motivation as Paul does here, they use a little or a great deal of legalism which acts as pressure, or they stoop to worldly, often rankly worldly, methods. So Christian voluntariness declines more and more. The odor of legalism and of worldliness makes the "gifts" so obtained nauseating in the nostrils of God. The harvest of real blessings is lost. See *The Active Church Member* by the author, p. 148, etc., on the entire subject.

All legalism in giving or in securing gifts is Romanistic. No one has yet surpassed Rome in this direction. Many who think they hate Rome yet imitate Rome, and they should give Rome due credit although they fail to do this. Tithing is Jewish. Applying a little Christian varnish changes nothing. Paul was reared as a Jew. If tithing could have been Christianized, the man who could and would have done it was Paul, and no better opportunity offered itself than this great collection which he planned for all his churches simultaneously. Paul shunned tithing. All the apostles shunned it. Not one word of Jesus favors it. His very mention of tithing is severely derogatory (Matt. 23:23; Luke 11:42; 18:12). The only other mention of it in the New Testament is purely historical (Heb. 7:5-9). Is this not enough? More than enough! "Each one just as he has chosen for himself in his heart!"

For a cheerful giver God loves. The Greek reverses the subject and the predicate and thereby emphasizes both: *God* loves him — God *loves* him. See the noun "love" for the real meaning of the blessed verb; also John 3:16. From ἱλαρός we have "hilarious." God loves the lighthearted, joyous, happy giver. He neither figures nor calculates. His faith is wreathed in smiles when another opportunity for giving greets him. The German *heiter* is good. Such a giver is himself filled with the love of God. No stimulus for giving can possibly exceed God's love in which grow all the fairest flowers of his blessings. Paul appropriates the thought and almost the words of Prov. 22:9 as found in the LXX: "God blesseth a man who is cheerful and a giver"; Hebrew: "He that hath a bountiful eye shall be blessed." The Hebrew actually has a beatitude.

8) Δέ adds another point: **Moreover, able is God to make every grace abound for you in order that, by having ever in everything every sufficiency, you may abound in every good work even as it has been written:**

He scattered out, he gave to the poor laborers;
His righteousness remains for the eon.

The verb is placed emphatically forward: "Able is God." Paul first presents his ability, what God *can* do, which implies his willingness; then in v. 10 what God *will* do. Paul's reliance is not based on his own ability to move the Corinthians as they ought to be moved but on God's ability alone. He tells the Corinthians that and thereby turns their hearts to God. Paul thus excludes the idea that he is belaboring the Corinthians with appeals of his own, for this is far from his mind. "God is able to make every grace abound for you" refers to χάρις in the broadest sense of the term. Note the complementary statement: "in order that you may abound in every good work." He makes every grace abound for you so that you may abound for every good work. The one abounding purposes another abounding. Abounding grace is to bring abounding good works.

"Every grace," like "every good work," denotes multiplicity. Grace is a unit, but as an active attribute of God it bestows many different gifts of grace, and each exhibits that grace. John 1:16: "grace for grace." "Every grace" is comprehensive in its multiplicity; it omits not a single gift of grace that we may need. Since it is "grace," every gift is totally undeserved — pure, sweet grace through and through.

We fail to see how anyone can restrict "every grace" to earthly possessions and say that God gives these so that we can give to others. What we need most of all is "every grace" for our hearts in order to do any proper giving. Here "every good work" extends far beyond giving. Paul wants the Corinthians to see that giving is only one of these good works. When he speaks about this one, it is quite necessary to view it in connection with all the many others, all of which are alike products of abundant grace that is freely bestowed upon us. In order to give we must first receive, namely receive grace from God. So every good work implies the necessary previous reception of grace. He who lacks the work proclaims that he has refused the grace of which that work would be the flower and the fruit.

Note the heaping up of "every" in *paronomasia*: *every* grace — *ever* — in *everything* — *every* sufficiency — *every* good work. God, indeed, knows no limit. Note the individualizing in "every" ("ever") which is combined in the multiplicity of completeness. Our versions mar the translation by interchanging "all" and "every." One may translate in either way, for when the article is omitted with this numeral, "all" and "every" flow together. But as the one adverb we have no "all"; so we use "every" throughout in order to match the "ever" used as the adverb.

The main feature is, however, to see that God's bestowal of "every grace" in abundance means our "having ever in everything every sufficiency in abundance for every good work." "Every grace" is thus practically defined for us. Here there is a stream that is full to the banks. All these many good works we need in our hearts: faith, love, tenderness, pity, strength, courage, energy, zeal, enlightenment, wisdom, etc., etc. Then for our hands we need earthly means for giving, helping, etc., place and occasion to confess, and so in every situation whatever any good work may require. All this sufficiency God is able to supply.

The Cynics and the Stoics used αὐτάρκεια to designate their favorite virtue "self-sufficiency" under all circumstances, the feeling of being satisfied with what one has as being sufficient, depending on nothing beyond it. The papyri use the word in the meaning "competency," a sufficient living. Some of the commentators draw on the pagan philosophers when they interpret this word. R., W. P., says outright that Paul borrowed the word from Greek philosophy and allows only this difference in Paul's use, that he did not approve the Cynic's avoidance of society. The philosophers themselves found the word and used it to denote a pagan *virtue*; Paul, too, did not invent the word but used it, as the common Koine papyri do, in the meaning "sufficiency," complete supply, one, however, that is provided by God. In I Tim. 6:6 Paul again uses the word. Although it is generally translated "contentment" in this passage and thus means a virtue, the meaning "sufficiency" is far more adequate.

God is able to provide us with such abundance that none of us ever needs to hesitate about dispensing it with full hands in all manner of good works. In fact, that we rely on his supplying us and thus engage to the limit in good works — this is his intention (ἵνα).

9) Most effective is the quotation from Ps. 112:9, which expresses the very same thought and uses even the figure of scattering seed. This psalm describes in detail the blessedness of the man who fears the Lord and delights in his commandments. One notable item in this blessedness is his great generosity toward the poor and needy. "It has been written" (perfect tense) = and is thus ever on record. The godly "scattered out" lavishly just like the sower who throws out his grain. The next proverb specifies: "he gave to the poor laborers," a simple but significant statement. One might use it as an epitaph upon a generous Christian's tomb. Four Greek words, yet how eloquent!

Plutarch distinguishes between πτωχός and πένης, the living of the former is living while having nothing, that of the latter living sparingly and depending on his labors. The one is a beggar who is wholly destitute, who lives on chance alms; the other is a poor, stinted workman. "To give" to the latter is not to hand him his pittance of pay but to make him a goodly present.

This godly man's righteousness remains "for the eon," the Greek idiom meaning "forever." The eon lasts until the Parousia, until time ceases and eternity alone is left. "His righteousness" is his *justitia acquisita*, the quality of righteousness that is due to the divine verdict which pronounces him righteous in God's court. This verdict of God's is pronounced on the man in regard to his works, the proper fruit of faith and the public evidence of faith. This righteousness thus "remains." The verdicts of men's judgment disappear as being valueless. But when the eon merges into eternity, Christ himself will publish this man's righteousness and the verdict from God before the entire universe: "Verily, I say unto you, inasmuch as ye have done it unto one of the least of these my brethren, ye have done it unto me," Matt. 25:40. This man enters heaven, and thus his "righteousness remains." The divine verdict on his works will never be reversed, will only be published to the universe at the end of the eon.

Chrysostom likened this man's beneficence to a fire which consumes the man's sins and thus prepared the way for the Catholic error that works justify. But these are the works that follow faith, the *justitia acquisita* which evidences the *justitia imputata*. The acquired righteousness is ever imperfect and obtains God's verdict only because its imperfections have been made good by Christ's righteousness, which is imputed to us even before we do a single good work. If the righteousness of life did not follow, this would be evidence that Christ's righteousness was never imputed to us, that justifying faith was never ours.

Paul's quotation is so effective because it brings out the thought of "every grace," first the grace that makes us God's own, then the grace that enables us to do good works, finally the grace that now and at the last day renders its public verdict on our good works as believers. Many a non-Christian and many a Jew also do great works of charity, and the world's verdict of approval rests upon them. But neither now nor in the final judgment can Christ render the verdict: "Ye did it unto me!" That verdict would be false. For whomsoever these do what they do, their intention is not to do them "for Christ."

10) From what God is *able* to do the thought proceeds to what God *will* do. His ability, of course, already implies his willingness even as his willingness implies his ability. God's purpose is "that you abound in every good work" (v. 8); this purpose God carries out, for Paul now says: "he will increase the fruits of your righteousness." Thus the final object is attained, namely great and multiplied thanksgiving unto God.

And he who furnishes seed to the one sowing and bread for eating will furnish and will multiply your crop and will increase the fruits of your righteousness — you being enriched in everything for all single-mindedness, which keeps working out thanksgiving to God through us.

What God does in the domain of nature he will in a higher, richer way do in the domain of grace. We see it every time a man sows grain; God provides that "seed" ($\sigma\pi\epsilon\rho\mu\alpha$). When it is sown, through it he provides "bread for eating" ($\beta\rho\hat{\omega}\sigma\iota\varsigma$ is "eating," the suffix -$\sigma\iota\varsigma$ denoting action; $\beta\rho\hat{\omega}\mu\alpha$ is "food," what is eaten or to be eaten). Ἐπιχορηγέω and the simplex have the same force: "to stand the expense of bringing out a chorus" at some public festival and thus in general "to furnish," "to supply." The connotation is that of great, free generosity. It is, indeed, with a lavish hand that God supplies seed and bread for mankind. God can even be named according to this generous action as Paul so names him here with the substantivized participle. In this way God attests his power and his beneficence to all mankind (Acts 14:17: "filling our hearts with food and gladness"). But we must note the connection between "seed for him who sows" and "bread for the eating." He does not drop bread from heaven although we know that he once gave the manna in the desert. "The one who sows" mentioned in v. 6 is repeated, but the bread that thus results is now added.

God will do the same for us in the domain of grace and do it even in a similar way, namely so that we must do the sowing and obtain a crop. Christ and the apostles see these beautiful and instructive correspondences between nature and grace and use them most effectively. Men generally and even Christians so often fail to see them. Worldly men fail even to see the hand of God in the domain of nature and talk only about "the laws of nature" and thus fail to let the beneficence of God lead them to repentance (Rom. 2:4) and do not even thank him (Rom. 1:21, 22). A covert argument underlies Paul's words, namely that he who is one to furnish so much for men's bodies certainly will furnish no less for us Christians in our spiritual life under grace.

"He will furnish and will multiply your crop and will increase (make grow or augment) the fruits of your righteousness." We now have no less than three verbs, first the same one that is used in connection with the seed and the bread and then two more that go far beyond this. God will not only "furnish" in the domain of grace, he will even "multiply," he will even "aug-

Second Corinthians 9:10

ment." To keep men alive with bread is a smaller matter for God than to load his Christians with the abundance of his grace. The bread which he furnishes to men is only "food that perishes"; he wants us to have "the food that endures to eternal life" (John 6:27). Paul calls the latter "the fruits of your righteousness," of that righteousness which "remains forever." John 15:8 adds that the Father is glorified when we bear much fruit of this kind and thereby show that we are Christ's disciples.

But let us note the terms used; Paul does not again say σπέρμα as earthly grainseed but σπόρος, "crop," a sowing that has been made and is in process of growing and producing. This is what God will multiply for us, not merely "seed" which we may never sow, but planted seed, a developing and a producing crop. When he multiplies the crop we have in the ground he thereby makes certain a multiplied harvest. So Paul adds: "he will make grow or augment your fruits of righteousness." We prefer the reading γενήματα to γεννήματα. The former is derived from γίνεσθαι and always refers to the fruits of the fields, the latter is derived from γεννᾶν and always refers to living offspring that is born of parents. The texts confuse the two, but we no longer should do so.

The future tenses are volitive: God *will* do these things; not merely futuristic: God *shall* do them. On God's part the will is always there to provide this increase of fruits of righteousness in the way indicated. If the increase is not forthcoming, this is due to our unwillingness. We do not let God multiply the crop we have or we do not even care to obtain the fruits. What a delight it is to any farmer to have many fields growing toward harvest! How pitiful it is if he has but a tiny patch! So it is with regard to you and to me in our spiritual life. Now God's will for us is literally to multiply our sowings, to increase the resultant fruits to the utmost. We regard "the fruits of righteousness" as an appositional genitive: the fruits constitute the righteousness. "Their works do follow them," Rev. 14:13.

We do not approve the long parenthesis found in the A. V. The A. V. follows an inferior reading when it translates v. 10 as a wish and changes the sense with its "both — and" and with its improper construction "minister bread for your food."

11) Paul continues with a plural nominative participle, regarding which our remarks on the similar participle found in 8:20 apply. Because the Greek participle has both case and number it is added with perfect clarity. Call it *ad sensum* if you wish but not an anacoluthon, irregular, independent as if it were an indicative, or reaching back across a parenthesis to v. 8 (A. V.). The present durative participle is just what Paul wants to express his thought, namely that in all that God will do for the Corinthians they are "being enriched in everything," etc. Their enrichment does not wait until all the fruit has matured, it begins when God starts to furnish his supplies and continues as the seeded crop is multiplied. A farmer counts himself rich when his abundant crops are growing and not only when the last load of the harvest is stored away. This present participle is exactly right.

Now this progressive enrichment is "in everything for all single-mindedness," namely that single-mindedness "which keeps working out (producing) thanksgiving to God through us." Here we have an exposition of what "the riches of their single-mindedness" in 8:2 means. Ἁπλότης is derived from the verb which means to spread out a cloth so that no fold in which anything may be hidden is left. See the fuller remarks in connection with 8:2. The riches consist in God's providing everything for the Corinthians so that they could put their minds on one single thing without having other conflicting considerations. Their one and only thought is one "which works out or produces thanksgiving to God through us." Their one aim is to get as much thanksgiving for God as possible, i. e., to have as many people as possible thank him. This is putting it in a beautiful and a true way. What a blessed thing to see how God is filling our lives with grace and help like growing crops so that our whole mind is bent only on multiplying thanks for him by what he is thus doing and will yet do for us! No worry about ourselves; no selfish greed to grasp earthly riches for us; only this one high and holy aim.

Your single-mindedness, Paul says, produces this thanksgiving to God "through us." God is furnishing even these ministers of his, Paul and his assistants, to the Corinthians, who are to aid the Corinthians in securing this rich harvest of thanksgiving to God. These ministers are moving the Corinthians to do their full part in this matter of the collection. The Corinthians ought to know how much they need this aid, for during recent months they have been very lax, have even become disaffected toward Paul. Their single-mindedness was marred by secret contrary and evil thoughts. If such a disposition had continued, little thanksgiving to God would have been the harvest but rather much pleasure for the evil one.

Paul writes only "through us," he is happy to be of some aid to the Corinthians in producing much thanksgiving to God. Rom. 1:21 combines glorifying God and thanking God, for we glorify him best when we thank his holy name. The highest aim for all of us should be this single purpose, to multiply thanksgivings to God. The minister's highest work is to aid his church in attaining this aim. How few rise to this vision of our Christian life and work? We see so much duplicity, so much *pleonexia* (v. 5), so much desire just for self.

12) With ὅτι Paul explains and elaborates his thought regarding this production of thanksgiving to God. **Because the ministry of this public service is not merely an adding** (something) **to fill up the deficiencies of the saints but** (is) **also an overflowing by means of many thanksgivings to God** — they, (induced) **by the test of this** (your) **ministry, glorifying God for the submissiveness of your confession as regards the gospel of Christ and for the single-mindedness of your fellowship with them and with all** — also they, **with pleading** (to God) **on your behalf, longing for you because of the exceeding grace of God upon you.**

Ὅτι is used as it was in 8:3. It is a mistake on the part of the Corinthians to think that, as far as their participation in it is concerned, this collection means no more than that they are only adding something to fill up the deficiencies of the saints which were caused by their poverty. They are, of course, doing this, but they are doing vastly more by doing this, they are causing an overflow of many thanksgivings to God. The latter should especially delight their hearts and make them eager to participate.

Paul brings out the distinctive feature of Christian charity. Worldly charity is at best happy only in relieving human distress. Pharisaic and work-righteous charity thinks it is acquiring merit with God. By relieving distress Christian charity delights in the multiplied thanksgivings that will rise to God from the hearts and the lips of those whose distress is thus relieved. This is what Jesus means: "Inasmuch as ye have done it unto one of the least of these my brethren, ye have done it *unto me,*" Matt. 25:40. This divine motive makes Christian charity a sweet odor to God.

We now note the details which are so rich in meaning. This is *diakonia,* service that is rendered with the sole intent of helping others; it is always a beautiful term. Paul makes it even more beautiful by means of the qualifying genitive "of this public service." Λειτουργία is public official service as when some official functions. Since priests function thus, some let the word mean "priestly service"; but the word itself never contains the priestly idea. Paul is not regarding the Corinthians as men who are engaged in priestly work. He sees them in a grand public work which is public because all these Gentile congregations of his are participating together. There is also an official feature about this collection, for it is the office of the church thus to help its needy members.

"Deficiency" is used in 8:14. The two present participles are especially interesting, for they are contrasts: προσαναπληροῦσα = by adding something (πρός) to fill (πληροῦν) up (ἀνά) — that is all that is done as far as the need is concerned; but περισσεύουσα = to make exceed, to make overflow, as when more is poured in than the vessel is able to hold — that is what is done by filling the hearts of the needy with many thanksgivings to God. The participles are to be construed with ἐστί as periphrastic present tenses. Paul says: "You are not merely helping to fill up the need of poverty, you are causing golden thanks to God to overflow."

13) He continues, as he did in v. 11, with a nominative plural participle that is used *ad sensum*. In v. 14 he follows with a participle in the genitive absolute when he is speaking of the same persons. The addition of the latter casts light on the former. As the one is the genitive absolute, so the other is the nominative absolute. Paul does not speak about how the poor saints at Jerusalem will thank the Corinthians for the alms bestowed upon them, nor how these saints will thank God for these alms. Such thanks are self-evident to Paul. As Paul conceives their reaction, the saints will glorify God in a much higher way. Induced

"by the test of this your ministry" to them, they will glorify God for the spiritual results which God has produced in you. This "test" is not one which these saints have originated; it is one that God is applying to the Corinthians. The genitive is objective: God tests out "the ministry" of the Corinthians in this case in order to see how genuine it is as men test out the metal and the weight of coins. The phrase speaks about a completely successful test which proves "this ministry" of the Corinthians a genuine ministry indeed that is in no way to be discounted. When the saints in Jerusalem receive the alms they will see this ministry, not only from the amount given to them, but from the entire spirit which produced that amount. Impelled by what they thus see, they glorify God.

Paul does, indeed, speak with great assurance in regard to the Corinthians. The test is yet to be made. How can he be so sure? What if the Corinthians fail in this test? Paul's trust is not placed in the Corinthians but in God who will move them. He trusts that God will surely bless the efforts he is making in writing to the Corinthians as he does and in sending them three good men to help them (8:16-24). Because he uses God's means, Paul is not the man to speak as though these means would fail. We fail when we resort to other means, when we do not trust the true ones which God furnishes us, and when we do not trust God enough to bless these means.

Paul sees the saints glorifying God for two things regarding the Corinthians. First of all, "for the submissiveness of your confession in (or in regard to) the gospel of Christ." The genitive is possessive: this feature, namely true submissiveness, belongs to the confession which the Corinthians are making regarding their adherence to the gospel of Christ. We need not hesitate about construing ὁμολογία εἰς (C.-K. 690 supplies other examples). It is also most natural to follow the word order as Paul wrote it. What is gained except involution by supposing that Paul means, "glorifying God for the submissiveness to the gospel as made by your confession"? Even the thought is better as the word order stands: "for the submissiveness of your confession in regard to the gospel." It is the actual submissiveness that shows that we are confessing the gospel aright. The gathering of the alms for the saints in the manner and the spirit set forth by Paul is a fine piece of the submissiveness that belongs to the confession of the Corinthians in regard to the gospel. This piece of the submissiveness is evidence that the rest of the submission is also present.

Secondly, the saints are seen as glorifying God "also for the single-mindedness of (your) fellowship with them and with all," i. e., all other saints. The word ἁπλότης is used in the same sense as before (8:2; 9:11); it does not mean "liberality" or "liberal" (our versions) but, as already explained, "single-mindedness." And κοινωνία means "fellowship" or "communion" as it did in 8:4 and not "contribution" (R. V.) or "distribution" (A. V.). Every thought of "contribution" is excluded by the phrases "with them and *with all.*" When we translate "liberality of the contribution *for them* (the saints) and *for* all," the meaning is misleading, for the collection was taken up only for the saints in Jerusalem and not for *all* saints everywhere. Yet this idea is defended, it is said that this contribution to the saints at Jerusalem is *as good as* a contribution to all saints everywhere; by helping some really all are helped.

Paul is speaking about something that is far higher than "the liberality of the contribution." The saints at Jerusalem are pictured as glorifying God "for the single-mindedness of (your) fellowship with them and with all," i. e., for your spiritual fellowship and communion. It is this fellowship of the Corinthians which extends not only to those saints who are being helped at present but to all God's saints, whether they are helped or not. This is "the communion of saints" confessed by us in the Third Article of the Apostles' Creed.

Paul even combines the two objects of δοξάζοντες, the ἐπὶ τῇ that is used with ὑποταγῇ should be supplied also with ἁπλότητι, and ὑμῶν should also be supplied with τῆς κοινωνίας. So we translate: "And *for the* single-mindedness of *your* fellowship." Let us consider the reason for uniting the two objects by means of one preposition, one article, and one genitive pronoun. The two objects always go together and form a whole. Submissive confession of the gospel means single-minded fellowship with all the saints, all of whom so confess and all of whom are in fellowship. The one is never separated from the other. The one is the basis, the other the result. Confession means fellowship, fellowship means confession.

For this reason Paul says "confession" and not merely faith. We know and recognize each other by our mutual and our identical confession. We cannot see each others' faith, but we do hear each others' confession. Confession is, however, the voice of faith even as fellowship is the evidence of this faith. The terms are perfectly chosen. For this reason, too, Paul employs two nouns for each of these related objects. He might have used two adjectives: "submissive" and "single-minded." The nouns are not only stronger than such adjectives would be, the nouns express the qualities which Paul wants to name: the quality of "submissiveness" and the quality of "single-mindedness." The one is the great quality which our confession of the gospel must have, the other the great quality which our fellowship must have. Ὑποταγή is not "obedience" (R. V.), the term for which would be ὑπακοή; it is "submission" (A. V.) or rather "submissiveness." This, too, makes plain that the two genitives "of your confession," "of your fellowship," are simple possessives: confession *has* the quality of submissiveness; fellowship *has* the quality of single-mindedness.

Still more. A confession that is not wholly and truly submissive is one that submits not only to the gospel but also to something else besides the gospel. It divides its allegiance. It tries to serve two masters. This is what we call unionism. On one occasion we confess with our brethren, then we turn around and confess with others who are not our brethren. At one time with those who accept all of the gospel as Christ gave it, then with those who alter that gospel at least in part. The sin of unionism is in the heart; it only manifests itself in the lack of proper confession in word and in deed. Christ ever requires complete submission to him alone, to his Word and gospel alone.

This is true with regard to the "single-mindedness in the fellowship" with the saints and true believers. "Single-mindedness" is exactly the proper word. It means a cloth that is spread out with no fold under which something may hide. Its opposite is "double-mindedness." Read Paul's own description of the latter in 6:14-18. Single-minded fellowship is found where the mind and the heart want only this one fellowship with the true confessors of the gospel of Christ. The other kind wants to fellowship the true confessors but at the same time also those who are not such confessors. Such fellowship is worthless. It has been likened to a harlot who is not for a husband but for several, perhaps, many men. He who can brother beyond the true confessors thereby reveals that his brothership means too little. This is the other side of what is termed unionism. We again see that it is down in the heart, and that it only reveals itself in promiscuous fellowshiping. We have already stated that Christ requires "single-mindedness" in our fellowship.

14) Paul intends that v. 12-14 should be regarded as one great thought: the public *diakonia* of the Corinthians and its supreme effects. He thus uses two participles: a nominative absolute in v. 13, a genitive absolute in v. 14. Since these are participles they express the effects as being dependent on the *diakonia* as a cause. It is a fine way of expressing this very thought. Paul could have made the second participle another nominative absolute, but that would have paralleled the two effects. Paul wants the second effect only appended to the first. This is exactly what the genitive absolute does. We see that v. 13 could not be expressed by a genitive absolute with a nominative absolute following in v. 14.

The second and secondary effect of the Corinthian *diakonia* is of a personal nature, the feeling which the saints at Jerusalem will have toward the Corinthians: "also (besides what v. 13 states) they, with pleading (to God) for you, longing for you because of the exceeding grace of God upon you." The dative is associative: the pleading for you accompanies the longing for you. This begging or pleading (δέησις) is intercession for the Corinthians. It accompanies the longing since the longing cannot be fulfilled, for the saints long to see their benefactors who are one with them in confession and in fellowship, long to embrace them and to thank them in person. But this is not possible; Corinth and Jerusalem are too far apart. So this intercession bridges the gap.

This longing is not the superficial one which beneficiaries have when they desire to meet their benefactors. The reason behind it is spiritual: "because of the exceeding grace of God upon you." R. 605 regards ἐφ' ὑμῖν as a dative: "grace to you." They who live in the grace of God long in brotherly fellowship to meet those who also live in this grace, the more so when personal gratitude for benefactions produced by this grace seeks for expression.

This very idea moved Paul to plan and to carry through his great collection. He had a higher object in view than the relief of personal suffering. He had that, too, in mind in fullest measure. But here was the opportunity to achieve far more, namely to cement the bond of confessional unity and fellowship and the bond of Christian love and attachment. The saints in Jerusalem were Jewish Christians, the majority of those in Paul's churches were Gentile Christians. How easy it was for these two to drift apart in thought and in feeling. What a blessed thing to keep them in closest fellowship.

This is not church politics in any sense of the word. This is spiritual statesmanship of the highest and the purest kind. It has nothing to do with outward organization in which church politics and mere ecclesiastical statesmanship spread themselves today. Would that more church leaders would feed on this text and then turn it into action for the present church!

15) Paul closes this part of his epistle and the grand thought expressed in v. 12-14 in a beautiful manner: **Thanks to God for his indescribable gift!** Note how "God" is found throughout this paragraph (v. 6-15). Paul turns all the thoughts of the Corinthians upward to God and describes the thoughts and the feelings of the saints at Jerusalem as likewise being turned to God. This is due to the fact that all of Paul's own thoughts are turned upward.

"His indescribable gift" fills Paul's entire vision. This is the immensity of God's gift of grace to all of the church and to all of its members. Such a "gift" God gave. But now let us not make the trivial application: "so we, too, ought to give," and then embellish that idea. From 8:1 onward Paul speaks of our giving, of all our good works, of all our motives in such giving and such works, of all our aims and our purposes in them, and of all the results and the fruits produced by them as being nothing but a part of God's grace *to us*, riches *for us*, blessing *for us*. All these are a part of this divine unmerited grace (see 1:2) which includes even vastly more. And it is this which he calls "God's indescribable GIFT." It is a pure gift *in toto*. When we rise to that pure plane as Paul did, the spirit of what he has said will shine in its full glory.

"Unspeakable" is not correct; it is "indescribable," for the simplex διηγέομαι = to recount, to describe, to set forth in detail. The fact that this word ἀνεκδιήγητος is not found in Greek literature before Paul's time and only in church writers after his time, is scarcely proof that Paul coined the word. Not every word that was used in those days found its way into writings that were preserved for us. But it is surely the proper word here.

CHAPTER X

The Third and Last Part of the Epistle

Chapters Ten to Thirteen

Paul's Answer to the Personal Attacks of the False Apostles. He Destroys the Last Effect of these Attacks so as to Complete the Preparation for His Happy Coming

Introductory
These Four Chapters an Integral Part of the Epistle

To what we have stated in the Introduction regarding the unity of the epistle we add the following.

(1) The first nine chapters involve what the last four contain to such an extent that the nine cannot be properly understood without the four. The reverse is also true: the last four rest upon the preceding nine to such an extent that these four cannot be understood without the nine.

All of the hints found in the first seven chapters in regard to opposition and opponents in Corinth leave us at sea until the last four chapters bring the complete answer to the questions raised by those hints.

The last four chapters reveal why the collection for the saints in Jerusalem began to lag, and why Paul wrote chapters 8 and 9 in order to expedite the matter of the collection.

Already this shows why the three parts of the epistle are arranged in the order in which these parts appear. The first seven chapters must come first; then must come chapters 8 and 9 in regard to the collection, and not until then the last four chapters about the Judaizers and their personal attacks on Paul, which included also Paul's assistants but chiefly the apostle himself.

(2) The first nine chapters are addressed to the congregation as such. The congregation as such has returned to its full allegiance to Paul. In these nine chapters Paul embraces the congregation, removes a few doubts from its mind, and stimulates it to full activity in the great joint work of all Paul's congregations for the relief of the saints at Jerusalem. Paul purposely puts all this first and does not interject it into what he has to say in answer to the personal attacks of the Judaizers who recently invaded Corinth and caused the disturbances in the congregation. No "psychological" question is involved in this arrangement of the material as the critics claim; it is simply good sense on Paul's part to postpone his answer to the personal attacks made on him by these outsiders, to attend to these attacks in the last part of his epistle.

All of these attacks deal with secondary issues, assaults on Paul himself. He vindicates his unselfishness, he reveals *in extenso* his sufferings while engaged in the work, he tells about the high revelations granted to him. Paul forces a comparison between himself and these attackers. The real issue, that of his apostolic standing, has already been decided as far as the Corinthians are concerned. The first nine chapters reveal that decisive fact. Only in the light of these chapters are we able to understand the last four chapters, for in these chapters Paul annihilates the last contentions and assumptions of the Judaizers and thus destroys the last hold which they will seek to maintain upon some of the Corinthians — we cannot say upon the congregation as such.

If we separate the first nine and the last four chapters, eliminate this vital connection between the two, both sections become fragments, buildings unfinished, curiosities. This is especially true regarding the last four chapters. If they are severed from the first nine, what are we to do with them, where shall we place them? They are not an independent unit; they must have had a connection with some other good-sized section. If that section is not the first nine chapters of this epistle, what has become of that section? Whatever preceded the last four chapters must have been more important, more fundamental than these four chapters. Would that become lost and the secondary chapters alone be preserved? And how were these secondary chapters attached to Second Corinthians if this originally consisted of only nine chapters? How does it happen that *all* texts have thirteen chapters?

More than this. If, as the critics claim, it is impossible that the thirteen chapters were written as *one* epistle, at *one* time, in *one* situation, would the people of whom it is claimed that they attached the four incongruous chapters to Paul's epistle of nine chapters not have seen this fact? Would they not have left the four chapters in the document in which they found them, where alone, as the critics assure us, they belonged?

3) The correspondences between the first nine and the last four chapters are decisive for both literary and historical criticism. The identical situation is reflected in both sections of the epistle. What the first nine chapters reveal regarding it comes fully to view in the last four.

If the epistle originally consisted of only nine chapters, why did Paul not go to Corinth at once on receiving the report from Titus? The last four chapters show why he still delayed. Without these chapters Paul owed it to the Corinthians to explain the continuation of his delay; yet no explanation would be offered. All is clear if this epistle has thirteen chapters.

In the four chapters Paul's defense is made *before* the Corinthians *against* the Judaizers *with* complete assurance on Paul's part. We understand that after we have read the first nine chapters. Without these nine the four, taken by themselves, would compel us to construct a fitting situation, and this would have to be the one that is portrayed in the nine chapters.

The verbal correspondences in the nine and the four chapters are marked. Leading terms are repeated just as they would naturally be in two parts of the same letter.

(4) But the great difference in tone! Brief doctrinal and ethical expositions of a general nature are interspersed throughout the nine chapters. No such expositions are introduced in the four chapters. Here, moreover, there are irony, satire, sword thrusts up to the hilt. The defense centers on personal issues. In the nine chapters we note nothing of this nature. The critics conclude that for these reasons the four could not have been combined into one letter with the nine.

The very restraint that is evident in the nine chapters shows that Paul reserved the demolition of the Judaizers for the final part of his letter. It was a wise thing to do that. When he comes to this demolition he makes a complete job of it. It is a sensible thing to do that. These Judaizers were most presumptuous; they were also outsiders; the Corinthians were to turn from them absolutely; they assailed the person of Paul with foul, slanderous means. Should Paul use half-measures? No. He annihilates this opposition. He breaks the last hold which these men have in Corinth.

But note how he dissociates these false apostles from the congregation. These chapters are not really a self-defense; Paul is saving the Corinthian congregation from these dangerous invaders who had already done so much damage, damage that, fortunately, Titus had already largely repaired. The purpose of the entire thirteen chapters is one and the same. Because the four chapters attack the enemies outright they properly form one part, and, of course, must attack. Must the entire thirteen chapters attack in order to constitute one letter? What canons of composition are these which the critics prescribe? We still feel free to write letters as we deem best in any situation, and we arrange the parts as we deem best for the situation. These parts are often very diverse. Some parts may be gentle, winning, explanatory, quieting, admonitory, instructive, and what not, and some part or parts — if such be the need — may be sharp, even denunciatory. Who will dictate to us what we dare or dare not put into a letter of some size? When, in addition, the letter writer is a man of Paul's size and Paul's spirit, is inspired by God's own Spirit, and the letter is one that the church of all ages has prized as inspired, shall we accept the findings of the critics? We believe not.

Paul Demands to Be Measured by His Word
Chapter 10

I. *It Is not Well to Challenge Paul's Courage or His Weapons*

1) **Now for my own person I, Paul, urge you by the meekness and gentleness of Christ (I) who, as far as appearance goes, (am) lowly (when) among you but when absent act brave toward you — now I beg (you) that when present I be not brave with the confidence with which I am counting on challenging certain ones, those who are counting us as walking in a fleshly manner!**

We see that in 9:15 Paul has concluded all that he has to say regarding the matter of the collection. With transitional δέ he turns to the third and last part of his letter. In sharp contrast with the entire preceding nine chapters, which he and Timothy (1:1) unite in addressing to the Corinthians, Paul alone now continues, for this last part of the letter concerns him personally in the most direct manner.

It is perfectly correct to say that chapters 1 to 9 are "we" chapters, and that these last are "I" chapters. Only incidentally does "I" appear in the nine chapters when Paul here and there refers only to himself. All the "we" refer to Paul and to Timothy, his assistant, this "we" occasionally includes other assistants. So in these last four "I" chapters a "we" appears here and there when something is said that affects or includes also Paul's assistants. This occasional "we" is entirely natural, for the attacks made on Paul include also, more or less, the men who are his official assistants. All the "I" and all the "we" in this entire epistle are thus perfectly clear. In the whole letter not a single literary "we" appears, which refers to Paul alone. The "us" in v. 2 is *not* Paul alone but he and his assistants. No careful writer, to say nothing of one as expert as Paul, would confuse "I" and "we" *ad libitum* when he is designating himself; here in v. 1, 2 they would occur in the same sentence. Such a mixture is out of the question when "we" is required, as it is in this letter, to include assistants.

The αὐτός, which is placed forward, adds great emphasis to the already emphatic ἐγὼ Παῦλος: "I, in my own person, I, Paul," in this new matter in which *I* am involved and my helpers only because of *me*. Paul begins the subject regarding his opponents in Corinth in a striking manner. He urges and begs the Corinthians not to put his courage to the test when he gets to Corinth, i. e., not to listen to his enemies who say that Paul is brave only when he is away from Corinth, brave only in his letters. It is very likely that some of these enemies even said that Paul was afraid to come to Corinth.

Paul tells the Corinthians that, when he comes, he will certainly use his bravery to dare and to challenge these enemies of his. It will not be good for those enemies when Paul comes and gives them a dose of his courage face to face, that courage of which they have been making sport. He certainly intends to demolish them completely. And he literally begs the Corinthians not to become involved with these enemies, not to listen to them or in any way to take sides with them so that, when he comes and makes short work of these enemies, he will have to deal equally with any of the Corinthians. Paul would very much dislike to do that to any of his Corinthians, to any of the congregation so dear to him; but he certainly counts on doing that very thing, most thoroughly too, to these slanderous and boastful enemies who in no way belong to the congregation, who have come from elsewhere just to invade and to disturb the congregation.

What Paul says is similar to 2:1, where he states that he does not want to go back to Corinth in grief because of the congregation or because of some of its members. It is even more like I Cor. 4:21, where he asks whether the Corinthians want him to come with a rod or in love and meekness. He knows that he will have to defeat those enemies. It is a task which he will not be able to avoid, and he intends to do it most thoroughly; but he certainly hopes and prays that he will not have to include any of his dear Corinthians in that painful operation.

So, to begin with, he urges them "by the meekness and gentleness of Christ" not to force him to use his courage also upon any of them. One article makes a unit of "the meekness and gentleness of Christ," for these two belong closely together. Note the use of "meekness" in I Cor. 4:21. Paul would delight to use that in Corinth as he always used it when he founded and built up a congregation. Jesus was ever "meek and lowly in heart" (Matt. 11:29; 21:5). "Meekness" is the quality in the heart, and its expression is "gentleness" in dealing with poor sinners. Both qualities were manifested by Jesus during his entire life. He is ever, also now, the gentle Shepherd who leads his flock, who gently carries the lambs in his bosom, who goes out and finds the lost sheep and bears it back to the fold.

Let no one tell you that Paul probably did not know how meek and gentle Jesus was during his earthly ministry; the very words he uses here regarding him show how fully he knew. Yet do not misunderstand this meekness and gentleness of Christ, as some do, when they think that Christ could never be anything but meek and gentle. He twice drove the traffickers out of the Temple. The woes with which he denounced the scribes and Pharisees to their very faces are no less than terrific (Matt. 23:13). Christ was also severe, scathing, fiery, and crushing. He was not an anaemic Jesus, whose every word was soft. The thunders of his denunciations are terrible. Yet this is true, he used severity only when he had to use it; he ever longed to use only gentleness.

We thus understand the appeal which Paul is making to the Corinthians. Think of that meekness and gentleness of Christ, Paul tells them, how sweet it is to you. Surely, you Corinthians want such meekness and gentleness extended to you and not their opposites. Let my reminding you of this meekness and gentleness draw you wholly away from these false apostles, who will be treated with severity. Paul is following the example of Christ in treating the flock with meekness and with gentle hands; but he also follows Christ's example when he is dealing with deadly severity with arrogant enemies and with those who second their enmity. May none of the Corinthians invoke that severity when Paul gets to Corinth.

With stunning effect Paul inserts the significant relative clause: "(I) who, as far as appearance goes, (am) lowly (when) among you but when absent act brave toward you." This is a quotation. This is what those enemies say regarding Paul: "Yes, when he is here with you in Corinth he puts on a lowly face and acts, oh, so humble! Brave? — well, only when he is away at a safe distance from you he becomes brave and sends brave, strong language in his letters! He has not the courage to face you in regard to anything; he struts courageously only when he is far away." So Paul tells the Corinthians: "I, about whom they say this, ask you by the very meekness and gentleness of Christ not to join in this challenge to my bravery when I come to face the fellows who thus insult me." Already when he wrote I Cor. 4:18 Paul knew that some boasted that he would never come to Corinth — he was afraid. And in that very connection Paul had replied that he would, indeed, come and would take the measure of these braggarts.

Κατὰ πρόσωπον, "according to face" = as far as his personal presence is concerned, and μέν balances that with ἀπὼν δέ, his being away or absent. The idea is: at one time, when you see him and have him face to face — again, when he does not need to face you, when he is at a safe distance. This shows how the contrast between the adjective ταπεινός and the verb θαρρῶ is intended, namely as a contrast in bearing. When he is face to face with them Paul is humble and lowly in his bearing, quite a coward; when he is away from people, his comb swells, he uses stern words. But that he does only when he is away. You do not need to be afraid of him; when he gets to face you again — if he, indeed, has courage enough ever to do that! — he will be as humble as ever.

When we note that two kinds of *bearing* are referred to, that one bearing is contrasted with an opposite bearing, we shall not regard the κατά phrase and the adjective as a reference to Paul's physical appearance, to the fact that Paul was a little man with sore eyes, at least a neurasthenic, some even say epileptic. Read what Paul writes and keep to that. A little man who is nothing as far as outer appearance is concerned and is even physically weak may be a lion in courage when he is face to face with you. What these slanderers say is that when he is face to face with them Paul is a lamb and a lion only when he is at a safe distance; he turns tail when you face him, he roars only when he is far off in the woods. Paul's appearance is not referred to at all.

2) Δέ is not "but" (A. V.), it does not begin a new sentence, it only repeats the δέ used at the beginning of v. 1 ("yea" of the R. V.). It introduces the stronger verb "I beg." Paul urges, yes, begs the Corinthians. Because the verbs belong together, the pronoun "you" is not repeated: "I urge you, yes, I beg (of you)." The object infinitive clause states what Paul urges and begs for, namely that, when he is present with the Corinthians as he soon will be, he may not have to turn his courage against them as he counts on doing even more against "certain ones," namely his insulting enemies. These he counts on challenging (τολμῆσαι, aorist, challenging decisively). The aorist θαρρῆσαι likewise refers to one decisive exercise of courage. No, no, Paul begs, do not make me use my courage against you! I want to use only my gentleness when I come to you. The sharpness used in my letters has only one aim, namely to remove anything that might need sharpness when I arrive in your presence. Παρών as a nominative is quite regular, its case is not determined by the infinitive; the reference is to the subject of the main verb, R. 1037, etc., also 490; B.-D. 405, 1.

The Corinthians shall, indeed, see Paul's bravery, for he speaks about "the confidence with which I am counting on challenging certain ones." He will not bluff, he has complete confidence. Τολμῆσαι refers to a decisive act of boldness: "to challenge decisively," and states how Paul will show his courage (θαρρῆσαι). Let none of the Corinthians be deceived by the remarks of these slanderers anent Paul's courage. These fellows will get their full dose of it; and Paul begs only that he may not have to include a few deceived Corinthians.

Paul scornfully designates the Judaizers as τινές, "certain ones," and then characterizes them with an apposition: "those who are counting us as walking in a fleshly manner." "I am counting" is followed by the infinitive while "who are counting" has the pronoun and the participle: "us as walking" i. e., that we make a practice of walking in a fleshly manner. Paul counts on demolishing what they count on. His challenge will defy these slanderers to prove their slander, and he is confident that they will be exposed. Ὡς marks this as being *their* slander. Yet Paul does not quote the slanderers, he states only what their slander is in substance and in effect. It amounts to this: "that we are walking according to the flesh" (see 1:12, "in fleshly wisdom"). These slanderers count on this as if it were a fact, as if they could prove it and show the Corinthians what unchristian men Paul and his assistants are. To be sure, they are hostile chiefly to Paul, but "us" does not refer to Paul; Timothy, Titus, and others who assist Paul are included in the same charge, for they would not serve as Paul's agents if they were not like him.

There is considerable difference of opinion regarding what this charge of walking in a fleshly manner means. Paul has just stated what this slander means, namely that he acts so lowly and harmless when he faces people and then acts so brave and powerful when he is away. At one time he plays the coward, then he plays the brave man. His assistants abet him in this and play the same game. This makes clear what Paul means by his confidence when his challenge faces the showdown. It will not be an argument or a defense on Paul's part. It will be the very act of bravery, the very act of the public challenge right in Corinth, face to face, before the whole congregation — if these slanderers will, indeed, dare to show *their* faces when Paul comes. It will be a dramatic *demonstratio ad oculos*. They will be confronted with the man whom they call a mere lamb when he is face to face with them, and they will find that they have run face to face into a lion. They will have to show what lions *they* are — they who stole into Corinth behind Paul's back and did their slanderous work which resulted in so much damage to the Corinthians. Brave fellows to do that while Paul is away! Will they be so brave when Paul faces them?

Paul herewith sends them his challenge in advance. It is the writer's opinion that they turned tail and left Corinth before Paul arrived there. All that we know about Paul's visit in Corinth for three months, of the plans he made to go to Rome and then on to Spain (Rom. 15:23, etc.), the entire tenor and tone of the magnificent letter which Paul wrote to the Romans in Corinth, lead to this conclusion. By getting out and never facing the man they had vilified these slanderers themselves demonstrated the kind of men they were so that the Corinthians thus also saw how much wrong they themselves had done to themselves and to Paul by ever having listened to such slanders and slanderers. It may well be possible that Paul counted on this effect and sent his challenge for this very reason, namely to drive these fellows out of Corinth. A wise move, indeed!

3) Paul states the reason that he urges and begs the Corinthians as he does not to allow themselves to become involved with these slanderers. The

reason in brief is that he and his assistants are ever warring with divine weapons. **For while walking in what is** (weak, bodily) **flesh we are not campaigning after the manner of what is** (weak, bodily) **flesh, for the equipment for our campaign** (is) **not fleshly** (weak, bodily, sinful) **but powerful for God,** (fit) **for wrecking of fortifications** — (we) **continuing to wreck** (foolish human) **reasonings and every height raised up against the** (real) **knowledge of God, and capturing every device** (of human thought) **for the obedience to Christ, and continuing in readiness to bring to justice every disobedience as soon as your obedience shall be completed.**

As poor, weak, human beings Paul and his assistants are, of course, walking ἐν σαρκί, in what is flesh. C.-K. 983 points out that "in flesh" does not mean simply "in the body," but that "flesh" includes the kind of thing it is. Neither Paul nor his assistants present an imposing appearance; they would frighten no one. They are just as weak as other men and lack even the show of outward power which some men are able to put on. But let no one for a moment imagine that in this great gospel campaign in which they are engaged they are campaigning "after the manner of what is (weak, bodily) flesh," i. e., with weak human skill which resorts to fighting "in a fleshly (sinful) manner," in the way in which worldly men seek to gain their victories. This second κατὰ σάρκα denies the first but obtains an added meaning from ἐν σαρκί. Paul says that we do not campaign in a sinful manner as men do who are only weak human beings and who as such know no other way in which to fight except such a weak and thus also sinful way.

That is exactly where these opponents are making their mistake regarding Paul and his assistants. They regard Paul and his assistants as being only men like themselves and thus think that in a fight they will be more than a match for this apostle and his little crew. These opponents imagine that they can outdistance them in trickery and underhand work. Their heavy artillery has thus far been vilification and slander. They were sure that they would win the day by this kind of bombardment. But Paul tells the Corinthians not to become involved in this fight. Paul and his lieutenants operate with a surprisingly different armament. Even to get within range of some shots from that as mere hangers-on is mighty dangerous.

Several things should be noted in this connection. Paul uses strong figures of war. The opponents want bravery, being so heroically brave themselves; Paul lets them get their ears full of war music. He is sending a declaration of war. The opponents say that Paul is mighty brave and warlike when he is at a safe distance. Ironically Paul justifies this talk; still at a distance from Corinth, he is using tremendously brave language. Let his opponents make the most of it. Let their courage rise, let them wait until Paul comes. Ah, but somehow this brave language of war on the part of Paul has an ominous ring for these opponents; there is a most disquieting confidence (v. 2) behind it. There is, indeed!

Paul also broadens his thought. Corinth is only one corner of the field of battle; Paul and his lieutenants are waging a complete campaign with a hundred objectives. This great general Paul regards the conflict at Corinth as only a little skirmish. He has been away from Corinth for so long a time simply because he is busy on a wide battlefront. Let his opponents catch what he is saying. They see him as a little, lowly man whom they can easily defeat; he is little, he is lowly, but a giant, the general-in-chief of a mighty campaign. All of this Paul writes to the Corinthians, only to the Corinthians; his opponents get it only indirectly. All that he asks of the Corinthians is not to get in the way lest they, too, get hurt. These few lines must have had a stunning effect on the opponents.

4) The grand figure continues. We prefer the reading στρατεία, "military service" (M.-M. 572); *Kriegsdienst, Feldzug,* "campaign" (B.-P. 1235); to στρατιά, "army." So also the plural ὅπλα = "equipment" and not really "weapons" or "arms" although they belong to the equipment of a campaign. R., W. P., calls "*we* war" in v. 3 a literary plural, but *our* equipment certainly does not refer to Paul's alone but also to that of his assistants. Some have "our" refer to all Christians. To be sure, all of us have this equipment; Paul, however, speaks only about himself and his aids in the campaign they are conducting.

To be sure, if they had no other equipment than one that is fashioned "according to (weak, bodily, perhaps even sinful) flesh" they could not possibly win against the opponents who were adepts at using this kind of equipment, the only one they had. But Paul and his lieutenants operate with nothing of this kind. Theirs is an equipment, every piece of which is "powerful for God" (ethical dative: to do God's mighty work), "fit for (πρός, R. 626) wrecking of fortifications." This has no similarity to Eph. 6:11, etc., which speaks of the armor of the Roman hoplite. To wreck fortifications mighty rams and ballistae are needed. Paul is speaking about divine artillery, about the greatest engines of war. This campaign is "for God," and God furnishes the whole equipment. It is folly to pit anything of a kind that is "flesh" against it.

Get the picture that is in Paul's mind with all its crushing irony. He paints the opponents as a handful of hostiles who, by harassing Corinth, imagine that they can defeat the whole military enginery of God which is employed in the great campaign that has been entrusted to Paul by God. Ps. 2:4 shows how ridiculous that is. Paul wants his Corinthians to see all of it in this light; then not one of them will ever again listen to these foolish opponents.

But is Paul's language not entirely too extravagant? Did he not worry about the outcome in Corinth (2:13)? Are these engines of his so invincible? Might he not have lost the battle in Corinth? One answer is that in less than three centuries the Roman Empire was stormed by these engines, the emperor himself was then a Christian. This war could not lead to anything but victory.

The other part of the answer is that this is war down to single places and even single persons. That at times does mean worry, especially when one has his whole soul in it as Paul did. It may thus also mean losses, never, however, defeats. Paul lost some whom he could not win or could no hold for Christ. He grieved over these. Jesus shed tears over Jerusalem. But none of these losses, not even the loss of Jerusalem and of the Jews as a nation, constituted a defeat of the gospel. The victories went on and on. Paul was leading them right now. Even those lost only attest the greatness of the victories that are actually won.

5) We do not make v. 4 a parenthesis. The three participles used in v. 5, 6 with their number and their case are by the Greek reader automatically connected with "we" in "we are campaigning" in v. 3. The more important point to be noted is the fact that Paul puts the whole mighty campaign into one grand sentence and inserts even the description of the equipment (v. 4) and with iterative present participles pictures the entire course of victory. The figures of battle and campaign continue, but they unroll before us the subjugation of some entire kingdom, the demolishing of its forts, the capturing of its soldiery, even the suppressing of any rebellious move that may linger or that may be renewed here or there. It is the picture of imperial Rome sub-

jugating one nation after another and incorporating it into the empire.

Those do not rise to the height of Paul's thought who think only of a Roman soldier or only of one battle or one siege. Paul has a far higher estimate of his work. Consider what he accomplished in that grand series of churches that had the gospel standard floating above them throughout all Galatia and along the Asian coast, across southern Europe, into faraway Spain. Here is the voice of the commander-in-chief of this far-flung campaign.

"For wrecking of fortifications" is a figure, but Paul now weaves in enough of the reality to define his figures. In his introduction to *The Parables of our Lord* Trench calls this interweaving of figure and reality "Biblical allegory." It is very beautiful, a cloth woven of two kinds of thread, the gold of reality, the silver of figure. John 15:1, etc., furnishes a lovely example; Ps. 23 another. "I am (reality) the vine (figure); you are (reality) the branches (figure), etc." We are at once told what the "fortifications" are: "(we) wrecking (poor human) reasonings" that men set up against the war engines of the Word and imagine that these forts are impregnable.

The absence of the article means that any and all such reasonings are included. They may be impressive philosophies, findings of science, or the arguments of the common man with which he tries to satisfy the little thinking that he is able to do. Paul says: "we continue to wreck them." And the engines of divine truth do, indeed, wreck them. The whole course of history is full of these wrecks. It is pitiful to see men trying to repair some of these wrecked reasonings today as if they could afford safe refuge in such repaired redoubts.

In this first participial clause Paul states *what* the fortifications are that are being wrecked ("reasonings") and secondly *against what* they are erected: "wrecking . . . every height raised up against the knowledge of God" to prevent this knowledge from spreading. Forts are erected on heights. *Gnosis* is the knowledge of true realization which involves a relation of the subject to the object, of the knower to whom or to what he knows (not the reverse as in mere intellectual perception). To know God, as Jesus states in John 17:3, is life eternal. Here, too, we see how the wrecking is done. The knowledge of God, against which the heights are raised, demolishes them. The Word of God brings this knowledge. Let us not confuse Paul's imagery. He is speaking, not about men as men, but about the reasonings which they set up as forts. These, Paul says, we wreck with the Word. Silly men may crawl into these wrecks and imagine themselves safe in such shelters; but their forts are just wrecks, and who does not know that such wrecks afford no safety whatever?

The second participle goes a step farther. When a fort is stormed, prisoners of war are taken. Paul uses the regular term for that idea: "making war captive of every device (of human thought or reasoning) for the obedience to Christ" (objective genitive). Again he does not speak concretely about so many persons won for Christ but more incisively, more in harmony with the figure of making war captives. Converts are not war captives. Read the exposition of 2:14. The senate granted a triumphal procession to some great commander after a glorious campaign. War captives were paraded in the procession to grace the the triumph; then, however, they were as a rule executed. Even apart from this bloodiness the figure would not fit persons at all. Paul's converts are not led as captives in his triumph; they become no exiles as so many war captives did, they are not sold into slavery, they are not even made a poor subject nation under foreign domination.

Every νόημα is made a war captive; it is the same word that was used in 2:11: the *noēmata*, "the devices" of Satan. Paul first speaks of "reasonings" that are set up against the knowledge of God and uses a plural; now he speaks of "every device" and employs a distributive singular which exposes what these reasonings are, each is a "device," a scheme, a concoction that is directed against the true knowledge of God. Paul is a master in combining singulars and plurals. Every such hostile device Paul pictures as falling a helpless and a hopeless war captive to a victor who abolishes that device. It is captured "for the obedience of Christ."

Let us keep to Paul's abstract thought. Persons have reasonings, and these consist in little groups of arguments, each being a device of human thinking that is set against the knowledge of God. Since they are just reasonings they are wrecked by the men who preach the Word. More than that. Being thus wrecked in themselves, in the case of every convert every device is wiped out by capture, wiped out "for the true obedience to Christ" to take its place. There are no more devisings of our own thinking. They are put into chains, dragged away, executed. Now there is only listening with hearts and thoughts that are completely obedient only to Christ. "The knowledge of God" is thus advanced to "the obedience of Christ." We know God when we obey Christ; and to obey Christ = to trust and to follow him alone.

C.-K. 766 has νόημα mean *das Denken*; others do better by translating "every thought" (our versions) since the suffix -μα denotes result, the result of thinking is an actual thought. It is a product of the νοῦς or intelligent mind. The interpretation would then be that by an act of the will we ourselves bring all our intellectual activity into complete subjection to Christ. R.,

W. P., follows this trend: "That is Paul's conception of intellectual liberty, freedom in Christ." It is true, we do subject our thinking and our thoughts to Christ. But Paul says that *he and his assistants* do the capturing. And he says that they make *war captives*. These war captives are put to the sword! That cannot apply to all our thinking or all our thoughts! That applies to "every device" of reasoning thoughts, every scheme they concoct against God's knowledge. This explains the singular: every one of these devices is led up and — off with its head! Thinking and thoughts? Most certainly, all your mind can produce! But never another "device"; now only delighted and happy obedience to Christ.

6) Paul's grand imagery can be carried a step farther: "continuing in readiness to bring to justice every disobedience," etc. We may translate "holding ourselves in readiness," etc. When imperial armies had subjected some nation, garrisons were installed. These were ever on the alert to squelch any incipient disobedience, to nip in the bud any revolt. When he was in Palestine the author saw a detachment of English troops rush by with machine guns. What was wrong? Oh, a little "disobedience" in Transjordania! So Paul and his lieutenants are ready to bring to decisive justice (ἐκδικῆσαι, effective aorist) "every disobedience" that may arise in the domain which they have conquered. "Disobedience" fits the preceding "obedience to Christ" but means any "device," any hostile "reasonings" that may again arise in any congregation under the control of Paul and his lieutenants. They are ever ready for this last task. "To bring to justice" is the proper verb. Such "disobedience" deserves to get its due. On arriving at the scene of disturbance the Roman troops took matters in hand, inquired for the disturbers, then meted out justice. That is exactly what Paul means.

The point of this clause is obvious. "Disobedience" had showed its head in Corinth. Rebels had broken into the congregation. Paul would have been a foolish commander if he had not taken measures to frustrate this movement, and if he would not plan to bring those rebel invaders to summary justice. He purposely speaks only about disobedience and about bringing to justice. He does not specify who the disobedient are or what the justice will be. Let the Corinthians think what they must. Paul has mentioned "certain ones" in v. 2 and also their contemptible actions. Do the Corinthians want to join them and get their dose of justice from Paul? Note the significant repetition: *every* height — *every* device — *every* disobedience.

"As soon as your own obedience shall be completed" (or fulfilled) applies to the Corinthians what the last participle clause states regarding every disobedience that may occur anywhere in Paul's fields. It answers the question as to why Paul did not at once rush to Corinth when he first heard of the disturbance occurring there. He did send First Corinthians, he followed this by sending Titus. He had refrained from coming himself because he did not want to bring to justice any of the Corinthians themselves — a most painful task for him. He trusted that the Corinthians would right themselves under the measures he was taking so that only the opponents who had come to Corinth would need to be served with due justice, if they, indeed, had courage enough to stay and finally to face Paul when he would come. For this reason he writes: "whenever (or as soon as) your obedience is fulfilled," i. e., you yet your own obedience into complete order again. It is what Paul has repeatedly said; he is giving the Corinthians time. This was wisdom. When trouble arises, it is not always well at once to leap in with all one's might in order to crush it. Christians often right themselves under proper advice and counsel if they are given time; they thus obviate the need of extreme measures.

The sum of this paragraph is plain: It is not well to challenge Paul's courage or his weapons; he is altogether too mighty and too victorious.

II. *It Is well for the Corinthians to Look at what Is before Their very Eyes*

7) The figures of war are ended. The asyndeton marks the turn of thought. **At what is right before your eyes, just keep looking at that!** The object is placed forward for the sake of emphasis; this removes the verb to the end and makes it equally emphatic. The present imperative urges the Corinthians to keep looking at what it is so easy to see. The A. V. and the R. V. margin translate this sentence as though it were a question, which implies blame: "Are you looking only at what is before your face?" The R. V. translates it as a declaration: "You are looking," etc., which implies the same blame. Both imply that the Corinthians ought *not* to look at what is before their faces, at the outward appearance of things. If Paul intends to state that he should say why it is a mistake for the Corinthians to look at what is before the eyes. Yet he does nothing of the kind, in fact, he does the opposite, he points to what is right before everybody's eyes and lets the simple, obvious, undeniable facts tell the Corinthians what the Corinthians should have seen all along. We regard the verb form as an imperative. It is the caption of this entire paragraph.

For this reason the elaboration starts with another asyndeton, and starts with the singular by addressing one of the Corinthians who, with the rest, is to look at a few obvious facts. **If anyone has been confident in his own mind** (the perfect implying and thus still holds this confidence) **that he belongs to Christ, let him count on this again before his own**

mind, that just as he himself belongs to Christ, thus also do we!

Paul is addressing one of the Corinthians, one who was impressed by the opponents of Paul, one who repeats their slander of Paul. He represents a number of such foolish Corinthians, all of whom do not see what should be so plain to them, which is lying, as it were, on the very surface. The person addressed is *not* one of Paul's opponents, one of the Judaizers, as some think. Paul never addresses them, he scorns to do so. He always addresses only the Corinthians, he speaks only *of* and never *to* the outside opponents, never speaks of them as belonging to the Corinthians but ever only as hostiles who have crept in.

This singular τὶς is continued in φησί in v. 10 and in ὁ τοιοῦτος in v. 11. All of these are the same person, one of the Corinthian members, one of those who especially ought to open their eyes and to see a few obvious facts. Not for a moment would Paul admit that the Judaizers belong to Christ. They are false apostles, deceitful workers, pretending to be apostles of Christ (11:13); they beguile as the serpent beguiled Eve, they are snakes to poison simple minds (11:3); they preach another Jesus, have another spirit, offer another gospel, all of these being contrary to what Paul has brought the Corinthians (11:4). Not for one minute does Paul admit that they are Christians. This τὶς is a misled church member. He is *not* one of the τινές mentioned in v. 2 and in v. 12, who are the false apostles. Paul always speaks of them in the plural: "certain ones," and always characterizes them by what they do.

The condition is one of reality (εἰ with the indicative). This Corinthian member has long been confident that he is "of Christ" (the predicate genitive with "to be"), i. e., that he is a Christian. The emphasis is on the reflexive pronoun: "has been confident (and is so how) *for himself,"* in his own mind and judgment. Paul does not dispute or question the fact that this Corinthian is a Christian. Paul does this: judging thus in his own mind regarding himself, this Corinthian admits that he thinks he knows what a Christian is; very well, then let him put his mind to work again: "let him count on this again before his own mind, that just as he himself belongs to Christ, thus also do we" (Paul and his assistants).

Ἐφ' ἑαυτοῦ corresponds to ἑαυτῷ, both thus being emphatic. This is the juridical ἐπί, "before" a forum or judge, this Corinthian being the judge. He knows what a Christian is, is confident that *he* is one. Then he must know what makes other men Christians, what makes Paul and his assistants Christians like himself. Paul just asks him to count in "also us." This Corinthian will certainly do that. Paul has no doubt about it; he merely asks that this be done.

The whole Corinthian congregation got its Christianity from Paul and his assistants. They learned from Paul what really makes a Christian. Any man in Corinth who thus judged himself a Christian would certainly not deny that Paul and his assistants were likewise Christians — unless he had been so deceived by these outside enemies of Paul's as to count them true Christians and had exchanged the Jesus, the gospel, the spirit preached by Paul for what these invading false apostles preached to tear down Paul's work (11:3, 4, 13). For this reason Paul writes "if"; but he writes it without fear on this score.

Paul puts this matter of being "of Christ" and a true Christian first. Only a man who is such a Christian will see the plain things that are right under his eyes, which Paul is about to point out. One who regarded the false apostles as Christians would be blind regarding these plain things. All that Paul intends to point out as being so very plain, so easy for any Corinthian to see, rests on these two things, that the Corinthian himself be a Christian and know it, and that, in the same way and judged by the same criterion, he knows that Paul and his assistants are equally Christians. This is the simple basis. For any Corinthian Christian who sees in Paul and his assistants fellow Christians it will be as plain as day that all the personal slanders against Paul and his helpers reveal only the gulf between them and the false apostles, reveal only that there is no comparison at all, that these false apostles are only invaders who break into other men's labors and make that their grand boast.

8) The close connective τε is in place because what Paul adds about his and his assistants' "authority" is necessarily closely bound up with their being Christians They were the Christians whom the Lord himself sent to build the church. "For" states that the reason for referring to their being accepted as Christians is that something is going to be said about their "authority."

For also if I boast of something beyond that, (namely) concerning our authority which the Lord gave for building you up and not for wrecking you, I shall not be put to shame — that I may not appear as if scaring you by means of the letters. For, The letters, he says, are heavy and strong, but the bodily presence is weak; and the word of no account. Let such an one count on this that the kind we are with the word by letters when absent just that kind also when present (we are) with the deed!

The texts vary between the aorist subjunctive καυχήσωμαι and the future indicative καυχήσομαι (a frequent occurrence in the texts); the Koine may use either after ἐάν. The punctiliar aorist is best, for it refers to some one instance when Paul may boast. He says "if I boast" (singular) and not "we"; but he says "concerning our authority" (plural, including his assistants). Paul will do this boasting, and he takes all the responsibility; but his boast will be about the authority which his assistants have as well as he. All of them act as a unit.

The comparative neuter with $\tau\iota$ = "something that goes beyond," something that goes beyond just belonging to Christ like every other Christian. What this is the phrase states, namely "concerning our authority," the right and power which we exercise in our office as ministers of Christ. If at any time Paul boasts regarding this authority he certainly "will not be put to shame." As far as he is concerned, he has so much of which he can rightly boast regarding the ministry of himself and his assistants that he certainly does not need to exaggerate; and no one will then be able to show that any boast he makes is hollow.

It is the Lord, Paul says, who gave us this authority of ours, gave it "for upbuilding, not for wrecking you" (objective genitive). We see why Paul prefaces this with the request that he and his assistants be acknowledged as Christians by this man who regards himself as a Christian. This man's Lord, who is equally the Lord of Paul and his helpers, established the ministry of the gospel, called Paul and his assistants into this ministry and thus invested them with the blessed "authority" which they have. In a little while we shall see how Paul points out that it is authority which first brought the gospel to Corinth and will also carry it far beyond. But the great point of this relative clause lies in the two $\epsilon\iota\varsigma$ phrases which denote purpose. Our whole authority as given by the Lord, Paul says, is "for upbuilding, not for wrecking you." In this way we use this authority, with this as the aim and object, ever to build you up spiritually in the Lord, never to tear you down and to wreck you spiritually. It is the aim which the Lord set for us; and when we boast of our authority, it is as having accomplished this blessed purpose, and no one can put us to shame for boasting thus.

Here there is a direct blow against the false apostles. What Paul and his assistants had built up so beautifully, a very temple of God, these apostles, stealing in later when Paul and his assistants were far away, went on to tear down, to wreck. Paul puts it personally: for upbuilding and not for wrecking *"you."* The false apostles reversed that. They used their spurious authority "not for upbuilding but for wrecking *you.*" Every reader felt that this is what Paul meant with reference to these pseudo-apostles as Paul indeed did. Note that καθαίρεσις is the same noun that was used in v. 4. Paul and his assistants were also to do some "wrecking," some tremendous wrecking with great engines of war. See the description in v. 4, 5. These false apostles wrecked the Lord's building, yea, wrecked it by stealthy undermining.

9) The ἵνα clause belongs to the entire preceding sentence. What Paul says about "our authority," about its being the Lord's own gift not for wrecking but for upbuilding you, and about his not being put to shame when he so boasts of it, all this is for the purpose "that I may not appear (as the false apostles would like to make me appear) as if scaring you by means of the letters" I write to you. Write a dash before the clause, and it becomes clear. The dash has the sense: "I am writing or saying this" that I may not appear, etc. Various attempts to connect the clause with only one word in v. 8 lose the thought.

Ἐκ in the infinitive is causative: "to cause you fear." Ὡς ἄν is not the classic ἄν with an infinitive used for the conditional optative or indicative with ἄν (B.-D. 396); here it = "as if." This is the only instance in the New Testament where it is found with a simple infinitive (B.-D. 453, 3; R. 969). The article "with *the* letters" refers to the ones which Paul writes and includes the present one. We know about two others, the first is mentioned in I Cor. 5:9, the second is First Corinthians. That makes three. Paul may have written one for Timothy's mission, another for the mission of Titus; if he did, we know nothing about it. The "tear-letter" which is found by the critics in II Cor. 2:3, is hypothetical. Nor would a tearful letter such as the critics have in mind frighten anybody, it would make the readers rather pity Paul.

10) Ὅτι states the point regarding scaring the Corinthians with letters. It is the slander which is bandied about in Corinth: "The letters are heavy and strong (so as to scare one), but the bodily presence is weak (never scares anybody), and the word of no account" ("contemptible," A. V.; a perfect passive participle with present connotation: "ever having been and continuing to be treated as nothing"). See v. 1: lowly and humble when present, bold and brave when far away, at a safe distance. Μέν and δέ contrast and balance the two parts of the statement. "The presence of the body" uses a genitive noun where we have the adjective "the bodily presence." Paul's λόγος is not only his delivery but also the substance of his oral preaching.

Instead of regarding Paul as a sorry-looking individual with sore eyes, a neurasthenic, epileptic, and what not, bald-headed, bowlegged, of unusually small stature, and not a speaker with either fire or thought, we should do better to get our picture from the hints which Paul himself furnishes and which Luke gives (Acts 14:12). Barnabas looked more imposing, but Paul was the superior speaker. In the next verse Paul says that he and his assistants would show themselves as being mighty in act as they showed themselves mighty in writing. The man who made the addresses which Luke sketches in Acts, which on occasion were very dramatic, some of them impromptu at that, was indeed no shallow, glittering Tertullus (Acts 24:1-8) but a real speaker. What else could a man be who stormed the citadels of the great pagan world with indomitable courage and established churches everywhere in spite of fierce opposition? Let no Corinthian slander deceive us in regard to Paul.

We prefer the reading φησί (A. V. margin), "he says," to φασίν, "they say." In v. 7 it is "anyone" (or "someone"), and in v. 11 "such an one," both are singulars. Between them the singular "he says" is correct as also the texts show. Paul is speaking about one of the Corinthians who is impressed by this slander, who himself also repeats it, silly though it is. Derogatory flings find such easy lodgement. People who ought to know better repeat them and often act as if they had to be true.

11) "Our authority," Paul says, about which I shall boast and shall certainly not be put to shame in doing so, is not brought forward as if I intend to scare you so that you need someone to tell you that I am brave and strong only in my letters, that you should not be frightened and take seriously what I write, that my bodily presence and my word when I am present amount to nothing. Just to silence such talk "let such an one count on this" so that he may not deceive himself and deceive others of you Corinthians who hear him talk so, "that the kind we are with the word by letters when absent" and away from you "just that kind also when present," when face to face with you, "(we are) with deed." This foolish member among you has only repeated what he heard the false apostles say about me in order to alienate you from me. He is wise if he counts on the very opposite of such talk. I will say to him that he had better count on this, and then when we meet face to face we will make good by actual *deed* every *word* that has been written in the letters. It will be much safer for him to count on this.

"Such an one" refers directly to the one who is speaking in v. 10; both are in the singular. Paul does not say: "The kind *I* am by word and letter when absent, that kind *I* am when present with deed." He uses "we"; his assistants are of the same kind with him, he would otherwise not have them as assistants. Paul's thought includes also his assistants. The reflection cast on him involves them. What kind of men would they be to be under a chief who frightened people with mighty words in letters and then did not make good his words by deeds when he came to face the people to whom he had sent those letters, these assistants at times even carrying the letters? By using the plural "we" Paul sets all of his assistants over against this man's foolish talk, the very fact of their being Paul's assistants testifies to the kind of man Paul is as well as to the kind they are.

Need we add how effective this reply is? To say that "Paul winced under the biting criticism of his looks and speech" conceives Paul as too little a man entirely. Here he merely pricks this bubble in passing in order to let the wind out of it, and he pricks it more for the sake of his assistants than for his own sake. Incidentally, Paul does seek to frighten this Corinthian a little by telling him that he had better count on seeing the word of the letters made good by the deed.

12) An explanatory γάρ goes to the bottom of this slander. When the false apostles started it they implied that *they* were better men than Paul, that although they wrote no letters, their bodily presence and their face-to-face speech were vastly superior to Paul's. The church member who echoed this slander implied the same thing: Paul was not very great when he was compared with these new apostles who had come to Corinth. For this reason Paul says in v. 8 that he intends to do some boasting. But before he begins he makes this explanation which is ironically deadly

for the comparison that was being made between him and the false apostles.

For we are not bold enough to classify ourselves or to compare ourselves with certain ones of those who (merely) recommend themselves; yea, they, measuring themselves (only) by themselves and comparing themselves (only) with themselves, are not (even) sensible. These are "the certain ones" mentioned in v. 2, the false apostles. Why, Paul says, I and my assistants would not dare to put ourselves into the same class with these men as though we were as high as they, or even to compare ourselves with them as if we were in anything as high and as great as they are, they who merely recommend themselves and never need anything more! The last assertion cuts the Corinthians deeply, for they received these men on such self-recommendation alone.

We could not think of it, Paul says, I especially who am looked down upon when one sees me present as ταπεινός, "lowly" (v. 1), as weak and of contemptible speech (v. 10). "To classify ourselves with" = *aequiparare*, as being on the same high level; "to compare with" = *comparare* so that at least some kind of a comparison can be made (Bengel). The irony lies in the fact that Paul and his assistants could not have done this in sober reality. They actually were *not* in the same class with these deceivers; there was not even one point of likeness for the purpose of comparison. For these deceivers belong to that great class which merely "recommend themselves." That is the mark of so many deceivers: they everlastingly sing their own praises. Yet they always find foolish people who accept them on that basis. This had happened in Corinth. So high they are, Paul says, and they put themselves there! We are counted out, not even a comparison is possible. For, of course, we could not possibly recommend ourselves in such a way.

'Αλλά is not adversative; by translating it "but" (our versions) a number of commentators turn off on the wrong track. They refer the statement to Paul and to his assistants and not to the false apostles and therefore cancel from the text οὐ συνιοῦσιν as well as the following ἡμεῖς δέ, for which procedure textual authority is entirely too slight. Συνιοῦσιν and συνιᾶσιν are only different forms of the same word. This conjunctive ἀλλά simply carries the story forward to another point and is thus at times climacteric, making the new point exceed the previous one; see R. 1185, etc. It does so here: "yea," they go as far as this, etc. It is no wonder that we would not dare to compare ourselves with these false apostles: *they* (αὐτοί) are incomparable. *They* know only one standard of measurement and comparison great and exalted enough to apply to themselves, and that is *"themselves,"* "measuring themselves (only) by themselves and comparing themselves (only) with themselves." Thus they always rate 100 per cent according to their own measurement and comparison. How could anyone class himself with them or even faintly compare himself with them unless, of course, he be or become one of them?

But when they are doing this, Paul adds, "they are not (even) sensible." Anybody can do this, namely make himself the standard and then find that he fully comes up to the standard. But that is silly. It is no measurement at all. It is like only recommending oneself, like singing one's own praises (v. 12a). This is irony, but irony that states only the cold, literal fact.

13) Over against this folly Paul places ἡμεῖς, what *we* do, Paul and his assistants; and now he starts to boast as he said he would in v. 8, after having cleared the way for this boasting by the intervening verses. **But we on our part** (when *we* now boast) **will** (of course) **not boast in regard to things that nobody can measure but** (will boast only) **ac-**

cording to the measure of the rule which as a measure God measured out to us, (namely) **our getting as far as even you. For not as not having gotten out to you are we overstretching ourselves** (in our boasting to you), **for as far as even up to you we were the first to arrive with the gospel of Christ** — **not making other men's labors our boast in regard to the things that nobody can measure but cherishing** (some) **hope, as your faith keeps growing, to be magnified in your midst according to our own rule for still more,** (namely) **for evangelizing the parts way beyond you,** (certainly) **not for making another man's rule our boast in regard to things already prepared** (by another man).

We, Paul says, have a standard, measure, and rule for measuring ourselves, not one that we set up, not our own selves, by which we always and easily rate 100 per cent; but one which God gave us, and by which you Corinthians and anybody who cares to do so can measure us. It is the distance and the extent of territory into which, by God's help, we have already carried the gospel and are about to carry it, from Syrian Antioch onward through Galatia, the province of Asia, Macedonia, even reaching to you in Corinth and in Achaia.

These are τὰ ἕτοιμα (v. 16), "the things already prepared," already done. It is the measure which God gave us to be measured by. Anybody can measure us by taking this yardstick. We expect to carry the gospel even far beyond you Corinthians, even into Spain (Rom. 15:23, 24), all of this being new territory. Measure us by that! We are not crowding into other men's labors, into Christian congregations which other men have built, stealing the fruits of their work, and then boasting about ourselves by making our own selves the standard of measurement.

This is what Paul has in mind in v. 7 when he tells the Corinthians to look at what is right before their eyes. A blind man could see this. But that is often the trouble: people do not see the forest for the trees.

The chapter is a unit. Paul is such a lowly fellow, and he cannot face anyone with manly courage, he is courageous only when he is at a safe distance (v. 1). The answer to that is the tremendous campaign which he is directing as commander-in-chief by demolishing the mightiest enemy fortifications (v. 2-6). Timid, little cowards who make fists at a distance do not wreck fortresses! Again, Paul is nothing in appearance, and his word amounts to nothing, and he scares you only in letters that are written from a safe distance (v. 10). The answer to that is the extensive territory into which Paul had actually carried the gospel by the authority which God had given him. He had certainly not established all of these Christian congregations by means of merely writing letters, to say nothing about letters that were intended merely to scare people. This Paul who is slandered as being nothing in appearance and nothing in face-to-face speech was the first on the ground in all of these lands and these cities and by his personal presence and personal speech accomplished all of these results.

Paul is not comparing himself with the false apostles, elevating himself above them, and casting aspersions upon them. There *is* no comparison. Paul could not make one if he tried. This is the thing, which is so evident in itself, that Paul asks the Corinthians to see, actually to see. If the Corinthians merely see it, this will be enough.

We, Paul says, are going to boast, "not in regard to things that nobody can measure"; we, as you Corinthians surely can see for yourselves, are not in that class of people at all. Such people, among whom are these false apostles, do as they please about setting up a standard of measurement as to what they really are, they make themselves the standard, measure and compare themselves with themselves. *They* are the 100 per cent standard, and then, of course, when they measure themselves by this standard, they always rate 100 per cent. How could they avoid it?

This is the trick that is still constantly worked. Religious fakes and imposters, pseudo-scientists and philosophers are arrogant specialists in this sort of thing. They make 100 per cent fit themselves so that, when they measure themselves, they always rate 100 per cent; and then they scoff at everybody else as these false apostles scoffed at Paul.

Is it so difficult to see that these men are merely tricking the Corinthians with τὰ ἄμετρα, with "the things not measured at all"? This word is sometimes understood as meaning *masslos*, "measureless," exceeding all measure. Our versions translate it "beyond our measure." The word means "the things not measured at all" because nobody really measures them, cannot measure them because they are tricked out of applying a real rule of measurement. It is not measuring at all to measure oneself by oneself. To insist on being measured thus is to prevent all real measuring. No, says Paul, we are going to boast, but never in order to deceive either ourselves or you Corinthians by such a trick, by offering a measurement that actually measures nothing at all. Εἰς = "in regard to."

We are going to apply a real norm of measurement (κατά), a norm that you Corinthians or anybody else can most easily apply to us. It is not a deceptive measuring that has been devised by ourselves in order to prevent a real measuring; it is "the measure of the rule which as a (genuine) measure *God* measured out to us." God himself stretched this tape by which he, we, you, anybody can take our exact measure. This is the tape that has the feet, the yards, the rods marked off so that anybody can see them: "our getting as far as even you." Look at the distance which we have come with the gospel, count the line of cities where we planted congregations, count onward to Corinth, "up even to you" — that is our measure! Is that not right under your eyes (v. 7a)?

"According to the measure of the rule" has the explicative or appositional genitive. Κανών has given us our word "canon," i. e., standard of measurement. It acts as the μέτρον or measure which one applies. Οὗ is attracted from ὅν; it is made genitive because of its antecedent; its predicative noun μέτρον naturally also becomes genitive. The second aorist middle infinitive is in apposition to "which as a measure" (R. 1078).

14) Paul and his assistants had certainly gotten as far as Corinth with the gospel: "For, not as not having gotten out to you are we overstretching ourselves" (in our boasting to you). We are not exaggerating in the least. But this is only the minor point which emphasizes the infinitive used in v. 13. R., W. P., thinks that Paul may have coined ὑπερεκτείνομεν since it has been found only in Gregory Nazianzen who lived years later.

The major point is brought by the second γάρ and the new verb: "for as far as even up to you we were the first to arrive with the gospel of Christ." This is the great point: not just getting there *first* with the gospel. The false apostles also got to Corinth. They made it their business to follow in Paul's tracks, to steal into his congregations, and then to undermine his gospel work. They had not even a commission from God, to say nothing of a mark of measurement that had been set by God, which they were to reach. Theirs was the devil's work (11:3, 4).

Note ἡμῖν in v. 13. The Holy Spirit set Paul apart for the special work of carrying the gospel to the Gentiles (Acts 13:2; especially 26:16-18). Thereby

God himself set the mark for measuring Paul and his assistants: "God measured out the measure *to us*" (v. 13). The farther Paul penetrated the Gentile world with the gospel, the nearer he came to the mark and the measure which God had set for him. Of course, God enabled Paul so that he got as far as he did. City after city he reached as the *first* herald of the gospel — "even as you." You Corinthians *first* heard the gospel from me. Measure me with this canon, which is the one God set for me!

The verb φθάνω should not be reduced in meaning from "to come first" (ahead of anyone else) to the paler meaning "to arrive" (no matter when). "We came *first* as far as even you" is in contrast with "getting as far as even you," in contrast because it says more. "As far as *even* you" means that Paul arrived *first* with the gospel also in all of the other places which he had evangelized.

Still more important is the fact that the false apostles broke into other men's work, where these other men (Paul and his assistants) had *first* built up the work. Their work would not have been so damnable if they had gone out into new territory as the first ones to preach their false Jesus; but no, they made it their business to invade other men's work. Our proselyters still continue this. The whole world is open to them in order to spread their errors if they must do so; but they make it their business and their delight to invade the congregations which were long ago built up in the true gospel. The devil could not remain in hell, he had to break into Eden (11:3).

15) Unifying his thought, Paul continues with two participles. Since these have case and number in the Greek they naturally refer to "we" (ἡμεῖς in v. 13 and the "we" in the verbs of v. 13 and 14): "(we) not making other men's labors our boast in regard to things that nobody can measure," etc. This is the

negative side. Both phrases are emphatic; both refer to the nefarious work of the false apostles. Comparison with Paul and his assistants? None is even possible.

The one thing which Paul never did was to build on another man's foundation, to preach where the gospel had already been preached by the Lord's preachers (Rom. 15:20). For this reason he told the Romans that he would only visit them on his way to pagan Spain. Paul's calling was ever to be *first* with the gospel, ever to conquer new fields. But these despicable false apostles never started a single new congregation of their own. Noxious parasites, they feasted on what other men, true men, had built up with arduous, wearying labors (κόποις, plural and with this significant sense).

Again, these fellows boast "in regard to the things that no one can measure" (the same phrase that was used in v. 13 and having the same sense). They, of course, have to do that, for otherwise people *would* measure them and would soon see through them. Craftiness is their game: *their* measure, which is *in no sense* a measure so that the things which they do remain ἄμετρα, *not* measured at all — that is where their boast lies. These two go together: breaking into other men's labors — preventing the things they do from being measured. Despicable? There is little that is more so!

Now the positive side of our godly boasting: "but cherishing (some) hope, as your faith keeps growing, to be magnified in your midst according to our own rule quite abundantly," etc. Note the spirit and the beauty with which this is expressed. Paul does not say "having *the* hope" but only "having hope." It is only hope, only some hope. He may be disappointed as he intimates. Boasting deceivers are so often magnified, praised to the skies. God's great apostles and true ministers may have to do without praise from men. "The Master praises, what are men?" Paul is not now hoping for praise. "As your faith keeps growing" looks to the future. The faith of the Corinthians will grow; deceivers will presently have a difficult time to get near them. The Corinthians have had one experience which ought to serve them for a long time.

But it would be normal for well-grown faith to fulfill Paul's hope that he and his loyal assistants "be magnified in your midst" and not, as hitherto, slandered. Yet magnified only "according to our own rule" (canon), the one just stated in v. 13, that by God's will and his grace we get as far as possible with the gospel. This "rule" does not glorify men as men, especially such as "recommend themselves" (v. 12) and do this by "measuring themselves by themselves" (v. 12 again); it glorifies God by using his rule with reference to the men who apply it to themselves as their own rule. It thus magnifies these men because of their faithfulness to God and because of the extent of work which he has laid out for them in the gospel.

Paul says: "to be magnified according to our own rule εἰς περισσείαν," which does not mean "to the highest height." Paul wants no extravagant praise. The noun means "surplus" (M.-M. 508). But the phrase does not mean "abundantly" (A. V.), i. e., magnified with a surplus of praise. The R. V.: "unto further abundance" comes nearer to the mark, though only nearer.

The idea of being magnified is not that the Corinthians may presently sing Paul's praises, that he may revel in this sweet music. He is not even thinking about having a bed of roses spread for him. He means "be magnified so as to be encouraged by the Corinthians for something more" than he has done thus far. This εἰς phrase denotes an aim or object. Paul hopes that the Corinthians will make him great for a surplus of work, a surplus he is already planning, for which he feels that he needs all the support that he can get. In a short time we see him writing to the Romans in the same way and asking also for their support to carry the work into Spain (Rom. 15:24). How could Paul go on into new territory and leave behind a congregation like Corinth that was still a prey to disaffection, still listening to deceivers? The old work must be safe before a surplus can be undertaken. The two phrases go together: "according to our own rule — for still more"; God's rule for Paul was: ever more and more new fields, ever a new surplus in territory.

16) It is plain that the negative infinitive is only the obverse: to evangelize those fields that lie beyond Corinth; hence not to boast in another man's work, in regard to things already prepared. Both are aorist infinitives, both are effective: actually to evangelize and certainly not merely to boast. Paul does not repeat "in other men's labors" from v. 15. He now uses a singular; he also advances the thought by not repeating labor but by now stating the rule according to which the labor is done. We see the force of this: to boast "in another man's rule" (canon again) is to try to reap credit from this rule that Paul follows, to build on virgin fields. These false apostles are so cunning, they let Paul go ahead, build up churches in pagan cities, and then steal after him and do their nefarious work in those churches. Would they, for instance, be the first to go to pagan Spain? That thought would not enter the heads of these parasites and proselyters! Deep scorn throbs in Paul's stunning phrase.

To make sure that we get its full impact he adds the εἰς phrase. He will never stoop to make his boast in taking advantage of another man's rule, the noble rule of going first into pagan territory, stealing in after that man, and then making boast "in regard to things already prepared" by that other true and noble man. Τὰ ἕτοιμα are the things which the other man put into condition at great labor, which he has carefully built up. Then these parasites make their soft nest in them, eat their way in farther and farther, and boast about it, try to get praise and honor for it. Disgusting! No, *not* thus Paul! Cannot the Corinthians see it all? It is so plain (v. 7a).

17) Now he who boasts, in the Lord let him boast! Note the emphasis. Let him make the Lord his boast. When the Lord sends and blesses him, when he really does the Lord's work according to the Lord's rule and method, then he may boast, not, indeed, as taking glory for himself but as praising the Lord. This is the true principle. Paul follows it in all of his apostolic work. But it applies to every one of us wherever the Lord has placed us, and whatever he gives us to do. Paul thus brings his discussion to a focus and a resting point. It is his way of doing throughout.

18) For he who (only) **recommends himself, not he is approved; but** (only) **he whom the Lord recommends.** We noted the great class of self-commenders in v. 12; the false apostles are excellent samples. All that needs to be said now is that self-recommendation never makes a man δόκιμος, a man tested and tried and found true and genuine. The emphatic ἐκεῖνος lends added emphasis: not *he*, not he at all. Drop the notion. Quite the contrary (ἀλλά), "he (alone) whom the Lord commends" (Luke 19:17). A man likes to flatter himself. Like the deceivers in Corinth, he may not even be honest. He may use false standards. The Lord sees through and through. Blessed is he whom the Lord recommends! In a phrase "Lord" may readily be used without the article; when it is a nominative it is more likely to have the article. It is fruitless to seek a difference in the meanings here.

CHAPTER XI

Paul Does some Foolish Boasting about His Own Person, 11:1 to 12:13

I. *Paul Asks the Privilege of Playing the Role of a Foolish Boaster because of His great Personal Concern for the Corinthians*

This section is unique in all Paul's writing. It has been well called the most magnificent and destructive thing that Paul has done in the way of ironical polemics. Like an actor on the ancient stage he puts on a mask in order to act a part, and the part which he acts is that of a fool, of a fellow who has no sense. But it is only he himself who feels that he is acting a fool. He asks his readers for once to allow him to do this. He feels that he is inflicting something on them. He asks them to tolerate it for a little while.

What makes Paul feel that he is acting the role of a fool is the fact that he boasts about his own person. This is what he dislikes. But the Corinthians themselves crowd him into assuming so unpleasant a role. He takes this role because of his great concern for them, because of the attacks made upon his person in order to injure not merely him but, most of all, the Corinthians themselves, their faith and their entire spiritual life. Paul's whole motive and aim are not self-aggrandizement but complete frustration of the attempts of the false apostles who have already done much to hurt the Corinthians. The assumption of this role while he is telling the Corinthians that he takes it only as a role, is the best means for completely overthrowing these ugly invaders and all the evil they have done or may yet attempt to do. A deadly seriousness thus underlies the mask which Paul assumes for a little while.

He feels like a fool also because he seems to descend to the level of the false apostles whose great asset was self-recommendation and boasting about themselves. Is Paul now not advertising himself in the same way, and that the more after he has exposed these men's folly as being senseless (οὐ συνιοῦσιν, 10:12)? Ah, but these men are *not* playing a role after informing the Corinthians that it is only a role; their whole life and activity are this very folly. Paul only apparently stoops to their level by now boasting about himself. Their boasts are entirely hollow. Behind the great show which they make is not only nothing, mere empty air; behind that show and pretense of great excellence and power is, in stark reality, only secret viciousness which they would not dare to let the Corinthians see. When Paul now takes the boaster's role, it *is* a role, just a role, because all that *he* will say in boast of himself is *not* sham, not pretense, not false and lying, but the straight fact and the simple reality from beginning to end, something which the false apostles would not dare to reveal about themselves. The Corinthians cannot verify a single boast of the false apostles; they have nothing but the simple word of these boasters, whose greatness lies in comparing themselves with themselves (10:12). Every word of Paul's boasting the Corinthians can verify, yea, most of what he will say they have long ago verified. Truth does not like to boast, lies must boast. Truth can truly boast, lies can boast only by lying.

All of this shows why Paul put on this mask, allowed himself for once to be driven into personal boasting. It shows what a deadly thing for his false, boastful enemies his true boasting was. In parts one and two of his letter Paul has prepared the Corinthians to be the audience of what he now does at the climax of part three. Since they are so prepared, there is no question about the effect of this section of part three. It will sink in as nothing else would do.

1) **Would that you would bear with me as to a little something of folly!** This wish and this assurance are the signature for the entire section (11:1-12:13). The sense is: "I hope you will bear with me." "Bear with me" implies that Paul is imposing a little on the patience of his readers by now offering them something that he himself admits to be "folly" or "foolishness." Yet he minimizes: it is only "a little something" of this kind, it will thus not be hard to bear with Paul. Assured that his wish, which is a kindly and an earnest request, will be granted, Paul adds as if expressing his thanks: **But, of course** ($καί$), **you bear with me!** You are gracious to do that. An imperative seems out of place after a wish: "Yea, even do bear with we!" Thus B.-D. 448, 6; Robertson is undecided, see his remarks 1186 on ἀλλά, also *W. P.* Opinions differ.

While ὄφελον is really a second aorist verbal form, the Koine uses it as a conjunction with a verb in the imperfect tense to express a wish regarding the present (thus in Rev. 3:15). We have the genitive μου to indicate the person: "bear with me," and the adverbial accusative to indicate the thing: "as to a little something."

2) Before proceeding with the foolishness which he desires to inflict upon them Paul tells what prompts his peculiar wish. It is his grave concern for the Corinthians. Back of the proposed foolishness lies the deepest seriousness. Paul reveals his motive and his aim at once and thus excludes all wrong ideas about "a little something of foolishness" that is now to be employed. When the purpose is so serious, any folly or foolishness which serves that purpose will certainly

not be frivolous, superficial, or objectionable in any way.

Three parties are most deeply concerned: Paul, the Corinthians, and Christ. What unites them is Paul's great and holy office. The figurative language in which Paul brings these three and his office together in one brief sentence is certainly admirable and highly effective. **For I am jealous over you with God's jealousy, for I espoused you to One as husband to present (you) as a pure virgin to Christ.**

Here we have Paul's blessed and glorious office in a new and most lovely light. Here there are the three that are concerned in that office, all in their actual relation. Here are the motives, here the purposes, all intertwined, so supreme for all concerned. I confess that I marvel at this expression of Paul's thought.

The picture is that of a father who has betrothed his daughter to the noblest of bridegrooms. Soon the nuptials will be celebrated. Soon the father is to lead his daughter to the altar (we use our modern language). This father can lead her there only as a pure virgin. The point and pivot of the whole imagery lies in this term: "a virgin pure." Hence we have the preamble: "I am jealous over you with God's jealousy." I watch over you with jealous eyes and see that you ever remain pure for that great day of presentation to Christ.

As far as we are able to say, this imagery is borrowed from the Oriental style of betrothal in which the bride was pledged to the groom by the parents, which made the two man and wife, yet so that a longer or a shorter interval intervened before the groom came to claim his bride, to carry her to his own home in grand state, there to consummate his marriage.

This way of entering marriage is much different from ours. The binding pledges were made at the time of the espousal or betrothal, none followed when the marriage was consummated; only the festivities and the feast took place then. In our day the marriage pledges are made on the wedding day. Today an engagement is only an advance promise to enter marriage and to take the marriage pledges at some future date. The ancient Oriental and the present Occidental customs have at times been confused. Engagements have been regarded as already constituting actual marriages. This was said to be a following of the Word of God. But the Scriptures know nothing about our present custom in this matter; they lay down no law, they only describe the custom that was anciently in vogue. It is well to note all of this.

The verb and the noun mean not only to be full of zeal but especially in this context to be jealous. "With God's jealousy" is certainly not "with godly jealousy" (our versions), merely a holy jealousy. It is much more. It is the very jealousy of God himself, about which the Old Testament has so much to say in reference to God's relation to Israel because this people was betrothed to him. The wifehood of Israel is not drawn into Paul's imagery, but there is merely a reference to the bridal state before the consummation of the marriage, the period between the solemn betrothal and the consummation to follow. "With God's jealousy" recalls all of the Old Testament statements about God and Israel. It fits so well because the Corinthians, too, were a congregation, a mass of people. God's jealousy has come to fill and to activate Paul who was acting for God in the betrothal of the congregation. The same feeling that filled God fills Paul.

The bride did not betroth herself. Her parents, her father, or whoever was the head of the house did that. Paul acts this part. He had founded the Corinthian congregation, he was its father. He had pledged this church in betrothal "to One as husband," namely "to Christ." Whereas in the Old Testament *Yahweh* is the bridegroom or the husband, in the New Testament it is Christ.

The verb is in the middle voice to indicate the personal interest which Paul has in this act: "I espoused you for myself." I as father, you as bride. Why translate: "to one husband" (our versions)? The noun is predicative to the numeral: "to One as husband." This "One" is emphatic and significant; it matches the other predicative noun "as a virgin pure." The idea is: to be faithful to this one as husband, to have not even a thought of another, and thus to come as a virgin pure to this One when the great festive marriage day comes and Paul as the father presents this his daughter to Christ.

Many think that the presentation takes place at Christ's Parousia; they also mix the presentation with the imagery of judgment. Paul has no special time in mind when the presentation will take place, for he is not writing allegory. He uses aorists as befits his figurative language: "did espouse" — "to present" once, definitely, completely. But this does not refer to single and momentary actions in the reality. Paul dedicated the Corinthians to Christ all along when he founded their church during the one and one-half years he labored in their city, when he presented them ever and ever as a pure, truly Christian church to One, to Christ alone.

By expressing it figuratively all the emotions and the motivations become manifest. The love of the father for his daughter; his great concern about her; the manner in which his honor is involved, etc. The love of the One for his bride; he has had himself espoused to this virgin; this pure and holy bond binds the two together. He is Christ, the Lord himself; the Corinthians are his holy bride. See what Paul thus stirred up in their hearts when he writes: "to One as husband — as a virgin pure." Dare the Corinthians befoul themselves with spiritual adultery? Do they ever intend to risk breaking their espousal to Christ? Could Paul have stirred up so many thoughts by means of so few words if he had not used this imagery?

3) Paul has cause for this parental jealousy regarding the Corinthians: the Corinthians themselves have made him uneasy. Paul says: I espoused you to Christ. **But I am afraid lest in some way, as the serpent deceived Eve in his craftiness, your thoughts be corrupted from your single-mindedness and your purity in regard to Christ.**

Πανουργία is the ability to do anything, and this word is used in the evil sense of stooping to use the basest means, any and all such means, to gain one's evil ends — "craftiness." The outstanding example is the serpent and his deception of Eve in the Garden of Eden; ἐκ in the verb intensifies: "completely deceived." Jesus used the same example in John 8:44. It is so effective because it is the first deception that entered our world, and because its results were so terrible. All other deceptions are the repetitions of this original, most fatal one, are the outcome of this radical deception.

Paul says "Eve" and not "Adam" in this connection because he wants to designate "the serpent" as the deceiver, and he dealt with Eve. He says "the serpent" and not "Satan" because he wants to bring out the full baseness of the act in its similarity to what the false prophets were doing in Corinth. They crawled into Corinth as Satan did into Eden, they were like serpents. They used the same "craftiness," they, too, intended to slay the innocent. These deceivers in Corinth were doing the devil's serpent work. Paul wants to arouse all the horror of the serpent in the Corinthians. Like a flash this word "the serpent" reveals all the **deadly danger from which the Corinthians should flee.**

Late Jewish fiction and speculation regarded the fall of Eve as a sexual sin. Some of the commentators collect all the Jewish statements on this subject on the supposition that they cast light on Paul's reference to Eve, that Paul *might* at least have had them in mind since he pictures the Corinthians as a pure virgin who may not be found pure at her presentation to her bridegroom. We decline to follow them. We decline also when pagan references are added regarding serpents' misleading women. There is nothing sexy in Paul's words. Eve was a married woman and not a virgin. The notion of the devil and of devils and evil angels having sexual intercourse with women is monstrous and found its ugliest form in the fiction of the incubus and the succubus in the days of the witchcraft craze. We mention this aberration only because it still appears in books.

In 2:11 νοήματα is used in an evil sense: "devices" or schemes; the singular occurs in 10:5. Here the word means simply "thoughts," the products of the νοῦς or mind. To corrupt them means to fill them with evil; the verb is the second aorist passive subjunctive, an effective aorist: "be actually corrupted." A phrase is added for the sake of precision: "from the (your) single-mindedness and the (your) purity in regard to Christ." The Greek articles emphasize: *"that* single-mindedness and *that* purity, *that* pertaining to your relation to Christ."

Here we have the literalness for what is stated figuratively in v. 3. Ἁπλότης is exactly the proper word, and it is used in the same sense as it was in 8:2; 9:11, 13: "single-mindedness." Despite our versions and others it does not mean "liberality" in these or in any other passages. Its opposite is duplicity. The picture is that of a cloth that is smoothly laid out so that no fold hides anything under it. Here single-mindedness refers to Christ; the mind and all its thoughts are set solely and singly upon him in love, loyalty, devotion, and there is no duplicity which secretly turns to another.

The addition of "purity" aids the thought by referring back to the figure of "a virgin pure." The thoughts are to be without a stain or a smudge of disloyalty of any kind. In his craftiness the serpent aims to introduce duplicity into our thoughts which are directed to Christ and thereby to defile our thoughts regarding him. We are no longer to be Christ's alone in our thoughts; secretly, in our hidden thoughts, we are to hanker after someone else. Figuratively we should thus no longer be a bride loyal and pure in heart for our blessed marriage presentation to Christ. An admonition underlies Paul's words which urges the Corinthians to flee any contact with the false apostles. What a shame to pretend to be loyal to Christ while disloyalty has crept into the heart through the serpent's agency which used the false apostles.

4) Γάρ states the ground for Paul's fear regarding the Corinthians. **For if he who comes** (to you) **preaches another Jesus, whom we did not preach, or you get a different Spirit, whom you did not get** (from us), **or a different gospel, which you did not receive** (from us), **you bore it well.**

This is a simple condition of reality and nothing more. If we prefer the reading ἀνέχεσθε, the present tense, all is exceedingly simple. If we accept the reading that has the imperfect tense ἀνείχεσθε, all is still simple, for this tense would say only that at different times the Corinthians bore this sort of thing well without rising up in arms, and it would imply that such complacent bearing is not yet ended. Worth-while textual criticism is undecided. The view that the apodosis is one of unreality with ἄν omitted is not acceptable. *If* we have unreality we have *one* situation in Corinth, namely no false gospel; *if* we have reality we have *another* situation, namely false gospel. All the other evidence is in favor of the latter's being true; v. 2, 3 are sufficient; v. 13 is more than that. Who ever heard of ψευδαπόστολοι preaching the true gospel? Men who preach the true gospel do not use the serpent's craftiness, do not produce the fear that the thoughts of Christians will be corrupted and turned into secret disloyalty to Christ, do not force a man like Paul to say to the Corinthians: "Examine yourselves, whether ye be in the faith!" (13:13).

Why does Paul then not attack these false apostles on what would thus be the chief issue, their false gospel? Why does Paul fight about the issue of his own person, as he does in these chapters, as if this were the chief issue? Paul tells us throughout. These false apostles made Paul's person the supreme issue. Unlike the Judaizers in Galatia, they used "craftiness" in this. They intended to establish themselves as the genuine apostles of Christ (v. 13). That is no marvel, says Paul, for Satan tries to appear as an angel of light (v. 14). They held their real teaching in abeyance until they should have destroyed Paul's standing in Corinth and have fully established themselves; this accomplished, they planned to come out into the open with their false gospel. For this reason Paul compares them to the serpent and to Satan. The Corinthians were still in the dark as to what these liars really taught in regard to the gospel. Paul rightly joins the issue which they drew on his own person. This alone stood in the open, the other was concealed, could thus be evaded if it were attacked by Paul. Yet Paul introduces it. The supposition that v. 4 decides the situation in Corinth in one way or in another is unacceptable. It would be strange for Paul to show in only one sentence — one that is put into a conditional form at that — how things really stood in Corinth.

We have μέν *solitarium*, the force of which is concessive or restrictive (R. 1151) ; there is no equivalent for it in English. The condition of reality speaks of an individual case as a real one, yet by means of the conditional form generalizes so as to include any such case. Ὁ ἐρχόμενος = "the man who comes" and visualizes that specific man. Several such have actually come to Corinth, and any others who may yet come are included in Paul's indictment. He comes and preaches to you "another Jesus, whom we did not preach" to you, "we," Paul and his assistants. You Corinthians know that it is not the same Jesus. What do you do? Avoid that man (Rom. 16:17, 18)? Nothing of the kind; you tolerate him, "well do you bear him!" You have done it already, and you thus show that you are this kind of people. Let another, let others come and do the same, and you will, no doubt, treat them well also. That is the reason, Paul says, that I am afraid that you may be corrupted from single-mindedness and purity of heart toward Christ.

"Another Jesus" — as if there were another! You Corinthians know there is but one, the "One" to whom "as husband" I did espouse you, the "One" to whom you know that you belong as a bride to her betrothed. Paul does not say "another Christ" although another Jesus would also be a different Christ. These false apostles were offering a different picture of Jesus as he lived and walked on earth, a Judaistic picture which stressed the Judaism of Jesus in a false way. Since Jesus lived as a Jew, so they preached, all his followers ought also to live as Jews. This is what the foolish Corinthians bear so well instead of rising up against it in indignation. By means of this Jewish Jesus these false apostles played themselves up as "the superlative apostles" (v. 5) who were vastly superior to Paul and to his assistants, whom they then vilified in all manner of ways. Astounding — the Corinthians "bear it well!"

The two "or" are conjunctive and not disjunctive. "Or" fixes attention upon each separate item; "and" would merely combine them. From "Jesus" Paul advances to the "Spirit" and then to the "gospel" because it is the Spirit through whom Jesus works among men, and because it is the gospel by means of which the Spirit does this work. The three occur in their natural and proper order. The false apostle, whom Paul describes, preaches "another Jesus" (ἄλλος); he speaks of the same person and uses the same name but makes him altogether "*other*" than Paul does. Thus "another" is in place. Such a Jesus would send "a different Spirit," who would also employ "a different gospel" (both times ἕτερος). These two are not just "other" with a different look and complexion as was the case in regard to Jesus but actually "*different*" from the Holy Spirit and the Christian gospel, namely a Spirit who is only called so, a gospel that is such only in name, each being nothing but a fiction. Indeed "another" Jesus could not send the Holy Spirit with the real, saving, divine gospel; what he would send, if he could send anything at all, would be "different," as different as fiction would be from reality. Note that λαμβάνειν has more of a passive sense, *bekommen*, "to get" (B.-P. 730); δέχομαι suggests the idea of acknowledging the gospel proclamation and hence means "to receive" so as to be governed by this gospel (C.-K. 379).

Note the careful wording: the false apostle comes and *preaches* another Jesus — you thus *get* a different Spirit, one that you did not *get* from us — and a different gospel (you *get*), which you did not *receive* from us. The Greek needs no object in the apodosis, but we supply one: "well are you (were you) bearing it!" Because in v. 1 we have "bear with me," our versions supply "him" in v. 4. Both of our versions do not seem to understand what Paul is saying, for the A. V. margin has: "ye might well bear with *me*," as though Paul is referring to the request he made in v. 1. The R. V. has: "ye do well to bear with him," but where is "ye do well" in the text? No; Paul registers the sad fact: You Corinthians stand this thing well, oh, so well, to have a man come and preach another Jesus, to get from him a different Spirit, a different gospel! For this reason Paul fears for the purity of the Corinthians.

5) "He who comes" in v. 4 is what Robertson calls a representative singular, one that is used to represent all who are like him. The condition of reality in v. 4 refers to the men who had actually come to Corinth and had preached another Jesus, etc.; it includes any others of this type who may yet come. Sorrowfully and with fear for the Corinthians Paul says to them: "you bear well" such men although you yourselves see that they bring you a Jesus we never brought, a Spirit and a gospel that are different from those you got from us. You evidently think these men superior to me and to my assistants who work under me. How can you otherwise treat such men so well after receiving what you did from us? You must think them superior because of their *logos* or because they make you pay for preaching their grand *logos*. An issue had been drawn on both points regarding Paul's great inferiority. Paul thus answers both points, the latter quite fully.

This is not a digression: Paul announcing his foolish boasting in v. 1 and then inserting so much before he starts that boast. Paul is stating the reasons which call forth the foolish boasting which he asks the Corinthians to "bear": 1) *their* attitude toward the false apostles whom they "bear so well"; 2) the attitude of *the false apostles* who give the Corinthians a plenty to "bear." This supposed digression in reality fortifies the succeeding boasting on the part of Paul. The Corinthians should not have forced Paul into this boasting, a thing that makes him feel like a fool. They should certainly not have pitted such men as these false apostles against him and thereby forced this boasting from Paul, a thing that was so disagreeable to him.

The connection is both true and close. First we have the general statement. **Well, I reckon that in regard to nothing have I come behind the superfine apostles!** Γάρ simply refers to all that v. 4 states. It is our introductory "well" or "well now." The very idea of treating these fellows who have come to Corinth and have brought what they did (v. 4) as "superfine apostles" after what the Corinthians have received from Paul! Well, if a comparison is, indeed, to be made where none can really be made, Paul for one reckons that he has had to take no back seat as far as these men are concerned. The perfect infinitive reaches from the past to the present: "have come behind so as still to be behind."

He ironically calls these interlopers who bring "another Jesus," etc., "superfine apostles"; verbs of excelling and their opposites take the genitive (R. 519). The compound adverb ὑπερλίαν is used as an adjective; see 12:11. "Superfine" hits the nail on the head. They came as grand fellows, indeed, who were vastly superior to any of the true apostles of Jesus, either the Twelve or Paul. Did they not bring "another Jesus" who was far superior to the one whom all other apostles brought? That alone was enough although we shall see that there is more to make them "superfine" as there naturally would be.

Our versions translate "the very chiefest apostles" as though Paul means that he is not inferior to the best among the Twelve, Peter and John and, perhaps, the Jerusalem James. Some have held this view. The next verse bars it out. Nobody could rate Paul as being inferior to Peter, etc., on the score of his *logos*, training in dialectics and rhetorical skill. Paul had sat at

Gamaliel's feet. He had all the rabbinical schooling of the Jews; Peter, John, etc., had none of it. They were the ἰδιῶται, "laymen," Paul the expert or specialist. Throughout this discussion there is nowhere a reason for comparison between Paul and any of the Twelve, least of all here and in 12:11. The whole clash is limited to Paul and the false apostles in Corinth. In no case would Paul fling an epithet like ὑπερλίαν at the Twelve, his honored fellow apostles, and then say no more about himself in relation to them. Softening the word when translating it does not change matters. It means "the excessive apostle," excessive as one who is trying to outdo all the real apostles. We have them right here in these chapters.

Paul calls these interlopers ἀπόστολοι, but only in the sense in which he calls them ψευδαπόστολοι in v. 13, "emissaries." The latter term brings out the fact that they had no commission from anyone. They were in the full sense "false apostles" who came with a sham commission, one which they themselves invented, by which to deceive people like the Corinthians. The supposition that they came from Jerusalem and that they bore credentials from any of the Twelve is unwarranted. We know of no men who were sent out by any of the Twelve to run around in the Christian congregations anywhere. That very idea is untenable. Any helpers of any apostle worked as did the assistants of Paul, under the eyes of that apostle.

These excessive apostles were not Jews from Jerusalem for the reason that such men could not boast about their *logos* as being vastly superior to Paul's. Paul had the best that Jerusalem could afford. They were Hellenistic Jews who had been trained in pagan schools and could thus boast about something that Paul did not have. Here the view goes on the rocks that Paul had attended the university at Tarsus, his home city. If that had been the case, no one would have looked down on him because of lack of Greek *logos*.

6) The first point on which Paul's standing is attacked he settles in short order. **But if, indeed** (καί), **I am a nonprofessional in regard to the** (matter of) **speech, nevertheless not in regard to the** (matter of) **knowledge.** This is the point of the slander referred to in 10:10: "His speech is of no account" (contemptible), it shows nothing of the rhetorician's dialectical skill and training. Some conclude that Paul admits this allegation. In view of the letters which he wrote, of the highest skill which he displays in their composition, of the rhetoric which he uses, the niceties of language which are of the highest order, the perfect word for each perfect thought, such a blanket admission on Paul's part would be strange. No; this is not such an admission, it is refutation. What Paul says is this: "What if I actually am what they say on the score of the *logos*, what does that amount to when I am decidedly not that on the score of the *gnosis* or knowledge?" We have two datives of relation. What a silly thing to quibble about a man's speech while disregarding what that speech contains in the way of knowledge!

This is an old trick: draw attention to the surface in order to withdraw attention from the golden things underneath the surface; fuss about the wrapping so that nobody will look at what is wrapped up. The Jews tried this trick on Jesus in John 7:15 in order to turn the people away from him because he was not graduated from the schools of their rabbis, but Jesus exploded their cunning; see the author's exposition. The same thing was tried against Paul. He uses only a slight blow or two to render the trick innocuous.

From his various addresses recorded in Acts we know what kind of speaker Paul was. Those addresses show the same ability which his letters reveal. Only in one sense was Paul an ἰδιώτης τῷ λόγῳ — he was not a graduate of a pagan university. The art which he employs is not the artificial technique of the Greek orators and rhetoricians. Their canons of art and their practice ill accorded with what Paul had to convey as an apostle. It contained too much artificiality. Paul's art was the native expression of the genuine *gnosis* or knowledge. In regard to that "knowledge" he admits no inexpertness: "nevertheless (ἀλλά) not in regard to the (matter of) knowledge." Both datives are specific, hence we have the article in the Greek. Nor is this mere assertion on Paul's part. With a continuative, confirmatory ἀλλά (R. 1185) he adds: **yea, (we) having in every way publicly shown it in all respects in regard to you.** In other words: You Corinthians know it! We prefer the reading φανερώσαντες to the passive φανερωθέντες, "having manifested" and not "having been manifested."

Follow this public manifestation through: 2:14; 3:3; 4:2; 7:12; and here. It has been said that Paul scorns the use of a special finite verb and just appends the participle. In the Greek the participle has number and case and is thus perfectly plain as a reference to all of Paul's assistants as well as to himself, for he operated to a considerable extent through them. All of them showed the *gnosis* which they had, showed it publicly. All of them dealt in public with their knowledge of divine truth: "in regard to you," ἐν παντί, "in every way," ἐν πᾶσιν, "in all respects." This is a telling *paronomasia*, one phrase being on each side of the participle, which is itself a proof that Paul was no ἰδιώτης when it came to expressing himself effectively. Our word "idiot" is derived from this term which meant "layman" in distinction from an expert. The R. V. renders ἐν πᾶσιν as a masculine: "among all men"; the A. V. is correct: "in all things," still better, "in all respects." That is that. No more need be added. Anybody who still wants to disparage Paul in regard to his *logos* is welcome to do so.

7) Now the next point. **Or did I commit sin in lowering myself in order that you might be exalted, in that I preached God's gospel to you gratis? Other churches I robbed by taking sustenance for my ministry to you.** It is merely misfortune when a man lacks dialectical skill, at least if somebody thinks he does; it is a different matter when he deliberately chooses an unusual course of conduct like this of Paul's. This might be doing somebody a "wrong" (ἀδικία, 12:13), committing a "sin," namely one against love (v. 11). The question about not taking pay for his preaching is treated at length in I Cor. 9:4-19, where Paul states that he has the fullest right to take pay and shows why he, nevertheless, makes no use of this right. But that, it seems, did not end the matter. When the false apostles came to Corinth they very likely utilized also this matter in order to injure Paul. They certainly took all that they could from the Corinthians — of course, just because they loved the Corinthians so much while Paul, who took nothing, showed that he did not love the Corinthians! This is the angle from which Paul now treats the matter.

He plunges right into it without the least preamble: "Did I commit sin," etc.? If there is any fault about this matter it could be only a moral one, the commission of a sin. Paul does not tone down this expression but at once formulates this "sin" so that the folly of calling it a sin is made strikingly apparent: "lowering myself in order that you might be exalted." This is what Jesus did with regard to the sin charged against him, that by healing on the Sabbath he desecrated the Sabbath. He asked: "It is lawful to heal on the Sabbath days?" Matt. 12:10. That question answers itself. To lower oneself in order to exalt others would be a saintly sin indeed. The sin is committed when one does the reverse. Paul lowered himself by taking no pay, by earning his own support, by thus risking disparagement on the part of the very people whom he served. Yet the Corinthians were exalted by his labors, were lifted to be children of the Highest.

Ὅτι is epexegetical: "in that." Note the impact of the Greek — great crime indeed: "gratis the God's gospel I gospeled to you." A sin to give you *God's* gift *for nothing*? By placing τοῦ Θεοῦ in the attributive position it receives the emphasis. So also the use of the cognate object produces both beauty and emphasis: "I gospeled the gospel to you." Are you Corinthians, to whom I gave so much in order to exalt you so highly, going to call me a sinner for doing this for you for nothing? Many a truth need only be put into the right words in order to rip away delusion and perversion. Paul has the *gnosis* for that. Here there is another case where he demonstrates it.

8) Paul causes this truth to smart: "Other churches I robbed by taking support for my ministry to you!" The Corinthians deserved this mortification in order to drive out their mean ingratitude. For what is meaner than to slander a benefactor for bestowing his benefaction *gratis*? But note, Paul says that he "robbed" other churches, he took from them what he should really not have taken, namely ὀψώνιον, "sustenance." "Wages" is too liable to be misunderstood as meaning regular pay, which Paul never took from any church, I Cor. 9:15, 18. This was a fixed principle with him.

The noun has no article and means "some sustenance." It denotes a gift that was sent to him after he had left those churches, which he could, therefore, not refuse. Yet even then he felt that he was robbing those churches, letting *them* press something upon him which he would not let the Corinthians press upon him. What made him feel thus the more was the fact that the other churches gave him this present by means of which he could come to Corinth and minister to the Corinthians. Thus, in a way, these Corinthians had the benefit.

9) Paul tells about it; καί is explicative: **namely, while present with you and having gotten behind, I was a dead weight on no one; for the brethren who came from Macedonia filled up my shortage; and in every way I kept myself nonburdensome for you, and I shall keep** (myself so). At one time, Paul says, during his stay of eighteen months in Corinth he really got behind (aorist participle), he did not really have enough; but even then he was a dead weight on no one. Vincent regards the verb as a transitive: "Paul did not benumb the Corinthians by his demand for pecuniary aid." The verb is intransitive: as one who is benumbed and helpless Paul was a dead weight on no one. The verb is derived from νάρκη, a fish that, like the torpedo or the electric ray, shocks its victim into numbness, the noun thus also means numbness. Paul did not become benumbed so that he fell a burden to a single person in Corinth. The verb is construed with the genitive.

The brethren from Macedonia came and filled up the shortage. These brethren had funds and came to Paul's assistance. This is sometimes taken to mean that they brought Paul a collection from Philippi or from Macedonia, but the words contain no hint of a collection. Windish finds in them a collection that Paul ordered in the Macedonian churches; in fact, when he first came to Corinth he brought a tidy sum with him but, needing a good deal of money for his travels, etc., his funds gave out, and he thus had more money collected for him *mit Nachdruck*. This contradicts what Paul says in I Cor. 9:9-14 and overlooks what

Paul says here. Paul, of course, registers only the fact that he in every way guarded himself and kept himself "nonburdensome" for the Corinthians.

Robbing other churches refers to the two gifts which the Philippians sent to Paul while he was at Thessalonica (Phil. 4:15, 16). The plural "other churches" generalizes, the Philippian church alone had sent the gifts. Later, when Paul was a prisoner in Rome, the Philippians sent him a third gift. We can easily surmise how Paul came to be out of funds during his stay in Corinth although he earned his living in Aquila's shop. We shall scarcely go wrong in saying that he had used up his funds, not only to pay for his own necessities, but also to provide for the necessities of his assistants, whom he sent here and there. That left him wholly destitute at one time while he was working in Corinth. But even under those circumstances he followed his principle: "I kept myself nonburdensome to you ἐν παντί, in every way" (or case), the same phrase that occurs in v. 6. He permitted the brethren from Macedonia to assist him. Paul adds significantly: "and I will keep (myself so)." Let the Corinthians mark it. Slander is the last thing to which Paul would yield.

10) **There is** (indeed) **a truth of Christ in my case so that this boasting shall not be dammed up in regard to me in the regions of Achaia.** Paul's case was different from that of any other apostle, totally different. He came into the church as an abortion, was not fit to be called an apostle (see the exegesis of I Cor. 15:8, 9). All the others were believers and Christians and as such were finally called as apostles. Not so Paul. Dead foetus that he was, fit only to be buried quickly out of sight, on the road to Damascus Christ called him to be an apostle even before he was converted to faith.

This is the truth of Christ "in my case." This imposed on him the obligation, which he felt so keenly, never to take pay for his work. This "truth of Christ," i. e., what Christ did by calling him into the apostleship while he was still such a hideous thing, Paul accepted as the stamp upon his entire apostleship. No church ever owed *him* anything, a man such as he had been, a persecutor of Christ and of the church. He felt that *he* could never make use of the right that they who preach the gospel should live by the gospel. He, too, had this right, but how could he ever think of using it? See the exegesis of I Cor. 9:16-18.

Ἔστιν, accented and placed forward = "there exists." "A truth of Christ" has the genitive of origin: a great fact which Christ himself produced in Paul's case. Ἐν ἐμοί = "in my case" (it is well explained by R. 587). Ὅτι is consecutive and states the consequence of this truth of Christ. The existence of this great fact in Paul's case involves "that this boasting shall not be dammed up in regard to me," etc. These slanders that were being circulated in Corinth about Paul amounting to nothing because he felt he was worth nothing and showed it by taking no pay should not dam up the boasting of the Christians in Achaia regarding Paul, that Christ had marked him in a most astonishing way.

His enemies might try to dam up and to stop this flow of boasting in Corinth. They shall fail there and shall certainly not succeed in the province generally. What these enemies consider so derogatory to Paul, Paul will advertise, and all Christians will continue to make it a boast regarding him even in all Achaia, Corinth included. Since in I Cor. 15:8, 9; 9:9, etc., Paul has stated what this "truth" or fact is, and since the Corinthians know it from other sources (the whole story of Paul's conversion being for a long time known to them), Paul does not need to expound what this "truth of Christ" is. Φράσσω means to fence in, dam up, barricade, or stop: "shall not dam up in the regions of

Achaia," silence it so that this glory about Paul shall no longer be heard there.

This passage has been variously interpreted. We see this in our versions. R. 1034 regards the first clause as a "solemn oath"; B.-D. 397, 3, and C.-K. 123 as *Beteuerung*, just a little less than an actual oath, and Wohlenberg speaks of "a strong expression of assurance." But such ideas are evidently incorrect. What is there that Paul should swear to? He says that in his case there exists a peculiar fact that is due to Christ. Paul's case is entirely exceptional; he has told the Corinthians so.

Next, Paul does not say: "stop *me* in this glorying (boasting)." Εἰς ἐμέ = "in regard to me"; see "in regard to you" in v. 6 and elsewhere. Paul is not running around in Achaia and boasting. He does not say: "*I* shall not be stopped," or, "*my* glorying shall not be stopped"; "no man shall stop *me*" (our versions) is not in the text. "This glorying *about me*," Paul says, "shall not be stopped," it shall be continued in all Achaia by those who appreciate what I am doing.

Some commentators interpret this passage contrary to I Cor. 9:18, where Paul says in so many words that he does all of his preaching "without charge." Nor was this done only in Achaia. The question as to why Paul should make such an exception of Achaia does not seem to occur to these commentators. Paul preached everywhere without charge; read I Cor. 9. Everywhere for the same reason. Everywhere he gloried in doing so; Christians likewise gloried "in regard to him." He had told them this "truth of Christ in his case." They appreciated it and what Paul did in consequence of it. Only in Corinth these invaders from the outside turned the whole thing into slander. Therefore Paul tells the Corinthians: "This glorifying shall not be stopped in the regions of Achaia."

11) For what reason? Because I do not love you? God knows (I do)! Διατί = "for what reason?" Ἱνατί would mean "for what purpose?" Does this insistence on the part of Paul that Christ made his case peculiar so that he will take nothing for his sustenance from anybody and will have this as his own boast and as the boast of others also "in regard to him," does this mean that he disregards the feelings of the Corinthians in the whole matter, that he does not love them? "God knows!" knows that I, indeed, love you with my whole heart. This is not: "God alone knows, I do not"; but the very opposite, the strongest assurance of love as God knows that it is. Regarding ἀγαπῶ see the noun in 2:4. This is not mere affection and liking but the love of full intelligence with purpose and actions according. Although Paul's case was peculiar it was one which comported fully with this truest love for the Corinthians and for all whom he won for Christ. Christ would not have made Paul's case what he did if that would have interfered with Paul's love.

12) That is settled. But in the case of the Corinthians others besides themselves are to be considered. Δέ brings up this other consideration. **Moreover, what I do and will do,** (I do and will do) **in order to cut off the occasion of those who want an occasion, that in what they boast they be found as, indeed, we** (are found).

Paul says that what he does and what he will do aims to cut off anything in the boasting which the false prophets do by which they can make it appear that they are what they are not, namely the genuine apostles that Paul and his assistants actually are. Paul's taking no pay while these false apostles take all they can get shall not serve as the ἀφορμή, "starting point or occasion" which they would love to have in the boasting that they are constantly doing. This is a hill which they cannot climb.

The second ἵνα states the purpose for which the false apostles want a starting point, namely "that in what they are constantly making a boast they may be found as, indeed (καί), we on our part (emphatic ἡμεῖς) are found." *They* would like to have people find *them* what people have actually found *us*. But the handicap which Paul has placed in their way is too great. They have a hard time explaining why they take all they can get while Paul and his assistants never take anything.

All of their explanations are bound to be lame. One, as it seems, was that Paul did not love the Corinthians (v. 11). But that was weak. "God knows I do" is the only answer needed. Another was that Paul took no pay because he knew that he was no real apostle. But that had the wrong effect. Perhaps that proved him to be real and his detractors spurious. Paul achieved his purpose: the false apostles had the starting point which they wanted completely cut off.

13) Paul drives home this point with an explanatory γάρ: **For such men are pseudo-apostles, deceitful workers, transforming themselves into apostles of Christ. And no wonder, Satan himself transforms himself into an angel of light.** Paul calls these men exactly what they are. "Pseudo-apostles" appears only here in the New Testament; some think that Paul coined this word after the analogy of pseudo-Christs, pseudo-prophets (Mark 13:22), and pseudo-brethren (Gal. 2:4). "False apostles" shows that the Jesus whom they preached, the Spirit and the gospel which they offered, were wholly pseudo or false (v. 4). "Workers δόλιοι" are such who deceive by putting out bait to catch victims; the original meaning of the noun δόλος is bait. The connotation is deception that kills.

They put on a σχῆμα, an outward form or fashion that makes them look like "apostles of Christ." They do not have the μορφή, the form that is native to the essence, the form which all true apostles of Christ have. Their own μορφή they dare not display, for then all Christians would run from them. So they put on a mask and thereby transform themselves into apostles of Christ.

14) Does this seem incredible? Does anyone ask why men who have no use for Christ should want to pass as true apostles of Christ? There is "no wonder" about it at all. "Satan himself transforms himself into an angel of light." Again, as he did in v. 3, Paul brings out the connection of all false apostles with Satan. He uses the same verb. The present tense is important: Satan does this again and again, it is his practice. He makes people think that they are dealing with an angel of light when, in fact, they are dealing with the prince of darkness himself. How else can Satan get his deadly lies across except by presenting them as God's words that are being spoken by one of God's angels (ἄγγελος = messenger)? In "angel of light" the genitive is qualitative.

In the apocryphal *Vita Adami et Evae* there occurs the passage: *et transierunt dies XVIII, tunc iratus est Satanas et transfiguravit se in claritatem angelorum et abiit ad Tigrem flumen ad Evam, etc.* The Apocalypse of Moses states: τότε ὁ σατανᾶς ἐγένετο ἐν εἴδει ἀγγέλου καὶ ὑμνεῖ τὸν Θεὸν καθάπερ οἱ ἄγγελοι καὶ παρακύψασα ἐκ τοῦ τείχους ἴδον ("I saw," namely Eve) αὐτὸν ὅμοιον ἀγγέλου. But the conclusion that Paul uses "an apocryphal mythical motif" here is unwarranted. In the *Vita* Satan transfigures himself *physically* and proceeds to the Tigris River; in the Apocalypse the same statement is made, he puts on the *physical* looks, sings like the angels, and Eve, leaning over the wall, *saw* him "like an angel." When angels appeared to men they used a physical form and bright and shining garments that were visible to the human eye. The apocryphal statements say that Satan imitated this. What Paul says is not that the false apostles dressed and made themselves look like Paul *physically*, or that Satan did that and made himself like an angel *physically*, but that they used "the craftiness" (v. 3) with which Eve was deceived, that they "corrupted the thoughts" of unwary men. There was no *physical* transformation of any kind, it was all *moral* deception.

We have at most only *an allusion* to the apocrypha, a reduction of the apocryphal statements to what is true regarding Satan and a stripping off of what is not true. Paul uses iterative present tenses to describe what is regularly done by these deceivers and not historical tenses to indicate what Satan is supposed to have done before the eyes of Eve. As to Satan and as to his false apostles — they still deceive in the way in which Paul states. Who ever saw anything that is similar to what these apocrypha allege regarding Eve?

15) **It is, therefore, no great thing** (at all) **if also his ministers transform themselves as ministers of righteousness — they whose end shall be according to their deeds.** There is nothing "wonderful" or "great" about this imitation. What Satan does he will, of course, teach his ministers. Paul significantly calls the false apostles "his (Satan's) ministers," men who voluntarily serve Satan for the sake of the aid they can give him; not "his slaves" (δοῦλοι) who are compelled to work for him. All false apostles and teachers serve Satan voluntarily. In order the better to do so, they pretend to be "ministers of righteousness" (compare 3:9, "the ministry of the righteousness"). The genitive is objective in both expressions: ministers who serve righteousness. "Righteousness," too, is to be taken in its full forensic, soteriological sense and not merely in the sense of our righteous living (called acquired righteousness) but as imputed to us by **God's** verdict for Christ's sake by means of faith.

We might expect the direct opposite to "his (Satan's) ministers," namely "God's ministers." As he does in so many instances, Paul here has no formal opposite but one which advances the thought and says more. The fact that "ministers of righteousness," who bring justification by faith and all that this includes, are ministers of God is self-evident. But this expression flashes into our minds all the blessedness of this ministry. This reacts on "Satan's ministers," for their work in serving Satan is to keep God's saving righteousness from men or to filch it from them if they have already obtained it by the help of God's ministers. The devilishness of this work is thus brought out and the devilishness of the method employed in this work, for these ministers of Satan pretend to bestow what God's ministers do bestow, yea, pretend while they really bestow the opposite, assured damnation.

When it is placed at the end, the relative often has strong demonstrative force. "Whose" = these who are the very ones whose, etc. They may play their game for a while, their "end will be according to their works." What that end will be need not be specified. The very restraint exercised in the brief expression is more effective than stronger language would be. "Their works" includes the constant deception which they practice by their lying transformation.

We are told that Paul ought to have told the Corinthians to sever themselves completely from these ministers of Satan, the more so since they were still active in Corinth. Is there any stronger way of demanding separation than by pointing to men as being ministers of Satan?

Others ask: "Was Paul's judgment regarding these men just? Should we not hear also 'the other side'?" The Oriental, the Jew, the Levantine are always ready with the denunciation: "Of the devil!" even when their own passion plays a strong part. The judge and the jury in this case are not we of today but the Corinthians, for this letter was written to *them*. "The other side" was before the Corinthians *in extenso* and for months. As to presenting sides, all the disadvantage lay with Paul. If Paul were just a Jew, an Oriental, a Levantine, why bother about this letter at all as though he were not fair to Satan and his emissaries? But Paul was Christ's apostle, and not a common Levantine who was uttering intemperate invective. Besides, he wrote these words under the guidance and the inspiration of the Holy Spirit.

II. *Paul Begins His Boasting as a Fool*

16) Reluctance is written all over Paul as he now crowds over the edge to fall into the pool of foolish boasting. He is ashamed to do this sort of thing and yet sees that he just has to do it. In y. 2-15 he has stated the grave reasons for his present strange proceeding. Now that he is about to begin he wavers a bit and tells the Corinthians how he wants them to understand it. He is not one bit happy about doing what has to be done.

Once more I say: Do not let anyone think that I am (actually) **a fool! But if** (you will) **not** (grant this wish), **think of me, even if** (you may think of me) **as of a fool, so that I on my part, too, may boast in regard to a little something!**

There is no need to assume that πάλιν, "again" or "once more," intends to repeat what v. 1 has said. The adverb states only that Paul is "again" speaking about his acting the fool. "To speak of it again," he says, "please, let nobody think that I am actually a fool!" Negative aorist prohibitions have the subjunctive and not the imperative. Although he is about to act as a fool by boasting like so many fools do, Paul is by no means a fool. Behind this apparent folly there is something that is vastly other than folly. This cannot be said about other boasters.

But Paul's wish will perhaps not be granted; the Corinthians will perhaps take him to be the fool he is acting. "Well then," Paul adds, "take me so and grant me the indulgence you grant a fool, let me do a little boasting!" The translation above fills the ellipses which make the Greek so neat but which the English is unable to duplicate. The negative μή γε cannot be used elliptically in English. Translations usually give only the sense and thus omit the negative.

17) What I am going to utter I am not uttering according to the Lord but as in folly, (namely) in this undertaking of my glorying. The two present tenses λαλῶ are futuristic (R. 869): "I am going to utter," the verb refers to mere utterance, the opposite of keeping still. Κατά does not mean that Paul is not going to follow the example of the Lord; it indicates norm. This foolish boasting will not follow the norm and principle of Jesus, for it will be done, not, indeed, *"in* folly," yet *"as in* folly." It will look like folly. It will thus stoop to a lower norm than Jesus used. If it were done in actual folly it would, of course, be stooping to sin; since it is done only in apparent folly it is not sin but is ethically on a lower plane than the one on which Jesus moved.

We thus see why Paul is so reluctant. We must admire him the more for overcoming himself. But see how he tells the Corinthians all about his reluctance. They must know it in order to appreciate what Paul is doing and thus to get the full effect of what he is doing. The second phrase is epexegetical: "namely in this undertaking of my glorying." It is difficult to find the right word for ὑπόστασις, a term that has various meanings. If we translate, "this confidence of my (Greek article) boasting," it would be the confidence or assurance which dares to do such a thing; if we think rather of the act, it would be *mutiges Unterfangen, Wagnis*, courageous undertaking, C.-K. 541.

18) Of his own volition it would not occur to Paul to stoop to boasting that would in any way comport with the part of a fool. He is forced into it. **Since many are boasting according to the flesh, I, too, will boast.** It is not the Lord's norm or principle but only that of men. The "many" includes the false prophets found in Corinth. Textually, "according to *the* flesh" is more assured than "according to flesh." Yet according to either reading the phrase does not mean "in a fleshly, that is, sinful way." To that Paul would never stoop. The phrase is to be construed with the main clause as well as with the minor clause. It need not be repeated, especially not in the Greek. In many connections "flesh" signifies anything that belongs to our human nature; *Leib, seine Art*, C.-K. 893. "The flesh" sums up all such externals and nonessentials. For a little while Paul will stoop to make "the flesh" in this sense the norm of his boasting and feel like a fool in order to be in the company of those who know no higher norm.

19) As far as the Corinthians are concerned, Paul says, he certainly need have no compunctions about boasting as a fool. **For gladly you bear with the fools, (you) being (so) intelligent!** This is irony. People of intelligence cannot endure fools. But these Corinthians are so intelligent that they not only bear them but bear them gladly. The verb is the same one that was used in v. 1 and governs the genitive. "The fools" has the generic article. Paul is proposing to enter this class for a little while. The remark that he cannot call the false apostles "fools" overlooks the fact that by "fools" Paul refers to "the many" mentioned in v. 18 who boast according to the flesh, and that Paul is now about to do the same thing. If the Corinthians tolerate fools so well, Paul certainly feels

encouraged: they will tolerate him and his foolish boasting, too.

In the Greek φρόνιμοι and ἄφρονοι are a pair, we cannot duplicate this in English. But the former are not "wise" (our versions), the term for which would be σοφοί, entirely too good a word. Even "intelligent" is too good. "Smart" comes nearer the sense. Since they are themselves smart, the Corinthians do not at all mind fools, they rather like to have them around. The sting in this remark is the implication that such smart people are bigger fools than the fools they indulge; and that, by getting such indulgence from people who think themselves so smart, these fools are smarter than the smart people on whom they impose.

20) Just how smart the Corinthians are in tolerating the imposition of fools gladly and with a smile is driven home with a vengeance. They are so smart that there is scarcely a limit to their folly. **Why, you bear it if one enslaves you, if one devours (you), if one captures (you), if one lifts himself up (over you), if one smites you in the face! I am speaking by way of disgrace that we on our part have been weak.**

Behold all that the Corinthians are willing to bear and even like! Paul lists the items and calls each one by its actual name. All of the "ifs" denote reality. All of them refer to past actualities that occurred in Corinth, but they cut more deeply: not only have the Corinthians actually tolerated such treatment on the part of the false apostles, but the conditional form also implies that they are ready to have it repeated again and again. So "smart" are they, smart fools! Such fools are the false prophets, mighty smart ones! The irony is devastating, but it is the irony of the cold facts — *that* produces the devastation. Irony is really of two kinds: one that aims only to wound and disregards facts, the other that lets the facts speak, to wound in order to help.

The five items make up one picture. Five is the half of ten, i. e., the half of completeness, hence it only sketches the fools that the Corinthians are to submit to this sort of thing. The picture is one of outrage of the most intolerable kind. That is the actual fact, but the Corinthians bear it as something that is perfectly in order. They submit to it "gladly."

Κατά in the first verb means "down": "if one makes abject slaves of you." The same is true with regard to the next verb; but we say, not "eats you down," but "eats you up"; the English is queer, for instance, "burn down" is also "burn up." The third verb means "to take," yet not "takes of you," robs you (A. V.), but "takes you captive" (R. V.) so that he has you where he wants to have you, to do with you what he pleases. These three involve the fourth: "if one lifts himself up over you" so that you simply have to submit. The last puts in the finishing touch: "smites you in the face," but not in answer to resistance which you may offer; no resistance on the part of the Corinthians is thought of, this smiting is the regular, everyday treatment. The Corinthians take it "gladly." Δέρει means literally "to flay." We need not resort to a figure of speech. Did Paul in I Tim. 3:4 not write regarding the bishop: "no striker" (not fighting), and in II Tim. 2:24, "must not be fighting"? Lords and masters freely used actual blows, and this custom persisted down the centuries to very recent times, and it persists to this day in many lands.

What an astounding picture of the false apostles, the superfine apostles, who had come to Corinth as high lords — and the Corinthians bowed in sweet submission!

21) But the worst cut of all follows in a sudden and wholly unexpected turn. The reader thinks: "What

a disgrace for the Corinthians!" and would stop at that. Not Paul, not Paul by any means. "I am speaking by way of disgrace," he says, "I am using this category or norm" (κατά); and now comes the sudden flash: "that *we on our part* have been weak!" What a disgrace for me and my assistants, poor, weak fellows who could not act the abusive lords like that so that you could submit to us with this gladness of yours! The disgrace is mine.

In 10:12 Paul has already admitted that he and his assistants are not in this class of high and mighty men and cannot even faintly be compared with them. In 10:10 he says, "My bodily presence is held to be so weak, and my word amounts to nothing." These false apostles know how real apostles ought to act so as to impress you with what real apostles are; *we* — why, we did not even know how to act as apostles. The perfect tense "have been (and thus still are) weak" is the correct reading, some texts have only the aorist "were weak," which omits reference to the present time.

Does Paul overdraw the picture? Then he would, indeed, be a fool and deliberately defeat his own end. His use of five clauses indicates that still more might be said. Four is used to indicate ordinary completeness; four is *not* used here in order to avoid this impression. It is worth while to note even such points in Paul's writing. Ὡς ὅτι is simply declarative "that," see 5:19 with the references. R. W. P., regards ὡς as implying that the clause "we have been weak" is quoted by Paul as the charge of others against Paul and his helpers; but see R. 1033 where Robertson himself is of a different opinion.

Here there is another place where Paul is charged with not being plain. The result is a guessing in regard to whose "disgrace" he has in mind, and the choice is assumed to lie between three: the pseudo-apostles, whose tyranny was a disgrace; the Corinthians, whose glad submission was a disgrace; Paul and his apostles, whose weakness in not having played tyrants is esteemed a disgrace. But Paul is as plain as plain can be with his most emphatic ἡμεῖς and his *own* admission: "*We*, we have been weak!"

And let it be noted that what Paul pictures here has been endlessly repeated. People will swallow anything on the part of false teachers. These men get their followers just where they want them; they love to put on lordly airs; they still get the huge salaries; they still act abusively. The only change that we note is a little modern veneer.

III. *The First Grand Gush of Foolish Boasting*

22) After having been pent up so long (since v. 1) the flood now bursts the dam and roars down in a torrent. Yet it is perfectly controlled. What other long lists found in Paul's letters lead us to expect is duplicated here. Read the author's study of the magnificent one in Rom. 12:7-21 which is perfect in every detail; also the one in this epistle, 6:4-10 which is briefer but equally perfect. For some reason the present one has found considerable appreciation among the commentators. It ought to find still more.

Here we have again a sample of the swift mind of Paul. When he began this list, the whole of it was already present to his mind. He did not start it and shape it as he went along. If he had he would have had the experience that we frequently have: we use some of the pieces too soon, and our design becomes faulty. Paul is a good teacher from whom to learn rhetoric. With perfect, unsought facility he combines his rhetoric with his material. Who except Jesus, the ancient psalmists, and the prophets have ever done as well?

Everything throbs with life. More than this, it burns with vitality and with power. There is not one false note. Only the high points are touched. There are so many that lesser things must be omitted. Only the most obvious things are used, those which it takes only half an eye to see. After the first three items regarding birth the pseudo-apostles are left miles behind. It is literally true as 10:12 has stated: Paul would not dare to put himself into the same class with these men, would not dare to draw a comparison. There was nothing in them with which comparison could be made. Paul's boasting and that of the pseudo-apostles appear like day and night. Verse 20 shows what they could in reality boast of.

Paul leaves out his assistants. He had to. They, indeed, shared many of these items; but if Paul had used plurals he would have seemed to appropriate what his assistants suffered for himself. At least the question would be raised concerning his share. Because this is all "I — I," it is boasting, foolish boasting like that of common, unspiritual men; Paul is blowing his own horn. Yet in a way it is not boasting; these are only the bare, unadorned facts which appear as boasting only because Paul himself recites these facts. For that reason Paul stoops to this fool thing as he calls it. The effect that was produced on the Corinthians simply had to be stunning.

The Corinthians had known many of the items long ago. This does not imply that Paul went about with a recital of them; but Paul's assistants and others who knew much of Paul's story had certainly talked in Corinth, had been asked to tell what they knew, and had surely told. The effect of the recital lies, not in telling a lot of new, startling things, but in putting together in briefest fashion this whole array of the facts. The effect produced lies in the mass. And the focus of this effect is not lost, the point is not blunted. Paul is not boasting about himself as being a superman, a mighty Atlas who is holding up a world of inflictions; it is

Paul's *weakness* which constitutes his boast. Yes, this is the man who is so weak, who lets all these inflictions roll over him, he it is who "has been weak" (v. 21) in Corinth and was unable to act the lordly tyrant, the role which the false apostles assumed, the role which the Corinthians liked so well in these false apostles because they regarded it as the one that was really proper in genuine apostles.

But in what thing anyone may be bold — I speak (only) in folly — bold am I also! The singular "in what" challenges any point that may be brought up by anyone, and ἄν denotes Paul's expectancy, he is ready, come who will. If anyone has the boldness to stand up and to make an issue on anything, Paul says, I will do the same, and we shall see if I fall down. But he just cannot help feeling like a fool when he does this boasting. The Corinthians must know: "I speak (only) in folly."

Hebrews are they? I, too! Israelites are they? I, too! Abraham's seed are they? I, too! The frequently used rhetorical three begins the list. Our versions do well to regard them as questions, which accords more with the challenging tone. The three terms are close synonyms, all are terms of honor among Jews and together express all that made the Jews so proud of themselves. The term Ἰουδαῖοι, "Jews," is, of course, not among them. The false apostles in Corinth were of genuine Jewish descent and made a grand boast of that fact. In this purely external matter — external as far as Christianity is concerned — they had no advantage over Paul. Let them call themselves what they will, choose what designation they please, "Hebrews — Israelites — seed of Abraham," they only include Paul, too. He is all these without a flaw.

"Hebrews" is the national name that was preferred by the Jews, and it names them according to their language. Some think that the word is here intended as a distinction from Hellenists. The "Hebrews" were the old type of Jews who preserved their Aramaic and used the Hebrew Bible, the Hellenists were the diaspora type who knew little or no Aramaic and used the LXX; even birth in Palestine has been introduced. But this overloads the word and dislocates the parallel with "Israelites" and "seed of Abraham," these two being only variants of the same idea. All three are just variants, all three are intended as boasting Jews intended them when they spoke of themselves with pride: they were of the choice Hebrew nation, descended from Israel, the father of the twelve patriarchs, born of the very seed of Abraham, the head of the covenant.

23) After this has been said, all the boasters in Corinth are left behind forever. **Ministers of Christ are they?** This question resembles the three that precede and is thus connected with them; but it is not intended as number four but as opening the new, astounding line which runs through to v. 31. The three questions are concerned only with birth and outward descent, which was a minor issue to Paul. But "ministers of Christ" is the supreme and in reality the only issue. All four designations are not terms chosen by Paul but terms that Paul caught up from these false boasters.

Do they arrogate to themselves the title "ministers of Christ"? Do they set up such a claim? Now Paul cannot say: κἀγώ, "I, too!" Now he says: ὑπὲρ ἐγώ, **Way beyond that I!** But he inserts: **I am talking as one beside himself!** He means: "That sounds crazy." Can anyone be more than a "minister of Christ"? But note λαλῶ and not, as in the parenthesis in v. 22, λέγω. The latter would be improper because it would refer to Paul's meaning; the former refers only to the sound of what he says.

This clears up a number of questions. How can Paul admit that the false apostles are in any sense "ministers of Christ" and even compare himself with them as being only more such a minister than they? Is he not comparing himself with the Twelve, the other real "ministers of Christ"? Paul is only quoting the claim of these false apostles. He has said that they "preach another Jesus" (v. 4); he has given them their right name (v. 13). They, of course, sail under the false flag "ministers of Christ," they would not dare to do anything else. That is *their* boast — take it for what it is worth; Paul puts *his* boast over against it. His boast is that he is "way beyond" what they are able only to claim. Paul's is not merely another claim that is only more extensive than theirs; Paul opens all the batteries of *the facts*, all of which prove overwhelmingly that he is in fact more than these false boasters ever even dreamed of including in their false claim.

Ὑπέρ is simply an adverb (B.-P. 1342); the fact that we lack other examples of this use need not disturb us. "I am beyond" means two things: 1) beyond because I have all the true marks of "a minister of Christ," have them in superabundance while they have nothing but their claim, against which the facts in their case, as stated in v. 20, cry out in horror; 2) beyond because I have the marks not only of "a minister of Christ," such as also Paul's noble assistants have, but even of *an apostle* of Christ. For in Paul's list of grand marks (v. 26-29) he brings in his extensive travels and what goes with these travels. One who was merely a minister of Christ might not be a traveller at all. But an apostle dared not remain in one place; the apostles had to "go to all nations" (Matt. 28:19), "into all the world, to all creatures" (Mark 16:15). Even in Corinth, Paul had to have the Lord's orders to stay one and one-half years as he did (Acts 18:

9-11). Throughout all of Paul's work we see how the ground burned under his feet; his aim was ever to cover as much new territory with the gospel as possible. We dilate on this point because it is sometimes overlooked and yet sheds so much light on the composition of the present list.

The fact that Paul should introduce a comparison between himself and the Twelve is so much beside the mark that we need offer no refutation of it.

Paul says that he is "beyond" all such as have no more than the claim of being "ministers of Christ," and that means completely beyond. An advance guard of four ἐν phrases that is coupled with adverbs shows how utterly he is "beyond" them: Way beyond (am) I: **in labors — excessively! in prisons — excessively! in stripes — beyond measure! in deaths — often!** These four are used to indicate ordinary rhetorical completeness and are arranged in an ascending scale: labors — prisons — stripes — deaths. These four are selected from Paul's life. Burdensome, exhausting labors (κόποι) are meant — the sham ministers of Christ have nothing of the kind. "Labors" is the proper word to place at the beginning; a genuine minister will do the heaviest labor for Christ. These sham ministers do not even work for Christ, to say nothing about labor. See Rom. 16:18 for information as to whom and what they serve (but compare the author's interpretation of this passage). With that combine v. 20 and note for what the false apostles use their strength. Not a bit for Christ!

The next three expressions belong together: labors and labors — but what a reward! "Prisons, stripes, deaths." Who of these sham ministers received a stripe for Christ, ever faced death for Christ? Never a one! The game which they play offers no rewards like this. Their "belly" would not endure it, Rom. 16:18. They enslave, eat up, lift themselves up, abuse others (v.

20). Is Paul ὑπέρ? So far that he has left them out of sight!

The adverbs are not adjectives, nor are they used in place of adjectives. They do not modify the phrases but the adverb "beyond": I am beyond them, not merely a little but *"excessively"* beyond them in labors, again *"excessively"* in prisons, even "beyond measure" when it comes to stripes, and "often" when it comes to deaths. This wipes out the idea that Paul means that he has *more* labors and *more* prisons to his credit than the false apostles, and that Paul drops the idea of "more" when it comes to stripes and to deaths.

Why this view? Because the first two are comparative adverbs, while the last two are not. R. 664 favors the idea that in every comparative adverb the comparative sense is somehow conserved. He has against him B.-D. 60, 3 who state that in some cases περισσοτέρως = ὑπερβαλλόντως. Here, where πολλάκις follows, this is surely the case. If, however, we *must* have comparison, it can be only this: "I am beyond them in labors as well as in prisons far *more* than I need to be in order to destroy all comparison; in stripes even excessively beyond them; in deaths often." The sense is that regarding these four points the false ministers have nothing whatever to exhibit. The last adverb "often" is a drop downward from the other three for the simple reason that "deaths" are the climax upward. "Stripes" are placed between "prisons" and "deaths" because scourgings were so severe as at times to cause death. Paul wrote from cruel experience. The backs of the false ministers showed not a single scar; Paul's back showed them ὑπερβαλλόντως.

24) **By (the hand of) Jews five times I got forty (stripes) less one; three times was I beaten with rods; once was I stoned; three times was I shipwrecked; a night and a day have I spent in the deep.** As was the case in v. 20, we have five items, the half

of total completeness which is ten. Paul recites only half of the whole story as to how he was often in the shadow of death. "By Jews" has the regular preposition of the agent with passives although "I got" is active. The Greek needs no noun, "I got forty minus one" being plain enough. Luke 12:47 likewise omits "stripes." When Paul says he got the thirty-nine five times he means that he got them. To suggest that on a few occasions he got less because this scourging was stopped before the full count was reached in cases where the victim was weak and had collapsed, contradicts what Paul says about his experiences. Five times he got the full thirty-nine; if he ever got a smaller count, it did not happen in these five instances. But this is true, he names these scourgings with the full count because each one brought him to death's door.

Deut. 25:3 fixes the extreme number of blows at forty. The Jewish judge might decree a lesser number, but he might not go above forty. Beyond that lay the death penalty. So Paul says he got the penalty just below death five times from Jewish courts. In later times the Jews fixed the extreme number at thirty-nine for fear of a miscount.

The victim was laid with his face on the ground, was held by his arms and his feet until the blows were administered before the eyes of the court itself. Originally rods were used. But later, despite the fact that the Jews were so scrupulous about not exceeding the number forty, the rod was exchanged for a leather strap made of calf's hide. The end of this strap was split into five strips, which made the penalty much severer. The Mishna states that the victim was bound to a pillar, the breast and the shoulders were bared, the body was bent, and thirteen blows were administered upon the breast, twenty-six upon the shoulders.

We have no record of these five Jewish scourgings which Paul experienced. It is evident that they did not occur in Palestine where the Jewish courts could unquestionably decree such penalties but in the Diaspora. This raises the question as to whether Jewish synagogue courts were allowed to administer such justice in pagan provinces. The *Jewish Encyclopedia* IV, 277, etc., states that this right was assumed by the rabbis.

25) Three times Paul was beaten with rods. This verb indicates that this was a penalty which was decreed in Roman courts and inflicted by lictors or, where a court was of lesser grade, by common court servants. Fortunately, we have Acts 16:22, 23 where one of these three scourgings is mentioned, where the same verb is used. The question naturally arises as to how Roman courts could scourge Paul since he was a Roman citizen, and heavy penalties forbade scourging of Roman citizens in the empire. The account given in Acts is valuable for showing that this *did* happen in Philippi where the judges lost their heads before the howling mob and Paul could not possibly assert his rights and thus, together with Silas, received we do not know how many blows. See the author on Acts 16 for the full story. The trouble was that a tumult was generally raised, and no orderly trial took place. Thus the *Lex Porcia* went for nought. How dangerous this *Lex* was we see from Acts 16:35, etc., where the judges were badly frightened when they discovered whom they had allowed to be scourged. We see the same thing in Acts 22:24, etc. Here Paul was able to assert his rights as a Roman. To assume that in the two other instances, concerning which we have no details, the Roman courts simply ignored the *Lex*, is not probable.

The one stoning which Paul mentions is fully recorded in Acts 11:19, 20. Paul was given up for dead. Shortly before this Paul barely escaped stoning at Iconium (Acts 11:5, 6).

We know nothing about the three shipwrecks. But that is not reason to cast doubt on Luke's Acts because he omits mention of them. He omits ever so much more because he does not write a biography of Paul. During one of these wrecks Paul was very likely adrift on the open sea for a night and a day and was in constant danger of being drowned, in danger also of not being picked up. We have no earlier use of νυχθήμερον, accusative to indicate extent of time. We have ποιέω in the sense of spending time in Acts 13:33; 20:3; James 4:13.

The tense is the perfect, the change to which after the aorists B.-D. 343, 2 call "without sufficient reason"; R. 897 calls it the dramatical historical present perfect, which is well enough as far as a name is concerned. But why not another aorist? Because extent of time in the past is to be expressed, and the perfect expresses that: I have done "a night and day" in the deep. That means twenty-four hours, but it also means that they began with the night, and that Paul was rescued only toward the end of the next day. Another night would probably have ended his life. "In the deep" does not mean under the water, another Jonah-miracle; it means on the high sea, on a raft or clinging to wreckage. These are a few of the almost fatal experiences of Paul. They reveal how much of the strenuous life of Paul is hidden from us.

26) The first dative ὁδοιπορίαις is different from the eight κινδύνοις that follow; the first governs the rest, and, therefore, in order to mark this difference and this dependence, κινδύνοις is repeated eight times. We have a similar construction in v. 27. There, too, a main dative governs the specifications, all of which are, however, cast in phrases. The eight dangers listed in our verse are grouped into 2 — 2 — 3 — 1. Two have genitives, two ἐκ phrases, three ἐν phrases of place, one an

ἐν phrase of place but denoting persons: "among false brethren." All of this is rhetorically perfect.

There was a reason that prompted Paul to list his travels with all that they entailed. The emphasis is usually placed on the "perils"; it ought to be on the "travels." The perils were incidental to the travels. But these travels marked Paul as a true apostle. We have already (v. 23) pointed out that "going" was the essential of apostleship. The apostles were to reach all nations, the whole world. It was their very commission to travel, ever to travel, and ever to travel into new territory and new lands. Obstacles, hindrances, dangers made no difference. It is in that sense that they are introduced here. But perils or no perils, an apostle had to do much travelling.

Ὁδοιπορίαις is the dative of relation: "as regards travels," and it depends on: "Beyond am I" stated in v. 23. Paul says: I am way beyond the false ministers as regards travels. He says that he is this πολλάκις and repeats this adverb found at the end of v. 23; he does this purposely in order to indicate that the thought developed in v. 26 is a continuation of that begun in v. 23. As Paul was utterly beyond the false apostles "in deaths," which was "often," namely every time he incurred mortal danger, so he was utterly beyond these false apostles every time he fared forth on an apostolic journey, and that was again "often." The false ministers could never take an apostolic journey, they were "pseudo-apostles" (v. 13). They had no commission "to go." They had, indeed, travelled to Corinth, but they were impelled to do this only by their own evil impulses (v. 20). On whatever journeys they undertook they, too, may have encountered perils, but none of *their* perils were like Paul's, could never be. Paul's were perils that were met with on *apostolic* journeys, theirs were perils such as the Pharisees encountered when they "compassed sea and land to make one proselyte; and when he is made, ye make him twofold more the child of hell than yourselves," Matt. 23:15. Compare v. 3, the serpent deceiving Eve, and v. 14, Satan.

It is thus that Paul brings this decisive evidence: **As regards travels — often! with perils of rivers! with perils of robbers! with perils from (my) race! with perils from Gentiles! with perils in city! with perils in wilderness! with perils in sea! with perils among pseudo-brethren!**

"Rivers" and "robbers" are genitives of source, the two genitives are a pair. Few rivers had bridges over them, many fords were dangerous, especially when the rivers had risen because of floods. Robbers infested the wilds despite Roman rule. They waylaid travellers, robbed, and often killed them. Remember the Samaritan who rescued the man that had fallen among "robbers" (the very word which Paul here uses, Luke 10:30, etc.). That poor man would have lost his life except for his rescuer. Christ's parable is taken from life. How many times had Paul and his little party been held up on the long and the frequent journeys which he had to undertake?

All of the "perils" which Paul lists were mortal perils, in anyone of which he might have easily lost his life. As v. 24, 25 specify instances to substantiate "in deaths often," so v. 26 specifies still further what some of these death perils were. Whereas v. 24, 25 have exact figures, the simple plurals used in v. 26 point to a large number of mortal dangers. During all of his travels Paul constantly took his life into his hands. Yet see how much he travelled! Divine providence alone preserved him. Yet he had many distressing experiences.

A second pair made up of ἐκ phrases follows. Deadly peril often threatened Paul from his γένος, his own race. Luke furnishes a number of such instance in Acts. The hostile Jews ever wanted Paul's blood. As they murdered

Jesus and Stephen, so murder was ever in their hearts — a lurid commentary on their morality. As Acts shows, the Jews often stirred up the Gentiles to murderous hate. They drove Pilate to crucify Jesus against his will; in the Diaspora they often found willing Gentile cooperation — in Acts 17:5, "certain lewd fellows of the baser sort."

The next are four ἐν phrases which are thus bound together, but the last is distinct from the other three. These perils occurred "in city" where one might think himself safe because of the protection of civil magistrates and their police; but, of course, also "in wilderness," on lonely roads, far from any habitation, and "in sea," in the small vessels of that day which were so easily wrecked by storms. Tourists are told of the wonderful "blue Mediterranean." It is lovely, indeed, when it is calm. But in 1925, in midsummer, the author's voyage from Sicily into the great fortified harbor Valleda on the island of Malta, even on a good French steamer, was made during a heavy gale which would have been dangerous to the sailing vessels of Paul's day.

City — wilderness — sea — pseudo-brethren. Critical eyes see a misplacement of the last, ascribe it to an early scribe, and correct it by transferring the pseudo-brethren to the place where the critic thinks this item should be: my own race — Gentiles — pseudo-brethren. The fact that ἐν would then be joined to two ἐκ does not cause hesitation. "Among false brethren" goes with the other three ἐν; "in city, desert, and sea" the worst dangers to Paul were those that threatened him "*in* (among) false brethren." The last phrase is exactly where it ought to be; no second phrase could be joined to it in order to make a pair.

Judas was in a class to which no other class has ever been added. Traitors are always in a class by themselves. And they constitute the worst peril of all. Judas betrayed Christ to death. Under the mask of "brethren" they who are pseudo-brethren have easiest access to their victim. Being but human, unable to see through a Judas as Christ did, such a victim is unsuspecting, takes no precautions, and unless the Lord delivers him, his fate is sealed. Paul writes φευδαπόστολοι (v. 13) and now ψευδάδελφοι. He puts these individuals into the same class. Both work secretly. Their power is destroyed once they are exposed. Paul discovered some of the pseudo-brethren and their dastardly work in Gal. 2:4.

27) **As regards labor and toil, amid sleeplessnesses often! amid hunger and thirst! amid fastings often! amid cold and nakedness!** The dative is exactly like the one that introduces v. 26. As all the "perils" modify the "travels," so all the ἐν phrases modify "labor and toil." The travels were connected with so many and such varied types of perils. The travels as travels were also "labor and toil." Whereas "travels" is a simple plural, two singulars now produce a similar effect: "as regards labor and toil." The singulars refer to mass, and both words bring out the strain and the effort of exertion which produce great fatigue.

Paul mentions four, the rhetorical number to indicate ordinary completeness. The second and the fourth items have paired terms like the first dative; the first and the third items are made multiple by "often," the adverb that has already been used twice.

Paul has mentioned "labors" in v. 23, but only as severe work. He is not repeating, for the emphasis is now on the hardships "amid" which all the labor and toil has to be accomplished. "And watchings often." The adverb modifies the phrase. It is distressing to be weary in body and in mind and then not to be able to get the rest and the relaxation of sleep. "Hunger and thirst" prevented sleep. "Cold and nakedness" did likewise. Those exhausting journeys led through arid places; on the long distances traveled food also gave out.

"Amid fastings" has nothing to do with ascetic fasting. That was a discipline which Paul certainly seldom needed. Such fastings would be ridiculous in this catalog. These are fastings that were caused by the fact that one had no food at all or had food but could not or dared not eat it. We have an instance from the later life of Paul (Acts 27:33, etc.); it certainly also illustrates sleeplessness and terrible weariness. "Often," Paul writes for the fourth time. What a tale it would make if we could get the details which this adverb covers!

The final touch is in "cold and nakedness," the latter meaning lack of sufficient clothes. Many a day is hot, but bitter cold is the night. When the road led over mountains, cold nights were frequent. Paul camped wherever he could. In the fall and the spring wet could be added to cold. Tourists complain that the cold is miserable during these seasons, even the hotels are icy. How little travellers could carry with them in order to keep warm. Paul's picture is only too true. When we note it we shall appreciate the various references to "being sent forward" by the brethren on some of these journeys. Their number means protection; they carried supplies, food, clothing, etc. They sometimes went even the entire way (Acts 17:15 is such an instance). Paul often had only two or three of his own assistants with him.

28) **Apart from the things** (that thus come in) **besides** (there is) **the press of a crowd upon me day after day, the worry over all the churches!** All the items mentioned from v. 24 onward are τὰ παρεκτός, the things that come in only "besides." They are not at all Paul's chief burden, they are only the extras that are thrown in for good measure. "Apart from" them

(χωρίς) lies Paul's real burden. In part those extras accompany his frequent travels, his arrival in new cities; in part they occur as extras when Paul is in the midst of his work in any place. They are always only "the besides." They deserve no better name when they are compared with Paul's real load.

This χωρίς phrase is astounding. We think that Paul has been heaping up all of his very worst troubles, during some of which he was even nearly killed. With the turn of a little phrase he now tells us that these are only the little extras, the greens that garnish the roast, the perquisites that are handed him in addition to his full salary. These things come "often," he now adds the big thing that comes καθ' ἡμέραν (distributive use of the preposition): "day for day." Those extra things Paul does not at all mind. They would, of course, frighten the false apostles in Corinth to death! Already that shows, as we have seen, how utterly "beyond" them (v. 23) Paul is. Paul uses five verses to describe the extras, to indicate his real load he writes one line. That is perfect psychology as far as the effect to be produced upon his readers and the exposure of the false prophets are concerned. The main burden is thus not minimized by comparison — quite the contrary. To expand on the main burden would have dissipated the concentrated effect at which Paul aimed.

The two nominatives are like an exclamation although we may supply "there is." The vivid word ἐπίστασις (R., W. P., aptly calls it thus) appears again in Acts 24:12 in the same sense: "collecting a crowd," causing people to halt; or "a collection of people." "Onset" is incorrect (R., W. P. on Acts 24:12). Paul refers to the number of people who in every city soon besieged him with a thousand and one questions that he should answer, a thousand and one difficulties about the gospel which he should solve. The apposition: "the worry over all the churches" (objective genitive) shows that all the questions and all the problems of all his churches found their focus in him. In Luke 10:41 we have the verb that corresponds to the noun μέριμνα, Martha "worrying" about many things; in Matt. 13:22 we have the noun "the worry of the world" smothering the good seed. Liddell and Scott, 984: "earnest care," with a note on derivations. This was the real load which Paul carried. All else was only "besides."

On the dative μοι see B.-D. 202. We have a compound verbal noun with the dative which is found only once in the New Testament; a few texts read "my." The A. V. has mistranslated the χωρίς phrase. Many wrestle with it as we see from the R. V. which offers two marginal alternatives. "The things besides" are the ones mentioned in v. 23-27, they are not "things without," things which Paul omits, or such as "come out of course."

29) In view of his main load (v. 28) Paul exclaims: **Who is weak, and I am not weak! Who is being trapped, and I on my part am not being burned!** No, not as a powerful man who is able to endure all this is Paul boasting thus. If the false prophets had even a few of the accessories to their credit, how they would boast of strength! For this reason Paul is so utterly beyond them (ὑπέρ, v. 23). He sees nothing in himself but *weakness*. He feels like nothing in view of this vast load. Is any man weak, too weak to bear his load, and am I, says Paul, not weak? Has anyone a burden that is greater than mine to make his legs give way?

The second exclamation is synonymous but a climax. Its sense is: Is anyone getting himself into a fatal trap, and I on my part am not doing even far worse, getting myself into fire? We may ask why we have ἐγώ only in the second question. It is because we have only a mere parallel in the first question: another is weak — then Paul certainly has a right to say that he, too, is weak (just ἀσθενεῖ and ἀσθενῶ). But the next two verbs are immensely stronger, both are deadly, the second indicates a death that is *worse* than the first; hence ἐγώ with all its emphasis must be used.

The verb σκανδαλίζω means to catch in a deathtrap, and the passive means to be so caught. The noun σκάνδαλον denotes the crooked stick to which the bait is affixed so that to touch the bait is to spring this trap that kills the victim. M.-M. 576. The point of comparison is deadliness. The noun *never* means "stumbling block," the verb never "to stumble," its passive never "to be made to stumble." When it is used metaphorically it means: "offense, to offend," etc., the idea is always *mortal* offense, offense that *kills* spiritually. Our versions misunderstand the word; dictionaries and commentators generally follow them. See the author on the previous instances of these words as found in the New Testament, Matt. 5:29; Mark 4:17; Luke 7:23; John 16:1; Rom. 9:33 (where πρόσκομμα, "stumbling block," and σκάνδαλον, "trap-trigger," are used side by side); I Cor. 8:13.

Πυροῦμαι is also passive. Both verbs are durative present tenses: "is anyone being trapped" — "and am I not (worse than trapped) being burned in fire?" Is there anyone whose work and whose burden are about to kill him as a trap closes down and crushes a victim? If there is, am not I, Paul, one who is literally being burned in the fire by my work? Both questions are sometimes misunderstood: Is anyone weak, and do I not in sympathy share his weakness? R., W. P., gives the second question the sense: "When a brother stumbles, Paul is set on fire with grief." The sympathy, the grief are introduced by the commentators. The sense becomes extravagant, a sense and a thought that Paul could never entertain, namely that in all Christendom there could be no weak person, no person getting caught in fatal trouble but that Paul feels it all on *his* back, on *his* heart. It has thus been said: Paul is here representing himself as almost equal to the heavenly *Christus consolator*. But such a thing is an impossibility for Paul, in fact, the opposite of what he says.

30) It is all weakness in the case of Paul, weakness that breaks down of itself as weakness, weakness that gets burned in fire by the load that is put upon it. **If I have to boast, in regard to the things pertaining to my weakness will I boast!** Paul is sure that he will leave most men behind in these things. Other men take pride in their personal strength and power, Paul's pride lies in the fact that he is weak, yea, nothing at all.

Δεῖ is used to indicate every kind of necessity, here that which forces Paul to boast like other men boast. Well, then, if it *has* to be, Paul says, I *will* boast, but only of things that no one else except some other good Christian would ever dream of using in a boast, of things that show how wretchedly weak I am! The very idea seems contradictory, paradoxical in the highest degree: boasting — weakness. But the greatest thing that Paul has come to see in himself is his weakness. He is himself astonished to see how great his weakness is. Men boast of the greatest thing they have; well, Paul says, this is my greatest, so this shall ever be my boast when boast I must.

31) Is this facetious? Is this pretense? **The God and Father of the Lord Jesus knows, he who is blessed to the eons, that I am not lying!** Paul is not lying by equivocation, by playing with words, by leaving an impression on his readers that is different from what he really intends. As he says in 1:13, he writes nothing other than what his readers read and what they understand when they read. Strange as it may

sound, his boast is nothing but his excessive weakness. God knows it is the truth.

Paul uses the same assurance which he voiced in v. 11 where he stated it in briefest form: "God knows"; here he expands the subject and merely adds the object. "God knows" is *not* an oath in v. 11 or here in v. 31 although it is called an oath by some commentators. There is neither the form of an oath nor the necessity for one. Paul is no profuse swearer. "God knows" states an assured fact, one that helps to assure others. Any additions to this brief basic formula do not change it into an oath. In v. 11 the object omitted is the one expressed in v. 31; with "God knows" no other object can be used than "that I am not lying." It really needs no expansion in v. 11. Nor does Paul Christianize this "oath" by adding to "God" what he does add. Does Paul not always refer to the Christian God when he writes "God," whether he adds something to the word or not? The addition "and Father," etc., intends to Christianize as little here in v. 31 as it does in the benedictions in 1:3. See that passage for the explanation that God is both God and Father of the Lord Jesus. The addition to ὁ Θεός only describes God, only bids the mind to dwell on who and what he is.

Ὁ ὤν κτλ. is an apposition; the participle is made a noun by means of the article. It is overstraining to say that ὁ ὤν is more than merely "he who is," that it = "the Self-existent One," and that εὐλογητός is another apposition as it would then have to be. Although Paul uses an apposition it embodies the common Jewish benedictions with reference to God: "blessed to the eons," exactly as in Rom. 1:25.

Εὐλογητός is the verbal with the force of the passive past participle "praised or blessed" in the sense of alone worthy of praise and blessing. The Greek has no word for "eternity"; it uses "eon" or the plural "eons" (here) or the intensification "eon of eons" instead. "Unto the eons," cycles upon cycles, means "forever."

Another word must be added regarding "weakness." See the exposition of 12:5, 9, 10. The more of weakness there is, the more room is there for pure grace and all-sufficient divine power; the less there is of our own weakness, the less room is there for divine grace and power. When we are reduced to nothing, God is allowed to be our everything. The world cannot comprehend such an experience. It was utterly beyond ($ὑπέρ$, v. 23) the false ministers and apostles in Corinth. But it is literally true: our greatest asset, our highest cause for boasting if we *must* boast, is this our weakness and all the things in our lives that exhibit this weakness: $τὰ\ τῆς\ ἀσθενείας$. Paul writes more than a God's truth, he writes a most instructive one.

Let us add the caution: this is not what is called "sinful weakness." Nor is the word used as it is in Rom. 14:1, etc., regarding a "weak" brother, weak in regard to the faith, weak in knowledge, grace, etc. Of this weakness one should be ashamed; he could never make it a boast. To be wholly weak, in absolute dependence on God's grace, help, gifts, etc., that is the weakness which God works in us by his Spirit and also fills with his power.

32, 33) Critics voice serious objection to v. 32, 33. Why a little story inserted here? Paul perhaps told several, and his scribe liked this one so well that Paul just let him insert it. Or the story is a gloss which was placed in the margin. Textually this brief story is assured. As far as Paul's asseveration of veracity in v. 31 is concerned, this certainly seals v. 30, it is not intended to fortify v. 32, 33, nor does it refer to 12:1 on the hypothesis that the Damascus story is an interpolation.

The list of items in Paul's first round of boasting closes with v. 28. The *addendum* found in v. 29, 30 points out what is essential in all of these items, especially in the real burden of Paul which is summarily stated in v. 28: it is that in all these things the readers are to see exhibitions of Paul's weakness, and that this his weakness, which is so exceedingly great, is his great boast. This astounding declaration is full truth and not a lie (v. 31).

The very career of Paul began with weakness, he had to run away as a fugitive. We say his career began thus, for the work in Damascus was not a part of his apostolic career. What work among the Jews he did there was abruptly discontinued. He tried a bit of work among the Jews in Jerusalem, but this, too, was soon interrupted. Then there follows a long period in which Paul is lost to view as he lives in Tarsus. Barnabas brought him to Antioch. There Paul at last really began to work until after this preliminary training in Antioch the Spirit sent him forth on his real work among the Gentiles in all lands. The flight from Damascus was the beginning. Paul's career began, like that of Moses, with flight and with a long period of waiting, waiting, nothing but waiting. This makes the flight from Damascus so significant. It forced Paul into the long wait in which he fully learned that he was nothing, that his mightiest asset was utter weakness, weakness which enabled God to do everything with him and through him.

The asseveration of veracity is supported by this historical evidence which began the night when Paul fled from Damascus so that he might learn the long lesson of his utter weakness, on the complete learning of which his apostolic success depended. For this reason the story is told here; for this reason a brief reference would not suffice. For this reason it is told at this most proper place. The tremendous energy of Paul, which at one time made him the worst ravager of the church, which after his conversion sought to make him the mighty disseminator of the gospel, must first of all be humbled in utter weakness and learn the only reliance which was at last learned by Moses: "*I will be with thee!*" Exod. 3:12; Matt. 28:20. More may be said; let this suffice.

In Damascus the Ethnarch of Aretas, the king, was guarding the city of the Damascenes in order to arrest me; and through a door in a basket I was lowered through the wall and escaped out of his hand.

This is the story related in Acts 9:23-25. But Paul and Luke relate it independently. Luke received his account from Paul. To make certain of capturing Paul, the Jews enlisted the aid of the Ethnarch by denouncing Paul as a dangerous disturber. This official posted special guards at the city gates, and, lest Paul elude them in disguise, the Jews, who knew Paul, helped to watch. But Paul escaped at night as both he and Luke describe this incident.

Along the city wall, where houses were built against it, one house was found which had a door that had been cut through the great wall high up from the ground; the door opened out from the upper story or from the roof of the house. This θυρίς was "a little door," *eine Luke,* and not a "window" as we think of windows. In a wall which served as a fortification houses that adjoined the wall would not have windows. This one little door was so exceptional that the hostile Jews and nobody else even thought about it even if they knew of its existence. It was, of course, always tightly barred. Paul was seemingly to be caught until some friend informed the disciples, and then Paul got safely away, and the soldiers and the Jews watched for an indefinite time at the gates.

The imperfect "he was guarding" already intimates that an aorist will follow which will tell about the outcome. Guarding the city means no more than what

Acts says, namely guarding the gates. We do not think that the Ethnarch surrounded the whole city. Aretas was the Nabataean King Harithath IV, the father-in-law of Herod Antipas. Aretas ruled from 9 B. C. to 39 A. D. How he came to have an Ethnarch in Damascus at this time, and just when this occurred, are questions for discussion. We think of this Ethnarch as an Arabian sheik.

An interesting point in the narration is the fact that after Paul names Damascus he does not say "guarded the city" but "the city of the Damascenes" (the adjective used as a noun). This sounds as though the city belonged to its inhabitants, and as though the king's overlordship through his Ethnarch was loosely exercised. It is a point for the historians to discuss; it is apparently one of the incidental touches that point to the absolute reliability of the historicity of Paul. Acts is full of such little tests. The "basket," too, is of interest since Luke calls it σπυρίς and emphasizes its roundness, Paul calls it σαργάνη and emphasizes the fact that it was plaited. In 1925 the writer was shown the hole in the air where the "window" was said to have been; the natives were making a new wall so as to enclose that hole again!

A lone, miserable fugitive is a man to be pitied. The flight from Damascus to Jerusalem was a long journey. Mighty Paul proposed to enter Damascus with a force of Levite police; he entered as a weak, stricken, blind man. When he left, never to return, he fled under cover of night. Weakness, weakness to learn so thoroughly as to allow God at last to use his strength in Paul.

CHAPTER XII

IV. *The Ultimate Extreme of Paul's Foolish Boasting*

1) It is necessary to boast. While not a furthersome thing, yet I will come to visions and revelations of the Lord. The reading thus translated has the best textual support. The δεῖ is assured. Moreover, the reading that has δέ would mar the sense by putting a false emphasis on καυχᾶσθαι as if Paul were now making a transition to boasting as a new subject when it has been the subject throughout and is mentioned as such even in 11:30. Our versions punctuate improperly. The first two words are an independent sentence. "To proceed with boasting is necessary." All of the rest is a second sentence that is tied together by the correlatives μέν and δέ. The μέν cannot be construed with what precedes but must be linked with what the following δέ brings. "While not a furthersome thing, yet I will come to visions," etc.

This verse introduces a new boast. It is added only under compulsion just as all of the previous boasting was. When he proceeds to the ultimate extreme in this matter, namely to the most astonishing sample in the great class of experiences that we label "visions and revelations of the Lord," Paul adds the preface with μέν: "while not a furthersome thing." He means that he expects to confer no spiritual profit upon the Corinthians by telling about this phenomenal experience of his. He uses it only in defense of himself as a man who is forced to boast. This is more true with regard to this experience than with regard to any item that is mentioned in chapter 11. We must agree with Paul. He is using a club to demolish the fake pretenses of the false apostles who play themselves up as "superlative or superfine apostles" (11:5; 12:11). The task of wielding this club is forced upon Paul. The Corinthians derive no profit from it. They are only to witness what Paul is doing to these fake apostles.

Robertson 1130 regards the neuter participle συμφέρον as an accusative absolute. We question that because of the μέν. We supply "is" and regard the participle as the predicate: "something furthering." Paul does not say whether what follows is a vision or a revelation; it may be called either or both. When he says: "Yet I will come to visions and revelations of the Lord" (genitive of the subject: the Lord is revealing), he implies that he has received a number of them and might relate several. Paul gently wards off the idea that what he now tells is all that he has experienced in this direction (Acts 16:9; 18:9; 22:17; 23:11; 27:23; Gal. 1:12; I Cor. 11:23; Eph. 3:3). Ὀπτασία = vision: seeing miraculously; ὅραμα = spectacle: a result of seeing; ἀποκάλυψις = revelation: act of imparting something hidden. The latter is the wider and the more important term. Many visions served for the purpose of revelation, but revelation could occur without a vision.

2) To the single incident narrated in 11:32, 33 another single incident is now added although this one has a sequel (v. 7, etc.). In 11:32, 33 we have the outer life, a lone fugitive stealing along through the night, a poor figure indeed. Here we have nothing but an ἄνθρωπος to whom God allowed something most astounding to happen so that he can speak of it only as if it were not he to whom it happened.

I know a human being in Christ, fourteen years ago (whether in the body I do not know, whether out of his body I do not know — God knows), such a one snatched up to the third heaven. And I knew such a human being (whether in the body, whether apart

from his body I do not know — God knows), that he was snatched into Paradise and heard unspeakable utterances, which it is unlawful for a human being to utter. On behalf of such a one will I glory, but on behalf of myself I will not glory, except in the weaknesses.

Paul says that he knows the human being and what happened to him. Paul has not the remotest idea how this happened to this human being. The thing itself was unspeakably glorious. That this person was Paul we, of course, note at once. Paul shrinks from saying so, he can scarcely believe it. He tells about it as though it had happened to another man and not to himself. The idea of Paul's boasting about *himself* is thus completely removed.

Another person might shout: "I, I have been in Paradise!" and exalt himself above all his fellow men. Another man might tell about it on every possible occasion. Paul kept it a secret for fourteen years; it is now forced from him only by utter necessity. Even under this compulsion he is able to tell about it only as though it had happened to another person. It seems incredible to Paul that it should have been *he* who had been in Paradise through such an act of the Lord's. Paul's humble character is here revealed. We have the rarest of all examples: a boastless boast. More than that, an extreme boast without a trace of common boasting.

"I know" and not "I knew" hints at the person to whom Paul refers. Ἄνθρωπος = a human being. The fact that a simple human being should have been in Paradise is so astounding. "In Christ" (see 5:17) is the one mark of this human being, for only his connection with Christ (ἐν) by faith would be essential in being transported into Paradise. The Greek says "before fourteen years," i. e., over fourteen years ago. Paul at last breaks that long silence. Fourteen years ago places Paul in Tarsus near or at the time when Barnabas came to summon him to Antioch.

Paul at once removes a question that will occur to his readers: "Was this a bodily transfer into Paradise similar to that of Enoch and of Elijah although it endured only for a brief moment, or was it a transfer only of the soul like that of the other saints at death and temporary, of course, in Paul's case?" The first phrase "in body" needs no article, the second "out of the body" has the article of previous reference; this is also the case in v. 3. Paul simply does not know. It was entirely miraculous. How could he, a mere human being, know? The thing is utterly beyond curious questions. "God knows," that is enough. This is a different "God knows" from those used in 11:11, 31. It is not a confirmation or an assurance to the readers but only a statement that God alone knows so that no one must ever press Paul for answers.

"I know a human being" is followed by the participle, the only instance of this construction in the New Testament (R. 1041). "Such a one" is added; he was nothing but a human being in connection with Christ who was "snatched" or removed by a *raptus* "as far as the third heaven." The first heaven is that of the clouds, the second that of the far firmament of the sky and the stars, the third is the actual abode of God, of the angels, and of departed saints in glory.

A mass of Jewish ideas about the seventh heaven is introduced by some interpreters, and they place Paul beyond the third heaven, viz. in the fourth. We consider all this Jewish material worthless for our interpretation. Are these Jews, who were never in heaven, able to shed any light on Paul's experience?

Man's mind is so constituted that it cannot function without the ideas of time and of space. Hence we always speak of heaven as a place, a ποῦ as the dogmaticians say. The Scriptures of necessity speak of heaven in the same way. Thus Jesus says: "*Where* I go" (ὅπου), John 8:21. Yet how little this is the space of our conception Rev. 21:16 shows, for it presents a city of equal length, breath, and *height,* the idea of space being carried to perfection in the cube. Here we have "till" the third heaven, distance, it is again our limited conception.

3) Paul repeats in solemn refrain, the words are almost identical until the last clause is reached. The old prophets often repeated with solemnity in the same way.

4) We now have a ὅτι clause instead of the mere participle, yet the same verb is retained: I know "that he was snatched," etc. In place of "the third heaven" we have "into Paradise." It is the word which Jesus used on the cross: "Today thou shalt be with me in Paradise!" Luke 23:43. Jesus himself tells us what place he referred to by that other word: "Father, into *thy hands* I commend my spirit!" Luke 23:46. We meet Παράδεισος once more in Rev. 2:7. In the Greek it has the meaning of a beautiful park, and it came to be used for "heaven" as a description that was taken from the Garden of Eden. The prophets at times pictured heaven in colors that were drawn from Eden and made heaven "Paradise Regained." Chiliasts regard these lovely passages of the prophets as references to their millennium. The Edenic tree of life appears even in the last chapter of the Bible, v. 2.

In Paradise Paul "heard unspeakable utterances, which it is unlawful for a human being to utter." Paul is indicating only a trifle of what he experienced in Paradise. Hence he says nothing about what he saw or what he felt but mentions only that he heard ἄρρητα ῥήματα (an oxymoron), "unutterable utterances"; this adjective is used only here in Biblical Greek. Its first meaning is "unuttered" and its next "unutterable," but the latter is defined by the relative clause "which it is unlawful for a human being to utter," λαλῆσαι, to say aloud. The utterances heard in Paradise were uttered there; Paul could otherwise not have heard them; but they were intended only for him and not as a revelation to be communicated to men in general. For this reason Paul had never revealed this experience. We may say that what Paul heard was for his personal encouragement, to be kept for himself alone lest it be used in a fanatical way by those who were not satisfied with what the gospel reveals.

The secrets of the Greek mystery cults were at times also called ἄρρητα in the sense that they were intended only for the initiate, all others being considered "profane." Paul's use of the word is frequently attributed to these pagan cults. The word has been called "technical" in these pagan cults. C.-K. 449 accepts the idea that ἄρρητα are such because they are to be kept from the profane. Ordinarily C.-K. repudiates this mass of paganism and all the Jewish apocalyptic ideas which have been drawn upon as shedding light on Paul's language. Paul is *not* an initiate, all other Christians are *not* viewed as "profane" and thus excluded. Paradise is *not* a hall of mystery cults. The whole pagan imagery is an abomination, from which neither Paul as an apostle, nor the Spirit of God, who guided his language, would borrow terms and expressions, to say nothing about "technical terms" for the sacred things of God.

The whole Greek language was open to the sacred writers to be used by them at pleasure. When they did use a word for *their* purpose, that does not mean that they had to include this or that purpose, connotation, side meaning of some *other* men. Such an assumption is false in the case of these as of other writers in the Greek and in every other language. With ἐξόν as a nominative we supply ἐστι (R. 881, 491). The negation would be οὐ whether it is construed with the copula or with the neuter participle (R. 1139).

5) When Paul adds that he will boast only "on behalf of such a one," such a one as he has described, he emphasizes the fact that all that he is saying is not to be taken personally. He is not boasting on behalf of *Paul*, that *I, Paul*, have been in Paradise. Though he was "such a one," no merit, no credit, no desert on his part were in any way involved. For when it comes to boasting (under compulsion, of course, v. 1), "on behalf of myself I will not boast except in connection with (ἐν) the weaknesses," which repeats 11:30 and thus needs no further exposition.

It has been remarked that Paul speaks as though there were two Pauls. That is true if it is understood as it is intended by Paul. At one time he sees himself as being highly distinguished by the Lord, as being granted even a glimpse of Paradise. Remember all the pain and the distress mentioned in 11:23-33. As if to forearm him against all of it so that he might not break down in his spirit under this frightful, never-ending load, the Lord let him have a taste of Paradise. About that Paul cannot and will not boast. He sees only the other Paul, the one depicted in 11:23-33, full of weaknesses, full of nothing that would ever be a boast for any man. That is the Paul of whom he will boast, and the boast will ever be "the weaknesses," these themselves and as such and not the fact that he bore them, that he did so much in spite of them and thus after all boasts about himself. We admire a man who does much despite great handicaps. Paul is not such a man. He is one who is nothing, whose boast is this very nothing.

6) Yet the fact that Paul makes his entire boast concerning his weakness dare not be misunderstood. **For if I shall ever want to boast I will not be a fool**

like so many are who actually make fools of themselves by exaggerating, by even outright lying just to aggrandize themselves, **for** in such a case **I will tell** nothing but simple **truth.** With ἐάν and the two aorists θελήσω and καυχήσασθαι Paul merely supposes a single instance in which he might want to make a single boast. The condition of expectancy is, however, not an actual expectancy, for in the next statement he adds **but I forbear.** The ἐάν only vividly imagines a case in which Paul might make up his mind to boast concerning something that is to his personal credit and not a great weakness and emptiness in himself. He would then tell the full truth. The Corinthians are to bear that in mind when they hear Paul making nothing but his weaknesses his boast. The trouble with the Corinthians might be that they suppose that Paul had nothing but weaknesses, and that he could not, except by lying like a fool, boast about anything else.

Even in his great humility Paul takes care to leave no false impressions. He *was* something by the grace of God (I Cor. 15:10). It would be falsehood to deny it even by implication, an implication which one might falsely deduce from the emphasis which Paul puts on his weakness as being his only boast. But why, then, not boast in truth about what Paul actually was? Here is the other danger: **lest anyone get to reckon in regard to me beyond what he sees me** (to be) **or hears from me.** The aorist is ingressive: "arrive at an estimate regarding me beyond what his contact with me warrants," i. e., admire me too highly. This Paul feared even more than to be despised because of his weaknesses. We know why: because it would rob the Lord of credit.

It is remarked that Paul here uses "fool" as indicating an actual fool and thus differently from "folly" in 11:1 and "fool" in 11:16 and 12:11. That is perfectly correct, and it is purposely done. It quietly makes plain how Paul might become a real fool, namely by boasting beyond the truth about his own person for such a man *is* a fool as everybody knows. What Paul actually does when he calls himself a fool for boasting in this unheard of way by bringing forward all his weaknesses which all other men would want to hide, is not real, is only assumed folly, call it a godly folly if you will. It is the Lord's own will that, despite the fact that he once elevated Paul to Paradise, he not only wanted Paul to remain utterly humble but also wanted no man to think of Paul beyond what one could see of Paul and hear from him in actual contact with him. However highly the Lord favors and blesses his ministers, for his work among men he is able to use none unless they be lowly as he himself once was when he walked on earth. Such alone are able to transmit his gospel as his, "that the exceeding greatness of the power may be of God and not from us" (4:7). The vessels dare be earthen only.

7) For this reason Paul adds the following. The man to whom the Lord had granted an actual visit to Paradise is the man to whom God gave a messenger of Satan to fisticuff him again and again. We omit διό before ἵνα. No one knows what to do with it; the textual evidence for and against it is evenly divided. The canon that the harder reading should be retained cannot be applied to a reading that is devoid of sense. Efforts to connect the dative that precedes διό with something that precedes in v. 6 or v. 5 are futile, and these do not solve the presence of διό.

In order that by the exceeding greatness of the revelations I may not be lifting myself up unduly there was given to me a thorn for the flesh, a messenger of Satan, to fisticuff me in order that I may not be lifting myself up unduly.

The dative is placed before ἵνα for the sake of emphasis. This is often done. It is a dative of means. Although the genitive is plural: "of the revelations," it refers chiefly to the one revelation which Paul has just described, when the Lord granted him a visit to Paradise. No revelation received by Paul exceeded this. This alone was intended for his own person; all other revelations, including the first one on the road to Damascus, pertained to his office. Most of the revelations were for the purpose of information, some directed Paul where to go or where to remain.

This one revelation, being so wonderful and intended for Paul alone, might tend to make him lift himself up unduly. For what other apostle had until this time been in heaven? The revelation granted to John came later. R., W. P., makes the verb passive; it is middle in both clauses, for it would be Paul alone who would lift himself up unduly and no one else. "There was given to me" must mean "by the Lord," and the aorist denotes a single act. "Was given to me" is surely to be understood as it stands: this fearful affliction was the Lord's *gift* to Paul. Rom. 8:28 helps us here.

As far as σκόλοψ is concerned, the wavering between "thorn" and "stake" may now cease. What of it if in Homer and in a few classical passages we have the latter meaning, the plural, for instance, for "palisades," even in the classics another word was usually employed to designate a "stake" (see Liddell and Scott). M.-M. 578, etc., shows that in the papyri the regular meaning of this word is "thorn" or sharply pointed sliver. So we should drop what Luther says regarding impalement, should drop any reference to crucifixion, to Gal. 2:20, and to likeness to Christ's crucifixion. "For the flesh" is the ordinary *dativus incommodi*. "Flesh" denotes the physical substance of which the body is composed. The *tertium compara-*

tionis in the metaphor "a thorn for the flesh" is the sharp, piercing pain that is produced when a thorn is driven deeply into the flesh.

A synonym elucidates: "a messenger of Satan to fisticuff me." In "thorn" we have the idea of something sharp and painful sticking deeply in the flesh so that it remains there and cannot be drawn out. And the Lord intends that it shall remain so. In the present subjunctive we have the iterative idea of blows that are struck with the closed fist. This verb is rare, yet it is used three times in the New Testament, figuratively in I Cor. 4:11 and literally in Matt. 26:67 where the Sanhedrists beat Jesus after they had condemned him. Derived from the word for "knuckles," it means to strike with the fist so that the hard knuckles make the blow sting and crush. "Slapping Paul in the face" (R., W. P.) is inadequate, for a slap is delivered with the flat of the hand.

These blows of the fist were delivered by "a messenger of Satan." This undoubtedly refers to v. 4 and is in extreme contrast with it: the man whom the Lord at one time took to Paradise is by this same Lord turned over to Satan's emissary to be beaten as a rowdy beats a helpless victim. "Is it possible!" one might exclaim. This thing occurs periodically. Every now and then there comes a frightful attack. Each is inhuman, is like an implacable demon who knocks a defenseless mortal to pieces with hellish glee.

We have Job 2:7 as an analogy. The Satanic agency should not be eliminated. The passage in Job is helpful in this that it shows us that God and Satan concur, but the motive of the two is opposite. God intends to try Job, to prove his faith victorious; Satan intends to destroy that faith. The solution as to how God can allow such attacks by Satan lies in the fact of Job's and of Paul's sinfulness in this sinful world. The fact that the devil's glee lies in the infliction of pain needs no proof.

Paul twice states the Lord's purpose: "in order that I might not be lifting myself up unduly," i. e., in order that I may ever be kept in deepest humility. The higher Paul's work was, the more he needed humility. The more divine his work was, the more necessary for him was the constant realization of utter dependence on the Lord; for if he withdraws his hand, Satan would have him utterly in his power. As it is, Satan's messenger can go only so far.

The question is constantly asked as to just what this figurative language means literally. Paul's letters as well as the Acts are searched for clues. The result is that no man knows. The supposition is widely entertained that the Corinthians knew what Paul meant, that his figurative language was clear to them. The writer must dissent. Paul tells about this thorn for the flesh just as he tells about his *raptus* into Paradise for the first time. In both he bares intimate secrets of his personal life which were never bared to the Corinthians before and are now bared only under compulsion.

It is really a question of forming a diagnosis. The data on which to base it are wholly insufficient. Paul intended them to be so. We have only two expressions: "a thorn for the flesh" — "to fisticuff me." Two symptoms or rather only one expressed by two words. Yet the theologians, who are mere laymen in the field of medicine and disease, proceed to diagnose the case like the most expert medics and insist on the correctness of their findings. These theologians are acting the part of quacks. To allow them to do so is to condone their quackery. To accept any diagnosis thus made is to honor quackery. If I had a common disease I should not call in one of these pretenders to diagnose my case, nor should I accept their diagnosis if it were gratuitously offered.

A few good medical men have examined our passage. Still fewer have ventured an opinion, and an opinion is about all that could be offered. Because the commentaries and other books about Paul so often dilate on this subject, we feel compelled to list the diagnoses that are on file, a mere look at which ought to be warning enough for any man. The first are Satanic suggestions: blasphemous thoughts — tortures of conscience — sexual temptations (after meeting the beautiful Thekla). The pathological filthy monkish imagination loves the latter down to the present day. Next, attacks on Paul by some persistent vicious opponent who made himself Satan's tool. Beside this we may place the generalization: all the afflictions and hardships that were incident to Paul's work. Finally, a diseased condition. Here the list is long: eye misery, headaches, malaria, ear trouble, sciatica, rheumatism, Malta fever, leprosy, some nervous disorder, hysteria or melancholia, epilepsy. Some men select something that would disfigure Paul, a few some ailment at sight of which the ancients would spit in their superstition.

8) Paul continues: **Concerning this I urged the Lord three times that it might** (permanently, aorist) **stand away from me. And he has told me: Sufficient for thee is my grace! For the power is brought to its finish in weakness.** Paul does not say when this thorn was first inflicted on him. All that one may surmise is that it may well have happened a short time after the visit to Paradise because the two are such opposites, and Paul narrates them together. Then Paul made three efforts that urged the Lord to rid him of the plague.

Παρακαλέω = to call to one's side, the context furnishes the special modification. Here it is prayer, the subfinal ἵνα clause states the substance of the prayer.

Some think that we should translate: "concerning *this one* . . . that *he* stand away from me," i. e., "Satan's messenger." The trouble with this is that "messenger" is only the elucidating apposition in v. 7 and not the main subject, which is "thorn." We prefer the translation of our versions which have the neuter: "concerning this," etc.

"Three times" means that Paul received his answer from the Lord the third time. Paul's petition comes under the class to which we must add: "Lord, if it be thy will." Hence it is incorrect to quote Paul's three petitions as an example of requests denied. In fact, there was a denial in no sense whatever, for Paul's petitions contained his readiness to submit to whatever the Lord might will. Paul does not need to record such details; they belong to the elementary essentials of prayer.

9) The perfect tense "he has told me" conveys more than the aorist "he told me"; it adds the continuous present effect to the past fact: once heard, the Lord's answer is ever in Paul's ears. Paul records exactly what the Lord told him, and we should not say that Paul uses his own language to convey what the Lord said to him. It is needless to inquire how the Lord spoke to Paul, seeing that many such direct communications appear in the Scriptures without specification as to how they were made. Those who received the communication always knew who spoke and understood the very words which he spoke.

The Lord's answer to Paul is weighty, indeed, and of the highest significance for the boast which Paul has been making. "Sufficient for thee is my grace," ἀρκεῖ σοι, emphatically forward, "it suffices for thee," for all thy life, all thy work, all thy suffering, also and especially for this distressing "thorn for the flesh." By placing the subject last it is made equally emphatic: "my grace." It is the blessed word χάρις (see

1:2) in the fulness of its meaning, the Lord's undeserved favor toward one who as a sinner has deserved the very opposite, this boundless favor with all that it bestows, pardon and peace, support and deliverance, comfort, strength, assurance, hope, joy, and every gift. That grace knows why it "gave" Paul this dreadful "thorn"; Paul has already indicated why. It permits Paul to be tried, but only in order that what the Lord had indicated by letting Paul see Paradise during his earthly life may be most perfectly accomplished. This grace cannot be insufficient; it will attain its τέλος or goal in Paul's experience. This grace cannot abandon Paul; it is mightier than "the thorn," mightier than any "messenger of Satan." It will support him in every ordeal and shine the brighter as pure, undeserved grace the more it is put to the test. What a sweeter reply from the Lord could Paul have desired?

This word of the Lord has been of untold comfort to countless saints of God, all of them sinners like Paul, many of them tried and tested as he was in the fires of affliction, all of them finding this same grace ever sufficient, yea, more than sufficient. If we are right in assuming that about fourteen years had passed since Paul made his prayers and heard this answer from the Lord we have these long years as evidence that the grace did prove sufficient for Paul. If the time was not that long it still covered a number of years.

That first sentence would have been enough; but the Lord added an explanation in regard to the very agony that had pressed the intense prayers from Paul's lips: "For the power is brought to its finish in weakness." The verb used is τελεῖται, the very verb that is employed in John 19:28, 30 where Jesus cried: τετέλεσται, which our versions properly translate: "It is finished!" literally, "it has been and is now finished." But in the case of our passage our versions translate the same verb with the present tense "is made perfect." This sounds like a translation of τελειοῦται, a different verb and an inferior variant reading.

One must distinguish between the two verbs. Jesus said: "It is finished!" the end has been reached, the last stroke has been done. The noun in the verb is τέλος, the end, the last point. He said nothing about his being τέλειος, having reached a certain maturity or perfection. The sense of our passage is not, as our versions have it, the power "is made perfect," comes to perfection only in the midst of weakness. The Lord says that the divine power "is finished," is brought to the end of its work in weakness. The present tense is not "linear" (R., W. P.) but gnomic (R. 866) as it is in all general propositions. We translate "the" and not "my" power although, as the next sentence shows, the Lord is speaking of his own power.

The Lord's power is certainly always τέλειος, mature, complete, and it cannot be made perfect, for it is ever so. But this power works and does things in us. It has much to do. When it has brought us to the point where we are utter weakness, its task is finished. It has then shaped us into a perfect tool for itself. As long as we sinners imagine that *we* still have some power we are unfit instruments for the Lord's hands; he still has to work on us before he can work properly through us. But when he has reduced us to utter nothingness, then the τέλος is reached; with such a tool the Lord can do great deeds. "The power" is generally identified with "my grace." Strictly speaking, the Lord's grace possesses power and works and operates in and through us with this its power.

This brief explanation showed Paul why the Lord gave him the thorn for the flesh. It was done lest he lift himself up unduly and thus become a tool that was unfit for the Lord. The verb ἐδόθη shows that the thorn was a gift to Paul, a blessing for him. It was the Lord's way of reducing Paul to total weakness so that he no more lifted himself up but lay prostrate and weak. So Paul became the wonderful instrument that we see him to be during all these past years, and the Lord worked great things through him. Paul bares the deepest secret of his spiritual life as an apostle. It was his weakness that made him so excellent a tool for the Lord. Nor is Paul an exception. The proposition is general. It is ever thus with the Lord's instruments although he uses various means to produce this weakness and its constant realization.

Very gladly, then, I will boast the more in my weaknesses in order that the power of Christ may spread its tent over me. The superlative ἥδιστα is elative (R. 670; B.-D. 246): "very gladly," "with exceeding gladness." Μᾶλλον is distinct (R. 664; B.-D. 246), "the more," "rather," since Paul had received this word from the Lord, which showed him the great value of all his weaknesses for the Lord's purpose. Paul will now make all his weaknesses his one and only boast. He now uses the plural. It includes the weakness of the thorn, which brought him down to the lowest point, and all the other weaknesses of which he has already spoken. All that he has said in 11:30 and 12:5 about his making only the weaknesses his boast, all that at first sounds so paradoxical and incomprehensible in these statements, is now perfectly clear. The Lord's answer to Paul's prayers brings the clarity. Paul's boast had ever to be "in my weaknesses"; yours and mine likewise.

Paul's purpose in boasting thus about his weaknesses is in perfect accord with that of Christ, "that the power of Christ (not: strength, R. V.) may spread its tent over me." The figure is beautiful. The power of Christ spreads its tent over Paul and all his weaknesses, does so once for all and permanently (aorist).

All Paul's weaknesses are covered and hidden away under that tent. It cannot be spread over one whose boast is in his own strength. The purpose clause does not mean that this is yet to be done, that Paul is still waiting for it after all these years. Paul will ever boast as he does so that the tent that was once spread over him may definitely remain over him.

We fail to see why this verb makes commentators think of the Shekinah or *Khabod*. This was not a tent or tabernacle at all but the cloud that rested on the ark between the cherubim that were on its lid. It never served as a cover. Other extravagant views have been added recently. This "power of Christ" is thought to be a hypostasis, an independent personification which subsists in itself. Paul desires to be "an incarnation of the power of Christ" just as Simon Magus was in Acts 8:10. The writer rejects all such views.

10) Reaching back into all that he has said and rounding it out in a final statement, Paul says: **Therefore I take pleasure in weaknesses, in mistreatments, in necessities, in persecutions, in distresses for Christ's sake; for whenever I am weak, then I am powerful.**

When he was boasting Paul spoke to others about all his great weaknesses, but for himself he takes pleasure in them. They look beautiful and lovely to him. He adds a few phrases by letting his eye run over four groups of evidence that exhibit his weaknesses even to other people. Four of the five ἐν phrases are specifications of the first. Any man is weak who has to submit to "insulting, violent mistreatments" instead of violently denouncing and bringing to justice such enemies; who cannot rise above "necessities," wants, and difficulties like the strong men whom the world admires; who flees from "persecutions" instead of turning against his pursuers with devastating power and wrath; who is ever in "distress," tight places, where he can do nothing but suffer. What a statement to say that all such situations are one's pleasure and delight!

But do not overlook "in behalf of Christ," for his sake, Matt. 5:11, 12: "for my sake." Paul thus enters the glorious company of the ancient prophets, to which none but such are admitted. This phrase puts a different aspect upon the whole statement. Blessed are they who are thus in utter weakness "for Christ's sake"!

And so we come to the end: "For when I am weak" as thus indicated, "then, then indeed, I am powerful," not with any power of my own but with "the power of Christ." It reverses everything that the world knows of power in a man but by that reversal reveals the only power that is power in the kingdom.

V. The Conclusion of Paul's Foolish Boasting

11) It is over with. **I have become a fool!** "I have gotten to that point by allowing myself to say what I have just said." The perfect is to indicate the completed state. Paul looks back to the point where he has gotten and is ashamed. The folly announced in 11:1 is now perpetrated. In what sense it is folly we have seen in 11:1. **You on your part compelled me!** "Not that this excuses me but it does say that I did not become a fool wilfully; and since my folly is recorded in a letter to you Corinthians, you are jointly guilty, which remember when you read." Μέν solitarium is either concessive or restrictive and has nothing to do with δέ (R. 1151).

For I on my part ought to be commended by you, for in no respect was I behind the superfine apostles even if I am nothing. At least the signs of the (real) apostle were completely wrought in your midst in all perseverance, both with signs and wonders and with power works.

Instead of forcing Paul to boast like a fool about himself and thus making him reveal all his weaknesses as his boast the Corinthians ought to be commending him. For this folly of Paul's boasting the Corinthians are as much to blame as is Paul. Ἐγώ is emphatically in contrast with the preceding ὑμεῖς and with the following ὑφ' ὑμῶν. The Greek uses the imperfect to indicate an obligation that was not met in the present. The obligation extends to the past and is still pending, for it has not as yet been met: "I ought to be commended" (συνίστασθαι, present passive infinitive). On this imperfect see R. 920; B.-D. 358.

For even if the Corinthians wanted to draw a comparison, in no respect does Paul fall behind the false apostles who had invaded Corinth, who boasted that they were "the superlative, the superfine apostles" in order to impress the Corinthians. The Corinthians should certainly know this, but they had forced Paul to act the fool by compelling him at this late date to show them how these superfine apostles were so far behind that they could not even be compared with Paul (see ὑπέρ in 11:23 plus what there follows). On "the superfine apostles" see 11:5.

It is a telling thrust when Paul adds "even if I am nothing." For this fact that he is all weakness and thus literally "nothing" is the very boast which Paul has been making at length. He made it in literal truth (see the assurance in 11:31 and the final proof in 12:9, 10), but the false apostles tried to make Paul out to be nothing. Paul takes their very slander from their lips and wields it as a double-edged sword.

12) Solitary μέν is restrictive in this instance and = "at least," although it has a lighter touch than our heavy English phrase (R. 1151). Paul points the Corinthians to what they could and certainly should use in commending him: At least, to mention nothing

more, the signs of the (real) apostle were completely wrought among you during the one and one-half years that I was in your midst, wrought in all perseverance (see 6:4). Three datives of means specify: "both with signs and wonders and with power works." They "were wrought" means by the Lord. "The signs of the apostle" = those that attest an apostle; "the apostle" is the representative singular (R. 408) and hence has the generic article (R. 757). Jesus himself tells us what the signs of the true apostle are by which he will be known anywhere: "Heal the sick, cleanse the lepers, raise the dead, cast out devils," Matt. 10:8 (his commissioning address to the Twelve). "Signs" = sure indications that men may see and read in their significance.

Among the outstanding signs which marked the presence and the work of a real apostle were what we summarize as "miracles," for which the Scriptures have the double designation "signs and wonders" and then also δυνάμεις, "powers," in the sense of "power deeds." Both are here used without articles. Σημεῖα may be used alone but never τέρατα. The former is the nobler name that has ethical content since "signs" point beyond themselves to the grace, mercy, divine power, and help that are operative in them, all speak about what the Lord wants to do also for the souls of men and not only for their bodies.

Paul uses the word twice, first in its broader sense, in which it may include more than miracles, next in its narrower sense, in which it is used with reference to miracles, especially when, as here, it is combined with the term "wonders." The latter term designates miracles as acts that make men wonder, fill them with amazement. But this is only its lower feature. Paganism, too, was proud of "wonders" or portents; and it seems that on this account the word is never employed alone in the Scriptures to designate miracles but is always combined with "signs." The third term refers to miracles as deeds that are wrought by the Lord's omnipotence. All three terms appear in Acts 2:22; Heb. 2:4. "Power works" are expressive here, where, in v. 9, 10, Paul has so significantly spoken of "the power of Christ."

Luke has no account of the miracles that were wrought by Paul during his stay in Corinth. But that accords with the object with which Acts was written, namely to show how the gospel made its course from Jerusalem to Rome. Hundreds of miracles were omitted, only those that were pertinent to Luke's object are mentioned, and a few are described. Now miracles were the most tangible evidence of the presence of an apostle. As μέν indicates, the least that the Corinthians could have done was to have pointed the false apostles to such miracles. But the Corinthians failed even in this. Not until now does Paul refer to miracles, and even now he does so only incidentally and not as pointing to the chief evidence of his apostleship. What miracles attested the false apostles? Absolutely none. As far as the chief evidence goes, Paul has already presented that in the most effective manner in 3:2, etc. The great monument to his apostleship which Paul had erected in Corinth was the Corinthian church itself, which was so great that every inhabitant and every visitor could see it and read its inscription.

13) Despite the fact that miracles were wrought perseveringly in Corinth, Paul finally asks: **What, then (γάρ), is it in regard to which you were treated worse than the rest of the churches except that I myself was not a dead weight on you? Forgive me this wrong.**

Even down to miracles the Corinthians had received everything from Paul that attested his being a true apostle. What could they, then, complain about as a treatment that was inferior to or worse than that which the rest of the churches received, those that had been founded by the Twelve, Peter, John, etc.? Paul can think of only the one thing which he has discussed already in 11:7-10, compare I Cor. 9:15-18, namely that he for his own person had not made himself a dead weight on the Corinthians (the same verb that was used in 11:9), i. e., had taken no support from them. Paul never did this as we have already seen. If that was a wrong which Paul had committed he here and now asks the Corinthians graciously to forgive him. This is the keenest irony. Ὅ is the common accusative with passives (R. 479); ὑπέρ occurs after a verb with the comparative idea: were treated worse "beyond the rest of the churches."

It undoubtedly cost Paul a good deal to assume the role of a foolish boaster and to play it through to the end. No more stunning answer could he have given to the mean attempts to disparage him. He absolutely outdoes all his vilifiers. They made him out as amounting to nothing; Paul declares that exactly that is his boast — I *am* nothing! I say it in utter truth (11:31), yea, the Lord himself has reduced me to nothing (12:7, etc.), and this is my joy and my satisfaction. But what have you Corinthians lost thereby? In my nothingness I did not ask even a penny of support. Pardon me for the great loss which you thus suffered!

The Impending Arrival of Paul

I. *He Will again Be of no Expense to the Corinthians*

14) **Lo, this third time I am ready to come to you, and I will not be a dead weight. For I am not seeking yours but you.** All that follows belongs under the caption of the first sentence that Paul is coming to Corinth and will soon be there. He announces that he will do as he has done before: be an expense to no one. On this matter see v. 13; 11:7-10,

the verb "to be a dead weight" in 11:9. Whatever objection cavilers had raised against this practice of Paul's, he will not alter his course. But what he now says on this subject is stated in view of his impending arrival. Paul wants it understood that he and his assistants will take nothing whatever from the Corinthians. The issue is to be considered as closed.

Ἔχω with an adverb = "to be." Τρίτον τοῦτο is not "this third time" (which should have τό added) but "as a third time this," and it amounts to the R. V.'s: "this is the third time." We see very little difference between "I am ready to come to you" and 13:1, "I am coming to you," since the present tense ἔρχομαι is constantly used with reference to a coming that will start presently. In fact, Paul was now on his way and had been for some time.

The question is not whether this is Paul's third visit to Corinth or the second, whether he has been in Corinth twice before this or only once. The question is concerned with this feature, whether Paul made a second brief visit to Corinth *after* he wrote First Corinthians. All the "critical" hypotheses need *this date* for the second visit to Corinth; all of them are overthrown when this date is not assumed. In order to secure this date the time between First and Second Corinthians is lengthened from a few months to about a year and a half, for a few months are too short a time to permit this date for the second visit. A further hypothesis is a third letter that was sent *after* the second visit, and this visit occurred *after* First Corinthians. Then there follow the hypotheses about the disgraceful scenes that took place in Corinth on the visit that is thus dated; Paul left thoroughly defeated and wrote a violent letter after he got back to Ephesus.

The interest of those who contend that Paul had been in Corinth only once before is not the point of the number of visits to Corinth but a visit that is dated *after* First Corinthians. If Paul had been in Corinth only once, the question is, of course, settled by that fact alone. But it is equally settled if Paul did visit Corinth a second time (even several times) at a date *prior* to First Corinthians. It is *this prior date* which the critics must face. This date clears the atmosphere. No critic has been able to lodge a single valid objection against it.

We thus understand Paul to say that his impending visit is his third. His second occurred some time during the two years that he spent in Ephesus. That second visit is of no importance whatever for either First or Second Corinthians. We have shown in 2:1 that it was not made in grief as is so often thought on the strength of πάλιν. That second visit was followed by a letter that is lost to us, to which I Cor. 5:9 refers and about which we know no more. We do not think that "I am ready a third time" refers only to the times when Paul got ready and includes one time when he got ready but changed his plans and delayed; 13:1 says: "I am going a third time." Τρίτον τοῦτο modifies "I am ready" or "I am ready to come to you." Why refer the adverbial modifiers across to the infinitive and even into the next clause: "to come this third time, and I will not burden this third time"?

Paul has already explained most fully why he took no support from any of his congregations (I Cor. 9: 15-17; II Cor. 11:7-12). What he now says is a kindly addition after the sting administered in v. 13. He is not seeking τὰ ὑμῶν, "the things of you," i. e., your goods, but ὑμᾶς, "you yourselves," i. e., your souls. The false apostles, of course, did otherwise. They cared for the wool and not for the sheep.

For the children ought not to lay up treasure for the parents, but the parents for the children. Paul speaks to the Corinthians as a father to his children.

His desire is to enrich them and to fill them with the spiritual treasures which he is able to provide for them and make their own. It is unfair to say that Paul should never have taken the present which the Macedonians sent him (11:9). Since when dare a parent not accept a little present from his grateful children? See that passage. It is also unwarranted to say that when a parent becomes unable to provide for himself, the children should provide for him. Paul was still fully able to provide for himself.

It is also stated that Paul is overthrowing the very law and principle which he lays down at length in I Cor. 9:6-12b, 14. But Paul himself distinguishes between the right that he had and his making use of that right. He did not make use of his right to support for a great and sufficient reason. Paul is here speaking about the spirit which animates him in foregoing that right, his readiness to act as parents do toward their children. Paul uses this relation of parents to their children as an illustration and as no more.

15) **Moreover, I on my part will very gladly spend and be myself spent in behalf of your souls.** The illustration of parents and children deals with ordinary obligation. Δέ goes beyond mere obligation. Paul is very glad on his part not only to spend of his energy and love but himself to be completely spent (ἐκ in the passive) for the benefit of the souls of the Corinthians. This is the spirit that animates him in his work: utter unselfishness and selflessness.

Both verbs go far beyond spending money. The second verb is so plain, for a person is himself utterly spent, not by paying money, but by using himself up. Here, too, Paul states for what he will spend and himself be spent, namely "for your souls." The illustration of parents and the fact that they spend money for their children is not retained. That illustration does not deal with any kind of spending but with the reverse, namely treasuring up, saving something to leave to children.

Paul now advances to the real motive: **If I love you more abundantly am I loved the less?** That would be strange, indeed! Love usually kindles love. This is "love" in the sense of 2:4, which see. The comparative adverb refers to ever greater evidence of love. A case occurs occasionally in which the more love is shown, the less that love is appreciated, and the less love is returned. Do the Corinthians want to be such a case?

16) Is something else hindering the love of the Corinthians? Paul openly states the slander. **But granted — I myself did not burden you; nevertheless, being a crafty fellow, I caught you with guile!** Is that the direction in which your suspicions run? Does that slander make you hesitate? On ἔστω δέ in the sense of "granted" see R. 948. It is rather too plain that when Paul himself was in Corinth he burdened no one. This is granted as being true by all the Corinthians themselves. But was that not merely a piece of craftiness, just a bait by which to take the Corinthians? It is the way of vicious slander to do this very thing: to make a virtue appear as cunning pretense whereby to gain selfish ends under cover.

17) Paul answers this with questions. Two have the interrogative word μή which implies "no" as the answer, and a double one has the interrogative word οὐ (repeated) which implies "yes" as the answer. **Anyone of those whom I have been sending to you, did I through him overreach you?** All of the Corinthians will have to confess: "No, never!" The perfect tense "have been sending" is to indicate repeated sendings (R. 893, 896). It is the very tense that is required.

The accusative τινά which is followed by δι' αὐτοῦ is called an anacoluthon (R. 488). It is a pendent accusative, it could also be a nominative. But the main point is the reason for thrusting this indefinite pronoun and its relative clause forward and then resuming it with διά: it places the emphasis exactly where Paul wants it. If Paul himself took nothing, is there anyone, anyone at all whom he has been sending to Corinth, whom he used as an underhanded means for getting something out of the Corinthians? In ὧν there lies τούτων οὕς.

The question includes all of the men whom Paul had sent to Corinth since he left the congregation. Just how many there had been we do not know; that point is immaterial. Some commentators introduce the matter of the collection but do not indicate how Paul could have overreached the Corinthians in regard to this money when I Cor. 16:2 makes it plain that none of Paul's assistants ever touched a penny with their own hands. Paul includes men whom he had sent before he asked that a collection be started. His question is this: Can any man in Corinth stand up and say that any person that had been sent by Paul in any way whatever asked for a single penny for Paul or, without asking, ever received a single penny? "Did I overreach you" means: take nothing when I was in Corinth but try to get something craftily later on.

18) The last two men whom Paul had sent were Titus and another brother. **I urged Titus, and I sent along the brother. Did Titus overreach you in anything? Did we not walk in the same spirit? In the same tracks?** The last mission of Titus' was not a pleasant one; Titus had to be urged to undertake it. Paul does not need to name the other man whom he sent along with Titus. He does not name the two to whom he referred in 8:18, 22; it is not necessary, the Corinthians know. "The brother" conveys only the

fact that the man was not one of Paul's regular assistants. Whether he was one of the two who are now being sent by Paul a second time (8:18, 22) we do not know. The view that "the brother" was to watch Titus is entirely unfair although it has been entertained. Titus was the main character, and hence Paul asks: "Did Titus overreach you in any respect?" Μή implies that the answer must be "no."

But negative answers would not satisfy Paul. He would end his questioning with two οὐ that call for positive answers. He now includes also himself together with all his assistants and others whom he had sent to Corinth: "Do we not all walk in the same spirit? in the same steps?" The A. V. is correct in translating "spirit" over against the R. V. which translates "Spirit." This is the dative of means or of norm. The Scriptures never speak of the Holy Spirit as a means or a norm that are used by us. By "spirit" Paul means the inner motivation, by "tracks" the outward, visible conduct. His double question is: "Are we not all alike inwardly and outwardly?" As I was when I was with you, taking absolutely nothing — have not all my messengers to you been just the same?

Objection is raised on the ground that Paul relies only on questions. In addition to that he is accused of arguing in a circle by proving himself by means of Titus and Titus by means of himself. Because he is honest and unselfish, his messengers must be the same; then vice versa. Paul does neither; either would be a farce. These questions are blanket questions that are addressed to the entire congregation and include every member. Their convincing power does not lie in argument, even as none is made; it lies in the fact that every Corinthian is challenged to point to a single instance where Paul or any messenger of his ever got a penny from any Corinthian member.

II. Paul Fears What He May Find when He Arrives in Corinth

19) All this time you are thinking that we are trying to defend ourselves to you. In God's sight in connection with Christ we are speaking (instead of keeping silence). **Moreover, beloved, everything is for the benefit of your edification.** Paul corrects a wrong impression that is prevailing in the minds of the Corinthians. He surmises that they are thinking that Paul is merely defending himself and his assistants, that he is writing in his own interest. The verb is apparently to be taken in the lower sense of "whitewashing ourselves," the present tense being conative, "trying to whitewash." Two things are wrong about this assumption: 1) any self-interest on the part of Paul and his assistants; 2) that Paul and his assistants are pleading their case before the forum of the Corinthians. The Corinthians had better disabuse their minds on both points.

In the first place, the forum before which Paul and his assistants stand is that of God: "in the sight of God," with him as the Judge "we speak." Let the Corinthians not think that *they* are the judges; they face that Supreme Judge as well as Paul and his assistants face him. "In God's sight in connection with Christ" makes plain the entire situation. Christ, his gospel, and his church are involved in all that Paul is writing. Hence, Paul says, "we speak," the verb means, "we are not and cannot be silent." The right way in which the Corinthians are to think about this epistle is that it is open speech before God himself and involves Christ who commissioned Paul and his assistants for their work. How could they dare to be silent unless they intended to abandon that work!

Δέ takes care of the other point. Paul and his assistants are not on trial, and the Corinthians are not the judges. The former are concerned about this matter in quite a different manner. Paul and his assistants are greatly concerned about the Corinthians, namely about their standing before God in Christ. "Everything" that Paul is writing is "in the interest of your edification," of your upbuilding in Christ. This is "edification" in the Biblical sense, which includes rebuke, warning, castigation, etc., and not in the modern sense of pleasant religious emotions. The idea is not that Paul is placing an indictment against the Corinthians before God, that he is putting them on trial before the Supreme Judge. The great Judge is looking down on all of them, on Paul and on his assistants and on all the Corinthians. Paul is speaking in his presence so that he may hear that all he is saying to the Corinthians is, indeed, for the benefit of building them up in Christ. He is not a dumb dog, he speaks and speaks plainly. As the Corinthians read this epistle they must realize that God's eyes are looking down on them, that all these things are connected with Christ and are said to them in connection with him. They will then stop thinking that Paul is on trial before them in a kind of self-defense. They will read this epistle as they ought to read it. Paul thus inserts the address "beloved" most effectively; it is expressive of his entire concern for the Corinthians.

See how simply Paul does this correcting of all foolish thoughts on the part of the Corinthians. Two little sentences are enough, but they go to the heart of the matter. But is Paul's epistle not in part an ἀπολογία or self-defense before the Corinthians? Yes, he is setting himself right in their eyes; he has even refuted charges and slanders made against him. But he has never done so in his own interest but only in the true spiritual interest of the Corinthians themselves. He wrestles with them in order to make them what they ought to be "in the sight of God in connection with

Christ." There is no difficulty whatever on this score unless we ourselves read this epistle with the wrong thoughts which Paul removes from the minds of the Corinthians.

20) "For" explains Paul's concern and does it in very plain language: **For I fear lest perhaps, on coming, I shall find you not such as I want, and I myself shall be found for you such as you do not want; lest perhaps** (there be) **strife, jealousy, angers, self-assertions, backbitings, whisperings, puffings-up, disorders; lest on my coming back my God shall humble me before you, and I mourn many of those who have been hitherto sinning and did not repent of the uncleanness and fornication and excess which they committed.**

The whole is one sentence: φοβοῦμαι followed by the three clauses with μή: "I fear lest — lest — lest"; the three heap up all that Paul fears. The first two are softened by πώς: "lest perhaps." The aorist ἐλθών indicates the moment of arrival in Corinth.

Note the skillful reversal of the thought in chiastic form: "not such as I want shall I find you — and I myself shall be found for you such as you do not want." If things were still awry when Paul got to Corinth or would get worse by the time Paul arrived, he would certainly not find the Corinthians such as he wanted. And that means that the Corinthians, too, would not find Paul such as they wanted. Congregations that are in a bad state seldom want a church official to arrive who intends to make thorough work in cleaning up their difficulties. Part of Paul's skill is evident in the use of the passive form in the second statement. Note the little difference: "not such as I want" — "such as you do not want." Even the placement of the negative is significant. Read R. 1161 and 1174 on οὐχ. The writer thinks that οὐχ οἵους and likewise οὐ θέλετε are each simply a single negated term; hence the negative is properly οὐ and needs no further explanation.

Paul states what he fears he may find in Corinth. We have four pairs. Four is used to designate ordinary rhetorical completeness, and the doubling of each of the four intensifies the completeness. Strife and jealousy — each sheds light on the other. In the Greek abstract plurals are used for concrete exhibitions or instances of what the abstract term signifies. This applies to the six plurals following. B.-D. 142. Thus "angry outbursts — cases of self-assertion" (C.-K. 444). These two are well paired. So also "backbitings — whisperings." Angry self-assertion bursts out publicly, but backbitings and whisperings circulate quietly. On the proud "puffings" note what Paul wrote already in I Cor. 4:6, 18, 19; 13:4, which show the relation between the two epistles. This was one of the failings that was prevalent in Corinth; it is here paired with "disorders."

Those who separate chapters 10-13 from Second Corinthians and call this "the Four Chapter Letter" which was written earlier or later than Second Corinthians make much of the eight evils listed here on the plea that the first seven chapters show that things were so far improved in Corinth that Paul could not have harbored these fears when he wrote those seven chapters. They do not note that those seven chapters plainly show that enough trouble is still active in Corinth, and that Paul might well have his fears about a *new* flare-up. He is setting these things down in plain words in order to head off this very danger. He tells the Corinthians that, when he comes, he does not want to find any of these shameful conditions. It was one of the wisest things he could do.

21) The two μή πως clauses are a unit, the second states the specifications for the first. The clause that has simple μή is an addition. Hence Paul again inserts

"on my coming back." On πάλιν see 2:1. In the interest of the hypothesis of a disgraceful visit of Paul to Corinth between First and Second Corinthians efforts are made to refer πάλιν across the participle so that it modifies the main verb: "lest my God shall humble me again." Paul puts it in a striking way: not that the Corinthians might suffer disgrace and humiliation, but that he, Paul, might be humbled by God before the Corinthians (πρὸς ὑμᾶς) at the sight of their disgraceful condition, that he might be caused to mourn over many guilty ones. Ah, yes, the *Corinthians* should feel that way, but would they? Well, Paul would! He does not use the plural and say that he and his assistants would be humbled and would mourn. His assistants would, of course, feel as he felt, but especially he would be affected.

"Lest my God shall humble me," the God whom I serve so earnestly in Christ, brings out the full poignancy of what Paul would feel — his own God bowing his head in the dust. That would be a sad, sad dispensation of providence for Paul. Jesus had labored in vain for Judas, for many others who then turned from him; that sorrow Paul, too, had often enough experienced, it would then be his again in Corinth.

But he is thinking also of the other and the older dangers in Corinth, of those mentioned in I Cor. 5:9, etc.; 6:9-20, the old pagan vices into which some of the Corinthians had been drawn and were ever in danger of being drawn. This final fear of Paul's so plainly reaches back into First Corinthians that it is useless to deny the fact. The fear is that Paul might have to mourn "many of those who have been hitherto (πρό in the participle) sinning and did not repent of their uncleanness," etc. Not repenting, they would, of course, be lost. This is sufficient reason for mourning without thinking of excommunication and the like. Paul speaks of that in its proper place. Paul uses first the perfect and then the aorist participle, each tense in its exact meaning. The sinning which started in the past is pictured as going on unchecked to the present (perfect), no decisive act of repentance at any time in the past causes a stop (aorist).

Paul uses the verb μετανοεῖν only here but uses it in the same sense as the noun is used in 7:9, 10, the inner change of heart by true contrition which turns to Christ for pardon. One article combines the three datives: did not repent over (ἐπί); we say: of "the uncleanness and fornication and excess which they committed." The three terms describe sexual sins plus what goes with them. See the remarks on Rom. 13:13 for details.

"Uncleanness" refers to the stench; "fornication" to the common type of this sin; "excess" to the unbridled action, ἀσέλγεια, *Zuegellosigkeit, Ausschweifung*. The sinners described here have been identified with those mentioned in v. 20. And they would, indeed, dislike Paul and cause the disturbances noted in v. 20. They knew what Paul did in I Cor. 5 and what he wrote in I Cor. 6:12-20. They had no use for him and would claim that Paul never intended to come (I Cor. 4:18). This identification seems to be correct.

"I fear, I fear!" is Paul's solicitous warning.

CHAPTER XIII

III. *Paul Warns the Corinthians regarding What He Will Do, if Necessary, when He Comes*

1) **This is the third time I am coming to you.** See 12:14. The repetition is emphatic. In 12:20, 21 and in 13:2 he also mentions his coming. All of these accumulated references to his coming, save 12:14, have the note of warning. I Cor. 4:18 indicates the reason; in Corinth some had puffed themselves up as though Paul would not dare to come. Such bold talk may not have died down as yet although Paul had been on the way for some time. The force of "this third time" would, then, be: I have been in Corinth twice, once after founding your church, and I shall come even a third time now that it is necessary.

Paul follows this reminder with a cold legal statement, which is abbreviated from Deut. 19:15: **By mouth of two witnesses and of three shall every matter be established.** That, Paul says, is what this my third coming means if there should be any in Corinth who need this procedure when I come. The corroborating testimony of at least two witnesses was required by the Jews when legal action was to be taken, that of three was considered a maximum. The same principle holds good in law everywhere. The Christian Church cannot possibly dispense with this principle when it deals with cases of discipline, and its action may be that of expulsion from the congregation. Jesus subjected himself to this principle of law, John 5:31, etc.; 8:17, 18; he prescribed it for us in Matt. 18:16; Paul holds to it in I Tim. 5:19. Paul's word is intended **as a warning.** He has just mentioned repentance

(12:21). He hopes that there will be no unrepentant sinners with whom he must deal when he arrives. They will get a fair trial, indeed, but a trial they will get.

Paul would, of course, not take such cases into his own hands and out of the hands of the congregation, he would not act as judge supreme and dictate the verdict by virtue of his apostolic authority. In I Cor. 5:3-5 he did the very opposite; in II Cor. 1:24 he declares the direct opposite. The congregation alone can expel. It hears the necessary witnesses, it passes every motion in every case. What would be Paul's function? The same as that which he exercised in his letters: to advise and to guide the congregation in the true spirit of Christ.

Since the time of Chrysostom Paul's word about the two or three witnesses has been referred to his two previous visits in Corinth and the third which is about to follow. We are told that τρίτον and τριῶν correspond, that "this *third* time" is repeated because it would be the *third* witness against the impenitent in Corinth. When it is asked how Paul could note a parallel such as that, we are told that this is "rabbinical" and therefore quite possible for Paul. Paul's stay of one and one-half years in Corinth took place prior to any trouble that had occurred there. His second visit took place prior to First Corinthians and had no bearing on recent developments. Two or three visits by the *same* man could not resemble two or three testimonies by *different* witnesses. The essential thing is that different persons serve as witnesses. No rabbi would regard the same man as three witnesses!

2) Pointing the Corinthians to Deut. 19:15 is itself significant, and this is followed by language that is just as plain if not plainer. **I have said in advance and I say in advance as present a second time and (as) absent now to those who have hitherto been**

sinning and to all the rest that, if I come back, I will not spare. Paul states in 1:23 that he had purposely delayed his coming in order to spare. It is an evangelical delay which allows the sinners who have merited discipline time to repent and to amend, which also does not hurry the congregation in its discipline. Paul now forewarns all concerned that his delayed arrival will bring this period to an end. "If I come back" (πάλιν as in 2:1) denotes expectancy and not doubt. It is the Christian's "if" which places the future into God's hands.

In I Cor. 5:3 Paul has used the same expressions which he employs here. There he wrote "absent in the body yet present in the spirit, I . . . as present"; hence he says here: "as present the second time and (as) absent now." In I Cor. 5:3 the time for sparing one impenitent sinner had come to an end; here the time for sparing a number of such sinners was now approaching its end. In I Cor. 5:3 Paul spoke ὡς παρών, "as if present"; here he speaks ὡς παρὼν τὸ δεύτερον, "as if present the second time." When he writes "the second time" he refers to I Cor. 5:3 as being the first time when he had to speak in advance to the Corinthians as he must now. The parallel is too marked to be denied.

Those who hold to the hypothesis of a visit of Paul's to Corinth between First and Second Corinthians disregard the connection of our passage with I Cor. 5:3. They let ὡς mean "when": "when I was present the second time on that hypothetical visit." All that which makes this second visit impossible should be repeated here. In addition we may note that in accordance with this hypothesis παρών is given the sense of an imperfect tense, ἀπών that of a present tense. Καί combines the two participles and cannot be deleted. This hypothesis separates the participles: "I have told you before when I was present the second time" on that hypothetical visit, "and I tell you before when I am now absent" What Paul plainly says is that when he arrives he will not spare, that he has been telling and is now telling the Corinthians this in advance "as if (already) present the second time though (καί) now (still) absent."

"Those who have been sinning" are the ones mentioned in 12:21 where they are designated by the same perfect participle with the addition that they had not repented. Impenitent sinners dare not be indefinitely spared. "And to all the rest" means all the rest of the congregation. If they do not take action against the impenitent sinners before Paul arrives in Corinth, Paul will not permit them to remain inactive after he arrives. We feel that Paul hopes that the congregation will take energetic action before he gets to Corinth. We decline to make "all the rest" mean still other sinners besides those mentioned in 12:21, such as 12:20 indicates. We have already seen that in all probability those mentioned in 12:20 and in 12:21 were the same persons. In addition to the sinners that call for action Paul warns also the congregation which needs to provide that action.

3) The statement continues: **I shall not spare since you are seeking a proof of the Christ speaking in me, (of the Christ) who is not weak toward you but is powerful among you. Yes, he was crucified due to weakness but he lives due to God's power! Yes, we on our part are weak in him, but we shall live with him due to God's power toward you.**

Δοκιμή is an actual "proof," the result of a genuine test. The Corinthians are seeking such real proof, and Paul says that they will certainly get it when he arrives. The proof is to demonstrate "the Christ speaking in Paul," the Christ "who is not weak toward you but is powerful among you." We take this to be Paul's own statement regarding what the Corinthians want to see demonstrated by Paul. He says that this Christ "speaks," makes utterance in him, i. e., is not silent. Paul calls himself Christ's mouthpiece. This speaking consists in the letters and the oral messages which Paul has been sending to the Corinthians and includes the letter which he is now sending. This speaking sounds strong (10:10). What does it really amount to?

The relative clause answers that question. Paul informs the Corinthians, both those who still raise such a question as well as all the rest who hear such a question raised, that the Christ speaking in Paul is certainly "not weak toward you Corinthians," a Christ who only utters (λαλέω) empty words through Paul's mouth, but a Christ who "is powerful among you." Both of the verbs are in the present tense. The Corinthians already have the greatest proof of the power of this Christ in all that he has wrought in the Corinthians; v. 5 points them to this proof. The Corinthians had better put themselves to the proof in order to realize what they themselves are, namely that Christ is in them with his blessed, saving power. But if they must, in addition, have proof of the opposite kind, proof of the disciplinary power of Christ, they shall get what they are seeking — "I will not spare." Paul has been sparing the Corinthians (1:25) in the hope that they would not need and require this proof which is bound to be rather painful. But since, after all, they seem not to be satisfied unless it is furnished them they shall get what they want.

4) The two καὶ γάρ are parallel; the one deals with Christ, the other with Paul and his assistants. Both are concessive (B.-D. 457); we translate "yes" or "and indeed" (the idea is not "for," our versions). Both concessions are wiped out by the strong adversative ἀλλά. "Yes, he was crucified due to weakness." Christ was certainly weak, so utterly weak and helpless that

his enemies triumphed over him, nailed him to the cross where he died the most painful and the most ignominious death. Paul names the extreme point of Christ's weakness. This, moreover, is the Christ whom Paul preaches, who speaks in Paul, this Christ crucified, whose earthly life ended in the most abject weakness. Well, then the sinners in Corinth have nothing to fear from such a Christ! Let such a Christ threaten through Paul's letters all he pleases!

Ah, "but he lives due to God's power!" God's power raised him from the dead, exalted him in glory and majesty, gave him a name above every name, etc., Phil. 2:9-12. "He was crucified" is one past act, "he lives" is eternal activity. The two ἐκ denote source, the death came "out of weakness," the living "out of no less than God's power," and no greater power than this exists. Do the sinners in Corinth and any others who are misled by them want a proof of this Christ's power? Does anyone imagine that it cannot or will not be furnished? Yes, it is the crucified Christ, the Redeemer and the hope of sinners, who speaks in Paul; but it is also this Christ of God's power, the divine Lord and Judge, the terror of all impenitent sinners.

The first statement deals strictly with Christ alone; the second, in close parallel, adds "us" (Paul and his assistants) to this Christ. "Yes, we on our part are weak in him." Because they are joined to him (5:17), his weakness, which is evidenced in dying on the cross, is in a manner repeated in all his true ministers. They suffer persecution and insult as he did, are hated by the world and all impenitent sinners as he was. Weakness, Paul says, is our lot "in him" (some texts have "with him"). We, too, look as if we might be easily derided and outfaced. Is this all?

"But we shall live with him due to God's power toward you!" That is the other part of the story. The tense is the future and might thus be dated at the final resurrection; but the final phrase "toward or in regard to you" forbids this. Due to God's power Christ's ministers now live together with him. This is called the logical future by some. As being weak in him we shall ever live with him by God's own power. It is the same power that raised up and exalted Christ. Eph. 1:18, 19. With this power you Corinthians have to reckon when you are dealing with us, Christ's ministers.

The last phrase "toward you" lends a startling turn to the statement. For the point to be noted is not that Paul and his assistants should live with Christ due to God's power (ἐκ again source) and enjoy this life merely for themselves. Their whole life by God's power makes its impact upon the Corinthians. Yes, it is in one sense nothing but lowly weakness (12:9, 10), and it does not even pretend to be anything else; but thus it shall ever be filled with God's own power toward the Corinthians in all that these ministers have to do with them.

Does anyone in Corinth seek proof of the Christ speaking in Paul? He should be satisfied, more than satisfied, with God's power in the weak, crucified Christ, with this same power in the weak ministers of Christ, whose voice is that of Christ, all his power coming to them through it.

5) In view of the conditions that have been existing in Corinth, where even impenitent sinners are found (12:21), the Corinthians should do something that is far more profitable to themselves than to demand proof of the Christ speaking in Paul. **Start trying your own selves whether you are in the faith, start putting your own selves to the proof! Or do you not fully know your own selves,** (namely this about yourselves) **that Jesus Christ is in you? — unless you, indeed, are disproved! Moreover, I hope**

that you will know that we on our part are not disproved!

This should be the real concern of the Corinthians. The present imperatives are conative. When it is used in an evil sense πειράζω means to "tempt"; here it is used in the good sense and has the meaning to "try" and is followed by the synonym "to subject to a test" as coins are tested to determine their genuineness and their full weight. Note the terms: δοκιμή in v. 3 — δοκιμάζω in this verse — also ἀδόκιμος three times — and δόκιμος once. We attempt to translate with English words that are also derived from the same root: proof — put to the proof — disproved (hence rejected; "reprobate" in our versions) — approved (tested out, proved and thus accepted as genuine).

The Corinthians are to apply the right tests to themselves as to "whether they are in the faith." We do not see how "the faith" can be anything but objective faith: the Christian doctrine and the confession which all believers have. The subjective feature is found in the copula and in the preposition "whether you are in." One is "in" the objective faith when he has personal, subjective faith and with his whole heart believes the objective faith. The assertion that "the faith" is never used objectively must be challenged as being incorrect.

To try and test oneself is simple enough. A few honest questions honestly answered soon reveal where one stands. There is "the faith" itself, the gospel with its contents. Does my heart receive that, receive it *in toto*, receive it without change of any kind? Do I reject that or any part of it? Does my heart truly believe this gospel of Christ? Do I trust it? Is my confidence full and strong?

"Or" is not disjunctive, it presents only the alternative: "Or do you not fully know your own selves,"

i. e., realize concerning yourselves this essential "that Jesus Christ is in you?" This alone could be the alternative. The Corinthians must have this realization "unless you, indeed, are disproved," i. e., tested and found false, spurious, either not believing the real gospel but something else or only pretending to believe the gospel while not really believing it. Our versions translate "reprobate," a word that is so forcefully used in I Cor. 9:27 by Paul regarding himself. Of course, if the Corinthians do not truly know that Jesus Christ is in them, if, in fact, they are spurious believers, they will not feel like trying and proving whether they are in the faith. Paul's question probes them. It does not mince matters in the least. True believers never resent that, only people who could not stand a real test are resentful. Εἰ μήτι implies that such a thing as the Corinthians being disproved or spurious cannot be possible. Note the expressions "to be in the faith" — "Jesus Christ in you." Each defines the other. He is in us when we are in him (John 15:5); this blessed fact may be expressed in either way. This is the mystical union, but ever as mediated only by the gospel (objectively) and by faith (subjectively).

"Jesus Christ" is the Savior's personal and his official name which includes who he is and what he has done and still does. Paul uses the simplest form of the name because the test that he wants made is not to be involved or difficult. We realize that Jesus Christ is "in" us when our hearts hold fast to him in trust and respond to the call and the prompting of his Word. Only the absence of these reactions could prove the absence of Jesus Christ in us.

6) Δέ = "moreover." The idea to be conveyed is not that, whether the Corinthians are approved or disproved, Paul hopes that they know that he and his assistants are not disproved; the idea is that the Corinthians are not disproved (spurious coins, rejected),

and that Paul hopes that for this very reason they will know that he and his assistants are likewise not disproved. Spurious Christians would not be able to know, their judgment would be worth nothing; but Christians who are able to test themselves and to realize their own genuineness, one may hope, will know the genuineness also of Christ's true ministers. If they are able to detect the presence of Jesus Christ in themselves they should be able to recognize others in whom Christ's power operates, especially those who helped to put Christ into their hearts. Knowing that Paul and his assistants are not disproved but approved of Christ, they will not listen to talk about a test to see whether Christ really speaks in Paul.

7) Now we are praying God that you come to do nothing evil, not (with the selfish motive) **that we on our part may appear approved, but in order that you on your part may begin doing the** (morally) **excellent thing while** (or: and that, δέ) **we on our part are as if disproved.**

Δέ adds this further statement about the intercession which Paul and his assistants are making for the Corinthians. Their prayer is "that you may come to do nothing evil" (ὑμᾶς is the subject of the infinitive, compare ποιῆτε). The aorist is important here: "may come to do." Paul is not speaking in general about doing any kind of evil; he is speaking about the specific act of siding with the impenitent sinners in Corinth so that when Paul arrives he will have to show himself approved by dealing unsparingly with them.

While they are praying thus, the great concern of Paul and of his assistants is by no means that they on their part "appear" before the eyes of the Corinthians as approved or genuine because of their success in keeping the Corinthians from making a serious mistake. Paul and his assistants know that they are approved of Christ, how they may appear to the Corinthians is a secondary matter. Paul has his hopes in regard to that (v. 6), and that is enough.

No; the motive behind this prayer is the thought that the Corinthians may begin doing the noble or excellent thing, the one that is pertinent to the situation, namely turning against the impenitent sinners in their midst. The tense is again important, it is a conative present subjunctive: "may begin doing." They cannot begin too soon. In fact, Paul hopes for a speedy answer to these prayers so that when he gets to Corinth he will find that the congregation has cleansed itself, that he does not need to use unsparing vigor upon it to get it to act.

What if "we on our part are as if disproved," as having no opportunity by disciplinary action and by taking the congregation itself unsparingly to task like a father applying the rod (I Cor. 4:21) to show that Christ speaks in us with God's power? What of it? Some may desire to see such a δοκιμή or proof (v. 3). Paul and his assistants will be glad to dispense with it. There are many pleasanter ways in which to show that they are approved and accepted of Christ. Note ὡς, "as if," which matches the preceding φανῶμεν, "may appear" (aorist subjunctive).

8) In order to explain somewhat this chief purpose of the prayer, which is directed entirely toward the end that the Corinthians may do the excellent thing even though Paul and his assistants get no special opportunity to appear as approved and genuine, Paul adds regarding themselves: **For we are not able to do a thing against the truth but** (are able to do something only) **in the interest of truth.**

The ἀλήθεια, "reality," "truth," does not mean the actual facts as they exist in Corinth so that Paul would say that he and his assistants cannot go counter to what these facts demand but can do only what these facts require. "The truth" = the blessed reality comprised in the gospel. Paul and his assistants are devoted wholly to this truth. They have no selfish interest such as thinking that *they* must stand before the Corinthians as approved, as tried and true. Just as their interest is only that the Corinthians may make no mistake, may do only the excellent thing, so their one interest is the divine, blessed truth of the gospel. Their arms are paralyzed so they cannot do even a single thing κατά, "against" that truth, but these arms are energized ever to do all that can possibly be done ὑπέρ, "in favor" of that truth.

We note how necessary it is that Paul rise to this highest plane. Κακόν and καλόν are only the moral aspects, "bad" — "excellent"; moreover, both refer only to the Corinthians. The interest which Paul has in the Corinthians as to whether they may make a moral mistake or not in their present situation is of importance for Paul and his assistants only in its connection with the truth, with the gospel, against which they could not dream of doing a thing, in favor of which they use their every effort. So, as far as they are concerned, all self-interest is barred completely, is replaced by the interest in the Corinthians, and even this interest in the Corinthians is one that is connected only with the great ἀλήθεια, the gospel truth, whose sum and substance is Christ, the Truth.

9) The very verb δυνάμεθα, "we are able, have power," recalls the opposites power and weakness that were used in v. 3, 4. So this explanation is added: **For we rejoice whenever we are weak while you are powerful; this, in fact** (καί), **we pray for,** (namely) **your complete outfitting.** The Corinthians must not worry about Paul and his assistants. They rejoice whenever they are weak, for they know then that they are strong (12:10), for God's power works in their weakness. Hence they are willing to appear totally weak. All that they desire is that the Corin-

thians may be powerful, i. e., that in their weakness, too, God's power may show itself most effectively (v. 4). For this also Paul and his assistants are ever praying, namely for the complete fitting out of all that the Corinthians may need.

The rare word κατάρτισις appears only here in the Bible; the verb is used several times (see v. 11). Κατά in the compound is perfective: a fitting out that is thorough and complete. Note the English "artisan." The genitive ὑμῶν is objective. Being completely fitted out, the Corinthians would again have their congregation in order as it should be; they would appear as the product of a good artisan.

10) **For this reason I write these things while absent in order that when present I may not deal sharply, according to the authority which the Lord gave me for upbuilding and not for wrecking.** Paul would like to see the Corinthians themselves put everything in good order in advance of his arrival. For this reason he is writing these things, in order to help them. If, in spite of everything, they prove dilatory, he will, when he comes, necessarily have to use sharpness. The aorist implies one decisive act. He will then wait and spare no longer (v. 2). He will then have to use the full authority given him by the Lord. This is no papistic, legalistic, or autocratic authority. The Lord never gave him anything of this kind. Paul defines it well: it is "for upbuilding and not for wrecking."

We may call it the gospel authority. See John 20: 21-23. Paul says the same thing about it here that he did in 10:8, that the Lord gave it to him for upbuilding and not for wrecking. The false apostles did the reverse; they wrecked what had been built up. Regarding the wrecking which Paul does see the grand passage 10:4, 5. The point to be noted here is that if after coming to Corinth Paul did not finally take strong measures by not using his divinely given authority he himself would be helping to wreck. To be guilty of anything like that is impossible to him.

IV. *The Conclusion*

11) Finally, brethren, farewell! Let yourselves be completely fitted out, let yourselves be admonished, keep minding the same things, live in peace! And the God of the love and peace will be with you. Our versions are correct in rendering χαίρετε "farewell," *valete*. Some commentators think that this is wrong because this is one of five imperatives. The number five should have been a clue to them. This first stands by itself: "good-bye." Then there comes a rhetorical four in two pairs. The two passives are permissive: "Let yourselves be completely fitted out, let yourselves be admonished!" See the noun in v. 9 regarding the first. As a meaning for the second our versions think of being comforted, but Paul has been admonishing, and he surely asks the Corinthians to let themselves be admonished, i. e., to accept the admonitions which will enable them to fit themselves out completely.

The next two also go together, for when they keep setting their minds on the same thing they will live in peace. By "the same thing" Paul means the one which he has been presenting in this epistle.

Paul seals these admonitions with the sweet promise that "the God of the love and peace will be with you." One article combines the two genitives and makes a unit of them. That is the purpose of the article. The article at the same time makes "love and peace" specific. It is not only love or peace but the love and peace of which God alone is the source. On "love" see 2:4; on "peace" 1:2. The view that this promise is Pelagian, that the Corinthians must deserve this presence of God before they can obtain it, is unwarranted. Paul writes to "brethren." He makes the same promise to them that Jesus made to the eleven in John

14:23. After we have been converted, God is with us; he will remain and not withdraw if we remain faithful, and the more we prove faithful, the fuller and the richer his presence in and with us will be.

12) **Salute each other with a holy kiss!** On this ancient custom see I Cor. 16:20; Rom. 16:16.

There salute you all the saints! These are all the brethren who are with Paul at the time of his writing. To say that this is the real "farewell" and not χαίρετε in v. 11 is, of course, not correct, for this is the greeting that is being sent by friends. On "saints" see 1:1.

13) Paul closes with what has come to be called and with what is used as the New Testament trinitarian benediction, the counterpart to the Old Testament trinitarian benediction found in Num. 6:22-27. **The grace of the Lord Jesus Christ and the love of God and the communion of the Holy Spirit** (be) **with you all!** The order of the persons as well as the order of their gifts are significant. We have "the Lord Jesus Christ" first, then "God"; we have "the love of God" second and not first. This benediction is pronounced upon people who are already Christians.

The love of God referred to is the love with which God embraces his own and not the love which reaches out to make men his own. God's love is able to bestow thousands of gifts upon believers which he could not possibly bestow upon people who are not yet believers or who are unbelievers. "The love of God" properly occupies the second place in this benediction.

"The grace — the love — the communion" are not conceived in the abstract but as including all gifts and blessings that emanate from them. Nor are grace, love, communion conceived as being separate from each other. We see that grace is only a form of love, love toward the undeserving. In 1:2 grace emanates from both God and Christ. So both grace and love toward believers also involve communion with them, and communion involves grace and love toward them. In fact, communion is the crowning form of grace and love. We should guard against intellectual distinctions. The rationalism which finds "communion" incongruous and not a true third in this trio gives evidence of the fact that it does not rightly understand what any of the three are.

Yet each concept is distinct in the union of the three, and each is in its proper place. It is pure, unmerited grace on which every believer depends until he draws his last breath. He is and remains a sinner until his end. The blood of Christ's grace must cleanse him daily. By grace alone he enters heaven at last. "Grace" keeps its full connotation of guilt and sin, of unmerited pardon in 1:2 and here at the end. It is always "the grace of the Lord Jesus Christ." To think that this dissociates it from the Father and from the Spirit is to think that it is dissociated from the love and the communion, neither of which is true or could be true. The Triune God is the fount of grace for us in Christ Jesus. Read the exegesis of John 1:16.

"The Lord" = he who has purchased and won us and to whom we belong; "Jesus" = the name he bore here on earth when he came to save us with his grace; "Christ" = this person in his saving office. Each part of his name glows with grace, and this form of his name has become infinitely precious to the church from the days of the apostles onward.

We have already shown how "the love of God" follows. It is again the love of full comprehension and corresponding purpose which in this benediction enfolds those who have been won by Christ's grace. Since it is here ascribed to "God," the infinitude of this love is emphasized. And this includes the infinitude of its blessedness for us. If the sinner bows his head at the pierced feet of the Lord because he is overwhelmed by the grace, shall he not be utterly lost in this ocean of the love which is as great and as blessed as God himself? Our little understanding staggers and falls, and only worship and adoration are left.

The third place in this trio belongs to the heavenly word κοινωνία, "union with," "communion" or fellowship. The Holy Spirit stoops down to us and enfolds us in his communion in which are found all the grace and the love. Not from afar are these extended to us but in a union which is beyond our comprehension. Yet we must not drift into what is called *Schwaermerei*, the false mysticism in which some revel. This communion is mediate, its means are Word and sacrament. In these the Spirit becomes one with us, and we with him. Apart from the means we are far from the Spirit.

The personality of the Spirit is often denied by rationalism. Only a person can establish communion. The Holy Spirit is here named beside the other two persons. So much for this passage. The full answer to unitarianism is compiled from the whole domain of Scripture revelation in any good dogmatics.

"With or in company with you all" is itself communion and fellowship. With the picture of the great apostle spreading his hands over the Corinthians with this profound New Testament benediction his voice sinks into silence. But the benediction remains upon our hearts.

Soli Deo Gloria

www.ingramcontent.com/pod-product-compliance
Lightning Source LLC
Chambersburg PA
CBHW071849290426
44110CB00013B/1085